THE RUNNING SHOE BOOK

Peter R. Cavanagh, Ph.D.

Illustrated by
Ann E. Vandervelde

Library of Congress Cataloging in Publication Data

Cavanagh, Peter, 1947-
   The running shoe book.

   Bibliography: p. 390
   Includes index.
   1. Running shoes. I. Title.
GB1061.6.C38   688.7'64'26   80-20365
ISBN 0-89037-182-2

©1980 by
  Peter R. Cavanagh
No information may be reprinted in any form without permission from the publisher.
                      Anderson World, Inc.
                      Mountain View, CA

Contents

	Acknowledgments	I
	The Road to Writing	VI
Chapter 1	What Happened to the Sneaker?	1
Chapter 2	The History of the Running Shoe	8
Chapter 3	A Runner's Anatomy	52
Chapter 4	The Biomechanics of Running	78
Chapter 5	How Running Shoes Are Made	96
Chapter 6	What Shoes Are Made Of — A Closer Look	122
Chapter 7	Shoe Testing and Shoe Surveys	137
Chapter 8	Gimmicks or Greatness?	157
Chapter 9	Fit and Comfort	186
Chapter 10	Shoe Gerontology	213
Chapter 11	Racing Flats	232
Chapter 12	Inserts, Arch Supports and Orthotics	241
Chapter 13	Can Shoes Prevent Injury?	261
Chapter 14	How To Buy a Running Shoe	277
Chapter 15	Groups With Special Needs	311
Chapter 16	Views on Shoes	320
	Index	386

Acknowledgments

In any task as extensive as writing a book, what starts as a solo performance rapidly turns into an orchestration of many talents, as the author becomes in turn composer, conductor, listener, recorder, and critic. In completing this book I have been fortunate to have the help and friendship of many people. Those mentioned in "The Road to Writing" were instrumental in moving the project along from concept to conclusion.

On a day-to-day basis, Tom Clarke, Keith Williams, Mario Lafortune, Rick Hinrichs, Rick Bunch, and Ray Feehery, all graduate students at Penn State, provided the intellectual stimulation that was so necessary to a successful research program.

A variety of people made important contributions to certain chapters of the book. Harvey Abrams assiduously pursued numerous historical leads, and John Lucas and Herb Juliano were both generous with their valuable historical documents. June Swann of the Northampton Museum was also extremely helpful. Malcolm Mitchell of Adidas (West Germany) hosted my tour of the Adidas Museum and the staff of ASICS (Tiger Shoe) Company provided interesting documents from Japan. Conversations with Jeff Johnson of Nike, George Birdsong of New Balance, John Thornton, and Lance Clarke were also useful in filling gaps in the historical record.

Marvin Ungar of Saucony was a patient instructor on shoe manufacturing techniques, and Paul Jones of Bostonian Ltd. was a ready source of wisdom on a wide range of topics. Saucony, New Balance, Nike, Brooks, Etonic, and Puma all allowed me to photograph the process of making running shoes in their factories. Norman Macmillan spent many hours at the microscope in the unselfish pursuit of photographs for Chapter Six, and Ted Porosky of C.S. Bergh gave me considerable insight into upper materials.

The chapter on shoe testing recalls the dedication of the people pictured on the back cover, who were all essential components of a mechanism that, like any other, works only with all its parts intact. Sue Williams,

Linda Clarke, Debbe Simkins, Rick Hinricks, Frit Cooper, Ray Feehery, Ginny Fortney, Michyoshi Ae, Carolyn Court, Mark Fischman, and Rick Bunch all worked until they must have seen running shoes in their sleep. Kate Bednarski and Greg Anson never did seem to sleep but carried on with the job regardless.

The technical expertise of Joe Johnstonbaugh, Tom Eby, George Sayers, and Robert Dillon were absolutely vital in designing, building, and maintaining the various pieces of shoe testing equipment.

Bob Alpert of Jones and Vining fielded many naive questions on last making and grading during the preparation of Chapter Nine. Greg Fredricks, owner of the State College Athletic Attic Store, was always a willing source of shoes and socks for various experiments, usually at the expense of short notice and poor credit.

Sheldon Langer and Justin Wernick of Langer Laboratories were helpful in preparing parts of Chapter Twelve, and Lloyd Smith and his colleagues at St. Elizabeth's Hospital, Boston, were both enthusiastic and generous in preparing their injury data for Chapter Thirteen.

Many of the people whose "Views on Shoes" are presented in Chapter Sixteen made a great contribution to the book through their helpful conversations. In particular, Steve Subotnick, Rob Roy McGregor, Jeff Johnson, Jerry Turner, Joe Henderson, and Dick Schuster all influenced my own views on shoes to some degree. Scheduling some of the interviews was rather like planning a military operation. Roger Vogel of Puma USA, Toshio Shigi of ASICS, Justin Wernick of Langer Labs, and Marty Liquori of Athletic Attic deserve special thanks in this regard.

As the writing of the book briefly threatened to close down every other aspect of life, Roberta Kurland managed to cope with the book as well as its oppressed author, and was also able to keep "business as usual" going with poise and warmth that was indispensible to survival.

Several individuals provided helpful comments on various drafts of the manuscript. Keith Williams, Tom Clarke, and Mario Lafortune were unfortunate enough to be asked to read the whole thing and did so with good humor and good comment. Marvin Ungar prevented some dire mistakes in the manufacturing chapter and Lloyd Smith gave helpful comments on Chapter Thirteen. Justin Wernick and Sheldon Langer reviewed Chapter Twelve and John Lucas read Chapter Two. Norman Macmillan's remarks on various early drafts, uttered between breaths at seven minutes a mile, were motivating. As deadlines drew near (and passed) Debbe Simkins proved to be a crack shot at split infinitives and other more serious abuses of the English language. Her perceptive remarks and creative editing made for a substantially improved manuscript.

Once in the hands of the professionals, the book quickly gathered momentum. Charles Tips was a source of enthusiasm and Steve Beitler provided good editing and good advice. The final copy, with so many illustrations, was a designer's nightmare, but Lynne Steele applied her craftsmanship and care to produce a fine end product.

I have always believed in visual communication as much as, if not more than, the written word. The contributions of the photographer and of the artist were therefore especially important. Brenda Palmgren spent many hours in the darkroom making most of the black and white prints which appear in this book.

Ann Vandervelde has been able to capture so many important ideas with the stroke of a pen. Her superb artwork has elevated the book well beyond what would it would otherwise have been. But she also did much more. She sustained, encouraged, nurtured, and loved in a way which made trying to succeed in this, and other projects, worthwhile.

Finally, our children Sasha, Jenny, and Chris can now breathe a collective sigh of relief. With one parent at the drawing table and the other feverishly scratching on a tablet of paper, they must have wondered at times if they were not orphans in their own home. The often repeated question, "After the book is done, can we...?" is now, happily, a thing of the past.

—P.R.C. August 1980

To Our Parents
who are friends and advocates

Dot and Jack
Evalyn and Van

The Road to Writing

Although only nine months in the writing, this book was seventeen years in the making. Mike Shaffery started it all with morning runs back in 1963. Eric Haslam, Mike Varah, and Dick Milne kept the spark alive with their encouragement of a meager talent during college, on the fringe of the varsity cross-country team. Dick Tibbot and John Williams were co-conspirators in planning strategies and counting training miles.

During the early seventies, running stopped but progress was astronomical, as an apprenticeship to Don Grieve showed me that science could be brought to bear on this sport called running.

Dick Nelson provided the means to change continents in 1972, and Steve Mahieu was there in 1973 to show me the long road down Commonwealth Avenue to the Pru (in three hours and too many minutes).

Mike Pollock was a catalyst in 1975, and twenty-six miles seemed a little shorter (and was considerably faster) that year. A lively discussion with Rob Roy

THE ROAD TO WRITING

McGregor in a coffee shop on the Avenue of the Americas planted the seeds of what was possible in 1976. John Larsen was there in the spring of 1977 to harvest the first growth of our studies of running and running shoes.

Bob Anderson showed interest in the summer of 1977, and Mario Lafortune pulled the ultimate "all-nighter" while tending old shoe testing machines for a long, long, week. The *Runner's World* shoe survey that year reflected his care and energy. Norman Macmillan and Dave Laananen were important links in the chain.

Art Boettcher never lacked clarity, friendship, or the desire for a hard run, and Hersh Leibowitz could be relied upon for inspiration and insight.

In 1978 Boston was a fast but foolish jaunt on too little training. Shoe test machines, computers, and force platforms had intruded too far into training hours.

By then Keith Williams and Tom Clarke were part of the team, both learning and teaching, prodding the science of running a few strides further with their own special talents. In 1979, at Dave Costill's prompting, Paula Apsell appeared on the doorstep with Bill Rodgers. Almost 800 shoes followed shortly after, destined to become the 1980 *Runner's World* shoe survey. At about that time, it seemed that the words were ready to be put down on paper. Mike Shaffery—just look what you started!!!

1
What Happened to the Sneaker?

Running is a simple sport. All you need is a body, a piece of ground, and the ability to put one foot in front of the other. But between the body and the ground is a piece of equipment that is far from simple. Only a few years ago, anyone but the most serious of athletes reached for their sneakers if they wanted to go out for a run. Today, the word "sneaker," and the shoe it represents, are definitely out with the running community.

But are "sneakers" obsolete for a good reason, or are we simply victims of a Madison Avenue myth, which says that running without a sixty dollar pair of running shoes will lead to sudden death, or at least shin splints? In this book we will put the running shoe on trial in an attempt to find out those things that every runner always wanted to know, but had no one to ask.

Running has seen an exponential growth in the last two decades. In 1964, slightly more than 300 runners toed the line at the start of the Boston Marathon. In 1979 there were 7,877 official entrants, plus thousands of unofficial runners who found the race just too good to pass up. But these legions are just the tip of an enormous iceberg. Some authorities put the number of people in the United States who run regularly at more than thirty million. That is about one in every seven Americans, or a number comparable to the whole population of Spain.

Most of these people run on the roads and sidewalks of America, and this book is about the shoes they run in, which are called training flats. As running has exploded in popularity, there has been a proliferation of choices for the consumer of running shoes. Finding the right running shoe in today's overcrowded marketplace ranks as high on a scale of difficulty as any other consumer decision we have to make.

In 1967, when *Distance Running News*, the parent of *Runner's World* magazine, published their first shoe survey, there were fifteen shoes in contention, from six different manufacturers. In the 1980 survey, 178 models were tested from thirty-four manufacturers. In the presence of such vast numbers of shoes with widely differing characteristics, some inside knowledge is essential if the right shoe is to be found.

Besides the sheer volume of running shoes, there are other factors which complicate the problem. Many important properties of a running shoe cannot be assessed by simply looking at the shoe. For example, the thickness of the protective material under the heel is not a good index of how well the shoe absorbs shock. So first the runner must know how he or she can find out about shock absorption, and then know how to match this capability of a shoe to their own requirements. Even features that are clearly visible need an eye that knows what to look for and a voice that asks a probing question or two.

What makes the situation still more difficult is that you cannot always rely on someone else's experience; what is good for one runner may be disastrous for another. If studied in the right way, a person's running style is as individual as their signature. Feet come in many different shapes and sizes, and even the left and right feet of the same person are frequently different.

The consequences of a wrong choice of running shoes go far beyond the money that is wasted. Bad shoes can cause bad injuries. But running injuries are not usually the bone-breaking, ligament-tearing trauma that are the lot of the football player. They are more insidious—slow to appear, and slow to disappear. So the first indication that a runner and shoe are mismatched might be a slight pain after a few weeks of running that becomes a disabling injury within a few months.

This book will provide all the information a runner needs to make a wise purchase when the time comes to buy running shoes. If you must have a pair before the sun sets tonight, I would urge you to turn to Chapter 14, which will tell you what to do and say when you walk into the store and are confronted by twenty brands of shoes and an eager salesperson.

Hopefully, most readers will have a little more time available, because this book is designed to be more than just a buyer's guide. I have tried to piece together a mosaic of information which should be of interest to all wearers of running shoes. The following paragraphs preview some of the ground that we shall cover together.

History

Our starting point will be a look backwards at history. The history of the running shoe is both extensive and absorbing. Early man in America was certainly a runner, and it is intriguing that the oldest known shoe was found in a cave in Oregon, the home of some of today's greatest runners. At the modern end of the continuum, the pedestrians of the late 19th century, the early Olympians, and the phenomenal growth of running in the 1970s were all factors which spurred the development of the running shoe. All of these and more are spotlighted in Chapter 2.

Biomechanics and Anatomy

Before we get lost in the detail of the running shoe, we will look briefly at the runner's body. The feet and legs make up the locomotor system, and it is clearly important to know something about what goes on inside the shoe and how the body works during running.

Runners are a cerebral bunch, anxious to digest every last piece of information about their chosen sport. Many doctors who treat runners have had the experience of a patient coming into the office and giving a long and learned discourse about the onset, symptomatology, and prognosis of their particular affliction, with a level of understanding that would make a medical student proud. Chapters 3 and 4 quench this thirst for basic knowledge with a consideration of anatomy and biomechanics.

Anatomy has long been the stock in trade of doctors and shoemakers alike, but biomechanics is something new. We shall see how new ways to study running can lead to important insights into shoe design that would have been impossible just a few years ago. In many respects the information in Chapters 3 and 4 provides an essential foundation for the whole of this book.

How Shoes are Made

A visit to a shoe factory has an impact on all the senses. The visitor smells the cements, hears the clatter of sewing machines, and sees the incredibly rapid movements of an assembly line worker who withdraws his hand only moments before a giant press comes crashing down. In Chapters 5 and 6 we make this visit, present a photographic essay showing how running shoes are made, and find out more about the materials from which they are made.

One of the best ways to appreciate the finished product is to see the component parts and how they are put together; here the reader can do just this without having to cut up his or her own shoes. We will also establish a system of names for parts of the shoe that will be used throughout the book.

Shoe Testing

Every October, *Runner's World* magazine publishes its shoe issue, describing what happened when a large number of running shoes were flexed, pounded, pushed, pulled, and generally insulted in the pursuit of hard facts about their performance. Shoe testing has become a tool that the consumer can use to find his or her way through the maze of look-alikes in the stores. But the numbers can be puzzling, and Chapter 7 gives some insight into what the tests are and how to interpret the results.

Gimmicks and Innovations

Inventors have long been fascinated by footwear, and running shoes have attracted more than their share of both genius and gimmickry. Often it is difficult to sort fact from fiction, when shoe advertisements claim to have gone beyond the bounds of perfection with some new innovation. In Chapter 8, we survey the current market for unusual features which sometimes make a shoe stand out above the crowd, but can also mean it should be left on the shelf. We will investigate the research and development process in the running shoe industry, with not altogether satisfying results.

Fit and Comfort

Although scanning the results of shoe tests is an important ingredient in the buying decision, it certainly does not guarantee the runner that his or her perfect shoe can be identified. One of the most critical properties of the running shoe is the way it fits the foot, and no one has yet devised a good way to test this, except by trying the shoe on. But fit and the all-important comfort of a shoe do have some underlying principles which we shall discuss in Chapter 9. Many people are surprised to hear that there may be up to half an inch difference in length between the same size shoe from different manufacturers, or that there are big differences in the thermal properties of different upper materials. We will discuss the significance of these and other facts about fit and comfort in Chapter 9.

Shoe Gerontology

Running shoes age faster than we realize. The obvious changes in the outsole and upper may appear too late to use as an indication of when to buy a new pair. The more subtle aspects of the aging process are decrements in the ability of the shoe to protect and control the foot. These changes, and some pointers on good shoe care, are discussed in Chapter 10.

Racing Shoes

After running perhaps fifty to one hundred miles a week in a pair of good training flats, many runners lace up a flimsy pair of racing flats when it comes time to race. The reason for the change is usually weight, since the average racing flat is about twenty-five percent lighter than the average training flat. But as we shall see in Chapter 11, the light weight can bring with it some less desirable properties, such as a drop-off in protection. For all but elite athletes, we shall reach the conclusion that at the current state of the art, most runners would do well to stick to their training flats for both racing and training.

Orthotics

Vast numbers of runners now have a secret weapon tucked inside their running shoes. This weapon, called an orthotic, is a custom-made plastic shell which cradles the bottom of the foot, and causes a subtle realignment of the bones of the foot and leg. By recognizing that many running injuries are caused by alignment problems, podiatrists and orthopedists have managed to get many injured runners back to their sport without resort to drugs or surgery. We will take a closer look at orthotics in Chapter 12, find out how they work, and how they are made. We shall also discuss the various "self-help" devices which the runner can either make or buy over the counter.

Running Shoes and Running Injuries

In the last ten years, runners have started to train over long distances, and during the same time running shoes have undergone some dramatic design improvements. One might hypothesize that the first change would cause more injuries, while the second would help prevent them. There is little doubt in the minds of most runners and doctors that the choice of running shoes can affect the incidence of injury, but finding hard data to prove this is difficult. The military has capitalized on its unique opportunity to study the effects of wearing different shoes during a training period. But otherwise, few well-controlled studies exist. There are two important questions we shall try to answer in Chapter 13. First, are runners as a group getting injured more than they used to? Second, are the kinds of injuries that runners experience changing? Many of the answers we arrive at are somewhat speculative—views which are useful temporary beliefs to be updated as better evidence turns up.

How to Buy a Running Shoe

By Chapter 14, it will be time to organize the information presented earlier into a strategy for buying a shoe. A ten-point plan is presented to guide you through a set of decisions about your particular needs. Running shoes should not be bought on impulse; some preparation is essential, and what you do before going to the store is just as important as what you do and ask in the store. Unfortunately, few running shoe stores have demonstrator models that you can run in to try them out. So a brief walk around the store is the most you can hope for. What if your shoe shows defects during the first few miles? And what if it doesn't suit you? We will tackle these problems and more in Chapter 14.

Special Groups

The shoe industry makes its product for that mythical "average runner," but there are several groups of people who need special attention. In Chapter 15, the needs of children, elite athletes, and habitually injured runners are considered. We talk more about women's shoes. Are they really made to suit a woman's foot? And what about walking in running shoes—is it a good idea?

Views on Shoes

Science has its Nobel Prize winners, politics its influential senators, and show business has its great film directors. But there are people who have been as important to the development of the running shoe as any of the above have been to their fields. In Chapter 16 we shall meet twenty-five people who have had a powerful influence on the evolution of the running shoe.

During 1979 and early 1980, I met with each of the people featured in this chapter to learn something of their ideas at first hand. Among them are counted athletes, doctors, businessmen, scientists, and journalists, but their common interest in running and running shoes, and their willingness to talk about it, allows us a glimpse inside the people who have helped shape our sport and the shoes we run in.

Questions Answered—Questions Raised

By the time you have finished this book, you will know answers to questions such as these:

- What kind of footwear did Greek athletes use?
- What does my podiatrist mean when he says I have hallux valgus?
- Am I a freak because my left foot seems to be a half size bigger than my right?
- What is a slip lasted shoe?
- How much force is generated underneath the shoe in running?

- What do shoe tests really tell me?
- When do I need orthotics?
- How do I look after my running shoes?
- What does Bill Rodgers think about running shoes?
- Are expensive shoes necessarily the best?

But for every question answered there is often a question raised. The shoe industry has come this far with surprisingly little research, and there are many important things about the running shoe that we know absolutely nothing about except how it feels in practice.

Anyone coming to this book in search of the perfect running shoe will leave disappointed. Such an animal does not exist. But those readers looking for a better understanding of the point of contact between the foot and the ground should find a lot to interest them. And they should end up prepared to sort the good from the bad in their search for a running shoe that is right for them.

2

The History of the Running Shoe

A history of running shoes must also be a history of running. It is one of those endless loops. Do the shoes make the runner or does the runner make the shoes? There have been some outstanding events in history which have shaped the course of the sport of running. There have also been important technical developments which have influenced the construction of running shoes. But for the most part, a clear separation of the sport and the shoe is not possible. So our journey through history will involve weaving the separate strands together into a greater whole. To trace the origins we have to begin earlier than you might imagine.

Sports psychologists tell us that, for many people today, running has become essential to mental well-being. The first runners ran, however, not for psychic hygiene but for sheer survival. Without good runners there would have been no food. Early man (such as Homo Erectus who lived approximately 500,000 years ago) was certainly an excellent runner. The animal bones found alongside early hominid remains confirm his success in hunting. The only evidence we have of the first homonids are fossil bones, tools, and a few footprints in the clay floors of European caves.

From such small clues anthropologists have reconstructed a fairly complete picture of the appearance of bipedal gait. Walking and running in an upright position were events so crucial to the continued evolution of our early ancestors that they have received much attention. We know that the body underwent many adaptations which made upright locomotion more efficient. The appearance of the lumbar curve in the low back, the broadening of the pelvis, and the convergence of the thigh bones were all important signs. Changes in the foot included a shortening of the long bones and most particularly the disappearance of the prehensile big toe.

It is almost certain that early man did not use footwear of even the crudest form. About one million years ago toolmaking began, and became widespread. Some of the later tools were probably used to scrape animal hides. This process led, perhaps 50,000 years ago, to the use of semi-prepared leather as clothing—probably little more than a single sheet used as a cape. Surely a similar crude covering for the foot was used but none has survived.

The earliest form of footwear that has been found dates back to the end of the last ice age (approximately 10,000 years ago).

These shoes, shown in Figure 2.1, were found in 1932 by archaeologist Luther Cressman in Fort Rock Cave in Oregon. Cressman, now an alert and engaging eighty-two years old, remembers the weeks of digging around a five ton fallen rock in the cave which convinced him that something important was underneath. Finally dynamite was used to break the rock. In the earth underneath was a cache of shoes like those in Figure 2.1 They were made of crushed sagebrush bark carefully knotted together. There is a complete outsole with added ridges for traction, a covering for the forepart of the foot, and straps to go around the back of the heel.

There is no doubt that these were running shoes. Their users probably spent the majority of their waking hours in the pursuit of food. A good runner was a good hunter.

By late stone age times (Neolithic period from 6,500 B.C.) all the basic skills for the manufacture of clothes and shoes had been developed. Prepared hides were being sewn together to produce skirts, tunics, moccasins, and boots.

The history of footwear from these early times is a fascinating subject, but adherence to our topic moves us forward to the Greek civilizations of the second millenium (2,000 B.C.) and later.

The evidence left by artists of the day show that, perhaps influenced by the culture of the Nile Valley,

Fig. 2.1 The earliest shoes in existence. A pair of sandals made of crushed sagebrush bark that belonged to an Oregon cavedweller over 10,000 years ago. (Courtesy of Luther Cressman, Ph.D.)

games and sports became an important part of life for ancient Greeks of both upper and lower classes. It is likely that the major purpose of the games was to provide spectacular entertainment, but there is little doubt that "the culture of a healthy body" encouraged the general population to exercise.

The earliest representation of runners in art comes from a vase painting dating back to the 13th century B.C. found in Cyprus. The main characters in the painting are fighters. But, quite incidental to the main theme, two runners, unshod and naked except for headgear, appear between the contestants, apparently engaged in a contest of their own. Since there are no written histories of this period we can only conjecture what kind of races these men ran.

By the time Homer began his compulsive documentation of Greek life and mythology in the 8th century B.C., running had taken its place alongside chariot racing, boxing, wrestling, armed combat, discus, archery, and the javelin toss in the funeral games that Homer reports as taking place in honor of Patroklos.

Homer also provides us with the first commentary on running style. He says that the winner of the foot race, Odysseus, passed his rival Ajax because he "...ran more lightly and held his hands and feet high."

THE EARLY OLYMPICS

The history of running and running shoes from the 8th century B.C. to the present can be best followed at either of its time extremes by the writing and art surrounding that most famous of sporting festivals—the Olympic games.

The first Olympics were held in 776 B.C. and the name of the winner of the footrace is still known to us today. He was Koroibos of Elis and it is no accident that his name survives. Victory in an Olympic event was considered to be the highest achievement which man (the games were for men only) could attain. Cities would glorify and often deify their citizens who became victors. The Greek ideal was of excellence in mind and body; early winners must have indeed been special individuals.

The longest race in the ancient Olympics was the dolichos. This race was most frequently run over twenty stades which at the principal site of Olympia, amounted to 3846 meters. This race is said by some historians to have been inspired by the messengers who carried the orders of war over long distances.

The runners in the dolichos would each line up in their own lane in a starting gate which resembled that of a modern day horserace. The starting line, still visible at Olympia today, shows two narrow grooves in stone, eighteen centimeters apart at right angles to the course. The runners competed barefoot and probably put their toes into these grooves to give some advantage in the start. They would then compete over twenty lengths of the straight course, turning at each end to retrace their steps.

Although clothes were worn in the early games there is no evidence to suggest that footwear was ever worn. The track surface must have been uncomfortable to the barefoot runners. It was rough and baked by the high temperatures since the games were held in mid-summer.

Clothes were abandoned by the athletes sometime near 776 B.C. for reasons which may have had religious significance or simple practicality as their basis.

Much Olympic history has been culled from the writing of Pausanius (3-2 B.C.) who seems to have been an ancient Greek combination of Howard Cosell and Walter Cronkite. In his descriptions of Greece he tells of the 200 meter stadion race held at the 15th Olympics. "(The winner Orsippus). . . won the foot race at Olympia by running naked when all his competitors wore girdles according to the custom." In the best traditions of journalistic skepticism and with the benefit of almost 500 years of hindsight Pausanius continues: "My own opinion is that at Olympia he intentionally let the girdle slip off him, realizing that a naked man can run more easily than one wearing a girt."

While other authors dispute the exact date when clothes were thrown away almost all the vase paintings of runners in action show them naked and without footwear. One beautiful example is shown in Figure 2.2 which shows distance runners in a typical pose matching each other stride for stride.

Women readers will no doubt be impressed already

Fig. 2.2 Competitors in a Greek distance race (the Dolichos—about 4,000 meters) without clothing or footwear. (Courtesy of the British Museum)

Fig. 2.3 Barefoot women athletes with flowing skirts from a vase painting of about 500 B.C. (Courtesy of the Vatican Museum)

by the sexism of early athletic competitions, probably reflecting that the current struggle for recognition of women's distance running at the Olympic level had early beginnings. It should come as a pleasant surprise, then, that a vase painting in the Vatican from about 500 B.C. depicts a women's foot race (Fig. 2.3). The contestants are wearing somewhat impractical long flowing skirts and shoulder-length hair slightly gathered with a small head scarf. There are clear ankle straps on some of the runners but these would appear to be decorative jewelry rather than functional footwear. The spartan woman athlete shown in Figure 2.4 is also barefoot and wearing a rather revealing outfit.

THE WAR MESSENGERS

We cannot leave ancient Greece behind without mentioning one of the most famous distance runners of all times—Pheidippides. Sorting fact from legend is at best difficult and at worst disenchanting. The original "Marathon Run," which the modern race is said to commemorate, took place in 490 B.C. It was a journey from the Plains of Marathon to Athens by a messenger

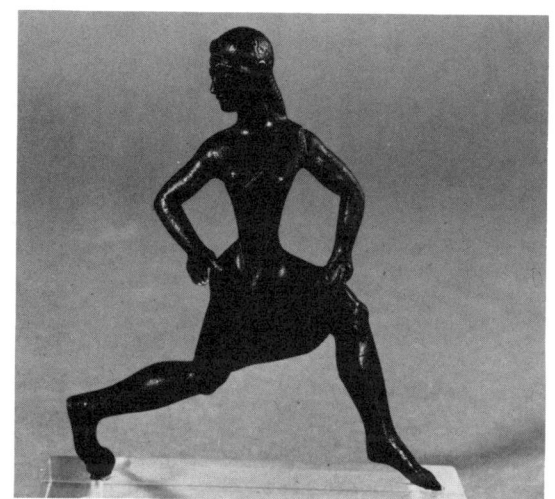

Fig. 2.4 A Spartan woman runner both barefooted and barebreasted. (Courtesy of the British Museum)

who joyfully proclaimed the victory of the Athenians over the Persians. His run is not documented by any contemporary writers. But hundreds of years after the fact historians described how he had burst in on the Athenian legislature, shouted "nike," the Greek word for victory, and promptly died. Another account says the messenger ran "in full armor" with footwear that we can only suppose was needed because the terrain was harsh.

But was this messenger Pheidippides? Historian John Lucas thinks it unlikely. He speaks for a majority of sports historians who feel that Pheidippides probably performed an even more impressive feat. As they marched out to face the Persians, the Athenian generals sent a messenger, apparently Pheidippides, to Sparta to recruit help. Completing this journey of 150 miles in less than one day, Pheidippides reportedly found the Spartans with more worthwhile things to do—it appears they were celebrating a religious holiday. The legend tells us that Pheidippides promptly turned around to carry the unfortunate message that help would not be available for almost a week.

It seems that conventional wisdom has taken the best athlete and the best story from two different incidents and combined them to produce a compelling legend.

THE END OF THE FIRST OLYMPIC ERA

As Greece came under increasing influence of the Roman Empire, the Olympic Games gradually declined in importance. Furthermore, as a highly visible symbol of conquest the Games were moved from the Sanctuary at Olympia to Rome. The spirit of athletic idealism which had fed the success of the Games for almost 1,000 years was subdued and infiltrated by the Roman passion for the spectacular, the dangerous, and the violent.

Although many Roman emperors were great supporters of the games, when finally abolished by decree in A.D. 393 they had changed so much that Koroibos of Elis, the first Olympic champion, would have wondered if he was on the right planet. Besides the influence of Roman bestiality, the Christians also did their share to try to destroy the Games. They equated participation in the Games with worship of gods other than theirs—which was not tolerated.

As one would expect of a nation which sought to conquer the whole known world, the emphasis of Roman sports and games was on combat. Participants were dressed in protective clothing and armor and probably wore footwear similar to that used by soldiers.

Shoemaking was a well-developed art in Roman times. There are many examples of fine workmanship in leather and hand forged nails in museums throughout the world. Styles ranged from finely worked sandals and mocassins to nailed boots for marching or walking (Figure 2.5). Separate shoes were made to fit the left and right feet, something that was not always a feature of earlier or later footwear. Shoes were also a means of showing rank, both by color and degree of ornamentation. The preserved or modelled heads of small stoats or ermine were sometimes worn by the nobility around the ankle as part of the sandal strapping. The Emperor Marcus Aurelius is said to have branded the colors yellow, white, and green as effeminate and to be used only by women.

Fig. 2.5   Examples of Roman footwear: a) Caliga in carbatine style, b) spiked caliga; and c) an Emperor's Campagus decorated with the head and fur of a small animal. (Adapted from *Mode in Footwear* by R. Turner)

The Roman armies also seem to have used runners to convey their messages. Mention of footwear for the runners occurs in an edict issued by the Emperor Diocletian (A.D. 248-313). He specified that runners should wear a *gallica* with a single sole for men, double sole for farmworkers, and without hobnails for women and mule drivers. Wooden shoes were also used in Roman times but it is highly unlikely that any running could be done in these early clogs.

FOOTWEAR IN THE DARK AGES AND MEDIEVAL TIMES

Games and sports during the Dark and Middle Ages retained the military flavor which had been injected by the Romans. Although the search for running shoes from these times will result in little success there were significant events in both shoe manufacture and shoe fashion which influenced later developments.

The use of nails in shoemaking seems to have been one of the technologies which, like glass windows, the Roman Empire took down with it. However, by the beginning of the Tudor period (1485) it is fair to say that, with the possible exception of high heels, most of the fashions and basic construction techniques we see today had been invented.

Shoemaking will be discussed at greater length in Chapter 5 but we should mention here that two enduring techniques, the turnshoe and welted construction, were in existence by the 12th and 14th centuries respectively. The turnshoe, as its name suggests, was made inside out so that when it was finished, the seams would be outside and the part of the shoe next to the skin was smooth. Early shoes for sports were certainly made by this technique.

The welt, described further in Chapter 5, allowed heavier materials to be used, since the shoe did not have to be pulled inside out after manufacture.

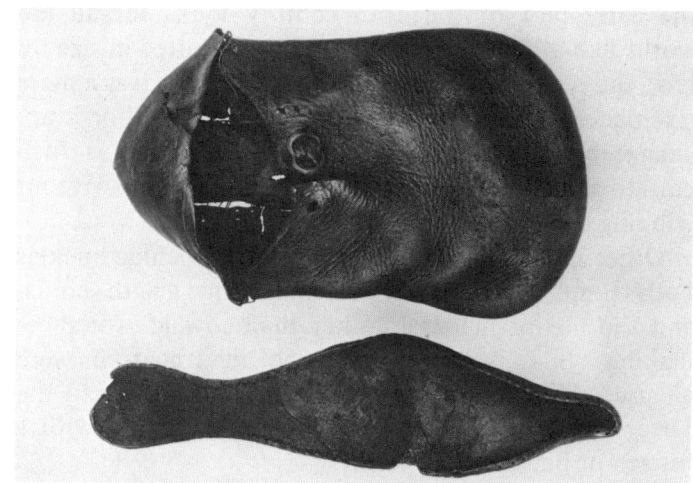

Fig. 2.6 The extremes of footwear made in Tudor, England (1485 onwards). A shoe almost six inches wide, and a pointed "pike." (Courtesy of the Northampton Museum, England)

Some of the more outrageous fashions of this period are shown in Figure 2.6. The toes changed with time from rounded ends, to square ends, to horned outriggers and even to points which were so long they were held up by chains around the knee.

Points, or "pikes" as they were known, became the subject of legislation as decrees passed in the reign of Edward III of England (1327-1377) limited their length to no more than two inches beyond the toes.

The massive "duckbilled" toe common in England in

the early part of the 16th century looks for all the world like a bicycle seat. It, too, was limited in size by law: the maximum width allowed at the toe was a mere six inches! The shoes seem to be "straights," or interchangeable between left and right sides, and it is difficult to imagine how one could walk in them without tripping over.

Other innovations of the middle ages include buckles both simple and ornate, thigh-and-knee-length boots, and the use of materials other than cowhide for shoemaking. Silks, velvet, wood, wool, and goatskin were all used. The legs were sometimes bandaged up to the knee with silk or cloth wrappings, terminated with a broach or buckle.

The use of the word "pumps" to denote slipper-like shoes began to appear in the English language in the 16th century. These were single soled shoes generally of turnshoe construction and were extremely popular as the footwear of courtiers. Their use as a light indoor shoe made them obvious favorites for games.

Pumps were to develop into Plimsolls in 19th century England. They were named for Sir Samuel Plimsoll because the line of rubber all around the usually canvas shoe was reminiscent of the line around ships which Sir Sam hoped would prevent overloading. By 1900 the form had developed into the sneaker which stayed a part of the American culture for the next seventy years.

THE ORIGINS OF MODERN TRACK AND FIELD

The basic simplicity of man running against man, woman against woman, is such that contests on foot seem to arouse a primordial resonance in the brain. The excitement of the early Greeks at the Olympic Games and the joy of the English peasants of the 16th century watching "the Running for Men Contest" at a country fair were timeless expressions of the same instinct.

In the early 1700s, footraces as part of the events surrounding a fair were common practice. Prizes frequently took the form of clothing and the competitors were, as often as not, women. One such race in Ireland inspired these lines in 1714: "Stript for the race how bright she did appear no covering hid her feet, her bosom bare and to the wind she gave her flowing hair". The parallel between the Spartan woman of 500 B.C. (Figure 2.4) and the Irish peasant of almost 2200 years later could hardly be closer.

Modern day track and field competition owes a considerable amount to the revival of "athletics," as it is known in England, in the nineteenth century. As American author Walter Camp was to lament in 1893, "...England has been in advance of us in track athletics ...having long ago learned the advantages of all outdoor exercises." The renowned Eton, alma mater of many

British Prime Ministers, conducted intramural track and field competitions in 1837. The first recorded dual meet was held in 1864 when Oxford and Cambridge competed in eight events.

At first it was not thought necessary to have special clothing or footwear for running. Advice typical of the period was given to the walker and runner in 1839 by *Walker's Manly Exercises:* ". . . the coat and all unnecessary clothes should be laid aside . . . the waistband of the trousers should not be tight, and the boots or shoes should have no iron about them."

Eighteen thirty-nine was an important year for footwear. It was the year Charles Goodyear finally hit upon the process that would allow rubber to be transformed from an imperfect curiosity to a universally used material.

The fact that certain trees yield latex had been known for almost 1,000 years but rubber had not been widely used because no one could find a way to stop it from becoming moist and sticky, under warm conditions and hard and brittle in the cold. The critical trick, which Goodyear discovered by the usual combination of luck and judgement, was to heat crude rubber with sulphur until everything melted. When the mixture cooled, the resulting product was stable and pliable. The process was named vulcanization and is still the basis for the natural rubber industry. Rubber began to find uses everywhere. It was particularly welcome in running shoes, where it provided some relief from the hard pounding that leather shoes inflicted.

By the middle of the century rubber shoes were being used for running and Sir John Astley, a famous patron of pedestrianism, wrote about ". . . india rubber shoes which fitted him like gloves."

Specialized footwear for sport was slow to appear. Pumps and sneakers, mentioned earlier, were a form of general recreational shoe and were used in running events.

Astley mentions a race in 1852 in which one of his opponents had "a lovely little pair of spiked shoes." Whether or not Sir John's reminiscences can be trusted is rather unsure. His memoirs consist largely of describing how much money he won on this wager or that. In the race mentioned he ". . . recommended the keepers and beaters to put their dollars on me, till quite a heap of silver depended on the result. . . " Fortunately for his backers he was as good a runner as he was a braggart.

The first spiked shoes were not made for running at all. The patent, issued in England in 1861, was for that grand old game of cricket. A statue of a young boy "waiting his turn to bat" in London's Kensington Palace shows what must be a very early version of a cricket shoe.

One of the most exciting finds during my own search of museums was made in Northampton—the center of the British shoemaking industry from early times.

Beautifully made, and extremely well preserved, the shoe in Figure 2.7 was displayed in a glass case, labeled "Running Shoe—possibly belonged to Lord Spencer c. 1865." It is likely that this shoe represents the earliest spiked running shoe ever made on a production basis.

The shoe can be dated with remarkable certainty. It bears the label:

"Thomas Dutton and Thorowgood, Castle Square Brighton, and at London, Stones End, Southwark 4, Martin's Court, Leicester Square and Beckford Row, Walworth."

The only dates on which these addresses coincide with listings for the firm in Post Office directories are between 1861-1865. This dating is also remarkably coincident with the first dual meet in track and field (already mentioned).

The Spencer shoe bears a definite relationship to early cricket shoes. The low cut design is of all leather construction but is nevertheless extremely light at 280 grams. There are three spikes under the forefoot and one under the heel, suggesting that the shoe was used as a distance running or cross-country shoe. It incorporates a broad toe band, which is a separate piece of leather, sewn into the welt of the shoe to add lateral stability.

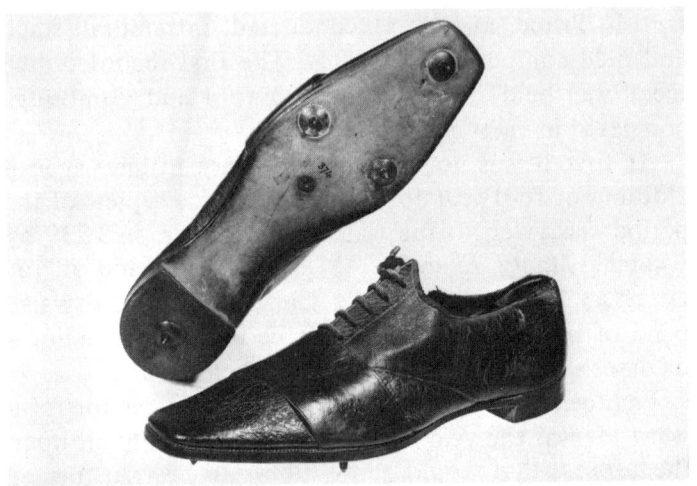

Fig. 2.7 The Spencer Shoe. Possibly the first pair of specialized running shoes ever made. (Courtesy of the Northampton Museum, England)

My own view of the Spencer shoe is that it pinpoints the first branch in the evolution of running shoes. From 1865 on, specialized shoes for running turn away from street shoes to form their own line of evolution.

The Spencer shoe was the precursor of track spikes as we know them today. The line was to branch again in 1896 as we shall see shortly. This second branch was bred by the needs of the "Pedestrians" and the protagonists of the Marathon Fever which gripped England and America at the turn of the nineteenth century. The 1896 branch leads directly to our modern day training flats.

TRACK AND FIELD FLOURISHES 1864–1896

The wearers of spiked shoes soon staked their claim as participants in a nationally popular sport. The first national championships in track and field were held in England in 1866 and America in 1876. By the time the first England vs. the United States meet was held in New York in 1895, America had overcome its late start in track and field and defeated England in all eleven events. The performances included an astonishing mile victory by Thomas Conneff in 4:18.2.

We have excellent evidence of the type of shoes worn by these athletes and the runners of subsequent times, for two main reasons. First, photography was a growing art particularly in the early days of track and field when the posed studio shot of the athlete prepared for action was to be seen in magazines and books. Second, the sporting goods business began to flourish by the end of the 19th century. There are catalogs and advertisements, notably from the Spalding Company, which give us much information. The first edition of the Sears Catalog was published in 1897. This catalog through the years is a storehouse of information about contemporary trends, including running shoes.

In 1894, the Spalding Spring and Summer Catalog offered runners three grades of spiked shoes at $6.00, $4.50, and $3.00 (Figure 2.8). To complete the track and field footwear line, jumping, walking, and cross-country shoes were also available, all with a $6.00 price tag.

Six dollars was no mean sum in 1894 when one considers that the average family of four earned $11.00 per week. The same $6.00 would have bought the family fifty pounds of steak which at the time was only eleven cents a pound.

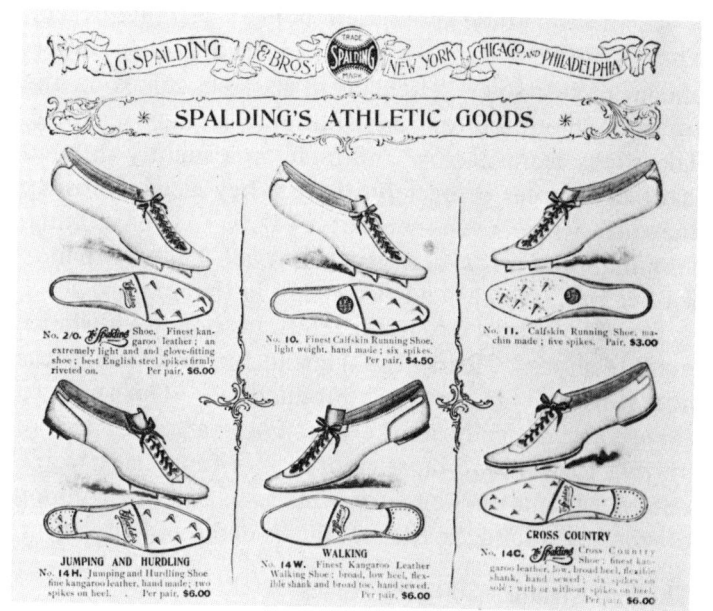

Fig. 2.8 Running and walking shoes from the 1894 catalog of A.G. Spalding. (Courtesy of International Sports and Games Research Collection, University of Notre Dame)

All the top-grade shoes were built to a similar design. They were low cut, made of kangaroo leather uppers and a leather sole. There were six steel spikes on the forefoot mounted on an additional leather half-sole. The shoes were narrow and built on a slightly inflared last (see chapter 9 for definition). They laced almost to the toe with seven sets of eyelets. The walking, jumping, and cross-country shoes all had a separate leather heel, which held two spikes in the jumping shoe.

Notably absent from the 1894 catalog are distance running shoes. Clearly the demand for these items was not sufficient to warrant production. This was to change dramatically in the next ten years. But before moving forward we must step back in time, back to the 1850s, when a phenomenon which was to bring running to the eyes and hearts of the general public began.

The Pedestrians—500 Mile Races

One of the rarest group of men ever to enter into athletic competition captured the attention of the public in the last half of the nineteenth century. The races were fixed at six days and six nights for a total of 144 hours of competition. The hardy competitors ran, walked, or slept in whatever blend they felt would keep them going. From contemporary accounts, this varied from warm tea to strychnine.

Olympic historian John Lucas has captured the excitement and agony of pedestrianism in an account of five special races in 1878 and 1879. These were sponsored by Sir John Astley, with large purses and a magnificent silver and gold belt offered as prizes.

The English Knight staged the series of 144 hour competitions between the best of two continents in what he billed as "The Long Distance Challenge Championship of the World." At Madison Square Garden in New York, and Agricultural Hall in London, spectators turned out in the tens of thousands to watch exhausted men walking and running around the sawdust and tanbark track for more than twenty of each twenty-four hours. The performances were truly phenomenal. In the first race, Irish-American Daniel O'Leary was victorious with a total of 520 miles completed in 139 hours. Before the series ended Edward Payson Weston, the "Father of American Pedestrianism," had extended the distance to 550 miles and his own pocket by $8,000. The greatest pedestrian performance of all time was logged in 1888 by Englishman George Littlewood, who covered an incredible 623¾ miles in 139 hours 59 minutes, an overall average of just over fifteen minutes per mile for six days.

The "Ped Races" were headline news in both London and New York papers. The fame of these iron men was put to good use by their shoe makers, as the advertisement from a contemporary newspaper in Figure 2.9 indicates. The shoes used by the pedestrians were high-top leather "boots" (Figure 2.10) worn over layers of

McSWYNY,

O'LEARY'S

CHAMPION SHOEMAKER,

419 BROADWAY,

N. W. corner Canal St., **NEW YORK.**

You can immerse my Water-Proof Boots and Shoes for any length of time, and if the water should get through, I will refund the money or exchange the Goods.

A Large Assortment of

Bengal Tiger, Alligator, Porpoise, and Seal Skins,

Tanned expressly for my use.

From Sir John D. Astley to the *Sporting Life*, London, England: "O'Leary had an ample supply of McSwyny's best made boots, which added materially to his grand success in the late tournament."

From the New York *Sun*: "O'Leary, interviewed by a *Sun* reporter, says—'I had shoes made on both sides of the Atlantic, and have never been suited until I met the Irishman on Broadway, and with his shoes I had no fear of being defeated by the great Weston.'"

From the New York *Herald*: "People passing the corner of Broadway and Canal Street have been attracted by McSwyny, the Bootmaker, who is exhibiting in his showcase the shoes of his manufacture which O'Leary wore in his great walk in which he defeated Weston. He covered 520 miles in six days."

Fig. 2.9 An advertisement from the "Pedestrian Manual" of 1880 using the endorsement of the great Daniel O'Leary, who "had no fear of being defeated" in a pair of McSwyny's shoes.

woolen socks. Keeping the feet in good condition must have been as difficult as staying awake for six days and nights. Each contestant had a team of handlers whose job it was to keep his body going come what may. Since such enormous sums of money were bet on the outcome of the races, payoffs and drug taking were common. The sport faded abruptly as the participants lost their credibility with the general public.

Despite the eventual decline of pedestrianism the public awareness of running competition had been heightened by these grueling races. But a race was to take place in 1896 that led to even more enthusiasm on behalf of the sport. It was also to lead to the birth of the marathon as we know it today.

THE MARATHON IS BORN

Athletic competition underwent a formal revival in 1896 when the first modern Olympic Games were held in Athens. The games were championed with great flair and passion by the French Baron Pierre de Coubertin over the somewhat lukewarm response of Greek politicians. At the suggestion of one of Coubertin's friends, Professor Michel Breal, a distinctly un-Olympic event was to be included on the program. This was a race of forty kilometers to be named the marathon. Its purpose was to commemorate the Pheidippidean legend.

The prospect of a Greek victory in the race captured

Fig. 2.10 Two competitors in a pedestrian race wearing what appear to be sturdy medium high cut leather shoes. (From *Ultramarathoning* by Tom Osler and Ed Dodd)

the patriotic spirit of the Greeks. They were determined to win the race along dusty roads from the plain of Marathon to the Stadium of Herodes Atticus.

The pre-race favorite was an Australian named Edwin Flack who had already won the 800 and 1500 meter races. But like many other starters in the race, Flack appears to have been completely unprepared for the distance and collapsed after being passed for the lead shortly after thirty-six kilometers.

The Greeks' desire to win had led them to conduct trials at or close to the marathon distance. This strategy proved successful. As the foreigners fell, due to their unrealistic early pace, the local runners gradually moved to the front of the field.

Two hours, fifty-eight minutes and 50 seconds after the start, Spiridon Louis, variously reported as shepherd or soldier in the Greek Army, arrived in the Stadium amid an ecstatic ovation from the home crowd. The day was crowned when eight minutes later Vasilakos arrived to begin a virtual procession of Greek finishers who filled first, second, third, sixth, seventh, eighth, and ninth places.

Although some authors refer to the "spiked shoes" of the competitors in the first marathon, it is unlikely that many of the entrants wore spiked shoes. The course was simply too rocky. Wearing spikes would have been uncomfortable and dangerous.

This first marathon race, on a March day in 1896, was to have a profound influence on the footwear that millions of distance runners wear today. The race itself was a first statement that running did not necessarily involve making laps around the track. The shoes for this new form of running would have to be different from track shoes. So the line of evolution of the modern distance running shoe made its second branch in 1896. Back in 1861, the spiked running shoe had split away from an everyday shoe. Now in 1896 the distance shoe has a small beginning. Following this line will lead us directly to today's running flats.

The marathon caught on like wildfire. The first Boston Marathon was run in the very next year with fifteen starters competing over a twenty-five mile course. By 1902 there were forty-two starters and an estimated 100,000 spectators lined the course.

In the 1904 Olympic Marathon in Saint Louis American Fred Lorz appeared in the stadium "almost as fresh as when he left it, over two and a half hours earlier." In the nick of time, as the laurel was about to be bestowed, it was discovered that Lorz had good reason to be fresh. He had actually dropped out at fifteen kilometers and ridden at least part of the way back to the stadium by car. Probably in penance, he ran the race of his life in the 1905 Boston Marathon to win in 2:38.25.

The London race of 1908 was the first one to be run over the modern distance of 26 miles 385 yards (42.195 kilometers). The curious extension of the previous twenty-five mile course was due to the wish of the organizers to start the race in the aura of royalty at Windsor Castle, and finish at the Olympic Stadium at White City.

Queen Alexandra started fifty-six runners on "the long grind", as journalists of the time liked to call the race. By twenty miles the early local hopes had been dashed as the English yielded the lead to South African Charles Hefferon. A massive four minutes behind came a diminutive Italian baker Dorando Pietri.

By a combination of heroic efforts from Pietri, and heavy fatigue overcoming Hefferon, Pietri took the lead in the last few miles. Entering the stadium, Pietri, on the point of collapse, turned the wrong way. As officials gestured wildly, Pietri fell to the track, exhausted. He was helped up, turned around, and before thousands of stricken spectators, fell a total of five times before being helped across the line by the chief clerk of the course and the medical attendant. (Figure 2.11)

Fig. 2.11 Dorando Pietri is helped across the finish line of the 1908 Olympic Marathon in London, only to be disqualified for receiving assistance. (BBC Hulton Picture Library photo)

Their help led to Pietri's disqualification, although there was photographic evidence that the St. Louis winner, Hicks, had also received illegal assistance. Thirty seconds after Pietri's ordeal ended with total collapse, American John J. Hayes crossed the finish line to become one of the most unwelcome and ignored medalists of all time.

Dorando's story made news throughout the world. He was feted as a hero and champion wherever he went. He was presented with the Queen's Cup by Queen Alexandra, and capitalized on his fame by turning professional as did Hayes. The two competed regularly before admiring crowds on both sides of the Atlantic with Dorando being the usual winner.

SHOES FOR THE MARATHONERS

The shoes worn by Dorando and his competitors were either heavy boots or shoes with leather uppers and soles which must have been very painful to wear. Rubber soling material was soon to be introduced.

Flexibility in footwear was not something the early marathoners got, or apparently wanted. Matt Maloney, who after his victory in a 1908 New York race was "now convinced that the Irish are the best long distance runners," had the following to say:

> Regarding running shoes, I like to have the soles of my shoes fairly stiff so as to keep the foot steady: if too pliable the foot bends on the inside and the result will be a blister on the foot and very soon it will begin to hurt, with the result that you are forced to stop and change your shoes—then you are through.

Fig. 2.12 The American Olympic Marathon team at the 1908 Games. John J. Hayes (far left) was declared the winner after Dorando's disqualification. Notice that only one runner is wearing high top shoes. (Courtesy of International Sports and Games Research Collection, University of Notre Dame)

The Spalding Company was one of the first to realize the reflected glory runners would feel by wearing shoes similar to the Olympic champions. In 1908 Spalding outfitted many of the American marathon contingent of six runners (Figure 2.12). They also dispatched Mr. G.L. Pearce, superintendent of the athletic shoe factory, with the team . . . "solely to give his expert experience in the matter of footwear for the . . .sterling athletes who competed for the Glory of America and the Stars and Stripes." This is reminiscent of Adi Dassler's travels with the West German soccer teams half a century later.

The 1908 race had created tremendous interest in the marathon. On his return from the Games, Pearce headed straight for the drawing board. In the first treatise on the marathon, a 110-page book by James E. Sullivan, published in 1909, we are told that:

> ". . . From his observations on the spot he (Pearce) has evolved the Spalding Marathon shoe which is already recognized as the only shoe on the market which is suitable for both indoor and outdoor wear. It is hand sewn with a flexible upper. The soles are of good weight and protected on the outside with rubber to prevent slipping and straining of the tendons or muscles.

The result of Pearce's labors is shown in Figure 2.13. "Good weight" certainly meant at least one pound per shoe and probably more.

The "top of the line" shoe was the high cut, black leather shoe which looks very much like an Army boot. The heel was reinforced with additional leather and the sole was a diamond pattern of "gum rubber".

The eight dollar expenditure is likely to have purchased a short-lived luxury, since the disclaimer printed in the advertisement advised the athlete: ". . . We cannot guarantee the soles on these shoes as they are pure gum, which, while the best and most costly

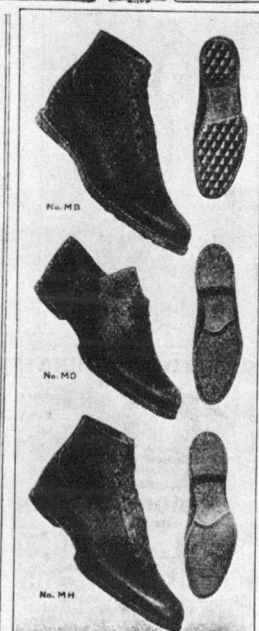

Fig. 2.13 These 1909 marathon shoes from Spalding were designed by Mr. G.L. Pearce from "his observations on the spot" at the 1908 Olympics. (Courtesy of International Sports and Games Research Collection, University of Notre Dame)

material for the purpose, is not, unfortunately, the most durable." Time does not seem to have helped much either. Boston Marathon mentor Jock Semple recalls the day in 1926 when he ran his first marathon in Philadelphia in a pair of Spalding Marathon shoes. They were too narrow for his feet and he reports "I wore them out in one race!" (see Chapter 16).

Despite the company's insistence that the shoes pictured ". . . represent the three styles most popular among American distance runners . . ." the photographic evidence seems to contradict the notion that high cut running shoes ever caught on. The picture of the 1908 team (Figure 2.12) shows only one out of six runners wearing a high cut shoe.

Indeed the cut of some marathon shoes of the early 1900s seems to be much lower than even the low cut Spalding shoe. The gum rubber sole disappeared from the catalog by 1911, leaving only the high and low cut shoe, both of which were fitted with a "cushioned leather heel" and a corrugated tap rubber sole under the forepart of the shoe. This version was now described as "the proper shoe for a long race."

Complaints from marathon runners about the durability of the outsole must have continued to flow into the Spalding offices. Rubber technology was not well developed in the early 1900s. In particular the techniques of reinforcing rubber to give better abrasion resistance were still unknown. So durability won the day over foot protection.

By 1913 the "Marathon" insignia had been dropped and the long distance shoes, now described as "Correct Marathon Shoes," featured all-leather outsoles. They were advertised at five dollars per pair with the stated virtue: ". . . Leather soles will not wear smooth". It is an intriguing comment on the gullibility of early marathon runners if in five years the "perfect" shoe could undergo such apparently negative changes and still be sold as the "correct" marathon shoe.

RUNNING BOOKS

The running boom brought with it running books. In addition to Sullivan's book mentioned earlier there were two other classics by great runners, one on each side of the Atlantic. In England Alfred Shrubb eclipsed most British and world records from one to eleven and three quarter miles between 1900 and 1908. His book in 1907 was written in the hope that it might ". . .prove of some slight assistance in redressing the balance" of American domination of international track and field.

In the States George Orton wrote a volume for the Spalding Athletic Library in 1911 called *Distance and Cross Country Running*. Orton was a 4:21 miler and noted in his book that American distance runners ". . . rank second only to the Englishmen whose climate and general upbringing have made them peerless in this one branch of the sport."

Neither man, at the time, was particularly interested in marathon running. In fact Shrubb thought the marathon had received "...a tremendous amount of attention – more, I think, than it deserves in some respects" and he added that marathon races "can hardly be called exciting affairs." Orton disposes of the event in ten lines, one of which implores the runner to cover no more than fifteen miles in training and "...depend on his general condition to carry him through the full distance."

It is perhaps not entirely surprising that neither book contains a paragraph of advice on footwear. Both men were essentially track runners who did not endure the agony of the marathoner. The many pictures in these books show runners in very low cut slipper-like shoes with no socks. The classic shot of Shrubb and two other runners in Figure 2.14 is a good example that we shall refer to later on (notice the ankle strap on Shrubb's right foot).

Sullivan's book does contain a half page on "The proper kind of shoes" for marathon running. The book was published in the Spalding series and, perhaps not surprisingly, the advice given by the author is to buy Spalding shoes. Sullivan noted that: "The firm is particularly pleased when a runner calls at their stores and

Fig. 2.14 The legendary British runner Alfred Shrubb (center) who held most world records from one mile to eleven and three-quarters miles. Note the ankle strap on his right shoe.

has his shoes made to order. In the long run that is the most desirable process, because one is then sure of getting a perfect fit."

As a final piece of advice Sullivan suggested that: "it is always safe to have two pairs of shoes, one for practice and one for running, and always be sure that your shoes fit right. Change the strings repeatedly and test them before you go to the mark in an important race."

Looking over the pictures of early twentieth century runners, it is striking that many of them do not seem to be wearing socks. This seems especially strange knowing that their shoes were stiff and heavy with large overlapping seams—the perfect environment for blisters. The problem is ignored by Sullivan in his 1909 book on marathon running, but leafing through the early sporting goods catalogs provides an answer.

The runners probably wore pushers. As a Spalding advertisement from 1894 shows (Figure 2.15) pushers were abbreviated bedroom slippers of chamois skin which were worn inside the shoe. Since they only covered the front part of the foot one is left to wonder at the size of the heel blisters that the runners must have had.

The second accessory that no well-equipped long distance runner would do without was a pair of running corks (Figure 2.15) sometimes known as "cork athletic grips." This is again something that the contemporary

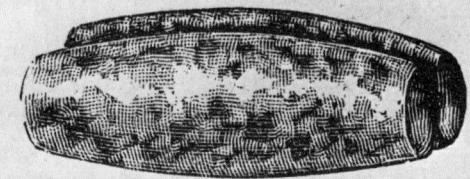

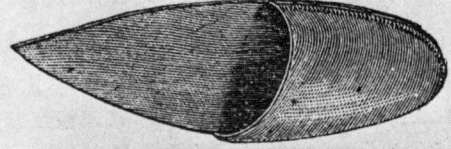

Fig. 2.15 Runner's accessories: corks to hold in the hand and "pushers" to go inside the shoes. Taken from the Spalding 1894 Catalog. (Courtesy of International Sports and Games Research Collection, University of Notre Dame)

texts on marathon running did not mention. Photographs and catalogs from 1894 through 1926 make it certain that their use was widespread. Later versions include rubber bands to hold them on to the fingers.

The grips were presumably something that would

allow one to maintain muscle tension in the finger flexors during running without completely clenching the fists. This doctrine would be strongly opposed by present-day thinking on the relaxation of muscles not directly involved in the exercise.

One of the most striking pictures of a runner using corks is shown in Figure 2.16. Here we see Kenneth McArthur winning the marathon at the Stockholm Olympic Games of 1912 in a time of 2:36:54 (on a course of 24.9 miles). Already garlanded with a winner's wreath thrown from the crowd, McArthur breaks the tape with his outstretched hands, and in doing so gives a clear view of his running corks for posterity.

MARATHON FEVER DECLINES

The years between 1895 and 1910 were years of marathon fever comparable to the 1970s. The number of entrants in marathon races grew each year. Anyone who ran wanted to try his hand at the ultimate challenge. Young boys tried to enter, but the authorities of the day campaigned hard against lowering the minimum entry age much below twenty. But the heights of public interest engendered by the 1908 Olympic Marathon could not be expected to last. Marathon running settled into a more stable phase of life. This is reflected by the entry count in the Boston

Fig. 2.16 The South African Kenneth McArthur breaks the tape in the 1912 Olympic marathon, giving a clear view of his running corks.

Marathon—always a useful barometer of marathon interest. Figure 2.16 shows that a record number of 193 runners started the event in 1910, a number which was not to be equalled until 1927. Who could have predicted that the first time more than 300 runners entered, 1964, would be followed by an onslaught of marathoners reaching an official 7,877 in 1979?

Despite the temporary decline of the marathon race from 1910 onwards, track and field gained ground. Schools in many countries of the world began to include Olympic track and field events in their sports programs.

The footwear industry responded to market pressure and "running shoes" became synonymous with track spikes. By 1915 the Spalding catalog displayed specialized spiked shoes for sprinting, middle distance, jumping indoors and out, and pole vaulting. They also sold an impressive array of track and field paraphernalia including a "harness for three-legged racing" and a "tambourine No. 1 required when throwing the fifty-six pound weight for height."

Other manufacturers entered the growing market. Sears Roebuck was already in the mail order business and their catalogs from 1897 onwards carried pages of sports shoes at prices consistently below what Spalding could offer. This led to a battle of words in print. Every Spalding catalog carried a long diatribe against cheap competition. For example, in 1911 the following appeared:

> "Beware of the Just as Good manufacturer, who makes "pretty" Athletic Goods (as if they were for use as an ornament) at the expense of "quality", in order to deceive the dealer; and beware of the substitute-dealer who completes the fraud by offering the "Just as Good" article when Spalding goods are asked for."

Sears responded with a play on price: "Our prices on sporting shoes are lower than any wholesale dealer on earth." Through the 1920s their marketing was low-key and clinical, a replica of Spalding's own approach, but by 1930 the Kiki Cuyler Jr. basketball shoes were out and endorsement by famous athletes had begun.

The late 1920s and early thirties were hard years, when putting food on the table was more important (and sometimes more difficult) than running marathons. Strangely enough there was renewed interest in marathon running in this decade. Boston entry numbers (Figure 2.17) reached a peak in 1928. The great Johnny Kelly was in his prime in these years and he is a living piece of the history of running and running shoes. Kelly tried anything he could get his hands on which was lighter, kinder to the feet, and cheaper than the Spalding shoe. He ran races in sneakers, bowling shoes, high jump shoes. And with no little success: his record is two victories and seven second place finishes in the Boston Marathon. Kelly also recalls the unfortunate Les Pawson, a three-time Boston winner, who made his own shoes in the Depression only to have his favorite pair stolen while he was in the shower.

Jock Semple, who has been connected with the Boston Marathon since 1923, also remembers the bad times. He tried patching worn out running shoes with rubber from car tires and early "shoe goo"-like compounds. One of his most vivid memories (see chapter 16) is of soaking his feet in beef brine for half an hour each night to harden them up. This strategy, together with patiently rubbing the shoes with neats-foot oil, warded off at least the catastrophic blisters which would force a runner out of the race.

But running shoes were still desperately hard on the feet. Semple recalls the clubhouse at the end of the

The History of the Running Shoe 31

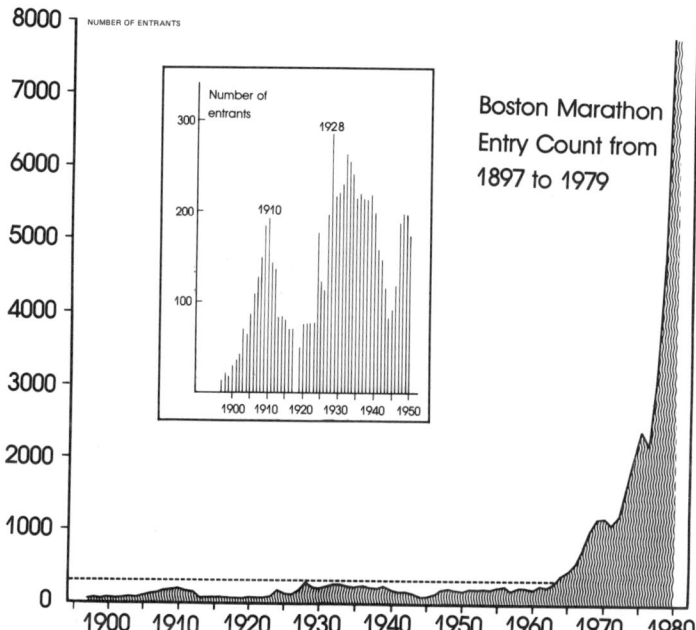

Fig. 2.17 The number of entrants in the Boston Marathon since its inception in 1897. Inset shows the early "marathon craze" peaking in 1910. Note that there were never more than 300 entrants before 1964.

early Boston Marathons as a "disaster area" with almost every runner in trouble with his feet.

The person who saved the day for both Kelly and Semple was an Englishman they both call "Old Man Richings." A retired shoemaker, Richings decided that, at seventy-five years old, he could make better shoes for runners than the youngsters were turning out. As a true Scotsman, Semple found the lure of free shoes irresistible—and what's more, they worked! Richings concentrated on a smooth seamless toe box and custom made the shoes for his clients. Semple was the guinea pig and recalls running over to Richings' house for adjustments. He had very wide feet and the Richings shoe was the best thing his feet had felt.

Unfortunately neither Kelly nor Semple had a pair of these shoes in their attic today. The closest we have is an advertisement from the 1940s (Figure 2.18) placed by Osborne Winslow, who continued Richings' tradition. The design is distinctive. The lacing was on the side of the shoe and an elastic "gore" helped the shoe fit well over the instep. There was a separate heel, a low cut

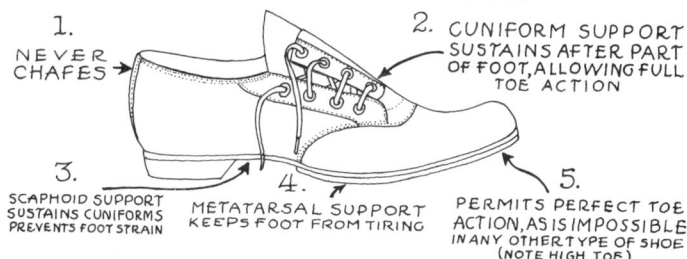

Fig. 2.18 An advertisement from the 1940s for Star Streamline Shoes, direct descendants of the original Richings shoe. The shoes were made to order after the customer provided a foot outline and some basic measurements.

rearpart without a counter and an "easy to repair" outsole. The shoes were probably at least five ounces lighter than their contemporaries. The success of the shoe speaks for itself. Nine of the first eleven men home in the 1940 Boston Marathon wore the shoe, which was to be the forebear of the New Balance line.

"Old Man" Richings apart, production running shoes made in America changed little during the 1930s. The 1935 Spalding catalog carried at least ten shoes for track and field but only a single long distance running shoe. The spiked track shoe of 1935 (Figure 2.19) has a striking resemblance to its forty-year-old ancestor that we met back in Figure 2.8. The shoes were no longer all hand-sewn, but the same patterns seem to have been used for cutting the leather uppers and the spike configuration was the same. The last had been slightly modified to give a more rounded toe box and the spike fixation had improved in the 1935 model. But in forty years, the spiked running shoe had hardly changed.

The single marathon shoe in the 1935 Spalding line was a low cut leather shoe on which rubber again appeared on the outsole (Figure 2.19). At a price of $8.60 inflation was obviously unknown. The shoe had increased by an average price of just over two cents a year in the previous quarter of a century! There was some decline in the quality of materials used, though. The leather was now described as "fine durable leather" —certainly not the "special qualtiy black leather" that had been used earlier.

Fig. 2.19 A track shoe from the 1935 Spalding Collection. (Courtesy of International Sports and Games Research Collection, University of Notre Dame)

The high top running shoe had disappeared for good at least ten years earlier. There was still a distinct and separate heel piece on the shoe. Matt Maloney, winner of the New York Evening Journal Marathon in 1908, had warned twenty-five years earlier that ". . . there is great danger in running without heels. The danger lies in breaking down in the instep. Once that happens the athlete is crippled for life." All twentieth century marathon shoes that I have seen heeded Maloney's warning.

THE EMERGENCE OF GOOD FOREIGN SHOES

During the 1930s athletes around the world first heard a name that was to become synonymous with quality and innovation in the athletic shoe industry. The name was Dassler.

Adolf Dassler began making shoes in 1920. He made slippers and dress shoes but, as a keen athlete himself, he soon gravitated towards athletic shoes. As the fledgling business grew he was joined by his brother Rudolph, and shoes bearing the name Dassler Brothers began to appear on the feet of successful German athletes. Figure 2.21a shows their first running shoe which appeared in 1925, probably made in the workshop where the young Adi Dassler is posing in Figure 2.20.

By 1936 Dassler shoes were becoming known internationally, and Jesse Owens won at least one of his four gold medals in the Munich Olympics wearing them.

From the very beginning the Dassler brothers were innovators; some of their other innovations include a shoe with an arch support lacing (Figure 2.21c) and an early form of speed lacing (Figure 2.21b) made in 1941. The original function of the stripes to support the foot is clearly apparent in this shoe. The first three stripe shoes also appeared in 1941 although the patent for the design was not submitted until 1949.

If Dasslers made marathon shoes in these early years, they have not survived. The glory was out on the track,

Fig. 2.20 The young Adi Dassler in his workshop during the early 1920s. (Courtesy of Adidas, West Germany)

and the Olympic track and field events were the focus of the company's efforts.

In 1948 the partnership of Adi and Rudi Dassler ended on a note of acrimony. After bitter family feuding Adi formed a company he first called Addas which soon became Adidas. From a small start with a

34 THE HISTORY OF THE RUNNING SHOE

Fig. 2.21A

Fig. 2.21B

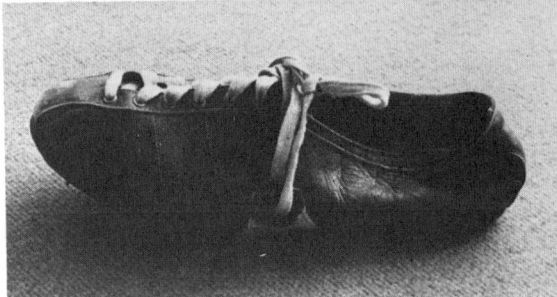
Fig. 2.21C

Fig. 2.21 Early running shoes from the Adidas Museum in Herzogenaurach, West Germany.

handful of employees, the company grew to become the largest athletic shoe manufacturers in the world. In the same small town in West Germany, Rudi formed the Puma Company and over the last thirty years the rivalry between the two firms has been a stimulus to the development of new ideas in shoe design.

Both companies are acutely conscious of their history. The Adidas museum in Herzogenaurach, West Germany (Figure 2.22) is perhaps the finest collection of track and field footwear since 1924. Puma also has examples of their early running shoes and shares an impressive record of patent disclosures for sports shoes. For both companies the competition regularly peaked at the Olympic Games. Each company vied with the other to outfit more Olympic athletes. Shoes became the currency of international track and field with Puma and Adidas the bankers.

Running in the 1950s benefited from a man who caught the attention of the world at the Olympic Marathon just as Dorando had done forty years earlier. When Emile Zatopek lined up at the start of the marathon in Helsinki in 1952 he already had the 5,000 and 10,000 meter gold medals in his pocket. Midway through the race Zatopek, already leading, turned to his nearest competitors, Jim Peters of Britain and Gustaf Larsson of Sweden, and said, "I've never run a marathon before, but don't you think we ought to go a little faster?" Although they didn't agree, Zatopek

The History of the Running Shoe

Fig. 2.22 Part of the running shoe collection in the Adidas Museum.

went faster anyway and came home for his third gold of the games in 2 hours 23:03.

To see what shoes marathoners of Zatopek's era were wearing we can turn to the archives of the Hyde Athletic Company which now includes Saucony. The Hyde Athletic Company had been making athletic shoes in New England since 1898. Football shoes were a company specialty but their running shoes were popular too.

Historian John Lucas recalls running in the 1953 Hyde ten-mile race and winning a pair of Hyde shoes for his efforts. Hyde "Spot Built" shoes were among the most popular domestic shoes in the 1950s, their ads claiming "they are used by more universities, colleges and high schools than other in the field." The 1949-50 Hyde marathon shoe was a fusion of Spalding's 1908 and Riching's 1935 shoes. Curiously, it was billed as a twenty-five mile marathon shoe although the marathon had by then been run at 26.2 miles for at least twenty-five years. The shoe was a welt construction made from kangaroo leather. It had the elastic "gore" closure with laces on the inside and a seamless toe box. The leather soles were covered in crepe rubber tap "for light weight, springy, surefooted speed so essential for those long grinds."

The picture bears witness that shoes of only thirty years ago bore little resemblance to those we use today. American shoemaking was on the verge of feeling the pinch of foreign competition. As if the German dominance of shoes on the feet of Olympic athletes was not enough, the Japanese Dragon was just awakening.

America first found out about Japanese marathon runners when nineteen-year-old Shigeki Tanaka won the Boston Marathon in 1951. Tiger, the best known of the Japanese shoes, made their first marathon shoe in the same year as Tanaka's victory. It is shown in Figure 2.24 and must represent, to a Westerner, one of the most curious running shoes of all time. The shoe has a

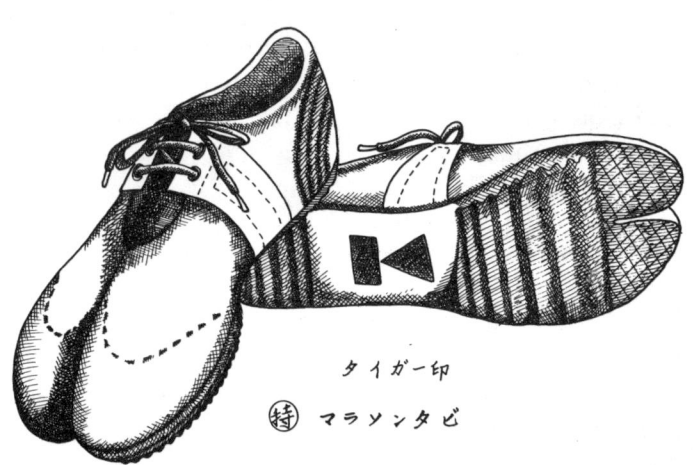

Fig. 2.24 A pair of Tiger Marathon shoes from the mid-1950s.

separate compartment for the big toe and was modeled on the traditional Japanese shoe the Geta. Presumably growing up with a thong between the big toe and second toe permanently spread these toes apart to the point where chafing was not a problem.

Tiger also made more conventional lines of running shoes, and by the mid-1950s were producing five different shoes all designed for road running. Their imports to the United States started in 1960.

A new product called training shoes also appeared during the late 1950s. The Adidas museum has six or seven shoes showing how these developed from 1945 onwards. "Training shoes" are not the same as our present day "training flats." They were intended as general purpose shoes for athletes in any sport to use while warming up, weight training, stretching, or anything else peripheral to the main activity. For sprinters a pair of "warm ups," as training shoes were called in England, were a status symbol not to be without.

One notable training shoe in the Adidas museum was made almost exlclusively of war surplus materials. The uppers were made from canvas taken from tents and the soles from material used in making gas tanks. Testifying to the fact that "training flats" were used to run in is a battered pair, much repaired, and autographed by their owner with the annotation that he had run over 8,000 kilometers in them!

Training shoes were very much like a modern day all-court shoe (Figure 2.25). They had shell construction rubber sole without much padding and with no heel wedge. The training shoe was the last development to fall into place before distance running shoes as we know them today emerged.

THE ENTRY OF NEW BALANCE

New Balance has a lineage which can be traced back to the Riley Company, which began making orthopedic shoes in the Boston area in 1906. Imbedded somewhere

Fig. 2.25 A typical "training shoe" or "warm up" popular during the 1960s and early 1970s.

along the line are the shoes Old Man Richings made for Jock Semple and Johnny Kelly in the 1930s. But the event that was to change the course of running shoe development occured in 1961. The now-retired owner of New Balance, Paul Kidd, and his design team thought that their spare production capacity could be put to good use by making running shoes.

As the product began to take shape it became clear that their greatest asset would be to translate the knowledge gained from orthopedic shoes into the running line. The absence of seams and adequate width in the forepart of the shoe were essential in making shoes for pathological feet. So why not do the same for runners?

With this philosophy, and the addition of the "ripple sole," the New Balance Trackster was born (Figure 2.26). This can truly be described as the first modern running shoe. It was the first running shoe of the twentieth century that bears any resemblance to our current shoes. And well it might, because its influence on subsequent development was profound.

When the shoe was first introduced in 1962, Paul Kidd remembers the response. "People laughed," he recalls, "it was so different from anything that had gone before. And the word 'orthopedic,' which we used to promote the shoe, was treated like a dirty word."

Despite the laughs, sales began to grow. New Balance was a small company; at first they were interested only

Fig. 2.26 The New Balance Trackster, introduced in 1962 and widely used for running throughout the next decade.

in the market offered by the Boston area. Athletes at Harvard, M.I.T., Tufts, and Boston University wore the shoe. As the teams travelled to compete, other athletes saw, tried, and wanted the shoe. But where could they buy it?

Retailers at first wouldn't touch the shoe. The width sizing, so prized by the customer, was a nightmare for the dealer. Carrying a full size and width range would mean massive inventories which only the larger dealers would contemplate. So New Balance built up a healthy mail order business and created a market which dealers eventually wanted a part of.

Competitors were surprisingly slow to catch on to what was to become the focal point of growth for the footwear industry. The ripple sole was copied by American Biltrite, and the subsequent litigation showed the Ripple Sole Company patent to be unenforceable.

THE HEEL WEDGE

Distance runners had made it clear to the shoemakers that they wanted the heel to be higher than the forefoot. With few exceptions this was a feature of the early shoes, and it was achieved by using a separate heel just the same as a heel on dress shoes. This had a number of disadvantages including a lack of arch support, pressure on the forefoot during mid-support, and being a source of danger due to tripping.

The solution which the New Balance Trackster offered was a continuous outsole as well as a wedge of rubber underneath the back part of the shoe. Besides increasing the heel height, this technique was found to produce a very effective shock absorbing mechanism. It is of course now a standard feature of running shoes. Notice that there was no midsole yet. In the forefoot the only protection was offered by the insole board and outsole. Separate heels lingered on until the early 1970s when they disappeared altogether.

The Aerobic Revolution

An important event had occurred in 1968 which was to influence the way Americans spent their leisure hours and the shoes that they wore during those hours. In that year Dr. Kenneth Cooper published his book *Aerobics*. The decade which began with President John Kennedy admonishing the "soft American" to get out of his armchair was to end with Ken Cooper offering the first practical and palatable prescription for fitness.

During his time at Harvard, Cooper's feet were being punished on his daily runs by the poor running shoes of the day. On a recommendation from the track coach, Cooper visited New Balance and was fitted with a pair of Tracksters. From that time onwards, he became the best (unpaid) booster that New Balance had, and the Trackster shoes became the symbol of the new fitness cult.

Fig. 2.27 The New Balance Speed Star, a beautiful racing shoe from the early 1970s.

New Balance added a racing shoe called the Speed Star (Figure 2.27) designed to be worn on both track and road. The shoe is a piece of artwork—light, flexible, and reasonably well-cushioned. There is one unused specimen still on display in the New Balance offices in Boston.

OREGON PLAYS ITS PART

While Ken Cooper was running along the Charles River in his New Balance Tracksters, events which were to provide the next impetus to shoe design and development were occurring on the other side of the American continent. Oregon track coach Bill Bowerman had always been known to his colleaues as a thinker. He was prepared to challenge the established order on training methods, recruiting policy, running shoe design, or any other topic of professional interest. He also had considerable skills as a shoemaker and frequently made shoes to suit his athletes' needs. He felt the shoes made in the United States were not good for runners and that European shoes were overpriced.

One of Bowerman's ex-athletes named Phil Knight came back from a European trip in 1963 with the idea of having shoes made abroad to Bowerman's specifications. Bowerman and Knight went to Japan and met with the Tiger people in 1964. The result was a line of Tiger roadrunning shoes including the original Marathon and Roadrunner. Knight became the president of the importing company which was called Blue Ribbon Sports.

But Knight had a full-time job as an accountant, and Bowerman was busy coaching. Someone was needed to sell the shoes; enter Jeff Johnson. Jeff was a bright young track nut who enjoyed selling shoes because it allowed him to do what he liked best—running races and talking track. Jeff started selling from the trunk of his car, later from a post office box, and then from a store in a suburb of Los Angeles. Through his efforts at the grass-roots level Tiger became the most popular running shoe by the time of the 1967 Distance Running News survey. Almost all the shoes in the Tiger

Fig. 2.28 World record shoes from Tiger worn by Derek Clayton for his first record of 2:09:36 at Fukuoka in 1967.

line had a cutout area under the arch similar to an ordinary street shoe. The Tiger Roadrunner was the most popular shoe, but the Tiger Marathon was the flagship of the line. This shoe had a very light rubber outsole with a separate heel and forepart, and a reverse leather upper. The pair shown in Figure 2.28 is particularly interesting. They belong to Derek Clayton and they are the shoes in which he ran his first world record of 2:09:36 in the 1967 Fukuoka Marathon. Compared to today's racing shoes Clayton's offered very little protection and less than a quarter of an inch heel raise.

Tiger followed their success in selling shoes to American roadrunners with a major new innovation. In 1967 they offered two shoes with an all-nylon upper. These were a new version of the Marathon shoe and an Olympiad XIX track spike. The advertisement urged runners "to just throw the shoes in a washing machine" when they needed cleaning. After this small beginning it took little more than ten years before virtually all running shoes on the market were made with nylon uppers.

As nylon moved into the marketplace, remnants of earlier days were still available. A pair of shoes which many of today's marathon runners remember is shown in Figure 2.29. These are the canvas-upper Converse Chuck Taylor shoes. Many promising first miles were run on two of these thick rubber heels and soles in the mid-1960s.

Jeff Johnson and his colleagues at Blue Ribbon Sports were also responsible for other innovations. When marathon runner Gene Conto complained that the cushioning in his marathon shoes was inadequate, he and Johnson set about trying to improve the shoe. They went to a drugstore and bought some Japanese shower slippers. They stripped the outsole off the Tiger shoe, then stuck on a shower slipper, covering the creation with a thin layer of rubber for an outsole. Although the shoe was very spongy and tended to take a compression set, the important thing was that the idea of a continu-

The History of the Running Shoe

Fig. 2.29 Converse "Chuck Taylor" running shoes, popular on the indoor circuit during the mid-1960s.

ous midsole had been born. The prototype was sent to Bill Bowerman, who liked it, and the shoe appeared not long afterwards as the Nike Boston. Like nylon uppers, the continuous midsole was soon to become a standard feature in the design of running shoes.

DISTANCE RUNNING NEWS

The late sixties were fertile years for running and running shoes. We have seen the importance of New Balance, aerobics, and Blue Ribbon Sports and we now need to add two more names—Bob Anderson and *Distance Running News*. In 1966 Anderson started a small quarterly newsletter while he was on the fringe of the distance program at Kansas State University. Most of the copy rolled off Bob's typewriter, although there was an impressive editorial board including Fred Wilt, Browning Ross, Burt Nelson, and Hal Higdon.

By April 1967 Bob felt the time had come for the fledgling magazine to survey what running shoes were available. He recruited Jeff Johnson's help and Jeff wrote a twenty-page article with a small narrative on each shoe. The market was not exactly extensive. There were fifteen shoes surveyed; four Adidas, three New Balance, five Tiger, one Puma, and a handful of unknowns. This covered the whole field at that time. Fifteen hundred issues of this first shoe survey were sold. *Distance Running News* was to grow into *Runner's World*. The first shoe survey was to be the start of a long line of issues which not only chronicled the changes in shoes but influenced the direction in which the developments were to go.

Joe Henderson—All About Distance Running Shoes

As booklet number one of a new *Runner's World* series, Joe Henderson picked up on the work of Jeff Johnson in 1970 and found considerably more to write about. The intervening four years had spawned more runners and more shoes. Henderson surveyed 800

THE HISTORY OF THE RUNNING SHOE

Fig. 2.30 A) The Tiger Cortez

B) The Adidas Olympia

C) The Tiger Boston

runners, asking for their shoe preferences and details of their injuries (which we shall look at in Chapter 13).

The most popular manufacturer of training shoes was Tiger, with almost seventy percent of the respondents owning Tiger shoes. This was followed by Adidas with a forty-three percent ownership. The only other companies making any dent in the marketplace were E.B. Lydiard with ten percent, and New Balance with eight percent. How things were to change in ten years! Brooks' share of the marketplace was 0.1 percent and Nike did not yet exist.

The top shoes themselves are pictured in Figure 2.30. They were the Tiger Cortez, the Adidas Olympia, and the Tiger Boston. This trio shows just what a transition point the early 1970s were. The Olympia was basically a direct descendant of the warmup or training shoe with little heel lift and rather poor cushioning. It was all leather, stiff and heavy (thirteen ounces), and had no midsole or wedge, just a thick rubber sole. One feature of the shoe which was to become universal was called the Achilles tendon protector. This feature probably developed in response to two forces. First, the low cut shoes tended to cause blisters on the top of the heel just where the Achilles tendon joins the bone (see Chapter 3). Next, early Tiger shoes had a simple pull-tab which was convenient for easing the shoe on. The raised area in the heel both prevented the shoe from cutting into the skin and served as a pulltab. Unfortunately it sometimes irritated the Achilles tendon making a mockery of its new name!

The most popular shoe in the 1970 survey was the Tiger Cortez. It featured a combined rubber midsole and outsole. Again, the upper was leather and the shoe was relatively stiff, although it was lighter than the Olympia at 10.4 ounces.

The Tiger Boston was the only nylon upper shoe included in the runners choices. Weighing in at 8.2 ounces, it also featured the complete cushioned midsole fashioned after the Jeff Johnson bathroom slipper experiment. Like most of the shoes in the 1970 survey, the Tiger Boston had no heel counter, had a low-cut heel, and no padding around the collar of the shoe.

OLYMPIC INFLUENCES

Americans had grown accustomed to seeing their marathoners do poorly in the Olympics. There were no great expectations in 1972 when Frank Shorter, Kenny Moore, and Jack Batcheler started their 26.2 mile journey. The thought of many people was that at least this tragic festival of sport, which had been marred by terrorism, would soon come to an end.

Few eyebrows were raised when first into the stadium was an unknown runner from some unidentifiable country, but like Lorz in 1904, the runner turned out to be an imposter. He was a local athlete who had just jumped into the run on the final lap. While confusion still reigned in the stadium Frank Shorter entered as the true victor. Shorter had outclassed the world after twice breaking the American record earlier in the week in the 10,000 meters. If winning the gold medal was not enough after so many years, minutes later Kenny Moore crossed the finish line to take fourth place (Figure 2.31).

There is nothing quite so close to the American heart as a winner, and Shorter's name soon became a household word. He became both the symbol of and the stimulus for the growing running movement. This one Olympic victory probably pushed the sport of running for the masses over the knife edge. From 1972 running grew like an uncontrolled nuclear reaction.

Fig. 2.31 Frank Shorter and Kenny Moore on a victory lap after taking first and fourth place in the 1972 Olympic Marathon (Mark Shearman photo)

The transition is clearly seen in the Boston Marathon growth back in Figure 2.17. From almost stable numbers of entries in the five years preceding Shorter's victory, the number of runners doubled within three years and tripled in four years. Runners were "created" out of nonbelievers in exercise. Running became first fashionable and then essential to the lifestyle of many Americans.

There is another image of the Olympics in the 1970s which many people still carry with them. After falling down in the 1976 10,000 meter final at Montreal, Finland's Lasse Viren went on to a world record and a gold medal. But as memorable as his victory was his victory lap (Figure 2.32). Viren took off his Tiger track shoes and, as the world watched on television, he waved them high about his head as he ran once more around the track trailed by a group of ecstatic supporters with an enormous Finnish flag.

But the shoes got considerably more air time than the flag, leading to accusations of professionalism and under the table payments. The rivalry among shoe companies had hit the headlines, and journalists uncovered the network of support for athletes that the shoe companies had built. Most stories were sensational; few were rational. Many people realized that the days of the independently wealthy sportsmen or women who played at sport as a diversion from counting their money were long gone. The athletes had to receive sup-

Fig. 2.32 Viren celebrates victory in the 10,000 meter final at the Montreal Olympics by waving to the world with his running shoes. (Mark Shearman photo)

port for their unique, dedicated pursuit, and the shoe companies were their lifeline. The trend of shoe companies providing financial support for runners was to become an accepted way of life in the 1970s.

RUNNING SHOES OF THE 1970s

In 1972 the name Nike appeared for the first time on running shoes. Knight and company made a sudden and dramatic split with the Tiger company after disagreement over distribution rights. From a base of absolute zero, Knight and Johnson went to Japan and specified exactly the kinds of shoes they wanted made by one of Tiger's competitors. By the time the 1973 *Runner's World* survey was published in the booklet *Shoes for Runners* in July 1973, Nike had already cornered twenty percent of the training flat market. The lawsuits surrounding the controversial split between Tiger and Nike smoldered for several years and generated volumes of interesting transcripts.

Nike pioneered shoes with nylon uppers which were fast becoming the rage. *Runner's World* estimated that seventy-five percent of all racing flats sold in 1973 were nylon and training flats were not far behind. There were few other major developments in the 1973 shoe survey. The front runner from Adidas was the SL72. Adidas was one of the few manufacturers putting a heel counter in their shoes and also introduced the wrapover heel which was slightly undercut (Figure 2.33). Cosmetically the shoe looked very much like the shoes of the 1980s but as far as weight (9.5 ounces), flexibility, and energy absorption were concerned it was worse than the shoes available today.

Before 1973 the outsoles of running shoes were a relatively simple affair. They were either flat one piece rubber generally ridged in some way to increase traction, ripple soles, or separate heel and forefoot units with nothing under the arch area (see Tiger Marathon, Figure 2.28). Bill Bowerman and one of his athletes,

46 THE HISTORY OF THE RUNNING SHOE

Fig. 2.33 The Adidas SL72, frontrunner in the 1973 *Runner's World* shoe survey.

Jeff Holister, decided that a change was in order. Bowerman did some initial experiments putting pieces of urethane into a waffle iron. Surviving the smell and the imminent danger of fire, Bowerman and Holister made a pair of racing shoes weighing less than four ounces (Figure 2.34). The original idea was to make spikeless racing shoes for track running, but the initial response of roadrunners was so positive that production training flats were soon made. A look at the outsole designs of running shoes in the store today will show how far-reaching the effects of Bowerman's experiments were.

An important event occurred in 1974. Looking for a combination of lightness and cushioning, Jerry Turner of the Brooks Shoe Company called in a chemical

Fig. 2.34 The original waffle outsole design on an ultralight pair of racing shoes, handmade by Bill Bowerman.

engineer. David M. Schwaber of the Monarch Rubber Company in Baltimore sifted through some of the more exotic polymers which had come through his laboratory. He came up with a compound called EVA— ethylene vinyl acetate. This material was made by a foaming process in which a chemical reaction generated gas bubbles which could be trapped in the material by high pressure. The resulting "closed cell foam" material was much lighter than microcellular rubber, and what's more it was a better shock absorber.

The new Brooks Villanova of 1975 had this material for a midsole and wedge. Brooks had a one year exclusive on the material. At the end of this year Schwaber had about every major running shoe manufacturer at his doorstep. Rubber midsoles and wedges were gone for good.

1975–RANKING THE SHOES

By 1975 Bob Anderson had decided to take the plunge and rank the available training flats one through thirty. The shoe survey was to become an annual feature in *Runner's World* magazine. Following the results of the survey gives us an excellent way to trace the final portion of the history of running shoes.

The criteria in 1975 were price, weight, number of users, and subjective assessment on upper softness, shank support, and sole makeup.

A revamped Adidas SL72 came to the top of the pile. It featured speed lacing (see Chapter 8), a different color, and a different name, the SL76.

Other new developments that year included a new line from New Balance, which finally ended their love affair with the ripple sole and leather uppers. The New Balance 3:05 Interval was for New Balance a revolutionary shoe (Figure 3.35). It had nylon uppers, a heel wedge, and an undercut heel with an outsole which wrapped around the back of the shoe. The most enduring new feature of the shoe proved to be the flared heel.

Fig. 2.35 The New Balance 3:05 Interval, first marketed in 1975, was one of the first running shoes to feature a flared heel.

This is a construction which makes the sole wider at the ground than at the heel counter. Theoretically this would give the shoe greater stability. Almost every running shoe today has adapted this technique.

The SL76, the New Balance 3:05, and most of the other shoes in the 1975 survey concentrated all of their protective padding under the rear half of the shoe. The forefoot received little attention because it was not considered a vital area. This assessment turned out to be incorrect. New entries in 1975 included Brooks, with a thirteenth place finish for its first attempt at a running shoe called the Drake and the enduring Villanova at twenty-second place.

As long as *Runner's World* was simply describing the shoes available, giving information on price and features, shoe manufacturers looked on from a distance with a tolerant smile.

But the ranking was a bombshell to the industry. They realized that the impact on the marketplace was substantial, and this was to have an important effect on the development of the running shoe. The pace of research and development quickened, and while footwear for other sports such as basketball and tennis lagged behind, developments in running shoes were fast and furious.

In 1976 the New Balance 320 was given the top ranking. This shoe was an improved 3:05 with more forefoot cushioning. Etonic entered the fray with a shoe called the KM, which was like a high-quality Villanova. Nike latched onto the flared heel idea in a big way. The LD-1000 had a massive heel flare which was to be seen in retrospect as a mistake.

The top fifteen shoes were all made from nylon weave uppers. A new feature in 1976 was the first use of a knitted nylon mesh in training flats. The Adidas Runner and the Osaga Moscow '80 both offered this innovation.

Lab Test Introduced

In 1977 laboratory tests were added to the *Runner's World* shoe survey. The tests measured qualities such as shock absorption, flexibility, and sole wear directly, and provided some baseline for manufacturers to use as design criteria and for runners to use in shoe selection.

Fig. 2.36   The Brooks Vantage, top shoe in 1977.

The top shoe in 1977 was the Brooks Vantage (Figure 2.36). The shoe had several notable features. Brooks was among the first shoe companies to do away with the arch support and replace it with a sockliner which they called a "soft support." This molded to the foot during the first few miles of running.

More revolutionary in a running shoe was the introduction of the varus wedge, which created an elevation on the inside of the heel compared to the outside. This was not a new technique in footwear design. It had been used in basketball shoes in the 1930s and tried under the heading of a pronation device in army boots in 1958. Podiatrist Steve Subotnick was a consultant to the Brooks shoe company and he suggested the addition. The rationale, was that many running injuries stem from excessive pronation which the wedge helps prevent.

Waffle soles became even more popular with runners. Since durability was important, Nike introduced a wear bar on the rear corners where the waffles were filled in to give additional wear. EVA was universally used but the Monarch Rubber Company was in search of even lighter compounds without compromising shock absorption. The density of these foams (mass per unit volume) tumbled over a four-fold range in five years.

By 1977 every shoe in the top twenty-five had a raised "Achilles tendon protector" at the heel, and all but four had flared heels. It was clear that many manufacturers were moving towards a consensus of design.

Running in the late 1970s continued to grow. Over 9,000 people lined up at the start of the 1979 Boston Marathon, while New York drew an astonishing 12,000 runners. The nation watched as President Carter jumped ashore from his Mississippi Riverboat Cruise to put in his daily five mile run.

As the number of runners grew, so too did the number of running shoes. The market proliferated at an exponential rate. The 1980 *Runner's World* shoe survey tested 178 different models of shoes compared to the fifteen that had been available in 1967. The number of shoes for women had increased dramatically with sixty training and ten racing shoes available. Not only were the numbers increasing but so was the quality.

Lab tests revealed dramatic improvements particularly in forefoot and rearfoot impact properties. Manufacturers were forced to go out and search for new technology to improve their shoes, and their search was fruitful. New tests of rearfoot control and traction allowed runners to gain more insight into their running shoes before making a buying decision.

The major innovation in this period was the introduction of air shoes. Rumors had been circulating around the shoe industry for some time that shoes with air midsoles were about to be produced. Pony, Adidas, Brooks, and Nike were all quoted as being interested, but it was Nike who first appeared on the market in 1979 with a shoe called the Tailwind. Besides the distinction of being the first fifty dollar shoe, it was the newest idea in running shoes in many years (Figure 2.37).

The shoe proved to have its strengths and weaknesses. Its forefoot impact properties easily outstripped every other running shoe on the market, but many runners found (and tests confirmed) early models of the shoe to be somewhat unstable in the rearfoot.

So Nike did not hit the right combination first time, but then neither did Charles Goodyear, who was almost

THE HISTORY OF THE RUNNING SHOE

Fig. 2.37 The first viable air shoe—the Nike Tailwind, introduced in 1979. The shoe has tubes in the midsole filled with pressurized freon gas.

bankrupt by the time he hit on the correct formula for vulcanizing rubber. The important thing was that the idea was out. Fertile minds, careful experimentation, and time will surely do the rest to perfect the idea of the air running shoe.

As designs have changed and quality has improved, prices of running shoes have changed at an even faster rate. The last fifteen years have seen the most dramatic changes as the graph in Figure 2.38 shows. In 1909 a pair of the best Spalding marathon shoes were

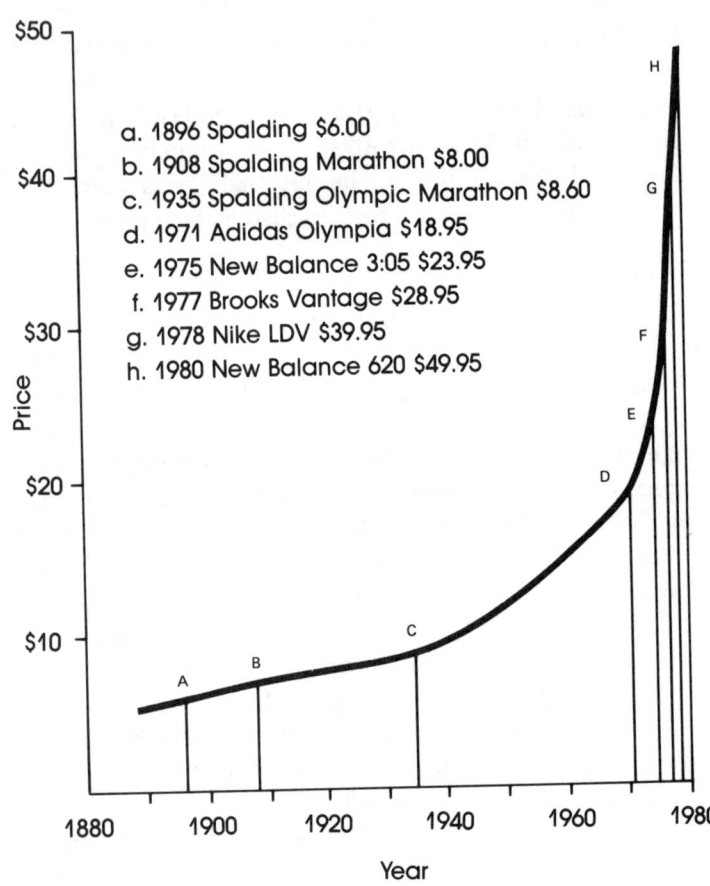

a. 1896 Spalding $6.00
b. 1908 Spalding Marathon $8.00
c. 1935 Spalding Olympic Marathon $8.60
d. 1971 Adidas Olympia $18.95
e. 1975 New Balance 3:05 $23.95
f. 1977 Brooks Vantage $28.95
g. 1978 Nike LDV $39.95
h. 1980 New Balance 620 $49.95

Fig. 2.38 The change in cost of a pair of good running shoes since 1880.

$8.00. Fifty years later for only ninety-five cents more you could buy a pair of Tiger Roadrunners. In 1980 several of the top shoes carried a fifty dollar price tag.

THE PAST AND THE FUTURE

If anyone thought that the evolution of running shoes was a short and simple matter, that idea must have by now been abandoned. The journey of almost 10,000 years has been long and involved. What is so intriguing about tracing this history is that it mirrors the growth of something that has become completely assimilated into our way of life. By a strange twist of economics, sociology, and psychology running has become a vehicle for fitness, relaxation, and for the expression of personal well-being.

Only fifty years ago old man Richings was custom-making shoes for a few top marathoners. Today over fifty million people own a sophisticated piece of equipment which is descended directly from Richings' work and those who went before him.

To think that we are at the end of the evolutionary process rather than at an intermediate way station would be foolish. The changes and improvements over the next ten years will probably dwarf all that has gone before. Technology has entered the running shoe equation to stay. We shall see better shoes, safer shoes, and faster shoes. But it is doubtful that the history of these future developments will make a more engaging tale than the events that have influenced our present day running shoes.

3

A Runner's Anatomy

Running shoes are worn on running feet, and running feet are attached to running legs. Trying to understand the design and construction of running shoes without a clear knowledge of what goes inside and above them would be difficult. This means that a look at a runner's anatomy is in order. But anatomy can be as dry as old toast. Despite spending three years in the anatomy department of a medical school (or perhaps because of it) I still have a strong tendency to fall asleep when reading books about anatomy. Spending hours learning things like which branch of the sural nerve innervates which region of the leg is simply no way to spend a Friday night.

But runners don't need a surgeon's grasp of human anatomy. They could care less about cutaneous nerves or anastamosing vessels. What matters is a working knowledge of what the parts inside there do, and what can be done about it when they don't work properly. If you are looking for detail, then go straight to *Gray's Anatomy*. But if you want a working knowledge of the part that's attached to the hip bone, read on.

It may seem perverse in a book on shoes, but we are not just going to talk about the anatomy of the feet. Footwear affects not only the feet but the whole body. A subtle change in design of the running shoe can cause everything from toe pain to back pain and headaches. So we will compromise and limit our coverage to the bottom half of the body.

BONE

We consider the bones first because they are the framework upon which everything else is built. Our framework is internal—an endoskeleton—in contrast to that of an insect, which is external—an exoskeleton.

The framework develops more slowly than almost any other tissue in the body. That's why there is such concern about young children engaging in vigorous sports at an early age. The x-ray of a child's foot (Figure 3.1) shows small dense areas and great expanses of emptiness. Development of the long bones proceeds from centers of growth spreading outwards, as the minerals needed to form bone are incorporated. Any injuries during this time of foundation building can seriously affect the final status of the bone.

Same Cell—Different Pattern

All bones are not equal. Some are dense and heavy, some are light and—apart from a hard exterior—spongy. Some are solid and some have "canals" down their cen-

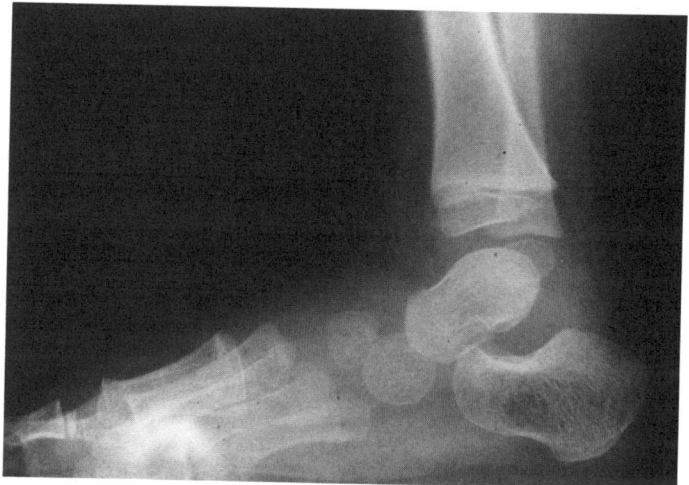

Fig. 3.1 An x-ray of the foot of a child showing incomplete ossification. (Courtesy of Dr. Jon Contompasis)

ters. The basic bone cells are the same, but the manner in which the cells are arranged reflects nature's adaptation to existing stresses.

One of modern biology's most beautiful techniques for investigating the structure of tissue is the scanning electron microscope (called SEM for short). With this tool we can travel inside the structures of the body as if, for a moment, we had shrunk in size and were walking through enormous caverns. The formations in the caverns are cells piled one on the other.

A picture of "spongy" bone taken with an SEM is shown in Figure 3.2b. The magnification is about

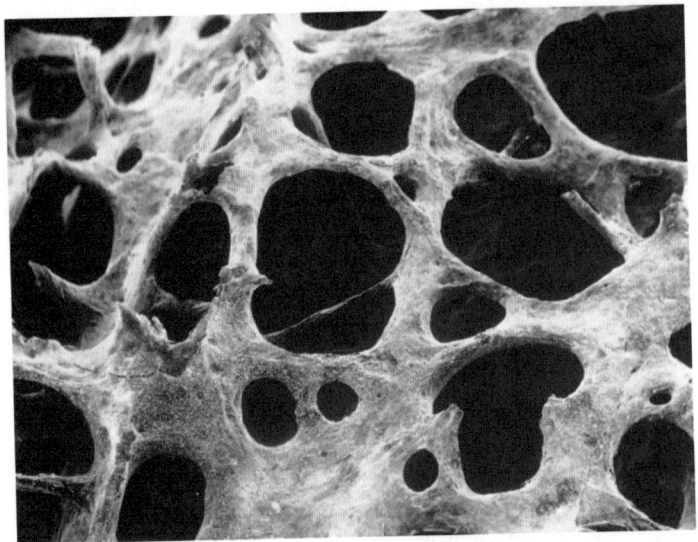

Fig. 3.2 Spongy bone seen in the scanning electron microscope. Magnification x 13. (Courtesy of Timothy M. Wright, Ph.D.)

thirteen times. This delicate structure has defied the efforts of engineers who have tried to duplicate its combination of lightness and strength. Spongy bone is found in places where the direction of stresses is continually changing. The cells are built up in small struts which follow lines of stress. These struts are called trabeculae, which roughly translated means beams. Most of the small bones of the foot are built in this way, and the ends of most long bones are also "spongy" underneath a thin shell of compact bone.

There is another specialized group of cells which forms the outer covering for bone. This covering is called the periosteum. It is important because the periosteum is a means of attaching the tendons and ligaments which both move and control movement of the joints. You never see the periosteum on old bones because it has been cleaned off like all the other soft tissue. In life it gives the bone a gleamy white look.

Injuries to Bone in Runners

As orthopedic surgeons and their bankers know, problems with bones and tissues attached to bones are by far the largest category of injuries which occur in sport. A survey of the specialty of team physicians would reveal an overwhelming number of orthopedists.

Fractured bones are not common running injuries, at least not the type of fractures that football players experience. Runners like to think their sport is more subtle—and indeed the injuries they experience definitely are! What do occur in runners' bones are stress fractures.

If bone is subjected to massive bending or twisting, it responds simply. It breaks like the branch of a tree, with a well-defined fracture pattern which can easily be seen on an x-ray. But take the same bone and insult it in a different way, the way the runner does, by applying smaller forces repeatedly, and a different but equally serious response occurs. The bone will first develop what some experts like to call microtrauma; small regions of damage which cannot be seen on a normal x-ray. Over a period of weeks these sites become the focal point for a small but definite breakdown in the structure of the bone.

By the time these small "cracks" can be seen on an x-ray, the runner has probably been continuing to pound the bone for perhaps three or four weeks and has a much more serious problem. He or she may have shrugged off the pain as simply another temporary ache and possibly disregarded the advice to rest.

Running with a stress fracture may soon be a thing of the past, thanks to a diagnostic technique called the bone scan which has recently been applied to runners. A small amount of radioactive tracer is injected into a vein. Within a few hours the limb is scanned to see if excessive amounts of the tracer have been taken up by bone. If there is a stress fracture, even in the early stages, the local inflammation will show as a "white out" on the scan.

Figure 3.3 is an excellent example. On the left is a standard x-ray showing no sign of trauma. On the right is a bone scan of the same patient showing clear evidence of injury. It might have taken three or four weeks before the x-ray would have given positive findings. This particular woman had run the Boston Marathon against the advice of her doctor and was only persuaded to stop running when she saw the bone scan.

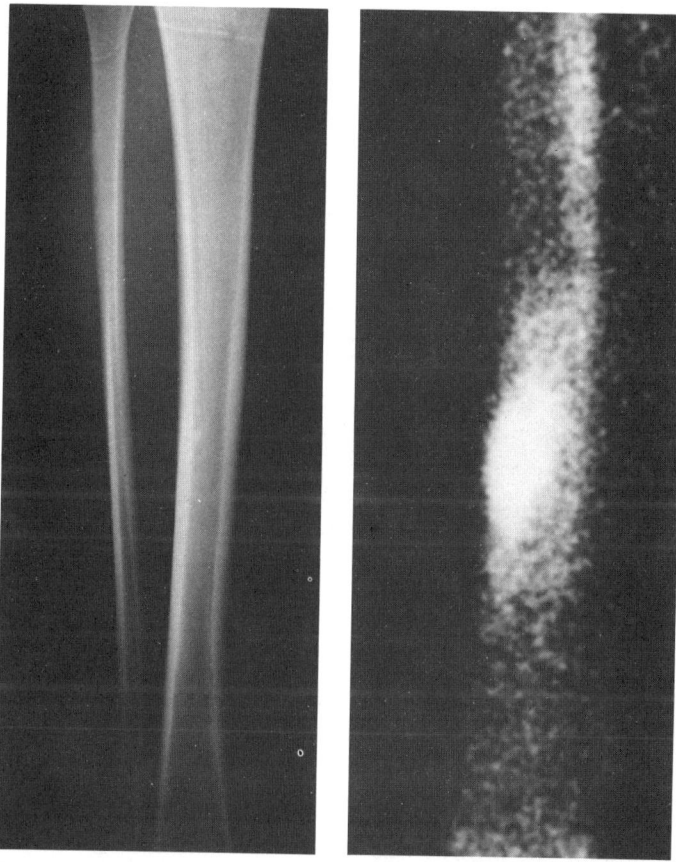

Fig. 3.3 A conventional X-ray (left) and a bone scan (right) of the same patient. While the X-ray shows no signs of trauma, the "hot spot" on the bone scan is clear evidence of a stress fracture. (Courtesy of Dr. Lloyd Smith)

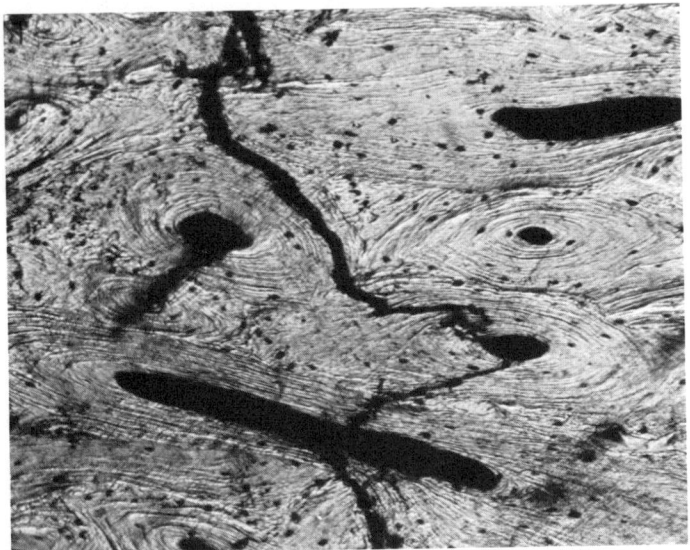

Fig. 3.4 An experimentally induced stress fracture spreading through a section of compact bone. (Courtesy of Dr. K. Piekarski)

Scientists have made attempts to induce fractures experimentally in slices of bone. Figure 3.4 shows the result of one such attempt. The crack followed the line of least resistance along the concentric circles of the bone cells. Such studies may eventually lead to a better understanding of how stress fractures originate, and to reducing their incidence. It is clear that changes in the design of running shoes over the last few years have reduced the incidence of stress fractures in certain bones. We shall discuss this point further in Chapter 13.

The Bones of the Lower Extremity

We move now from bone in general to the bones of the lower extremity. In one leg there are thirty bones; in one foot twenty-six. That's far too many to be on first name terms with. Throwing conventional terminology to the wind, we will divide the structures of interest into nine parts and give the various units names of our own, paying only parenthetic respect to the five millenia of established anatomical terminology.

Figure 3.5 shows the complicated truth. This is an x-ray of a healthy leg—at least I hope it's healthy because it's one of mine! In Figure 3.6, generous license has been taken with conventional anatomy. This diagram is a highly schematized artist's impression of the skeleton of the bottom half of the body and is labelled according to our simplified scheme.

The abstraction is not without its reason. Important elements of the real system have been accentuated. Certain dimensions have been expanded or compressed to suit the purposes of description. This should help in describing the way the system works without getting submerged in detail.

All of the power in human running and walking is transmitted from the legs upwards. But the legs only add up to about thirty-five percent of total body weight, so a firm framework for transmitting forces to the rest of the body is required. The hip bones do just that.

The hip bones or pelvis are the key to linking the

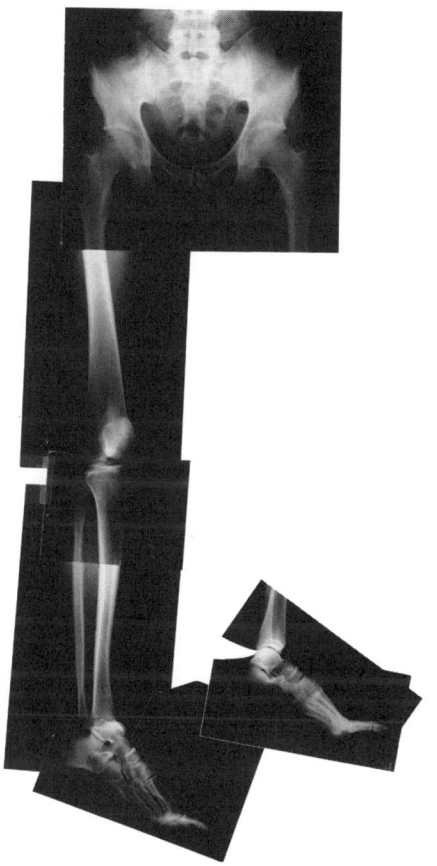

Fig. 3.5 Lower extremity x-ray (Radiologist Ann Heasley)

A Runner's Anatomy

power which the legs generate to the body. The legs join the hip bones through one of the most robust and well-protected joints in the body, and the backbone or vertebral column also has its origin firmly seated on the hip bones.

As is well known, the adaptation to childbearing has made the female pelvis wider than the male counterpart. This difference, although essential for giving birth, has left the woman athlete with a few unpleasant consequences which we shall discuss in the chapter on biomechanics.

The Thigh Bones

None of our apelike ancestors ever had "knock knees"! One of the modifications which accompanied upright walking was a tendency for the thigh bones to come together at the knees. This allowed foot placement to be more underneath the body, so that during the period of one leg support in walking and running the body was not drastically off balance.

The result is that the thigh bones angle down from the pelvis with what is known as a "carrying angle" of between five and ten degrees. The shaft of the thigh bone is made up of dense, cortical bone. At each end there is a specialized region where the shape and structure is modified to match the shape of the unit with which it interfaces.

We are accustomed to thinking that bones are rather similar to those the dog might dig up. Nothing could be further from the truth. The thigh bone, for example, is a virtual cellular factory with a rich blood supply and a capacity for producing red blood cells. An inert framework it definitely is not!

The Kneecap

The kneecap or patella is an unusual bone. It is called a floating bone because it is submerged in a layer of tendon. As you see from the diagram in Figure 3.6, the end of the thigh bone has a slot in which the kneecap rides. This is the site of the notorious injury known as "runner's knee," which is the single most common injury in runners.

The purpose of this curious lump of bone is to make the muscles that straighten the knee more efficient. The kneecap simply moves the tendons, to which these muscles attach, further away from the center of the knee joint. It is a fact of mechanical life that the same force applied further away from a point of rotation will produce a greater torque or turning effect.

When the thigh muscles are relaxed the kneecap can be moved about freely, particularly in a side-to-side manner. But as soon as knee movement begins, the kneecap is pulled down firmly into its groove on the front of the thigh bone. Any lateral movement of the kneecap during normal activities can be disastrous.

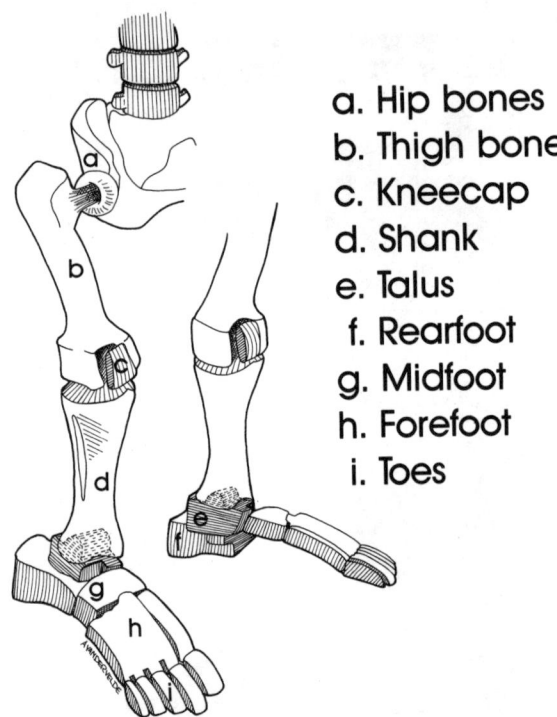

a. Hip bones
b. Thigh bone
c. Kneecap
d. Shank
e. Talus
f. Rearfoot
g. Midfoot
h. Forefoot
i. Toes

Fig. 3.6   A simplified anatomy of the lower extremity.

The Shank

There are two bones in the shank, even though the smallest of the two, the fibula, does not really do anything that the larger tibia couldn't do by itself.

The blame for this overdesign is on the shoulders of evolution. It is simply not fast enough to keep up with changes in the function of body parts. Perhaps that is just as well. Many people might lose the ability to reach above their heads, simply because they hardly ever do it!

Being on the road to the evolution of the perfect shank causes nothing but problems. The two bones have to be bound together by ligaments which can tear. Instead of being tightly attached to a bone, many muscles beginning in the leg are joined to a band of connective tissue stretching between the bones. This is like putting guy lines in sand rather than soil.

Both bones are smaller than one single bone doing the same job might be. Also both are remarkably susceptible to stress fractures, and it is tempting to connect the two observations.

There is one other curious fact about the shank that we should mention. Most of the muscles that are important in control and movement of the foot have their origin somewhere in the shank. This is one of the many reasons why problems with feet and footwear may be reflected in pain somewhere else.

The Talus

If we had to pick one bone that runners and makers of running shoes ought to know something about it would probably be this small chunk which is about the size of a child's building block. Not because the bone itself is of great significance, but because an understanding of the interface of this bone with those above and below it provides a key to the understanding of foot function in running. In this section we shall do little more than note its position and structure. Its joints are what make it critical and joints are discussed later in this chapter.

The talus is at the junction of foot and leg. On top of it is the shank. Underneath it is the rearfoot. There is no way to apply forces to the floor and on to the body without these forces being transmitted by the talus. Surprisingly, cases of failure in the talus are rare. This is due to the sturdy structure in which the bone cells are embedded, along lines which correspond to lines of stress as the joint between the shank and talus moves through its range of motion.

THE FOOT

The foot has twenty-six separate bones which we are going to divide into three groups. This division is somewhat artificial because the joints of the foot allow much less movement than most other joints of the body. This is particularly true in the midfoot, where ligaments bind the parts together so tightly that little movement is possible. So movement of one region will inevitably influence the other regions.

Nevertheless the distinction into rearfoot, forefoot, and midfoot is a useful one and is widely used by podiatrists and orthopedists.

The Rearfoot

This unit contains only one bone, the heel bone or calcaneus. It is the first bone so far in our journey through the leg that makes contact with the ground. It is the point at which the powerful calf muscles, responsible for the thrust we associate with running, find their home in the foot. It also has articulating surfaces with the talus and the midfoot. The rearfoot is home base for the infamous plantar fascia (in which plantar fasciitis is born) and is the site of heel spurs (Figure 3.7). There are fat pads around the rearfoot which help to protect against damage.

With so much going on around it, it is no wonder that this bone has received more attention than any other from the designers of running shoes. The "heel wedge" so characteristic of running shoes is placed to give the heel bone a soft life. The heel counter is there (among other reasons) to prevent it from moving laterally. Elaborate rearfoot control systems from the "stabilizer" to the "varus wedge" have been developed to control its motion. As we shall see in Chapter 4, keeping the rearfoot in a normal alignment with the talus is an important factor in injury-free running.

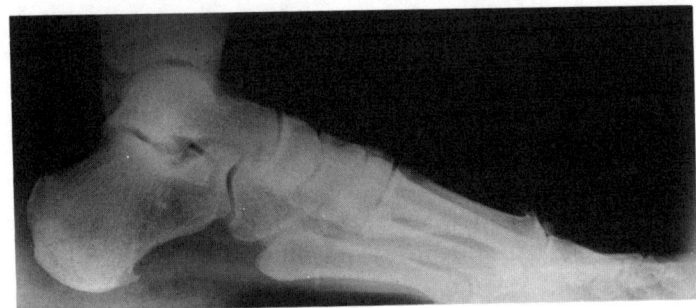

Fig. 3.7   A bony spur on the front surface of the heel bone. Spurs are also visible on the upper surface of the forefoot. (Courtesy of Dr. Jon Contompasis)

The Midfoot: Keystones of the Long Arches

This region is made up of five small bones which look—and fit together—like pieces from a Chinese puzzle. The simplicity of one bone joining the next at a single joint is gone.

Each of the five bones in the midfoot touches at least four others, and the movements within the whole unit are very difficult to assess. The bones resemble building blocks, and the function of the five as a system is more important than their individual characteristics.

The way in which the five bones of the midfoot are arranged is important because they form the beginning of all three arches within the foot. We will call these arches the long outside arch, the long inside arch, and the transverse arch. You may find the first two of these referred to as the lateral and medial longitudinal arches, respectively.

The long arch on the inside of the foot is considerably higher than the outside arch. This is obvious from footprints and is confirmed by an x-ray of the normal foot. You can see back in Figure 3.6 that the midfoot joins the rearfoot at a much higher level on the inside of the foot. This is the arch that requires an arch support in running shoes. It is also clear from Figure 3.6 and the x-ray in Figure 3.7 that the complete midfoot is well above ground level. Since we know that both the rearfoot and forefoot contact the ground, it follows that the individual bones of the midfoot form the bridge between these two contact areas. They are the keystones of both inside and outside long arches. This is shown schematically in Figure 3.8 where foot and ground are shown to make contact at three points—one in the rearfoot and two in the forefoot. Architecturally, the importance of the midfoot in the long arches is clear.

The transverse arch is not so obvious, and some authorities argue that it doesn't really exist in the normal foot. Finding it in your own foot is complicated by the fact that the bones are heavily wrapped in the soft tissue of muscles, ligaments, and fat. Where it does exist, this arch is formed by a bowing upwards of the bones in the middle of the midfoot and forefoot. The cross sections in Figure 3.8 show how individual bones in the midfoot also act as keystones for the transverse arch. Of course the arches don't stay in place, like early bridges did, just because the building blocks were correctly placed. The arches of the foot are sustained by a large contingent of ligaments and muscles which are continually called upon to fight against deformation.

The arches, tightened by their supports, are thought to be important as natural shock absorbers during running. The exact amount that they deform is difficult to

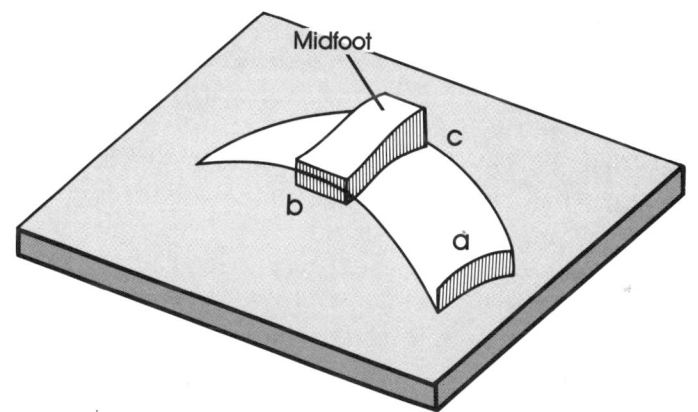

Fig. 3.8 A schematic representation of the arches of the right foot. (a) is the transverse arch, (b) the long outside arch, and (c) the long inside arch. Notice how the midfoot plays a critical part in maintaining the long arches.

measure, but the idea of the arches acting as shock absorbers is a compelling if unproven one. The logic does not extend to "the higher arch the better." In fact many high-arched feet have a rigidity which makes them poor shock absorbers. The absorption comes from relative movement among the bones of the foot. If this movement cannot occur the body will receive more than its fair share of impact from foot strike in running.

The Forefoot

After the complexity of the midfoot, the long slender "rays" or metatarsals of the forefoot come as pleasant relief. The five individual bones are miniature replicas of the long bones such as the thigh. Their difference in structure from the midfoot bones signals a difference in function. They start, each bone squashed up against its neighbor, with firmly bound joints on the midfoot. The first four (counting always starts with the inside of the foot) are well supported, but the fifth hangs on to its midfoot connection perilously, with half the bone hanging in space.

To fulfill their role as the third component in the long arches, after the rearfoot and midfoot, the metatarsals resist compression, something that long bones are particularly good at.

Because of their shape it is tempting to see the bones of the forefoot as part of the toes. But the toes do not begin until after the metatarsals have made their next joint in the chain. Certainly their front ends have a freer life than the bones of the midfoot. As the forefoot bones fan out toward the toes, the relative movement permitted between them increases. This can sometimes be a problem when the first ray, which gives rise to the big toe, drops much lower than normal, affecting the balance of the whole foot.

The Toes

Like the evolution of the shank, that of the forefoot and toes is way behind the functional adaptations that we are forcing upon these parts. The toes still bear the mark of the days when manipulating and climbing with the foot was as important as doing the same with the hands. Certainly the toes are critical to our being able to make quick balance adjustments. They carry large pressures inside the shoe. But the gross overdesign which leaves us a total of fourteen separate bones in the toes is nothing more than another souvenir of evolution.

The same could be said about other features of the foot. As we saw in Chapter 2, humans have been wearing shoes for a mere 10,000 years, or something like one percent of the time since upright locomotion began. During the previous time, the foot became well adapted to walking and running on uneven surfaces, with the arches well equipped to accommodate surface changes.

But the modern foot does not meet uneven surfaces.

All it meets is the inside of a shoe, which is usually smooth and rigid enough to render the elaborate mechanisms within the foot unnecessary. We can guarantee that evolution will take the hint and, if our species lasts long enough, future feet will be considerably simplified.

Surface Landmarks

The foot is so tightly packed that it is difficult to just look at your foot and identify some of the structures we have been describing. Figure 3.9 shows some of the surface landmarks labeled on a photograph of the foot.

CLASSIFYING FEET BY THEIR ARCHES

So far we have described the normal foot and paid no attention to the individual differences which are so important both in the selection of a running shoe and from an injury standpoint. There are many ways to classify feet into various types. One common method uses the height and condition of long arches to identify three groups—normal, flatfeet, and high-arched feet. One of the simplest and most telling indications that feet differ considerably are footprints. Figure 3.10 shows the footprints of three people, all with approximately the same length feet, taken during easy, comfortable standing on both feet.

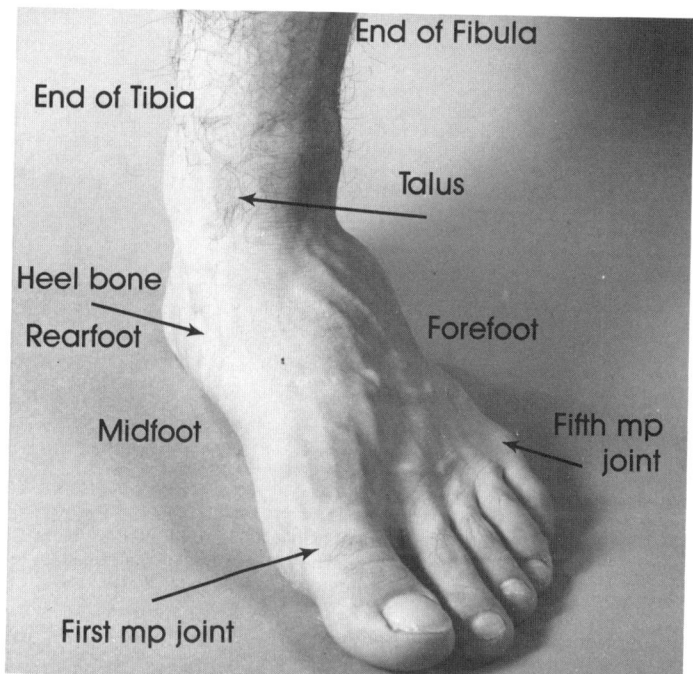

Fig. 3.9   Surface anatomy of the foot.

Normal Foot

The outline of subject one (Figure 3.10) is generally considered the normal footprint. The high, long, inside arch leaves a crescent-shaped gap while a thin peninsula joins the rearfoot and forefoot. The direction of the area joining rearfoot and forefoot can be deceiving since

A RUNNER'S ANATOMY

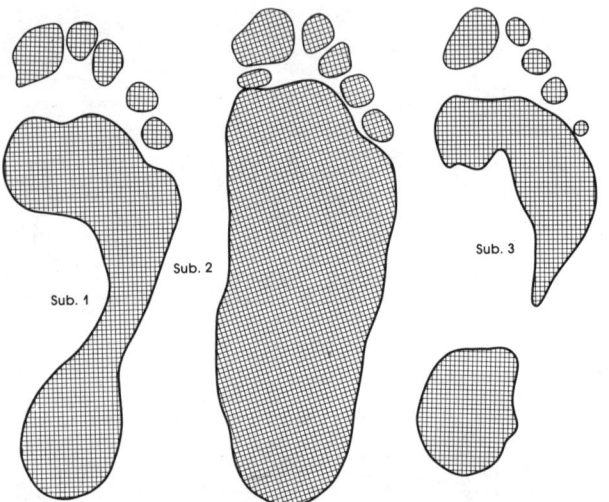

Fig. 3.10 Footprints from normal (subject 1), flat-footed (subject 2), and high arched (subject 3) runners. The contact area of the three feet are 112.2, 190.7, and 83.9 square centimeters, respectively.

it looks as though the person is toeing out. But the foot does not flex in this direction. Anatomists call the axis of the foot the line joining the center of the rearfoot and the tip of the second toe. Notice also the large gap between forefoot and toes where no weight is supported.

Flat Foot

Subject two in Figure 3.10 has a classic flat foot. Not only has the long inside arch completely collapsed, but the soft tissue under the area bulges out, adding to the contact area. The area between the forefoot and toes is almost all used for bearing weight, and the foot is turned out (abducted) during stance and during running. Just because a runner has a footprint like subject two does not mean they should run for treatment. There are thousands of flatfooted runners functioning without problems. Some people have their flat feet from birth and manage very well. The flat foot considered most problematical is the hypermobile flatfoot that seems to have too much motion at its joints. A runner with this foot type will probably end up using an orthotic.

High Arch Foot

The other end of the spectrum from the flat foot is the high arch or cavus foot, shown by the print of subject three in Figure 3.10. In this foot type both inside and outside long arches are so high that the footprint is split into separate rearfoot, forefoot, and toe regions.

There are, as you might expect, a number of types of cavus feet. The one that causes the most problems in running is the rigid cavus foot. The joints in this foot are so tight that the normal shock absorbing functions are greatly reduced. Sometimes cavus feet have a forefoot which naturally assumes a lower position than the rearfoot, even when the forefoot is pressed to try to bring it deformity, and brings with it special problems for the running shoe wearer which we will discuss in Chapter 14.

High Arches Mean High Pressures

If we assume that the three subjects all had about the same body weight and that weight is equally distributed over the whole contact area we can make an estimate of the average pressures underneath their feet. The last assumption is questionable, but let's proceed anyway. The actual areas under the right feet of subjects one, two, and three were 112.2, 190.7, and 83.9 square centimeters respectively. Pressure is calculated as force per unit area. If we use the normal foot as the standard of 100 units of pressure, the average pressure under the high arch foot will be 134 units and under the flat foot only fifty-nine units. Add high pressure and poor shock absorption, and we can guess that the high arch foot is a potential source of trouble to a runner.

Shoes for Foot Types

What we are leading up to is that different foot types will need different shoes. Not too much has been made of this idea in books and magazines because it assumes that runners could identify their own foot type. I believe such identification is possible, and will go into more detail on the subject in Chapter 14.

THE JOINTS

Where two bones come together, movement is generally required. This seemingly simple statement is true only if we are willing to be extremely broad about our definition of movement. The relative movement between two bones varies from a few millimeters of sliding between the two bones of the shank up to the tremendous freedom of movement that exists between the thigh and hip bones.

There are several different types of joints in the body, but some common features can be seen in most of the joints of the lower limb. The three most important are surface coating, lubrication, and muscle or ligament support. These are illustrated in Figure 3.11.

Synovial Joints

The joints between almost every bone we have considered in this chapter are called synovial joints. The synovial joint is always "sealed" by a special bag called a joint capsule. Within this bag cells generate small amounts of synovial fluid. It is easy to get the idea that our joints are swilling with lubrication, but that is not the case. The knee, which is one of the largest synovial joints in the body, has only about one-half of a cubic centimeter of synovial fluid inside it. This is about one-eighth of a teaspoonful, but it is enough to produce the desired effect.

A RUNNER'S ANATOMY

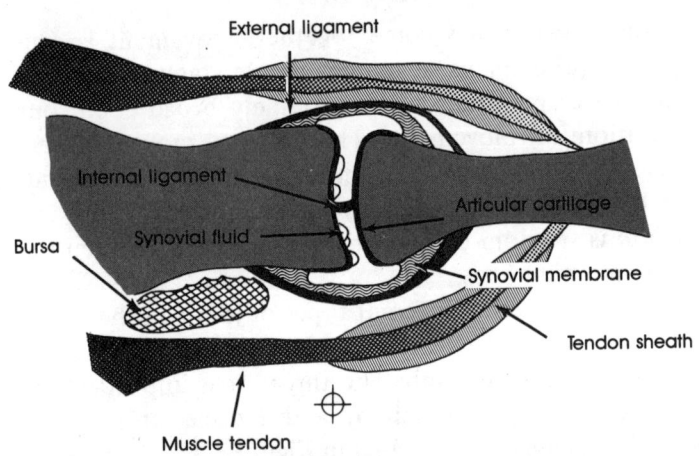

Fig. 3.11 A schematic view of a typical synovial joint.

The surfaces of bones which meet in a joint are coated with a smooth lining called articular cartilage. This layer is very thin and somewhat elastic. It is there both to lessen the friction between the sliding surfaces and to provide a small amount of shock absorption as the bones butt into each other. As our joints age, this layer gets worn and fragmented, one of the many reasons why we become more "creaky" as time goes by. Sometimes there is also a disc of cartilage between the two bones which is a great deal thicker than the articular cartilage. The two menisci at the knee joint, frequently torn in traumatic impacts to the knee, are good examples of this type of structure.

Ligaments

Ligaments are basically stiff, elastic bands which bind together bones forming a joint. They have a good blood supply and are composed principally of a substance called collagen. Several bundles of collagen fibers can be seen in the SEM of a ligament in Figure 3.12. Ligaments on the outside of a joint, called external ligaments, are invariably present. The most notable of these are the collateral ligaments of the knee and ankle, both of which are easily injured. Only some joints have internal ligaments. The hip has one small ligament inside the capsule, and the knee has two, called the cruciate ligaments. The capsule of most synovial joints begins in the external ligaments.

Although ligaments are important for joint stability, without muscle action joints would be damaged much more frequently than they are. When a doctor prescribes exercise to tone up muscles around a damaged joint, what he or she is doing is to try and provide more protection for the ligaments. Stresses which are anticipated are much easier to cope with. Nature has designed reflexes which "recruit" muscles to cope with unexpected disturbances, but these are often not fast

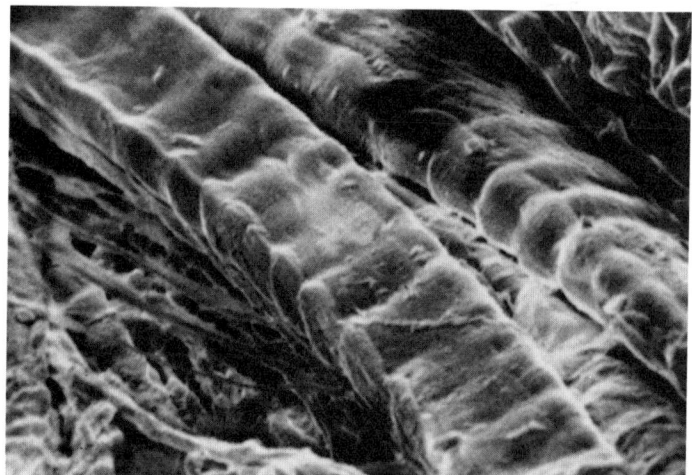

Fig. 3.12 A knee ligament seen in the scanning electron microscope. (Courtesy of Dr. David Butler)

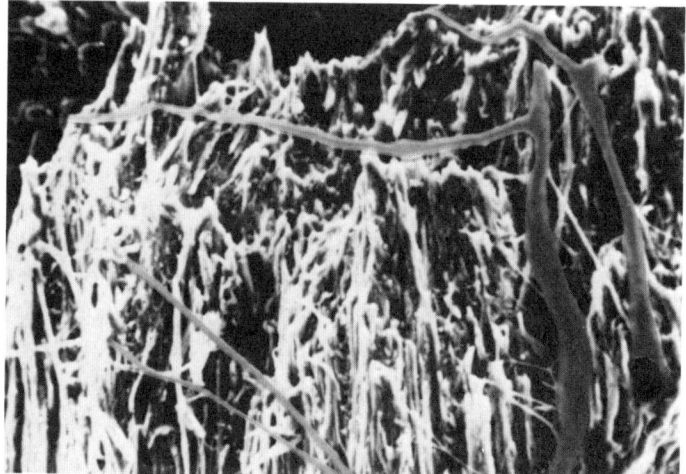

Fig. 3.13 A ruptured ligament also showing ruptured blood vessels. (Courtesy of Dr. David Butler)

enough to prevent injury to ligaments. The full load in the case of rapidly applied stresses must be carried by ligaments which may rupture as the load exceeds their strength. This is what happens when you turn an ankle. A ruptured ligament and its broken blood vessels are shown in Figure 3.13.

Tendon, Sheaths, and Bursa

All muscles end in tendons, which can be considered specialized ligaments joining muscle to bone. Tendons are also mainly collagen fibers but show a higher degree of organization than ligaments. Blood supply is also considerably reduced.

Some tendons have to move through large ranges to do their job and are provided with lubricated sleeves, called synovial sheaths, to help them move easily. While the sleeve is tied down with connective tissue, the tendon moves freely inside.

Runners rarely rupture tendons, but irritation of the sheath caused by pressure from the shoe, overuse, or an alignment problem leads to tendonitis which, as a class, makes one of the largest group of running injuries (see Chapter 13). The Achilles tendon and the tendons on the back of the leg are particularly susceptible to this injury.

Some joints include structures which we can think of as closed bags of fluid called bursa. These allow relative movement of one structure over another, perhaps a tendon on a tendon or muscle over bone. We never know much about bursa until something goes wrong. An inflammation of the bursa, a bursitis, can be a particularly troublesome running injury.

The Hip Joint

The hip is often characterized as a ball and socket joint, and it is the strongest joint that the body has. It gets its great strength from both ligaments and muscles, and from its bony architecture. Movements in running do not tax the hip joint as far as its range of motion is concerned. The most usual movements are flexion and extension, which occur when you raise and lower the knee, respectively. However, other movements are critical to correct foot placement, weight transfer, and adequate stride length.

For example, during standing the right and left feet are on both sides of a line drawn through the middle of the body (Figure 3.14). This is also generally true during walking. Sometime when you are running, look at your

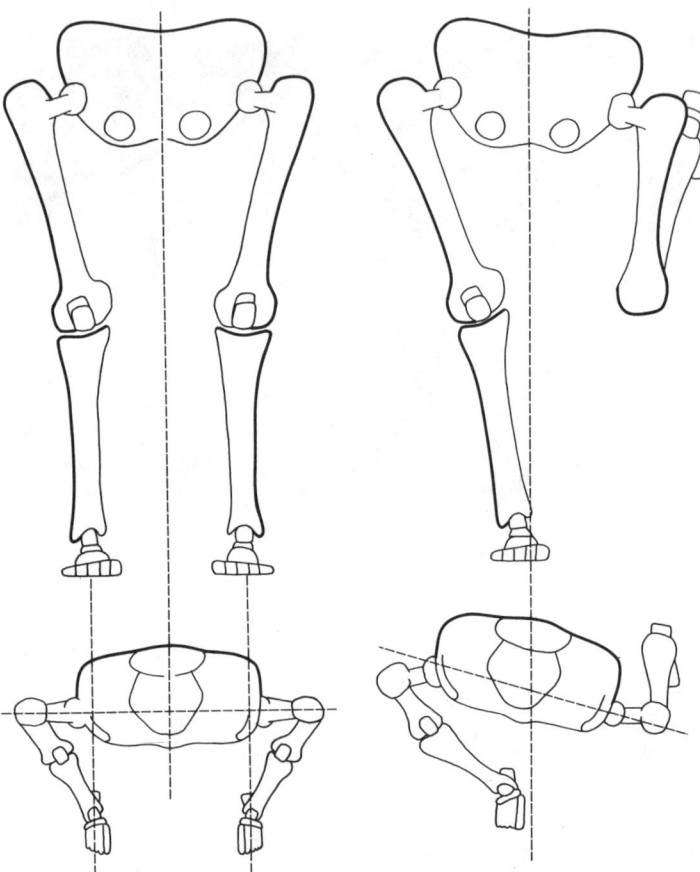

Fig. 3.14 The lower extremity from the front and from above during standing and running. Notice how the foot comes across toward the midline of the body in running, and how the hip bones rotate around the supporting thigh.

footprints and you will see that the left and right feet tend to be placed more on a straight line. Indeed, sometimes the feet will cross over to the other side of the midline. It is the hip joint which allows the movement of the foot and leg over toward the midline. This particular movement of the hip is called adduction and is shown in Figure 3.14. Recovery to its initial position would involve the opposite movement called abduction.

A further movement of the hip allows the thigh to rotate about its long axis, or, if the thigh is fixed, allows the pelvis to swing forward on the thigh. Notice from Figure 3.6 how the joint is not at the end of the thigh bone. The bone sends out a sideways beam which ends in a ball for the joint. During the support phase of running, the pelvis swings forward about the supporting leg in a movement called internal rotation at the hip (see Figure 3.14). The hip joint of the swinging limb in the diagram is experiencing the opposite called external rotation.

Joints Around the Knee

There are three joints that you can grasp within one hand's distance of the knee. The most important one, usually called the knee joint, is between the thigh bone and the major bone of the shank, the tibia. This must rank as one of the weakest major joints in the body, and it is very susceptible to injury. The reason for this is that the way the bones are designed does not add much to the stability of the joint. What strength the knee does have is due to the powerful muscles and ligaments.

A second joint at the knee is the one we've already mentioned between the thigh bone and the kneecap.

Finally there is the joint at the knee between the two bones of the shank, and it is relatively unimportant. The small shank bone, the fibula, is bound extremely tightly to the tibia and very little movement can occur.

The movements of the knee joint are basically flexion and extension, bending and straightening, particularly when the whole leg is straight. Despite appearances the knee is not a hinge joint. The joint axis moves around in different parts of the range of motion. Sliding of the thigh bone over the tibia also occurs.

Many people are surprised that when they stretch their legs out and turn the toes in or out this is actually external and internal rotation of the hip and not a movement of the joints of the knee or the foot. When the knee is flexed some inward and outward rotation of the shank is possible.

Runners don't get the massive knee joint trauma experienced in contact sports. Runners' injuries are much more subtle. But knee pain is not rare; in fact it is more common than any other running injury as we shall see in Chapter 13. The most common knee pain is labeled "peripatella pain" which is pain around and underneath the kneecap. We shall characterize the cause of this injury later on as principally due to overuse and misalignment of certain structures in the lower extremity. Running style and the design of the running shoe exert a considerable influence on the problems at the joints of the knee.

In running the knee has to resist forces which try to bend it in two directions that it cannot go. With placement of the foot under the midline of the body there is stress on the outside of the knee joint. The tension tends to force the outside surfaces of the joint apart. This is resisted by the lateral ligaments and is a potential source of pain. There also is a tendency for the thigh bone and the shank to rotate in opposite directions, and we shall examine this further in the discussion of the biomechanics of running.

The Ankle Joint

The true ankle joint is between the shank and the talus. It is a very simple joint in that its movement is restricted to one plane. We can see from the schematic diagram in Figure 3.6 that a mortise is formed by the shank into which the talus fits, so if all other joints of the foot are fixed, motion at the ankle joint simply raises or lowers the toes. No other movement is possible at this joint. The ankle joint is a fairly frequent source of injuries in runners. What happens is that a sudden unevenness in footing occurs, and the rearfoot is forced to turn inward before the muscles can do anything to save the ankle joint ligaments. The capsule and the ligaments of the ankle are so closely related that swelling soon follows the initial damage.

The Subtalar Joint

The joint between the talus and the heel bone is called the subtalar joint. Its motion is very important because it is the site of pronation and supination, words often heard between runners and their physicians. The movement of the subtalar is often made to sound complicated by calling it a "triplanar movement." In fact it is only complicated when described in terms of the three planes of the body.

The axis of the joint is tilted up at the front and over toward the inside. The pin through the parts of our simplified model in Figure 3.15 shows this. Note that this arrangement is completely different from the ankle joint axis, which is basically in a side-to-side position (Figure 3.15). The best simplification of subtalar joint action is that shown in Figure 3.16, as proposed by Verne Inman.

The diagram represents the subtalar joint as a simple mitered hinge with a diagonal axis connecting the leg to the foot. The model is set up first to simulate the time during running when the support foot is in the very early stages of contact with the ground. The second position shows what happens to the leg when the subtalar joint pronates excessively; the leg is forced to rotate inward. The oblique axis that we described earlier

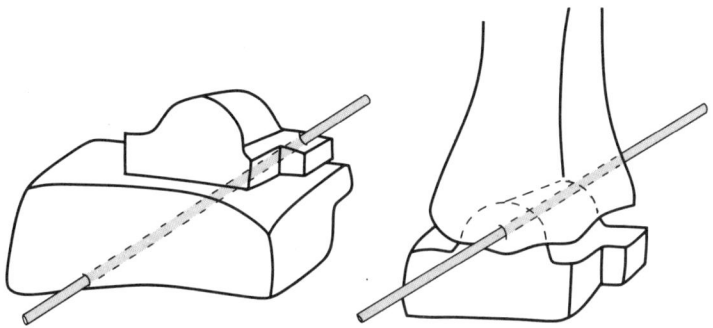

Fig. 3.15 The axis of the subtalar joint (left) represented by a pin. Notice that this axis is not oriented in a simple side-to-side alignment like the axis of the ankle joint (right).

means that motion at the subtalar joint must involve both the leg and foot.

The concept of subtalar joint action is important in understanding how too much pronation can adversely affect the knee joint. Figure 3.17 shows our anatomical model in the middle of right foot contact during running. As the subtalar joint pronates the leg rotates inward. If there is too much pronation a large amount of inward rotation will occur. The result at the knee joint is a screwing type of motion that the knee is not designed to resist. Pronation is a normal and necessary part of running. It is only when excessive amounts of motion at the subtalar joint occur that injury is likely.

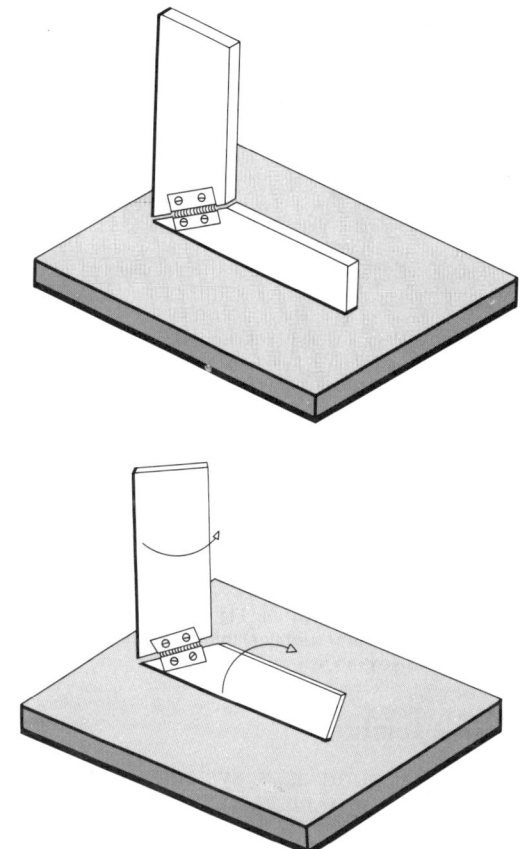

Fig. 3.16 A simplification of the subtalar joint showing that, because of the orientation of the axis, the shank (upper segment) will rotate inward when joint movement occurs.

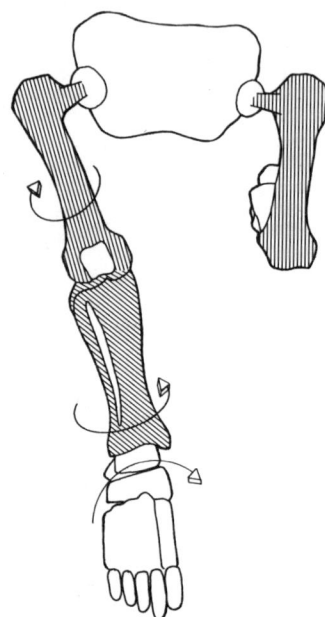

Fig. 3.17 The principle shown in Fig. 3.16 but now applied to the simplified skeleton. As the subtalar joint pronates, the shank rotates inward, causing stress at the knee.

The Midtarsal Joint

The midtarsal joint is a system of two joints masquerading as one. Both the talus and the heel bone join the bones of the midfoot, and these joints are collectively called the midtarsal joint. When the subtalar joint pronates, the midtarsal joint has to adjust to accommodate the new position of the rearfoot. Some authorities believe that laxity of the midtarsal joint is as much a problem to runners as excessive pronation at the subtalar joint. A number of structural deformities of the foot are also associated with midtarsal joint misalignment.

Joints Involving Midfoot and Forefoot

Trying to bend and twist your own foot will tell you that only small amounts of movement are possible between the midfoot and forefoot. There are several joints connecting these two regions but they allow limited movement.

What is perhaps more important than the movement is the relative stability of these structures even in the absence of muscle forces. It has been shown that even when the muscles of the leg and foot are anesthetized so they cannot exert force, the arches of the foot retain their shape and strength. This shows that the ligaments and bony structure can act alone as the primary source of stability, although it is unlikely that any of the more severe stresses are carried without the help of muscles. Certain muscles are placed in a position which leaves no doubt that their functions are to support the arches of the foot.

The Big Toe

The big toe and the bones in the midfoot and forefoot which support it are known as the first metatarsal segment. You will notice that in the main anatomical diagram (Figure 3.6) the section of the forefoot behind the big toe has been given a separate existence. This is because it is responsible for more abnormalities than any other forefoot segment. The two major problems are that it is either too short or too flexible.

When the big toe is short the condition is referred to as Morton's toe (to be distinguished from Morton's foot) after Dr. Dudley Morton, author of a book written in 1935 called *The Human Foot*, which is still a classic. About half the book is spent discussing problems consequent to a short first toe. Morton's theory was that if the first metatarsal is too short to bear its portion of the load, the next bone in line across the foot, the second metatarsal, must do more than its share of work. It responds by growing more sturdy, and this added responsibility may be more than it can take, leading to a variety of complications.

Exactly the same problem exists if the first segment has too much mobility. As it hits the ground in a situation where it would normally accept load, the metatarsal continues to move upward and other parts of the foot must do its job.

Another problem with the big toe is the formation of bunions. These are pressure-related growths between forefoot and toe which can be extremely painful. Usually in this condition the first toe does not point in the same direction as the rest of the toes. In the most common problem, known as hallux valgus, the big toe tries to climb up on its neighbor.

Joints Out of Alignment

While anatomy books show joints in perfect alignment, the reality for many runners is less than perfect alignment. Together with overuse (simply more wear than the body was designed for) alignment problems of the lower extremity have been identified as one of the principal causes of running injuries. Two words you will hear often from physicians and sports scientists who talk about running are varus and valgus. Varus means turning in toward the midline of the body while valgus means turning away from the midline. These terms can be applied to any part of the body, but they are frequently used in connection with the rearfoot or forefoot. They also imply a starting point for measurement.

In the rearfoot the starting point is the neutral position of the subtalar joint. This can be described as the point where the line bisecting the leg and that bisecting the rearfoot (heel bone) are parallel. For the forefoot, the neutral position is when a line across the bottom of the heel and a line across the metatarsal heads are parallel, when slight pressure is applied to the fifth metatarsal head. These conditions are shown in Figure 3.18. From these starting points rearfoot and forefoot valgus and varus are defined as depicted in Figure 3.18.

The alignment of a runner's lower extremity will

A RUNNER'S ANATOMY

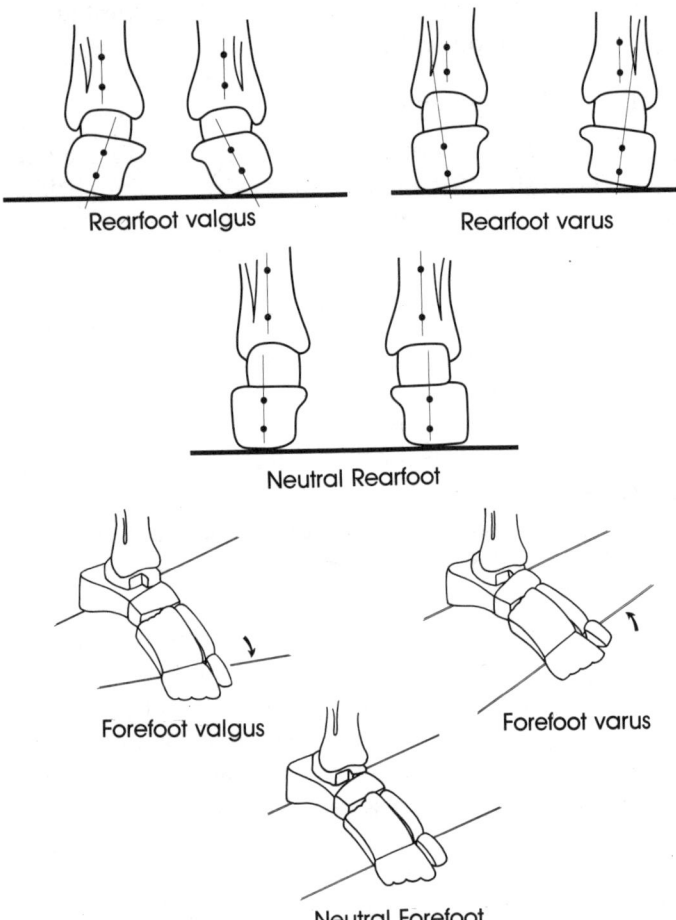

Fig. 3.18 Alignment problems with the joints of the leg and foot.

have implications for the type of running shoe needed, a topic which is discussed further in Chapter 14. Both static (standing) and dynamic (running) alignment are important. The dynamic case requires an understanding of the biomechanics of running which we shall cover in the next chapter. Grasping the various concepts will also be a great help in following the treatment process at the time of any injury.

MUSCLE—MAKING THE PARTS MOVE

Muscle tissue is fascinating to study because it does something besides just sitting still under the microscope. When a muscle cell receives an electrical signal an elaborate chain of events is set in motion.

The electrical changes at the cell surface cause chemical changes in the cell's equilibrium. Like floodgates suddenly swinging open, small channels in the membrane open up. These channels briefly allow an inward rush of substances that they usually repel, and a complex interaction among parts which are both framework and engine at the same time begins (Figure 3.19). The end result is that force is generated, either to accelerate a part of the body, slow it down, or simply hold a certain structure rigid.

Muscle action during running resembles the interplay of instruments in an orchestra. The muscles are not switched on for long periods of time, but come in brief-

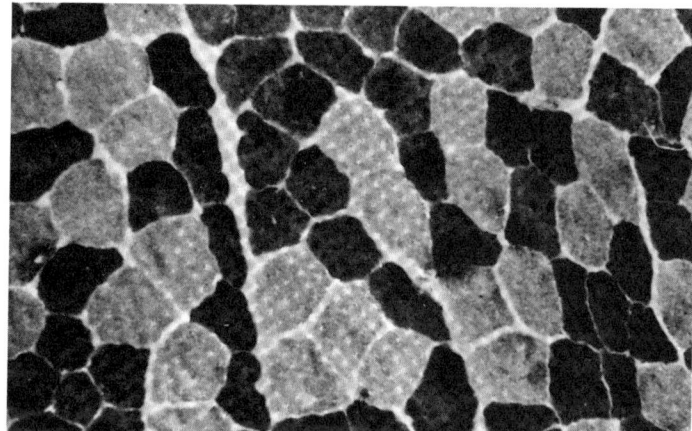

Fig. 3.19 A cross section of a piece of human muscle. The darkly stained fibers in this section are slow twitch fibers, the lightly stained fibers are fast twitch. This subject has a preponderance of slow twitch fibers, but the fast twitch fibers are generally larger.

ly in sequence for perhaps one tenth of a second, do their job, and then switch off as other muscles take over. The individual muscle fibers are specialized according to their resistance to fatigue (Figure 3.19). Distance runners typically have more fatigue resistant fibers (slow twitch) while sprinters have more fatigable fibers (fast twitch).

Major Muscles

Some of the important muscles in the lower extremity are shown in Figure 3.20. We usually describe a muscle by the joint action it has when shortening or contracting. But in running the things muscles do as they lengthen are equally important.

Let's take two examples. The quadriceps are four individual muscles on the front of the thigh that merge into the patella tendon and finally terminate on the front of the shank. During running the quadriceps perform two important and completely different tasks. As the swinging limb comes through, they straighten the knee in preparation for foot strike. During this action they are, of course, shortening. But once the foot strikes the ground the quadriceps are forced to lengthen as the knee flexes or bends to cushion some of the impact of landing.

Another muscle with a dual job in running is called the tibialis anterior (Figure 3.20), located on the front of the shank. During the swing phase the foot has to be brought into a position for foot strike with the toes raised (known as dorsiflexed). As you can see from the diagram, the tibialis anterior is well-placed to perform this task. It can exert an upward pull on the whole foot which will then rotate about the ankle joint. As soon as the foot strikes the ground, the tendency, if the runner is a rearfoot striker, is for the foot to slap down on the ground. So the tibialis anterior just keeps on working, controlling the way the foot is placed. It is just like lowering a weight on the end of a rope.

Such dual muscle actions like those that the quadriceps and tibialis anterior perform are the rule rather than the exception in the lower extremity during running.

Hip and Knee Joint Muscles

Some of the largest muscles in the body control the motion of the thigh. To move the thigh from side to side, the adductors on the inside of the leg and the abductors on the outside (Figure 3.20) are called into action. One of the abductor group, called the tensor fascia lata, sends a long band of tendon down the outside of the leg; this tendon is sometimes a site of injury to runners.

The hip flexors and extensors (Figure 3.20) interact to move the hip forward and backward. Although the quadriceps and their counterpart on the back of the leg, the hamstrings, extend and flex the knee, respectively, they also cause hip movements because they cross both hip and knee joints.

Most of the muscles responsible for major movements of the foot are attached to the shank, as you can see from the diagram in Figure 3.20. The fleshy parts of the muscles generally end above the ankle joint, and long tendons curl down to an attachment in the bones of the foot. The tendons run, as we discussed earlier, in synovial sheaths, which are held in place by a band of connective tissue shown schematically in the diagram. Many of these tendons use the bony projections of the ankle

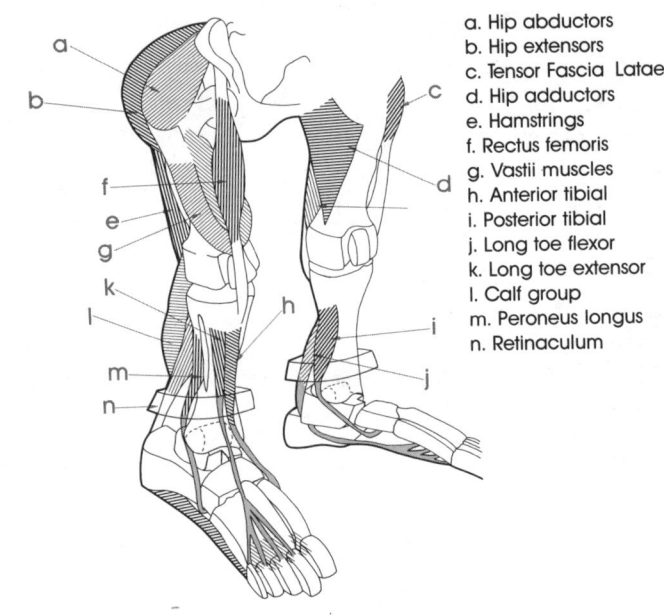

a. Hip abductors
b. Hip extensors
c. Tensor Fascia Latae
d. Hip adductors
e. Hamstrings
f. Rectus femoris
g. Vastii muscles
h. Anterior tibial
i. Posterior tibial
j. Long toe flexor
k. Long toe extensor
l. Calf group
m. Peroneus longus
n. Retinaculum

Fig. 3.20 The major muscles of the lower extremity represented in their approximate locations on the simplified skeleton.

as pulleys on their way to the foot. Good examples of this type of action are the long flexors and extensors of the toes. The biggest muscles on the shank are the calf muscles. These are actually two separate muscles, one starting above the knee and one below it. They merge into the Achilles tendon to provide the powerful pushoff or plantar thrust required in running.

Two other muscles starting on the shank deserve our attention. These are the tibialis posterior and the peroneus longus. As you can see from the diagram, these don't simply terminate on the first foot bone they see. The tendons wrap around underneath the midfoot, one on each side, providing important support for the arches. The tibialis posterior is well placed to try to resist pronation. In runners who pronate excessively this muscle is frequently overworked and the tendon becomes inflamed. Such injuries are a major component of "shin splint syndrome."

The foot has its own network of muscles which start and end in the foot itself. There are muscles which move the toes up and down and from side to side. The big toe generally has its own set of muscles for each separate job, while the remaining four toes usually share the same muscle but have separate tendons which transmit the force.

SUMMING UP ON ANATOMY

I hope that the original promise of a straightforward description of the major components of a runner's anatomy has been fulfilled. Of course, the system is considerably more complex than I have suggested. All the muscles are supplied with a network of nerves, veins, and arteries which thread their way delicately through the leg. The spaces are filled with connective tissue, fat pads, and bursa. And I haven't even talked about the elaborate "computer program" in the brain and the sensors in muscles and tendons which make the whole assembly move in a coordinated pattern.

But there is a basis here which will help you understand the movements in running and ultimately the way different running shoes will affect certain parts of the body. Next time you are told that you have posterior tibial tendonitis, rearfoot varus, or hallux valgus at least you'll know which part to look at.

4

The Biomechanics of Running

From our brief look at anatomy we now know the major components of the running mechanism. But knowing the components and understanding how they function in running are two very different problems. To study the movements of the parts and how they are affected by different shoes, we must turn to one of the fastest growing branches of sports science—biomechanics.

In biomechanics, the movement of the human body is studied in mechanical terms. Typical applications in running include measuring the movements of the limb segments, measuring the forces and pressures underneath the foot and the shoe, and calculating what muscle forces are responsible for the observed movements. In a way, then, it can be seen as a scientific system of coaching and designing equipment such as running shoes. Despite its great potential, not everyone in the running community has welcomed biomechanics, or indeed the other sports sciences, with open arms.

DOES SCIENCE SPOIL RUNNING?

Some people feel that science should stay as far away from running as possible. Running, they reason, is a pure activity. The intrusion of hypothesis, experimentation, and inference will tarnish this purity and turn running into yet another mechanized activity in which input and output can be simply related. And to some extent they are right. Much of the joy of running is in its simplicity. Take this away and a major attraction disappears.

Yet talk to the same purists when they are injured, and they will likely lament the fact that their search for a cure has been fruitless, or perhaps lay blame on a new pair of shoes that they had been trying out.

Science cannot be a fair weather—or in this case a foul weather—friend. To understand the complexity of running, to explain the subtleties of injury, to design shoes which will help us run longer without injury, we need constant inquiry. Science is not a stop/start process which can be called upon in times of need. Each experiment typically raises more questions than it solves. Data are often inconclusive and difficult to interpret. Each study adds a fraction of one percent to the overall picture—a picture we desperately need more pieces to complete.

Proletarian Science—The Lowest Common Denominator

The science in this chapter is distinctly proletarian science. We are not trying to explain how some people can run marathons in two hours and ten minutes while others only manage to complete the course in four hours. We will present details of the lowest common denominator of the running gait, the contact of the foot with the ground.

The foot strike and the subsequent ground contact phase have certain features in common in all runners. Having said that, we must immediately add that when studied in fine detail the pattern of ground contact can be as individual as the runner's voice, something unique and identifiable. We call the initial contact foot strike, not heel strike, because many runners do not strike with the heel but with the midfoot or forefoot.

How Is Foot Strike Studied?

The science of sport biomechanics had ridden to success on the crest of inadequacy—the inadequacy of the human eye to study movements which occur as quickly as running. Coaches are forced to attempt such visual analyses and by concentrating their attention carefully on a single part of the body at a single time can sometimes identify problems. But frequently events happen

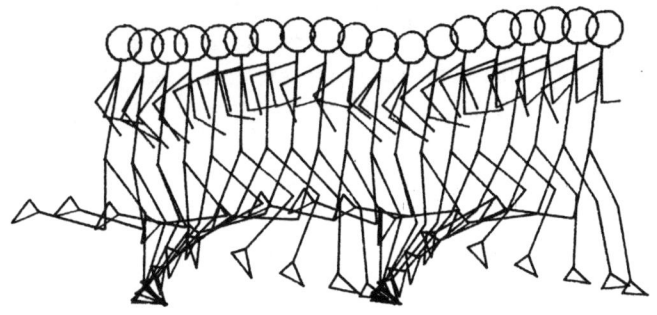

Fig. 4.1 Computer drawing of the movements of Bill Rodgers' body during one complete cycle of running.

far too quickly to allow visual analysis to produce meaningful results.

Look for a moment at Figure 4.1, which is a summary in one plane of the movements which Bill Rodgers' body goes through between two contacts of the same foot. This unit is referred to as one cycle of running. Clearly there is a vast amount of information to assimilate in this figure even after the computer, which drew the picture, has done the hard work of reconstructing the position of various body segments.

The basic information, from which this figure and others like it are drawn, comes from high-speed photography. Runners are filmed at speeds up to 500 frames per second. If we wanted we could therefore make about 300 separate prints which would record the successive positions of body segments during one running cycle (since a cycle lasts about 0.6 seconds). The change between each print would be imperceptible since they are only 1/500 of a second apart.

Film Analysis

Fortunately, there are better ways to extract important information from film than simply looking at photographs. If such was not the case, biomechanics labs throughout the land would soon disappear beneath a deluge of photographic paper.

The process of film analysis is laborious but simple. A high grade projector moves the experimental film through one frame at a time, stopping the film for as long as the operator requires, sometimes up to thirty seconds or more. The image is projected onto a table in front of the operator (see Figure 4.2).

Usually markers are placed at points of interest (on the running shoe, over the ankle or knee joints for example) before filming takes place. The markers provide the operator with the targets which must be measured. This is done by lining up a small device which has crosshairs, like the sight in a rifle, with the targets you see in the figure.

The table in Figure 4.2 is perhaps 100 times more

The Biomechanics of Running

expensive than the simple drafting table that it might appear. Beneath its surface is an array of precision wires that are able to sense the exact location of the crosshairs and turn it into a pair of numbers—x and y coordinates. These numbers are immediately digested by the computer; the operator then moves to the next target or the next frame. It may take several hours and not a little eyestrain to go through a complete cycle of running in this way, digitizing the positions of a dozen or so body markers on every frame of the film.

So the important leap has been made. Movements of the runner's limbs, too fast and complex for the eye to see, have been converted into numbers. Thousands upon thousands of numbers are held by the computer in a fragile set of magnetic dots. These numbers give us the potential to unlock some of the secrets of running.

But potential has to be realized. The really creative steps are still to come. The computer must be programmed to do the right calculations, and the results must be scanned for significance. Most important of all some presentation must be devised which will allow the results to be communicated. Not just to other doctors and scientists, but to Joe and Joanne Runner.

The Approach to the Ground

As your foot gets close to a landing on the ground, chances are that the inside border of your shoe is higher off the ground than the outside border. This is shown

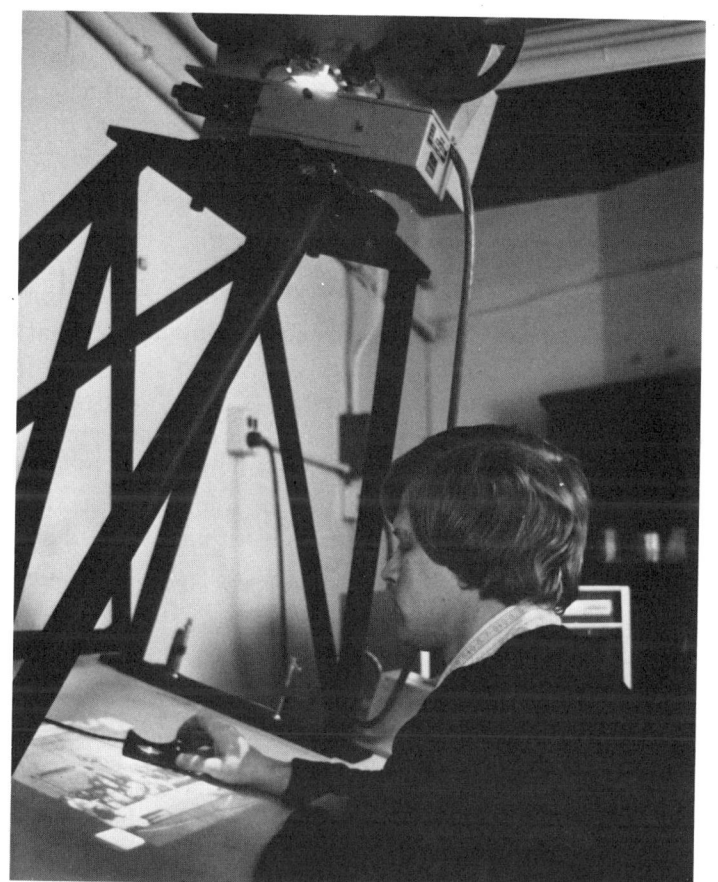

Fig. 4.2 A film being digitized. The image is projected onto a table, which converts a location on the film into numbers which can be read by a computer.

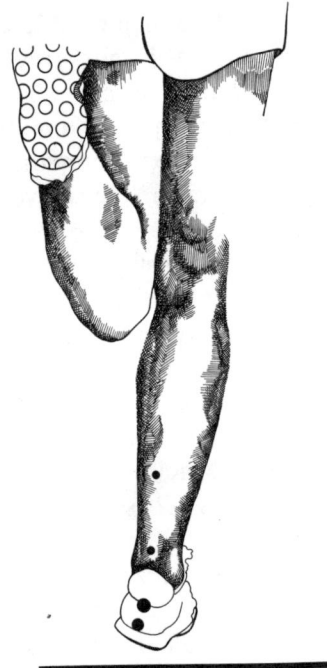

Fig. 4.3 A typical landing position in distance running. The foot is placed toward the midline of the body and it is oriented (in supination) so that the outside border of the shoe will touch the ground first. The targets on the leg and shoe are typical of those used in film experiments.

in Figure 4.3. This occurs for two reasons. During the swing phase, the subtalar joint has been moved by the muscles on the front of the shank into a supinated position. This brings the toes up toward the shank and raises the inside border of the foot slightly.

The second reason for the orientation of the foot at landing is that most people place their left and right feet almost along one straight line when running at typical distance running speeds. This means that the foot will be placed underneath the midline of the body rather than to one side, as it is in walking. So even if the subtalar joint was in a neutral position, the adduction of the leg produces what is known as a functional varus of the foot. Remember that varus means turning in toward the midline; you can see from Figure 4.3 that the foot and shank both have a varus tilt just before ground contact is made. The varus is called "functional" because it occurs as a result of normal movement rather than pathological alignment of the joints of the leg. If the pelvis is wider, as it is in some women, the angle of the leg needed to place the foot under the body will be greater. This will lead to much more pronation during stance, as we shall see below. Runners whose right foot "crosses over" past their body's midline will experience a similar effect.

The Myth of Heel Strike

The result of this functional varus is that ground contact is first made with the outside or lateral edge of the shoe, and not the back edge as some shoe manufacturers would have had us believe in the past. If by heel strike we mean contact between the back edge of the shoe and the ground, then heel strike is a myth. It hardly ever occurs in level running although it is quite common in walking. This is the first part of a concept I'll call the LMF pattern of running. The L stands for the "lateral" edge of the shoe, where contact with the ground is first made. More on M and F shortly.

Pronation After Foot Strike

Now landing on the lateral border of the shoe is like landing on a knife edge, albeit a soft knife edge. The natural response is that the foot and shoe tend to shift quickly into a flat position.

This flattening out of the foot involves the subtalar joint in the movement of pronation. Many people have the idea that any amount of pronation is undesirable, because pronation is mentioned so often in connection with injury. But without pronation, the foot could never assume a flat position on the ground and thus perform the necessary functions during support.

The trouble arises when pronation does not stop within what might be considered the normal range. Too much pronation, or pronation at the wrong time in the contact phase, are the conditions that can lead to trouble. As we discussed in Chapter 3, pronation at the subtalar joint inevitably involves internal rotation of the shank which, at this point in the contact phase, is bad news for the knee joint.

All of this happens within a fraction of a second after touchdown, and film analysis allows us to measure rather exactly how far this process of pronation goes. As you might guess from the anatomical account of the subtalar joint, a full analysis of its motion would be quite complex. So we settle for measuring the alignment of the rearfoot and leg, and for the purposes of illustration will equate this with subtalar joint motion.

Markers are placed on the back of the shoe and the back of the leg and the subjects are filmed while running at the chosen speed.

The graphs in Figure 4.4 show some results of these measurements from three kinds of runners. One runner (subject A) moves slowly from about ten degrees of supination to just past the neutral position, about .06 of a second after touchdown, which is roughly one-third of the total contact phase. The second runner (subject B) pronates more than subject A and reaches a position of maximum pronation at about .045 seconds after foot strike. This pattern is quite close to the average of the many subjects that we have examined. The third runner, a female varsity athlete (subject C) shows rapid movement into a position of extreme pronation within .033 seconds after foot strike. She has gone about fifteen degrees beyond the neutral position.

Watching a slow-motion film of a runner who pronates excessively makes one wince with pain. The picture in Figure 4.5 is a print of one frame taken of a subject with excessive pronation. Bad as it looks, it cannot quite convey the same feeling as watching the

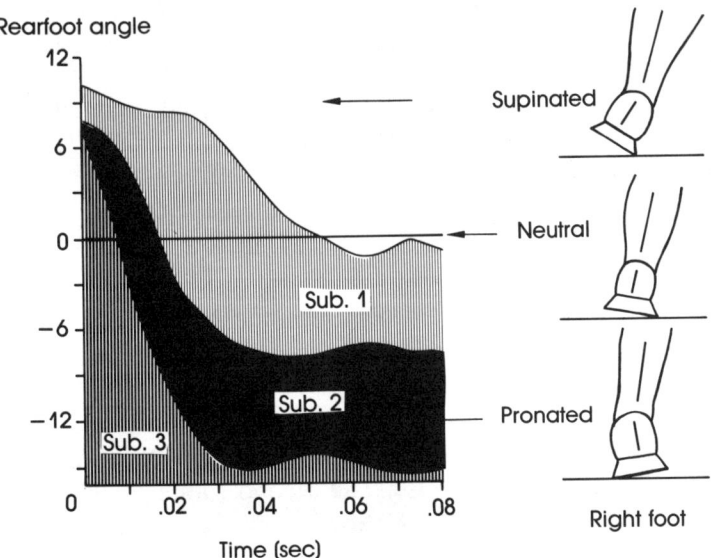

Fig. 4.4 Rearfoot movements of three different runners during the early support phase. The drawings of a right foot show supination (positive angles), the neutral position (zero angle), and pronation (negative angles). Notice that all three runners start out in about the same supinated position at foot strike, but differ dramatically in the amount of subsequent pronation.

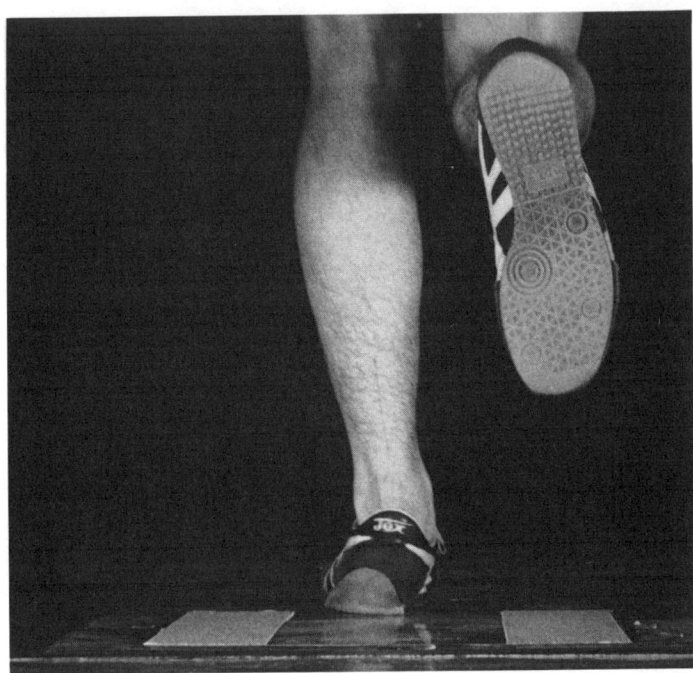

Fig. 4.5 A single frame from the early support phase of a runner who pronates excessively.

movement relentlessly and painfully unfold in slow motion.

The reason measurement is so important is that your opinion of what is overpronation and mine may be poles apart. A standard system of measurement is needed so that doctors can communicate with each other and so that they can measure the effect of various treatments.

Pronation in Different Running Shoes

From a research point of view, the measurement of rearfoot motion has allowed us to make statements about how well different running shoes help prevent overpronation. There is no doubt that the amount of pronation that occurs is dependent on a number of features in the design and construction of the running shoe. This is demonstrated clearly by the graphs in Figure 4.6 which show pronation by the same subject in two different shoes. Orthotics will result in even more dramatic control of rearfoot movements. This topic is covered in Chapter 12.

This important feature in a shoe is called rearfoot control and we shall talk more about it in Chapter 7. The study of rearfoot motion has also paved the way for the design of machines which will test the rearfoot control provided by a shoe without having to go through the long and expensive process of filming, film analysis, and the production of graphs.

Forefoot Control

It would be wrong to leave the impression that all runners' problems are in the rearfoot, or that excessive pronation is the only notable misalignment which occurs. A look at Figure 4.7 will confirm that this is not the case. The runner in this picture shows a pattern of movement which causes him to literally almost fall off the outside edge of the shoe at every foot strike. The outside border of his shoe is both worn and compressed to a greater degree than the inside border.

The alignment problem here is a combination of fore-

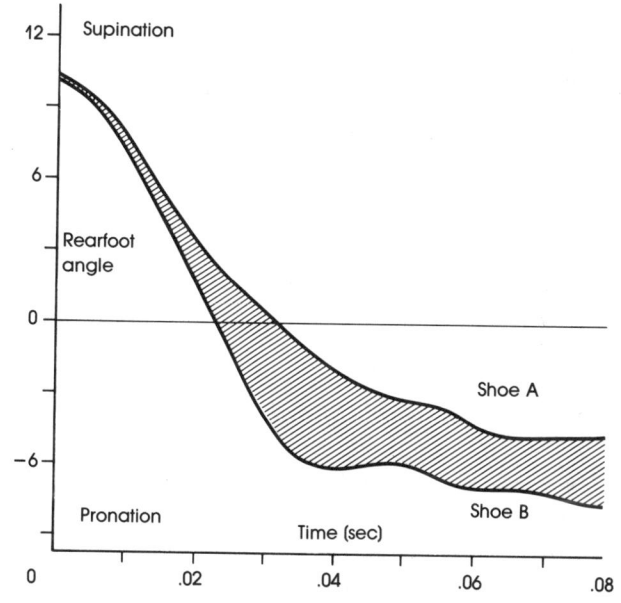

Fig. 4.6 Average rearfoot movements from a group of runners each wearing two different shoes. One shoe prevents the runners from pronating much better than the other. This property is known as rearfoot control.

foot varus and bow legs (genu varum). This runner's forefoot needs just as much control and attention as the excessive pronation of the subtalar joint of the runner in Figure 4.5. There are other such conditions which you will find described in *The Foot Book* by Harry Hlavac, D.P.M.

Fig. 4.7 This runner has a rigid foot which not only does not pronate, but does not reach the normal flat position during support. Most of the pressure is under the outside border of the shoe.

What Kind of Runner Are You?

Although the movements during early support, such as pronation, occur too quickly to observe by eye, the end points of these movements are held for quite a long time. So you can, in effect, make an approximate visual estimate of what kind of runners your running partners are as far as their rearfoot and forefoot movements are concerned.

One of my favorite ways to run a race, when time is not particularly important, is to start slowly and then pull up through the field watching runners' patterns of movement. Later on I talk to them about their associated aches and pains.

From this rather unscientific survey of perhaps 100 runners during races, it is clear to me that misalignments of the joints of the foot and leg are not always associated with pain or a high incidence of injury. That is not to say that the cumulative effect of overpronating, for example, on every stride of hundreds of miles of running won't eventually catch up with the runners. The injury surveys provide overwhelming evidence that injury and misalignment go together.

THE MEASUREMENT OF THE INVISIBLE

Although sport biomechanics really began with cinematography, it soon graduated to higher art forms. There are some features of human movement for which high-speed film and its associated analysis are completely useless tools of study. The two principal areas that I have in mind which are of great importance to running and running shoes are the measurement of force and pressure underneath the foot.

Forces Under the Foot

Next time you get onto your bathroom scale, try an experiment of your own. First get on as slowly as you can, and you will observe that the needle or digital indicator will slowly rise to show the value of your body weight. Now step on faster, but not so fast that you will be unable to see the numbers on the dial. You will see that the scale registers values greater than your body weight, perhaps enough to take the scale beyond its range if you step on fast enough.

The high values on the scale are not a sign of malfunction. They really do mean that the forces pressing up on your foot are greater than your body weight. How can this possibly be? The understanding of this phenomenon goes back to a famous apple which is supposed to have fallen on the head of Sir Isaac Newton in the 17th century.

When you are standing still on the ground, the maximum force that can be exerted on your feet is the combined weight of your body and whatever you are carrying. If it were any other way you would float off into space.

But as soon as you move the forces will change. Large forces can exist both as you jump upward and as you jump downward—as in landing from a height. It is clearly not the direction of movement, then, which causes large forces.

The key factor is acceleration, or change in speed. When acceleration is considered, getting more upward speed (as in jumping up) or less downward speed (as in landing) both amount to the same thing—an acceleration upward. This acceleration is responsible for the increased force under your feet.

Forces in Running

We might seem to have drifted rather far from the topic of running, but the brief lesson in physics was necessary because it turns out that both of the situations just described occur in quick succession during contact with the ground in running. There is a device called a force platform which can measure variations in forces under the foot during running. Even though forces are in a sense, invisible, the force platform allows us to visualize them.

In Figure 4.8 the results of an experiment on a woman distance runner who clocks in at seven minutes per mile are shown. These results, and the figures showing various body positions during ground contact provide tremendous insight into running mechanics.

As soon as the lead foot touches the ground, the forces rapidly build up to a value greater than twice the runner's body weight. This happens because not only is the body weight being supported but the downward movement of the body must be stopped by an upward acceleration. There is then a brief period when the forces fall slightly. At this time the first acceleration phase has stopped and the second has not yet begun. Soon the smooth rising phase of the force begins and the body moves upward. The rising force is a reflection of upward acceleration in preparation for takeoff.

So for the second time in the brief contact period (which does not last much more than one quarter of a second), the force under the foot rises to somewhere between two and three times body weight. The size of the force is dependent upon speed, but not to the extent that you might imagine. The force falls rapidly in the late stages of support until it is zero at toe-off.

Standing With Two People on Your Back?

So, the effect on your feet of running (at typical distance running speeds) is as if—temporarily—you were to stand holding two people weighing the same as you do on your back, first taking one foot off the floor, and then standing on the forefoot of the contact foot.

Put in these terms, the possibility for injury to the foot becomes overwhelmingly clear. These large forces at the foot result in even larger forces at the joint surfaces. The force between the bones of the shank and the talus, for example, may be greater than ten times body weight. This enormous force is produced by muscle action which tends to compress the joint surfaces even more.

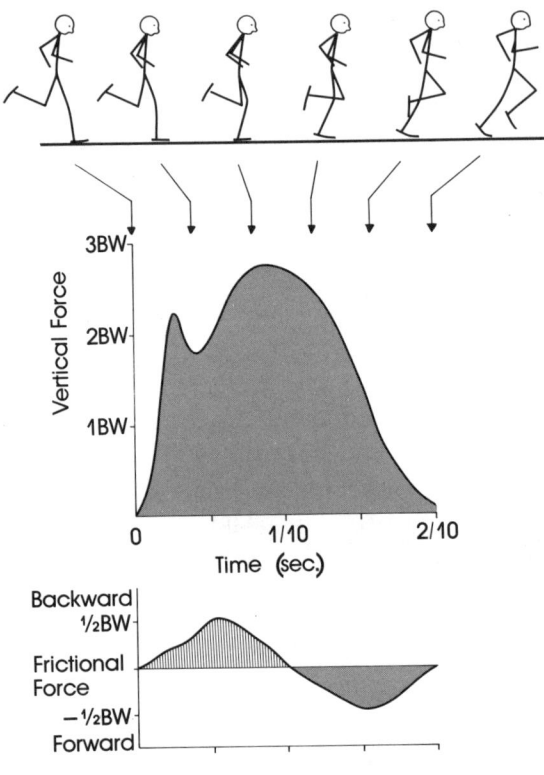

Ground Reaction Forces in Running

Fig. 4.8 The vertical and front-to-back forces during the period of ground contact in distance running, which typically lasts 0.2 seconds. The positions of the body at various times during the contact phase are shown by the stick figures. The vertical force has a first peak associated with landing greater than twice body weight. It rises to almost three times body weight during midsupport. The front-to-back forces show first a braking phase and then a propulsive period, both with peaks of one half of body weight.

Friction Forces

Although we most often think of the force components that act upward on the foot, those that act in a front-to-back direction are also very important. The objective of efficient ground contact is to lose as little forward speed as possible. Some speed must be lost; as soon as the foot touches down, a braking force equal to half a body weight pushes back on the body. This is shown by the upward hump of the frictional force curve in Figure 4.8. The force is referred to as "frictional" because if the surface were smooth the force could not exist and normal running would be impossible.

In the middle of the contact phase, the force temporarily falls to zero. The speed that has been lost in braking must be made up on propulsion, and the downward hump in Figure 4.8 shows the body accelerating back up to speed.

So running at a steady speed is not a reality. With every foot strike a runner is going through a cycle of slowing down and speeding up.

Spotting the Pressure Points

It is one thing to know how big the forces are, but it is equally important to find out where the forces are applied. The force platform can give us some information about this too. Figure 4.9 shows the outlines of right feet as if they had been left as footprints by three different runners each running at six minutes per mile. You

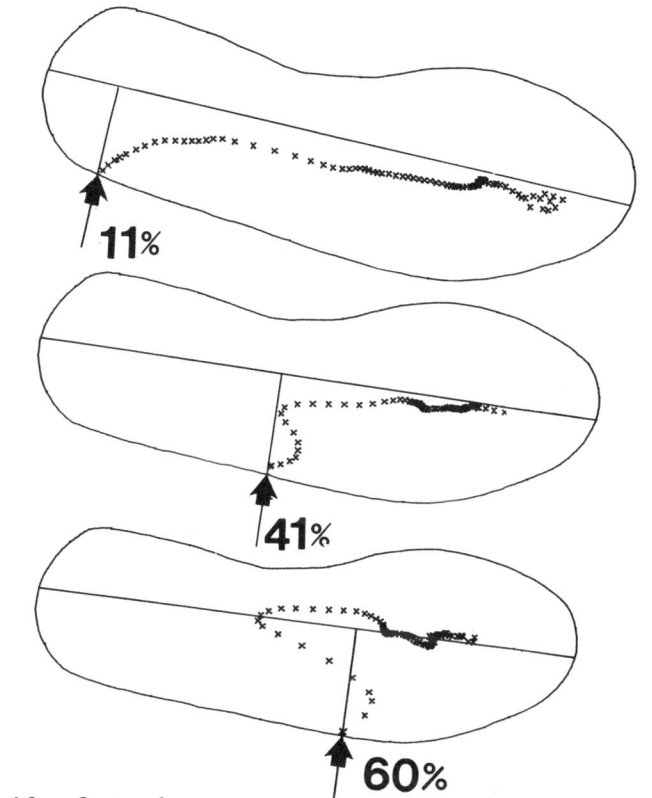

Fig. 4.9 Center of pressure patterns from three runners running at six minutes per mile. Imagine you are looking down at your own right foot, and can see how the center of the pressure distribution moves underneath the shoe throughout the contact phase. The arrows indicate the point of first contact between shoe and ground, and the number alongside the arrow is the strike index. (See text for further details.) Notice that the strike indices are very different in the three subjects despite the matched running speeds.

can see that runner A toed out much more than the other two.

During any instant in the contact phase the forces under the shoe are applied to a wide area. The small crosses on the foot outlines represent the best estimates, calculated by a computer, of where the center of the pressure distribution is located.

We should repeat that all three runners were running at the same speed, but as you can see their patterns of pressure distribution were extremely different. Runner A is a classical rearfoot striker. The first cross appears on the rear lateral border of the shoe showing where first contact was made. Runners B and C would be classified, on the basis of the first point of contact, as midfoot strikers, since they both made initial ground contact in the middle third of the shoe. The strike index shown in Figure 4.9 is a way of being more precise about the point of first contact. It represents the percentage of shoe length, measured from the heel, where the first center of pressure point appears. On this basis the rearfoot striker has a strike index of eleven percent and the two midfoot strikers indices of forty-one and sixty percent. This kind of evidence about foot strike patterns is much more conclusive than looking at films since it really shows where the pressure is acting.

Very quickly after the first contact the pressure center in all three subjects moves toward the midline of the shoe, as shown in Figure 4.9. Subject C is a rather extreme pattern since her pressure center actually moves beyond the midline.

When the pressure center enters the front third of the shoe the crosses fall on top of each other so that it is no longer possible to distinguish one from the next. Now the crosses are drawn at equal time intervals so when they are widely spaced the pressure center is moving fast and when they are close together it is almost stationary. Looking at the diagrams in this light we see a fast movement to the midline, and a very slow movement under the forefoot.

The LMF Pattern Explained

What we have discovered through the film and force data presented here is that running does not involve a simple back-to-front traverse of pressure on the bottom of the running shoe. Although the distribution of pressure, even at the same speed, is extremely different among runners, what they all have in common is what I call the LMF pattern.

The runner first makes contact on the *lateral* border; the pressure moves immediately toward the *midline* and then stays in the *forefoot* for a long period of time.

It seems to me that running shoes to date have been designed as if running was a simple back-to-front transfer, which is certainly not the case. Many shoes are modified at the rearmost part of the heel but hardly any shoes have special features which allow them to cope with the first contact on the lateral border. We may well see some major developments in this respect in the future.

The forepart of the running shoe is a particularly important region, but before beginning our discussion, let's take more time to look at data from biomechanical experiments.

The pictures in Figure 4.10 combine the force and pressure center data in a way which gives the most effective visual idea of the interaction between the shoe and the ground in running. Instead of looking at individual runners we will examine patterns from a group who were also running at six minutes per mile.

First some words of explanation about the diagrams. You must imagine that you are looking at someone running from left to right across the page. Just as they are alongside, you get the opportunity to look underneath the runner's right shoe, because the outside border has been lifted slightly upwards for the purpose.

As the contact with the ground occurs, arrows begin to appear. The arrows contain three important pieces of information. The length of the arrow is proportional to the size of the force; the bigger the force the longer the arrow. (See the One Body Weight scale in the corner of each diagram.) The arrow points to the center of the pressure distribution. If the arrow is slanted backwards the runner is still in the braking phase of contact with the ground. When it rolls around and points forward then propulsion is underway.

Rearfoot Strikers

The group of twelve runners whose data make up Figure 4.10a all make first contact with the ground with the rear lateral border, and are therefore classified as rearfoot strikers. Note that at the time of first contact the arrows are relatively small, which means that the forces are small. By the time the first peak of two and one half times body weight is reached the distribution is centered approximately twenty-five percent of shoe length from the heel. This tells us that the very back part of the heel is not as important as we might think in protecting the foot from the first impact in running.

As the support phase continues, the arrows get smaller, reflecting the drop in force we noticed earlier. This is a brief respite between landing and propulsion.

By the time the center of pressure reaches the forepart of the shoe the arrows grow larger and finally get close to vertical. Both of these findings are somewhat counter-intuitive. First, the size of the arrows means that the forces are larger than on any other part of the shoe. We might have thought that initial impact forces would be largest, but Figure 4.10a shows that is clearly not the case. Second, the fact that the arrows were leaning in a backward direction means that braking was occurring the whole time that the pressure center was in the rear two-thirds of the shoe. Only when the pressure center was firmly under the forefoot did propulsion occur. The time and place where the arrows show the frictional forces changing from braking to propulsion have important implications for tread design. The appropriate variations in tread can prevent slipping and maximize propulsion, particularly under adverse conditions.

Midfoot Strikers

We used to believe that when you ran slowly you landed on the heel, when you ran at a middle-distance pace landing occurred on the midpart of the foot, and fast running required a forefoot landing.

The rearfoot strikers that we met in the last few paragraphs show that this view of ground contact is not correct. They were running at a middle-distance pace yet landing on the rearfoot.

The five runners whose data make up Figure 4.10b give further evidence against the theory. Their speed of running was also six minutes per mile. You will see from the figure that their first contact with the ground occurred almost exactly at half of shoe length—hence the term midfoot strikers. This probably represents almost a flat foot plant in some of the runners.

There is a brief backwards movement of the center of pressure, reflecting the fact that this style of running in-

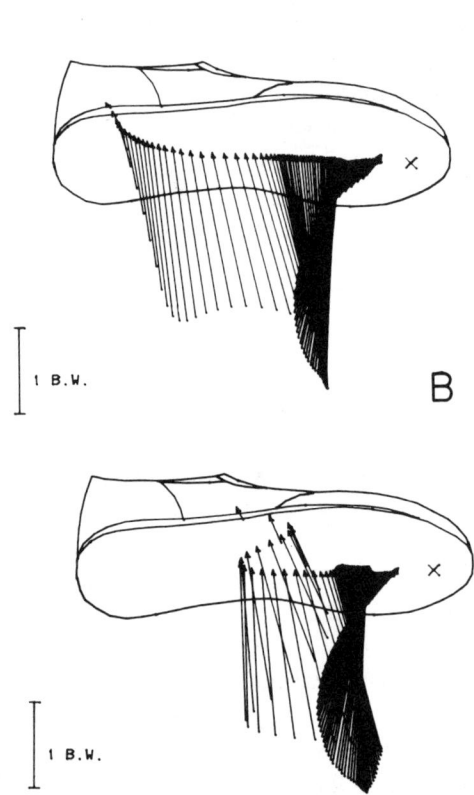

Fig. 4.10 Forces underneath the shoe of rearfoot and midfoot strikers. The outside edge of the right shoe has been lifted, so that we can represent the force by an arrow whose tip points to the center of pressure. The scale factors of one body weight should be compared with the length of the arrows to determine the size of the force. Notice the different requirements that the two runners have in their running shoes. Reproduced with permission from *The Journal of Biomechanics*.

volves a tendency to land on the middle of the foot and then put the heel down.

In fact, as the wide space devoid of arrows in the rearfoot shows, the rear part of the shoe is much less important to a midfoot striker than it is to a rearfoot striker. The midfoot strikers clearly make great demands on the front half of their shoe. It must be able to cushion the impact of landing and be capable of protecting the foot from the large forces involved with support and propulsion.

The Importance of the Forepart of the Shoe

Notice how the front part of the shoes in Figure 4.10 is crowded with lines which become almost indistinguishable one from the other in both rearfoot and midfoot strikers. This means that for most of the ground contact, the pressure is centered in the forepart of the shoe.

Notice also that the forces are largest underneath the forefoot in both groups of runners. These are extremely important findings. For many years, makers of running shoes felt that all they had to do to make a good shoe was to put a sizeable wedge in the rear part of the shoe; this would provide all the protection the body needed.

Figure 4.10 shows how wrong this was. It is likely that many of the forefoot injuries suffered by runners were simply a function of lack of protection in the front part of the shoe. Certainly the initial force of impact has different characteristics compared to the later peak. But both forces will affect the body in different ways and no one is yet able to say which is the more damaging.

Future Shoes

Force and pressure analysis are two keys to better shoe design. A major effort in my own research group is directed toward the development of a system capable of a complete mapping of pressure distribution inside the running shoe.

Figure 4.11 shows some early results. The height of the "mountains" indicates the amount of pressure, in this case, between shoe and floor. The idea is to have a

Fig. 4.11 A three-dimensional map of pressure underneath the shoe. The higher the "mountain" the higher the pressure.

computer create a display, such as the one in the figure, for perhaps 100 instants during the ground contact phase. The images would be displayed in quick succession on a television-like device so that the eye would see a continually changing surface.

These kinds of techniques will allow us to learn about the subtleties of individual running patterns. They will also be useful for the prescription of orthotics (see Chapter 12), the diagnosis of running injuries, and the evaluation of new shoe designs. Future shoes should be based on a good deal more scientific inquiry than those that have been built to date.

Leg Weight and Shoe Weight

Since shoe weight is considered important by many runners it is appropriate to include a brief discussion of why weight is important. The only weight you are used to considering is body weight. But one of the important areas of biomechanics deals with finding out what the various parts of the body weigh. This is necessary information for many of the mechanical calculations that are performed to try to understand human movement.

Although there are tremendous individual variations in body dimensions there are some approximations which will get us reasonably close. Your thigh, shank, and foot will weigh, respectively, about ten, five, and two percent of your total body weight. Notice how the weight decreases as the body part is further from the "middle" of the body. There is good reason why evolution has made us this way, since there are several types of movement that cause energy to be expended. We will consider two contrasting forms.

The first type of movement consists of raising a body segment against gravity. Technically this is called increasing the potential energy of the part. It is very easy to calculate since it is equal to the weight of the part multiplied by the distance it is moved upwards.

The important thing to realize is that it does not matter where the weight is placed on the body. The change in energy will be the same as long as the height change is the same. Thus a one pound weight on the head or on the foot would involve the same energy change if it was moved through the same vertical distance.

But a second type of movement is very different. This is rotation of a body segment; how the weight is distributed is critically important. The energy here is called rotational kinetic energy and what is most important in this calculation is how far the weight is away from the axis and how fast it is rotating.

Now consider the leg swinging through during the recovery phase of a running cycle; let's look at the effects of adding some extra weight to each segment of the leg in turn. The whole leg is rotating about the hip joint and the foot is farthest away. So adding weight to the foot will be much more important than adding it to the shank. Adding weight to the thigh will have even less effect on energy cost and theoretically, adding a weight at the axis of the hip joint would make no difference whatsoever to this form of energy. The foot will be traveling faster than the shank, which travels faster than the thigh, so the effects of distance and speed combine to maximize the importance of the parts furthest away from the hip.

This explains the old axiom that an ounce on the foot is like a pound on the belt. Moving the ounce on the foot increases both the potential energy and kinetic energy, while the pound on the belt only increases the potential energy.

A typical training shoe weighs about eleven ounces for men and nine ounces for women, so the effect of putting on a shoe is to increase the weight of the foot by about twenty-five percent. But this extra weight is added in the worst possible place as far as energy expenditure is concerned. We will look at the exact effects of different weight shoes on running efficiency in Chapter 11.

Summing Up on Science

This chapter has presented a brief introduction to some of the things that sport science can do for the runner. I shall refer back here many times because the material represents a rationale for much of the speculation in later chapters.

While it is by no means complete, what I have tried to do is to show that the days of opinion not backed up by evidence are numbered, if not already over.

There are now techniques available which can provide a detailed analysis of the events which occur as the runner's foot touches the ground. Experiments such as those described in this chapter have already had an important influence on the shoe industry. The runner has definitely benefited by having a wider selection of shoes on the market which are designed to protect the foot and not just to look pretty.

5

How Running Shoes Are Made

The intricacies of design and construction of many space-age gadgets we use daily are well beyond the comprehension of most of us. We don't know why they work, we just know that they do. There are no such mysteries about shoemaking. Building a running shoe is a logical, straightforward process where the function of each part is obvious from its physical form. There is no need to understand solid state physics or the theory of relativity to understand shoemaking. What's more, the process is like putting together an erector set, and that appeals to the builder in each of us.

It is important for the runner to know how running shoes are made. There is good shoemaking and bad shoemaking. Knowing how various operations are done enables you to look for quality in a running shoe. You can develop an eye for good workmanship and an awareness of shortcuts that are sometimes taken and mistakes that are made.

Shoemaking is still heavily labor intensive. Labor costs are about equal to the value of the materials used in the shoe. The import battles that are still going on between running shoe companies who make their shoes in the Orient and those who make them in the United States are bitter and ruthless. Domestic manufacturers feel that the advantage of cheap labor enjoyed by importers gives them an overwhelming price advantage.

In this chapter we will find out why so many hands are needed to make a running shoe. Coverage of initial design and special features of certain shoes will be saved for later. Here we will show what the basic parts are and how they are put together.

PARTS OF THE RUNNING SHOE

As a prelude to talking about shoemaking, we have to agree on a set of terms to describe the shoe. Figure 5.1 is a composite of the features found in most shoes. The more exotic extras will be dealt with in Chapter 8.

The two main parts of a running shoe are the upper and the "bottom," as shoemakers like to call it. The upper is the part which covers the foot while the bottom provides the interface between foot and ground.

The Upper

In traditional shoemaking terms the part of the upper covering the forefoot is called the vamp, with the remainder known as inside and outside quarters. The vamp is often made from one piece of material to minimize the number of seams which would cause irritation to the foot. The edge around the shoe on the upper, where the upper and sole meet, is called the featherline.

The upper is the site of attachment for many other parts, and as we shall see in Chapter 6 it is generally multilayered. If the upper is nylon it starts as one large piece to which leather parts are gradually added to reinforce critical areas. The anchor point for the lacing system is called the eyestay, which forms the throat of the shoe. The suede covering at the back of the shoe is called the foxing.

The front of the upper, often referred to as the toe box, has a leather overlay called the wing tip (see Figure 5.1). A stiffener is sometimes placed underneath the wing tip. If the leather tip only covers the rim of the toe box and does not go up to join the throat it is called a mudguard tip or a moccasin toe box. A padded vinyl or stretch nylon covering around the upper, where contact is made with the foot just below the ankle, is called the collar, and the projection above the heel is known as the pull tab or Achilles tendon protector. (Its function is to help pull on the shoe and it can sometimes irritate the Achilles tendon.) In a pocket at the back of the shoe is a stiffener called the heel counter which helps control the rearfoot during running.

At the level of the center of the long inside arch there is frequently reinforcement sewn on the upper. If it is on the outside, it is called a saddle and often supports

HOW RUNNING SHOES ARE MADE

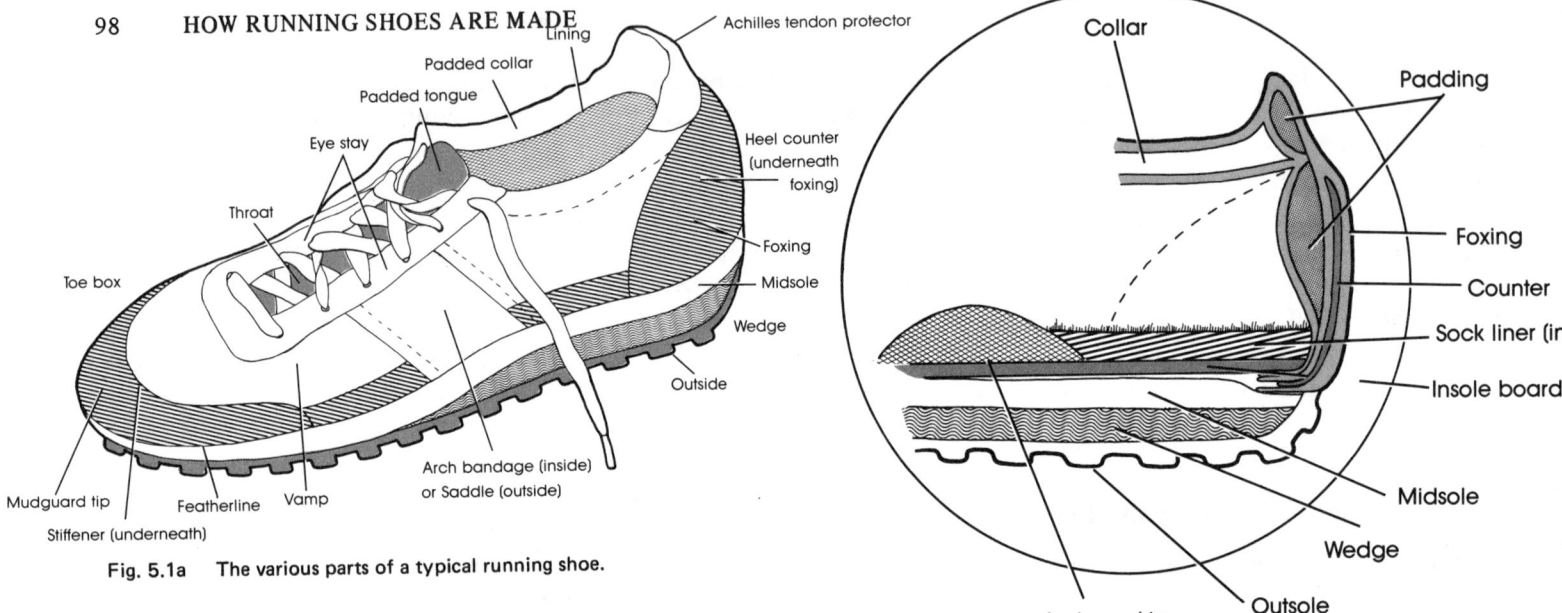

Fig. 5.1a The various parts of a typical running shoe.

Fig. 5.1b A cross section of a shoe showing the various layers in the bottom and heel counter area.

the eyestay (as in some New Balance shoes). This type of construction is often called an Oxford shoe. If the reinforcement is on the inside it is called an arch bandage.

The Bottom

The main components of the bottom are the outsole, midsole, and wedge (see cutaway view in Figure 5.1b). The outsole is designed to give durability and traction but also contributes to shock absorption. The midsole is designed exclusively for shock absorption, and the wedge for both shock absorption and heel lift.

Lying on top of the midsole in most shoes is an insole board which, as we shall see shortly, is an essential component in cement-lasted shoes. Shoe manufacturers use many different devices to cover the top of the insole board and thus line the inside of the shoe. The generic name for these devices is the "sockliner," sometimes called the "insole." Sockliner materials range from terrycloth to foam and differ greatly in their properties.

In some shoes the wedge is on top of the midsole, but usually it is underneath as shown in Figure 5.1. Some manufacturers will make the midsole-wedge unit one piece by skiving (shaving the material) or molding.

Putting the wedge on top of the midsole gives somewhat better results than putting it underneath. When the wedge is underneath it often forms a ridge on the underside of the shoe, which is frequently visible through the outsole.

The cross-section of the back part of the shoe (Figure 5.1b) shows the various layers between the foot and the ground, and how the heel counter fits into the pocket underneath the foxing. The half-moon shaped piece of foam rubber intended to provide some support for the arch is also visible. Runners usually call this the arch cookie.

METHODS OF MANUFACTURE

Running shoes produced as far apart as South Korea and New Hampshire are made by remarkably similar techniques. Shoes of all types are classified by the way in which the upper is attached to the sole. The three processes used for most running shoes are cement lasting, sliplasting (or moccasin construction), and injection molding. The better injection molded shoes usually have polyurethane bottoms. Since cement lasting is the way more than ninety-five percent of running shoes are presently made, it will be our principal focus.

Of course, there is more to shoemaking than simply putting the parts together. Unless the parts are properly designed the shoe will neither fit nor perform well. All aspects of design and fit will be covered in Chapter 9. We will assume in this chapter that the designer's work has been done and concentrate on the business of shoemaking.

The Moccasin

Although the oldest shoes mentioned in Chapter 2 were made by braiding strands of sagebrush bark together, most of the 10,000 years of shoemaking history has been a search for better ways of fixing the leather upper to leather sole to give good fit and durability.

An early technique, usually associated with the Indians in the United States, was the moccasin (Figure 5.2). The foot is simply wrapped in a sheet of leather which is gathered over the instep and around the leg in

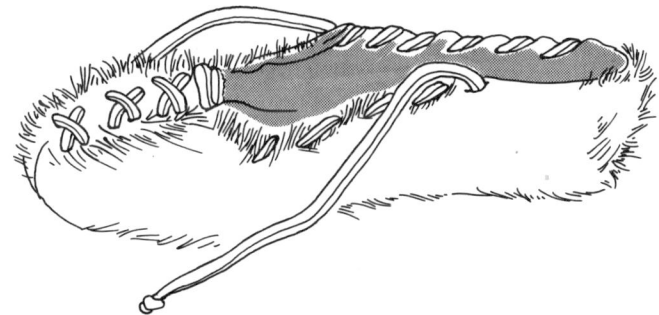

Fig. 5.2 An early moccasin used both in Europe and North America, made from a skin which had not been tanned.

any reasonable way. This method was also used in prehistoric Britain. It required a minimum of pattern cutting, and the shoe was finished in one manufacturing operation. The principal disadvantage was that the same leather was used for the sole and the upper although the requirements of the two regions are quite different. This was overcome by putting an insole inside the shoe. Note the fur on the outside of the moccasin in Figure 5.2, showing that the shoes were made of rawhide or leather that had not been tanned.

Shoes Made Inside Out—The Turnshoe

The joining together of a sole and upper that were made of different materials was done first by leather thongs and later by thread. Because of the need to prevent the stitching on a shoe from being worn out through abrasion with the ground, an obvious thing to do was to put stitching inside the shoe. The only reasonable way to do this was to make the shoe inside out and when it was finished, turn it. Thus the turnshoe was born some time in the first millenium A.D. (Figure 5.3).

Little did the inventor of the turnshoe know that the first man to run a four-minute mile would be wearing a running shoe made with this technique. Roger Bannister's shoes were made on the turnshoe principle by the Law family in England.

The turnshoe technique had several disadvantages when used to make running shoes. First, it left seams

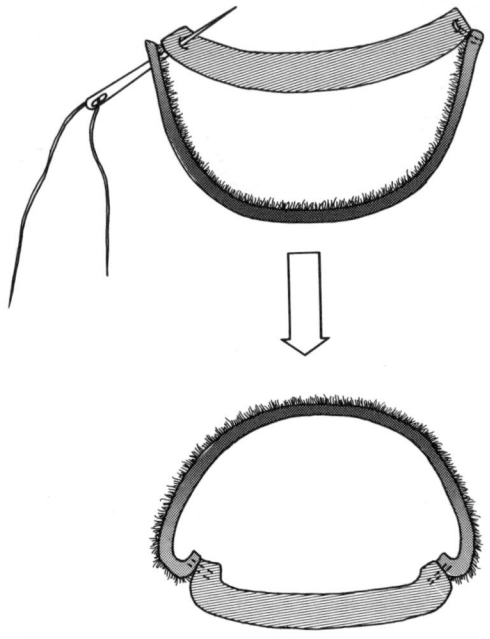

Fig. 5.3 A cross section of the front part of an early form of construction called the "turnshoe;" the sole was made inside out and then turned. The shoes used by Roger Bannister in the first four minute mile were made this way.

inside the shoe exposed, and this means blisters for runners. Also, a good fit could not be guaranteed because the turnshoe was not usually made on a wooden pattern called a last. Its fit therefore depended upon the accuracy with which the parts were cut and sewn.

The Need for Shoe Repair—The Welt

Several forces led to the development of new techniques for making shoes. First, when the bottom of a turnshoe wore out, the whole shoe had to be thrown away. The shoe also must have let water in. Finally, it just isn't possible to turn heavy shoes inside out. Like all good inventions, the answer now seems obvious. Simply sew on a thin strip of leather at the same time as upper and insole are joined together. Then the thick and replaceable outsole is joined to this leather strip known as a welt.

In fact, the method evolved by putting the new piece on the inside of a turnshoe (Figure 5.4). Only later was it realized that there was no need to turn the shoe if the welt was on the outside (Figure 5.5).

The Last

The art of shoemaking soon became heavily dependent upon the skills of another craftsman—the lastmaker. Early lastmakers started with a crude chunk of maple wood, and painstakingly modeled it into a shape around which the upper of the shoe was fitted as tightly as the skin on a banana. This carefully shaped mold, called the last, held all the secrets of fit that the shoemaker possessed.

Historically many shoemakers made their own lasts for special customers, and today some of the world's

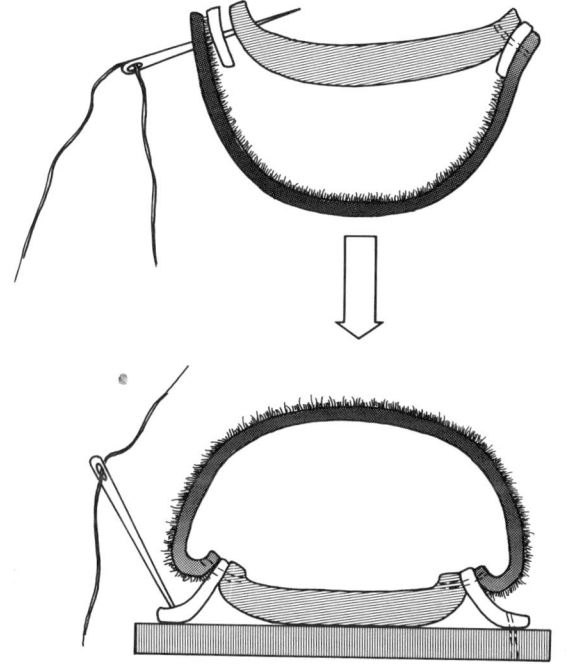

Fig. 5.4 A modification of the turnshoe, to allow a separate sole to be added. Small pieces of leather called welts were sewn in between the upper and the inside so that a replaceable outsole could be added.

elite runners have lasts specially made to the shape of their feet.

Wooden lasts have now virtually disappeared, since modern versions are made of high-density polyethylene

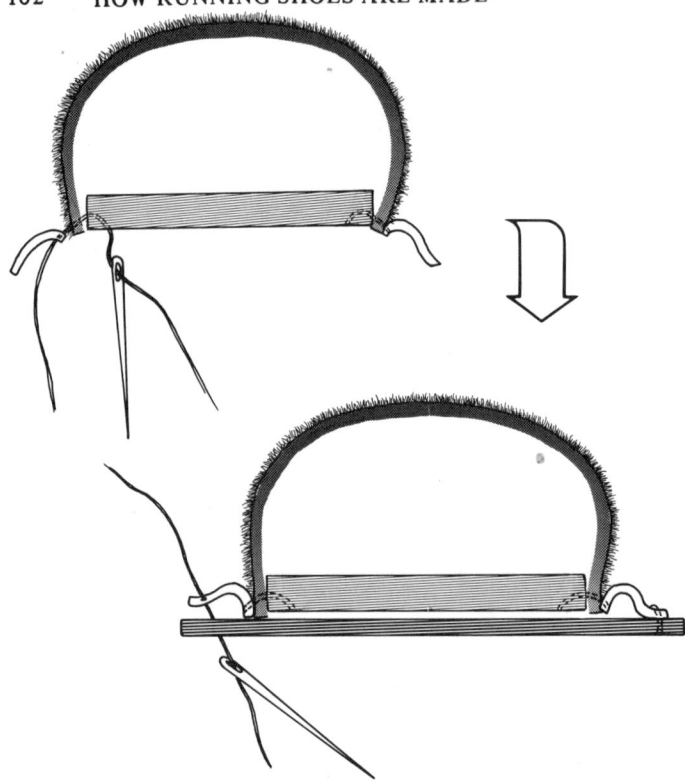

Fig. 5.5 The final stage in welt construction, where the shoe did not need to be turned inside out after sewing.

like the one shown in Figure 5.6. The last has been a vital part of shoemaking over the years and it still is, as we shall see shortly in our visit to a modern running shoe factory. We shall discuss lastmaking in Chapter 9.

Development of Shoe Machinery

The industrial revolution was created or accompanied —depending on your point of view—by a massive growth of automation. The development of the sewing machine in the nineteenth century had a dramatic effect on the shoe industry, moving it from a cottage industry into the factories. Sewing machines were just too expensive an item for individual workers to own.

The McKay Stitcher and later the Goodyear Welt Stitcher were important because they allowed upper and sole to be attached without any handwork. By 1900, the machinery available to the manufacturer was not so different from what it is today, especially in the fitting room, where the various parts of the uppers are pieced together as they are stitched.

Chemistry to the Rescue: Cement Lasting

While there might be more than 2,000 stitches in the upper of a typical running shoe, an equally important part of the construction is the cement used to hold many of the layers together. As we shall see, once the upper is finished the rest of the running shoe depends entirely on cement for its integrity.

In most modern running shoes a part of the upper, called the lasting allowance, is pulled down onto the last and cemented onto an insole board which had previously been put on the underside of the last. This process is called cement lasting.

How Running Shoes Are Made

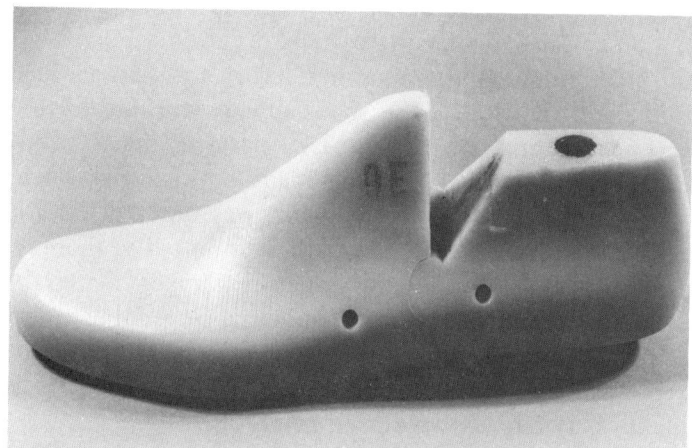

Fig. 5.6 A running shoe last: a modern plastic former that is the foundation around which the shoe is built.

The chemistry of adhesives has advanced so far that this bond rarely if ever fails. Adhesives are also used to cement the layers of the outsole-midsole-wedge combination together and to join the upper and board to the midsole.

Nails have virtually disappeared from running shoe manufacture except when used for added stability in the heels of some training flats.

Sliplasting

Some shoes have no insole board. In this design, called sliplasting, the top and bottom of the foot are entirely wrapped in a continuous piece of fabric. The ends of the upper are either drawn together underneath and sewn as in a moccasin, or a separate liner in the shape of a footbed (called a slipsock) is sewn onto the margins of the upper. Then, in the process which gives the shoe its name, the last is slipped into the shoe for the remaining soling operations to be completed.

The principal advantages of sliplasting are that the abrupt transition between upper and insole does not occur since the same piece of fabric is used for both. Thus the shoe tends to wrap the foot, whereas cement-lasted shoes are always "flat" on the insole. Also, the hard insole board is absent in a sliplasted shoe, and this sometimes leads to a more comfortable fit. Some running shoes are half sliplasted. That is, they are a closed bag at the back and cement lasted at the front, or vice versa.

Injection Molding—String Lasting

Several running shoes on the market have been made with injection molding of polyurethane. Often the upper is held onto a metal last by the process of string lasting. In this technique, loops of thread around the edge of the lasting margin enclose a length of string. When the string is pulled either by hand or by machine, a tight fit between the upper and last is obtained.

The injection molding machine encloses the string-lasted shoe with a mold, both underneath and on the sides. The reaction to form the polyurethane occurs when the two (or more) components are driven into the mold under high pressure. The material solidifies in the mold, bonding to the upper through its own adhesive characteristics and, some seconds later, is released to form the finished outsole.

The process of polymerization causes the material to foam. This gives it a cellular structure and dramatically reduced weight for a given volume. The better injection molded shoes are flat lasted where the regular cement last upper is presented to the machine for the application of the bottom.

There are several reasons why polyurethane construction has not spread further into the running shoe market. Injection molding machines are expensive and complex, and they almost need a full-time chemist to keep them running smoothly. Also, performance, particularly shock absorption, can be improved with materials lighter than polyurethane.

A VISIT TO THE SHOE FACTORY

Shoe factories may well be the last bastion of the skilled hand worker. If you have a vision of shoes being made by computer controlled machines in a sterile twenty-first century atmosphere, forget it. Certainly shoes are made by machines, but more important than the machines themselves are the skilled hands which guide the parts through the various stages. Let me take you on a visit to a shoe factory.

By the time we arrive at the factory the designer has done his or her job. He or she is already working on the next generation of shoes. The patterns have been specified, the cutting dies are made up, materials have been ordered, and hopefully what was ordered has arrived at the factory. Like any other commodity, there is cheap upper material and expensive upper material, cheap outsoles and expensive outsoles. Depending upon how much profit the manufacturer expects to make on a given shoe and how many shortcuts have been taken, quality may already have been compromised.

The Receiving Room

The materials from which the shoe will be made are stored in the receiving room. Looking through this section of a large shoe factory reminds one of being in a carpet store. There are rolls and rolls of this and that synthetic material all stacked up and labeled. The rolls are a little narrow for carpet though, generally three to five feet wide and from thirty to fifty yards long. In most factories making running shoes, synthetic materials are more in evidence than leather. But piles of split and suede leather are there, dyed the latest fashionable color, and ready to become foxing, lacing stays, and wing tips.

Cutting Out the Parts

As we shall see shortly, the rolls of material are already made up or combined into a sandwich of upper material, foam layer, and a lining. The first operation in making the shoe is to place the rolls of combined upper and the sheets of leather on a flat surface and stamp them out with cutting tools (Figure 5.7a) in the same way Christmas cookies are made. Notice that the parts are not cut one at a time but up to twelve at a time; this can lead to some differences in size between the parts on the top and bottom of the pile.

The process of cutting out the parts or clicking, as it is known, requires considerable skill. The first rather basic skill is to keep your hands out of the way as the arm of the hydraulic press or clicker comes crashing down on the carefully machined cutting tool or die. The more refined skills enable the operator to choose where on the sheet or roll the parts can be cut out with minimum waste. Efforts to duplicate by machine what a skilled operator can do by eye have involved extremely complex mathematics and have not been entirely successful, particularly in the cutting of irregularly shaped suede leather skins. Machinery does exist to cut the uniform nylon material expeditiously with little waste.

With leather there are additional problems, since variations in the properties of different regions of the skin must be matched to the requirements of different parts of the shoe. We shall investigate this problem further in Chapter 9.

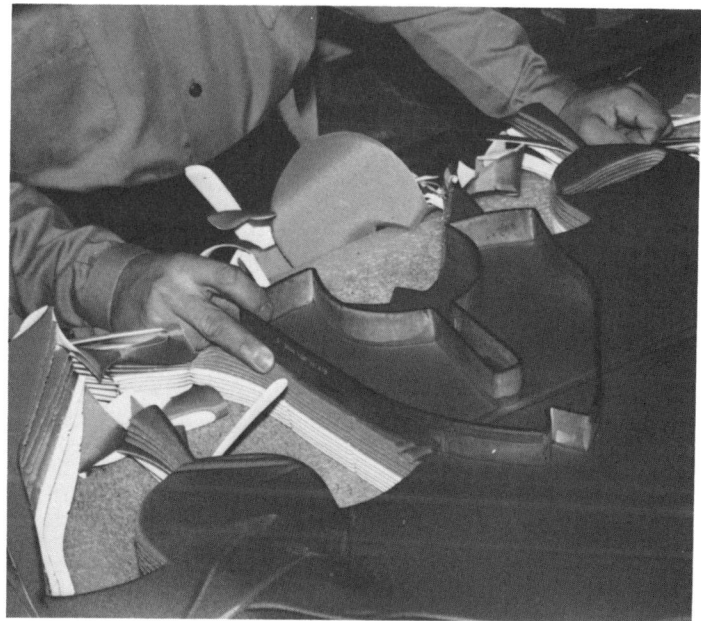

Fig. 5.7a Stamping out the upper components from rolls of the upper package.

The Size Headache

The headache of different sizes has already started. The plan usually calls for between ten and twenty sets of components to be made for one size of shoe. These

106 HOW RUNNING SHOES ARE MADE

groups will stay together until the completed shoes are put in the box at the end of the production line.

Besides cutting the material to the correct shape, the cutting tools leave behind two important sets of marks—in-nicks and out-nicks. The in-nicks contain coded information on what size shoe the component is for, and the out-nicks are cues for the sewing machine operator to align various parts during assembly.

When the cutting operation is complete the ten major parts shown in Figure 5.7b are in existence. They are bundled up, labeled, and moved into the fitting room where all the stitching is done.

The Fitting Room

The fitting room is the heart of the shoe factory. Sewing machines throb in an endless symphony as the process of sewing all the different components onto the upper takes place.

It is in the fitting room that an observer is first struck by the number of different people that actually touch the shoe on its journey from being a roll of material to a finished product. In one of the larger running shoe factories there might be 200 women with their heads down and their feet on the sewing machine pedal, moving almost faster than the eye can follow. One shoe might visit twenty of these women, becoming a little more recognizable with each stage. The work is incredibly repetitive and monotonous, so incentives

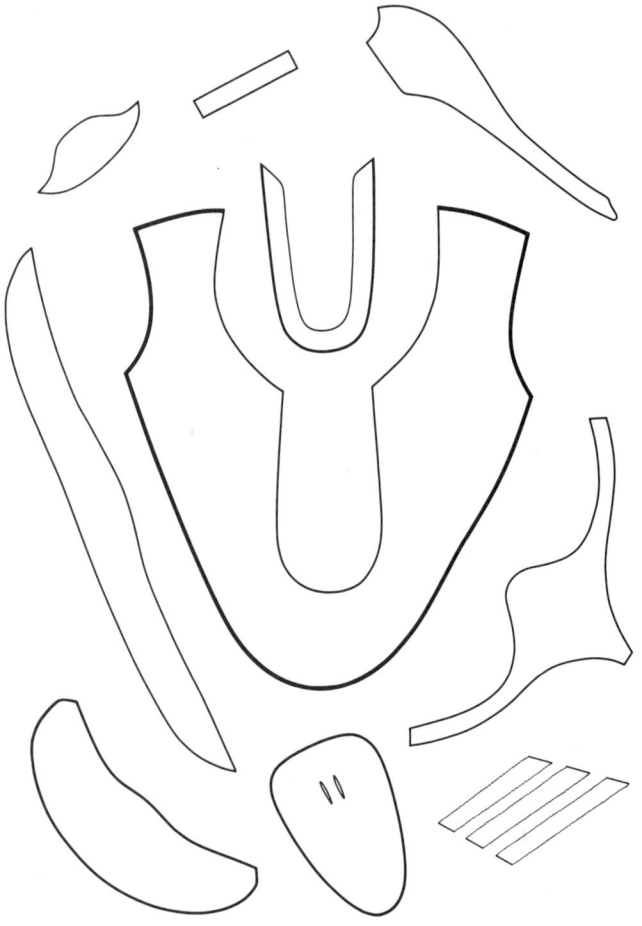

Fig. 5.7b An assortment of parts which emerge from the cutting room.

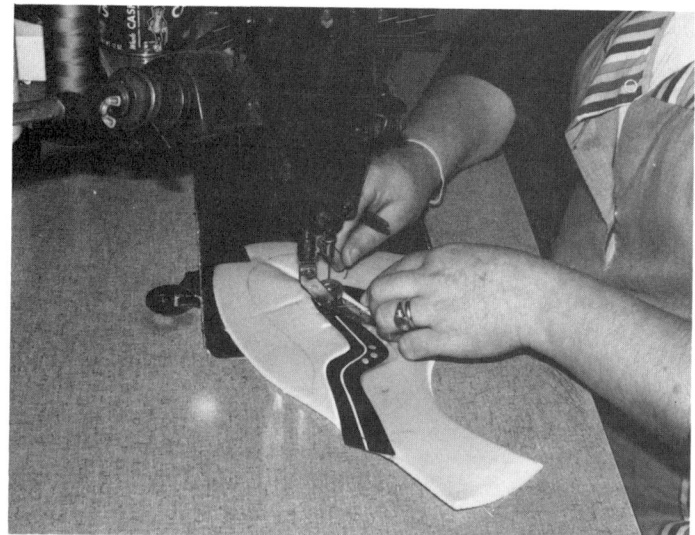

Fig. 5.7c The stitching process begins, as a machinist aligns the logo with previously drawn chalk lines and puts the resulting combination under the needle.

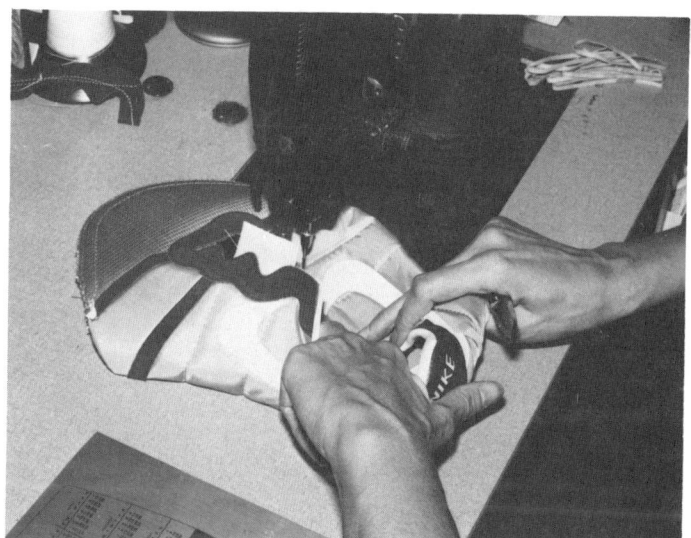

Fig. 5.7d The upper is now almost complete as the eyestay is sewn in place.

for both quality and quantity are important aspects of motivating the workers.

There are many shortcuts that can be taken during the fitting operations that will lead to an inferior shoe. The quality of the thread and the length of the stitches play an important part in keeping the shoe alive throughout its hard life. In good shoes vital areas will have a double row of stitches. In addition to the skill and motivation of the workers, the methods used by the manufacturer for quality control are also critical. In some factories every single batch of shoes is inspected by a supervisor, and poor work will eventually be reflected in a low paycheck.

Figures 5.7c and d show uppers at the beginning and end of the closing process. The chalk marks, visible in Figure 5.7c, are put on the upper so that the operator can place the parts correctly on top of each other before sewing. The eyestay is being sewn on to the completed upper in Figure 5.7d, after the foxing, the stripes,

108 HOW RUNNING SHOES ARE MADE

Fig. 5.7e   The lace holes are punched out of the completed uppers.

Fig. 5.7f   A completed upper of a cement lasted shoe. The additional material, which will not be visible in the completed shoe, is called the lasting margin.

the logo, and in this case the different toe box have all been sewn together. The holes in the eyestay will be created in the punching operation shown in Figure 5.7e.

The Finished Upper

The finished upper of a cement-lasted shoe is shown in Figure 5.7f. It looks a lot like a hat or cap, and an oversized one at that. You will recall that the edges of the upper have to be folded underneath the insole board during the cement lasting process.

For the sliplasted shoe there is one more operation to go. This upper does not have the large lasting margin because a slipsock is sewn directly onto the upper as shown in Figure 5.7g. An alternative method of sliplasting involves wrapping the upper underneath the shoe and joining the two parts together. This is shown in Figure 5.7h which is destined to be a half sliplasted shoe. The rear part of the upper has been folded and sewn down the middle, while an insole board will be inserted to last the front part of the shoe. The schematic

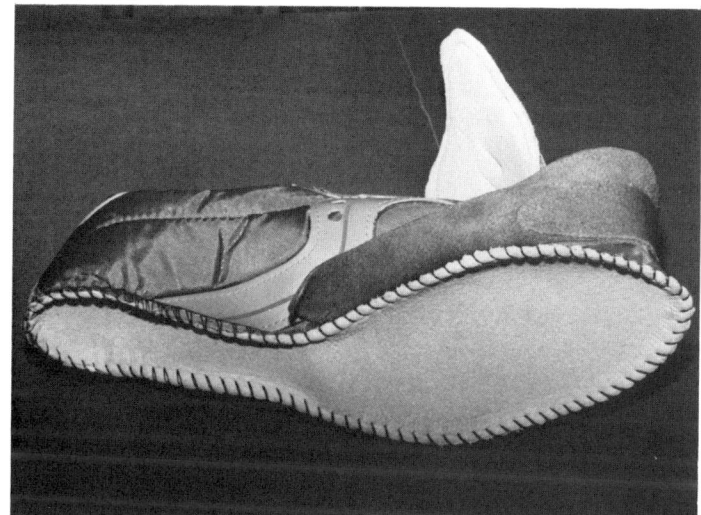

Fig. 5.7g A completed upper of a sliplasted shoe. The slip sock is sewn in place and the upper forms a closed bag.

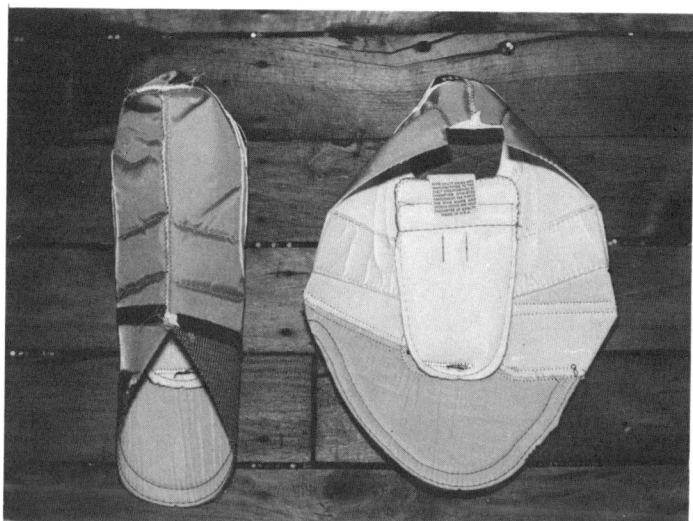

Fig. 5.7h Alternative finishings of a slip lasted shoe. The outer margins of the upper are drawn underneath and sewn. This example is known as half slip lasted, since an insole board will be used under the front part.

drawing of these two types of sliplasted uppers in Figure 5.8 should help to demonstrate the difference between them and the finished cement last upper in Figure 5.7f.

Hanging Around

With the fitting operations finished, the completed uppers are hung in same-size batches waiting to meet up with a last. Figure 5.7h reminds one of a fishmarket where the day's catch has been hung up for sale.

The Lasting Room

When their turn comes, the finished uppers move into the lasting room. There they will be stiffened and shaped tightly around a plastic mold or last in the shape of the final shoe and firmly cemented to the insole board.

The transition from the fitting room to the lasting room is a striking one. First, it's a transition from clean, intricate handwork to less subtle, heavy machine

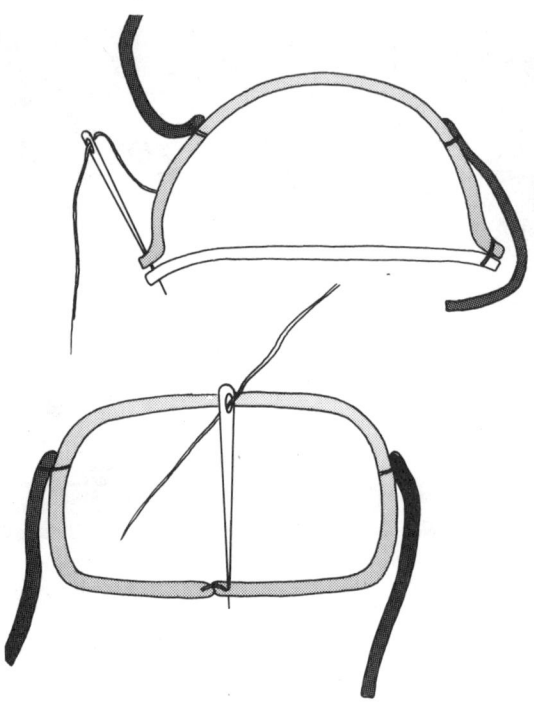

Fig. 5.8 The two different slip last constructions, shown schematically in cross section: top with a slip sock, bottom with an upper folded underneath the shoe and sewn.

Fig. 5.9 Hanging around! Completed uppers waiting their turn to be lasted.

work. The smell of cement is in the air, and the soling room is staffed almost exclusively by men, whereas women operate almost all of the sewing machines in the fitting room.

The Lasting Operation

Lasting is the name given to the process of putting the upper over the last and fixing it underneath the last so that the shape is retained.

The process can best be understood by looking at the shoe cross-section in Figure 5.10. Here you see how the insole board is temporarily held on to the underside of the last, and the extra part of the upper has been pulled underneath and cemented to the insole board.

Let's take a step-by-step look at the lasting process.

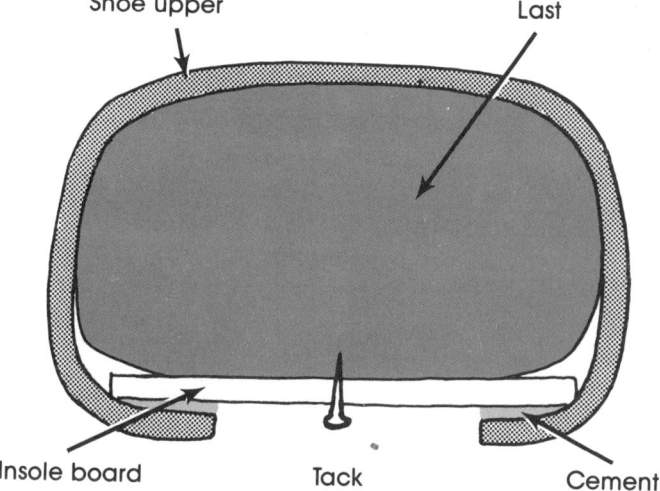

Fig. 5.10 A cross section showing the lasting operation. An insole board is tacked or stapled to the last, and the upper is wrapped over after cement has been applied to the board.

Stiffening Toe Box and Heel

Good running shoes have additional stiffening in the heel region and the toe box. In Figure 5.11a the preformed fiberboard heel counters which will stiffen the rear part of the shoes have been dipped in cement, and will be inserted into the pocket between the foxing and the upper. We will discuss various heel counters in the next chapter.

The toe box stiffener was put onto the upper in the fitting room as a flat thermoplastic band. When it is heated and allowed to cool it will hold its new shape.

How Running Shoes Are Made 111

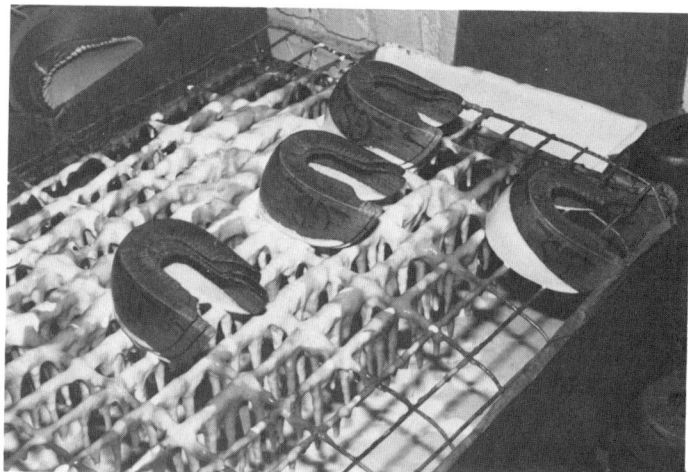

Fig. 5.11a Preformed fiberboard heel counters, left to drain off excess cement before they are placed inside the pocket at the back of the upper.

Because the shoe is made out of flat pieces of material but must fit around a curved object, it is necessary to precondition the upper before pulling it over the last. There are a number of ways of doing this. One, shown in Figure 5.11b, involves the forepart of the shoe being held above hot water. Besides making the upper more pliable, such steaming will soften the toe stiffener so that it can harden in the form of the last during the next operation.

In the cement-lasted shoe an insole board is first placed on the last bottom and temporarily tacked down

HOW RUNNING SHOES ARE MADE

Fig. 5.11b Uppers in a toe steamer to soften the toe box stiffener before lasting begins. When it hardens again, the stiffener will take the shape of the last.

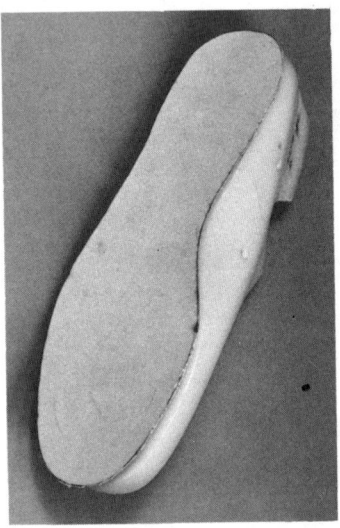 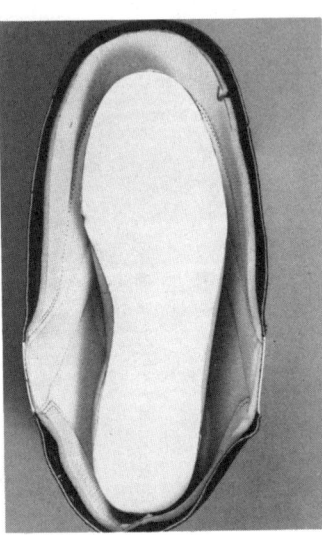

Fig. 5.11c (left) The insole board in place on the last. Fig. 5.11d (right) The upper in place on the last, ready for the lasting operation to begin.

in the correct place (Figure 5.11c). The insole board is extremely important because it forms the backbone of the shoe during lasting. The preheated upper is then carefully positioned on the last (Figure 5.11d) and then brought to machines which secure the forepart (Figure 5.11e), the back part and the waist or midsection. The last will now stay with the shoe until the entire manufacturing process is almost complete and the shoe is nearly ready to wear.

Lasting Machines

Gone are the days when the shoemaker had to pull the sides of the upper over the last and nail them down in place. Modern lasting machines are about the highest level of automation in the shoe factory and are fascinating machines to watch. In a series of carefully sequenced operations, mechanical pincers first pull the upper firmly down over the last to give the shoe the re-

Fig. 5.11e The first step in lasting. The shoe is placed into a toe lasting machine, which grips the lasting margin in the forepart and pulls it down over the last after applying cement.

quired shape. Next, a hot, automatic cement nozzle moves on a precise curvilinear path, spreading cement between the upper and the insole board. Finally, an array of mechanical "fingers" moves in like a well-drilled army battalion (Figure 5.11f) to press the upper and insole board together for a prescribed period of time.

When all the arms and levers of this intricate machine withdraw, the embryonic shoe has taken on the exact shape of the last (Figure 5.11g).

Fig. 5.11f The "fingers" of the lasting machine at work pulling the upper tightly down over the insole board. The cement nozzles are also visible at the bottom of the perforated V shape.

Nail Seating

One or two manufacturers still use small nails on some of their shoes for the rear part lasting operation (Figure 5.11h). The last is reinforced by a steel plate

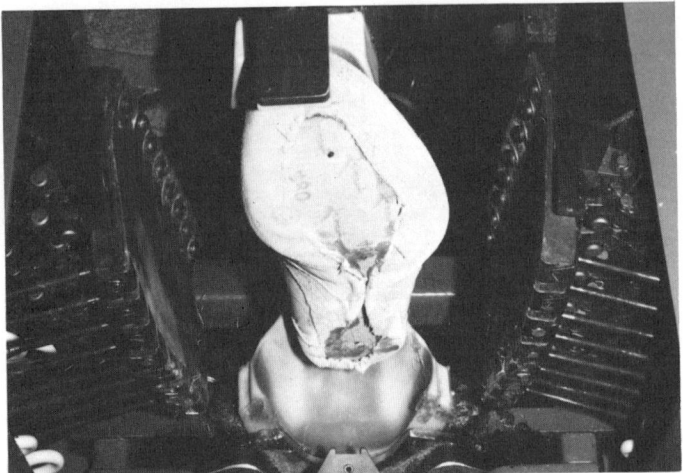

Fig. 5.11g The endpoint of lasting. The upper now fits onto the last better than a skin on a banana.

which turns the nails over on the inside of the shoe. For the procedure to be effective, the heel counter must be very tough and rigid. Otherwise the base may remain secure but the counter itself will be useless.

Sliplasted Shoes

The sliplasted shoe follows a different sequence from the cement-lasted shoe. In the operation which gives the shoe its name, the last is slipped inside the "bag" formed by the fully closed upper (Figure 5.12a). The fit is a tight one and a shoehorn is used to ease the upper into place. The shoe then goes through an abbreviated lasting operation since there is no insole board to last the upper to. The edges of the leather trim are tightened and cemented onto the slipsock (Figure 5.12b).

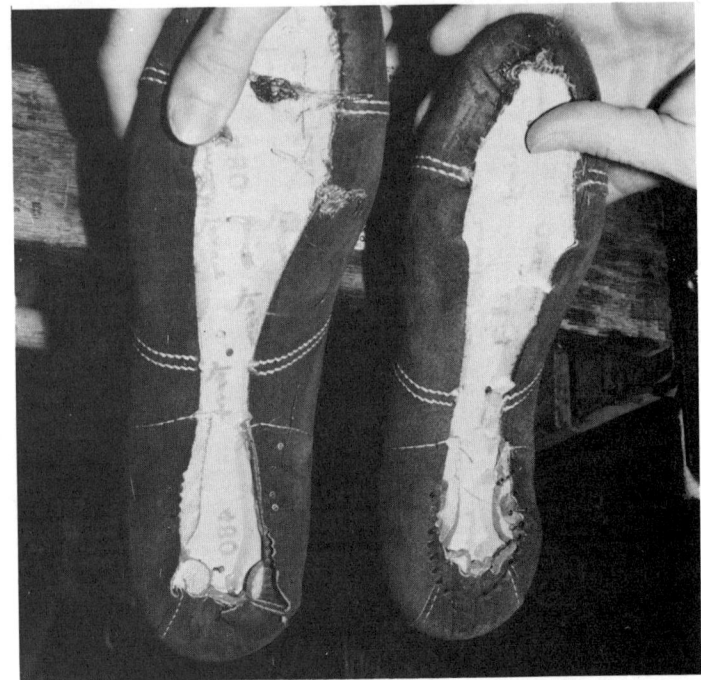

Fig. 5.11h Nailseating. Some manufacturers put small nails through the heel counter margin, which was wrapped underneath in an effort to stabilize the shoe.

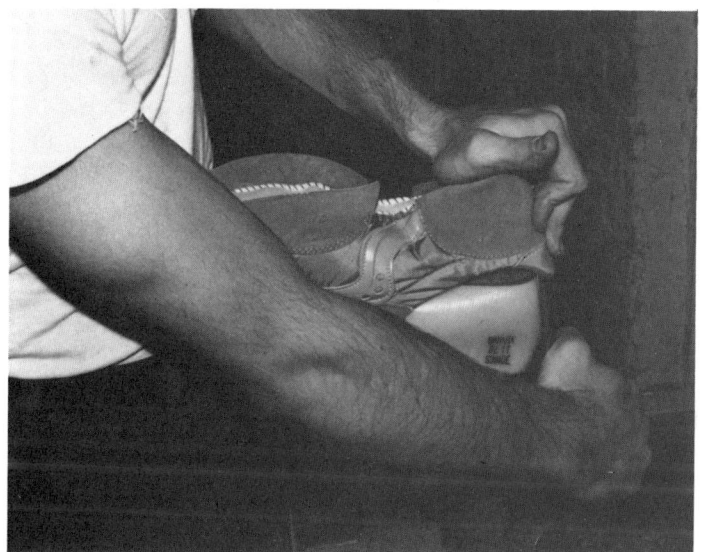

Fig. 5.12a The last is slipped into the shoe in the process that gives the shoe its name.

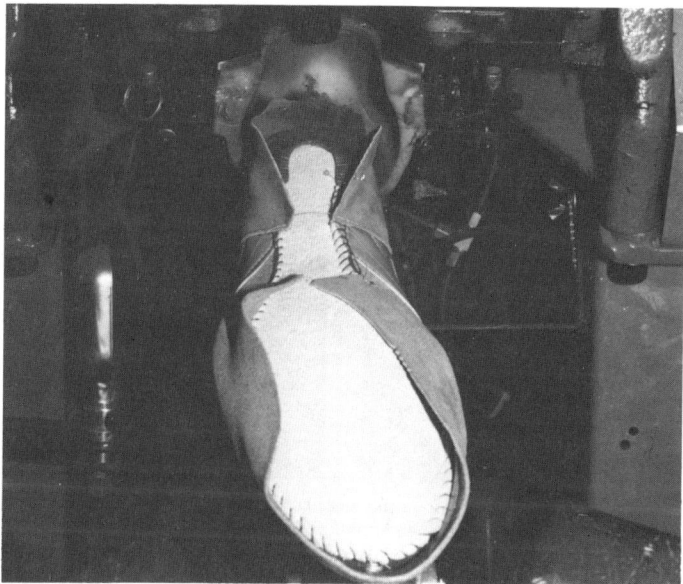

Fig. 5.12b The leather margins from the foxing are drawn underneath the slip sock and cemented in place.

The half sliplasted shoe, as the name implies, is a mixture of the cement and sliplasting techniques. Generally the forepart of the shoe is completely closed, with the rearpart cement lasted over a small insole board. The reverse is also seen occasionally.

What Can Go Wrong With Lasting?

Although the process of lasting is machine dominated, the human factor can still affect the final quality of the shoe. The line along the side of the shoe where the upper and midsole will eventually meet is called a featherline. Creases along the featherline are a sign of a poor lasting operation.

If the upper is not put evenly onto the last, the shoe will have a tilt which will affect the alignment of the foot during the support phase. This will most likely show up at the seams on the rear part of the shoe,

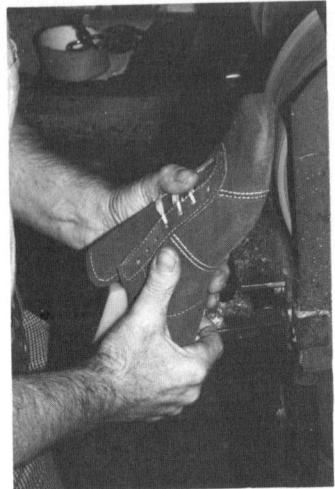
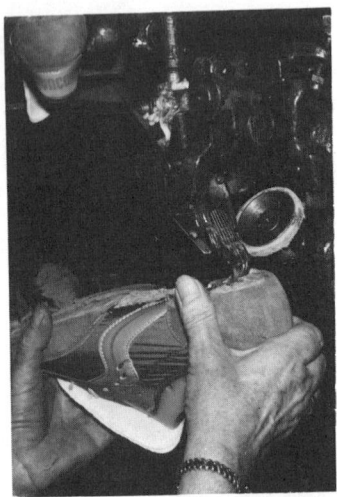

Fig. 5.13a (left)   Roughing; the leather turned under during lasting is smoothed out to give an even surface onto which the midsole is applied.
Fig. 5.13b (right)   Cement is applied to the complete underside of the shoe, which is then set aside to give the cement time to cure.

which do not align vertically when the shoes sit on an even surface.

If the cement is not well applied a poor bond will be formed and the sole may loosen with wear. Conversely, if too much cement has been used the uppers themselves may be stained.

Roughing, Cementing, and Filling

Preparations are now made for the major operation of applying the sole to the upper. The operation called

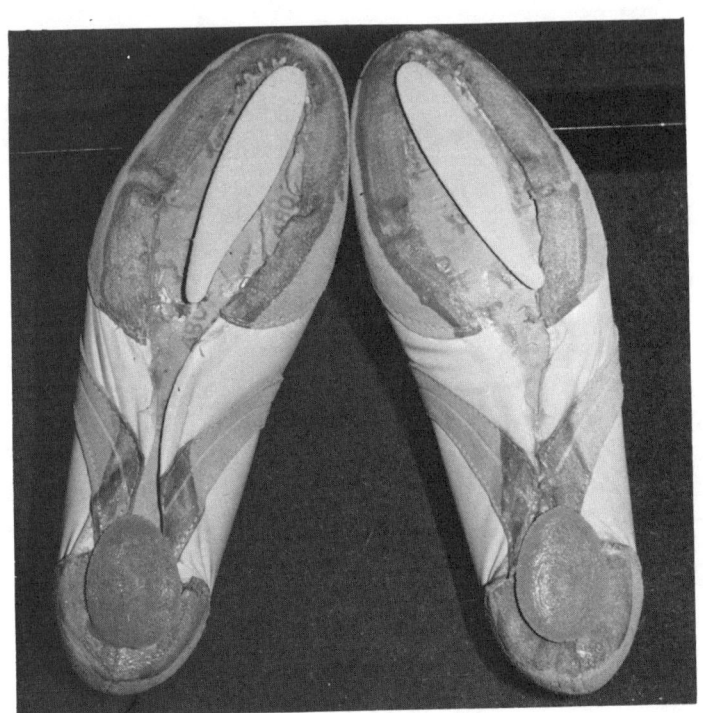

Fig. 5.13c Small pieces of filler placed over the insole board to avoid a step between upper and board. The runner would probably feel the step as the shoe aged.

roughing (Figure 5.13a) involves removing the top surface from the leather which has been folded underneath the shoe. Some folds and creases in the lasting allowance are inevitable, particularly at the toe (Figure 5.11i), and these are ground off during roughing. If the roughing operation is carelessly done, part of the upper may be damaged, or an insufficient amount may be taken off, leaving a poor surface for bonding.

The cement used to attach the bottom to the shoe has to dry before contact on both the last bottom and the midsole. It is applied by a pressure extrusion device (Figure 5.13b) which squeezes cement over the prepared bottom. The shoe is then set aside to allow the cement to dry.

When the lasting margin was cemented to the insole board two steps were created down from the leather overlap onto the insole board. This is clearly shown in the schematic diagram in Figure 5.10. If this gap between steps is not filled it can lead to discomfort because the part of the shoe on which the foot rests will be uneven. Some manufacturers choose to forget about this, but others put a filler into the gap. The filler is sometimes little more than waste scraps from the cutting room, but it serves the purpose of giving an even surface underneath the insole board. It is put in place (Figure 5.13c) as the cement is curing.

THE SOLE ASSEMBLY

While the upper has been traveling through many hands in the cutting and lasting operations, sole assembly has proceeded with much less fanfare.

Sheets of polymeric foam material (see Chapter 6) are bought by most shoe manufacturers; they are al-

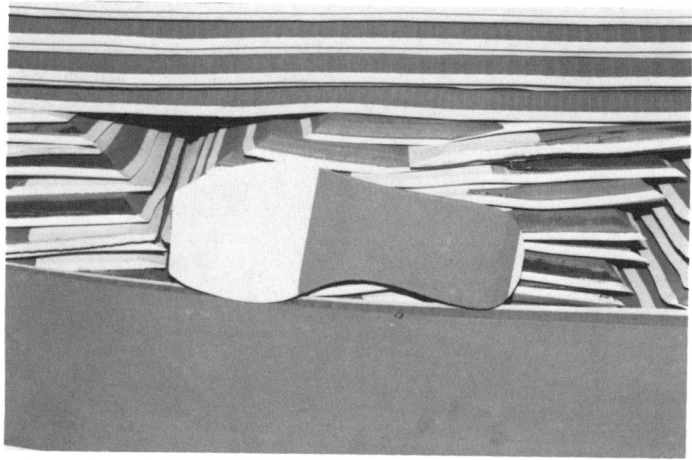

Fig. 5.14a Sheets of EVA (ethylene vinyl acetate—a polymeric foam) already bonded together in two layers for the midsole (white) and wedge (dark). The complete unit (shown center) is simply stamped from the sheet.

ready made up into the two layer system which will become the midsole and wedge (Figure 5.14a). From these sheets, single units are stamped out to the correct size, and skived to make the required edge contours such as flare in the rear part, undercut at the back of the shoe, or a tapered thickness in the forepart.

There are two basic kinds of outsoles. Some, like waffle patterns, which have certain features in specific regions of the shoe must be cut precisely from the molded sheet. Others can be cut anywhere on a sheet rather like the upper components. Often an outsole

Fig. 5.14b Outsoles stamped from rubber sheet are lined up on a midsole and wedge unit and placed on a conveyor, which takes the complete bottom through an oven to activate the previously applied cement.

Fig. 5.15a The complete bottom and upper are placed over a heating element to activate the cured cement. Notice that the last is still in the shoe.

which should be precisely cut is not stamped out accurately, leading to asymmetry in the finished shoe.

The outsole and midsole wedge combinations have cement applied separately (Figure 5.14b). They are then set aside to allow the cement to cure and meet again after heat activation. The outsole is aligned under the midsole and pressed to form a firm bond. The sole unit is now complete. The cement which will eventually hold this unit to the upper is spread over the exposed midsole, which is taken to be matched up with an upper of the correct size.

Sole Laying

Despite all the intricacies that preceded it the final major operation is a simple one. The sole unit and completed upper, still on its last, are placed over a heater (Figure 5.15a) to activate the cement. They are then carefully aligned so that the midsole meets the featherline all the way around the shoe (Figure 5.15b). Before the cement cools, the upper and bottom unit are com-

How Running Shoes Are Made 119

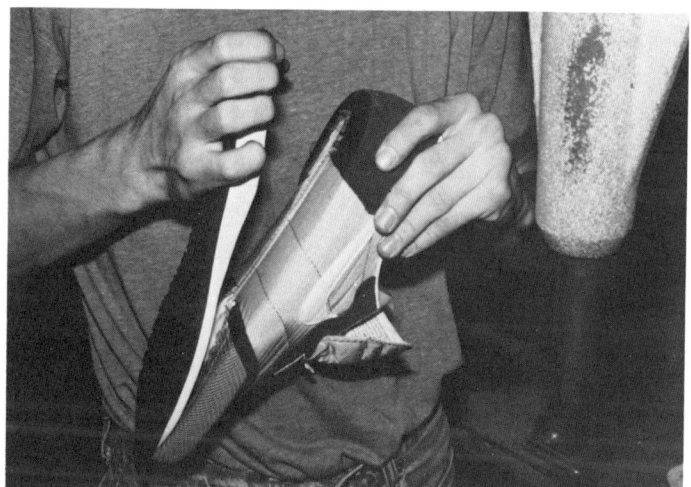

Fig. 5.15b The upper and bottom are carefully lined up so that the midsole meets the featherline all the way around the shoe.

Fig. 5.15c Sole laying. A high pressure press squeezes the two units together and holds for a brief period of time.

bined by a press which exerts a predetermined pressure for a specific amount of time (Figure 5.15c).

The product suddenly looks like a complete running shoe, and is almost at the end of its long journey through the factory. The cross-sections in Figure 5.16 show the composite as it now appears in a cement lasted and a slip-lasted shoe.

Finishing Operations and Inspection

One common point of failure in the running shoe is the bond between the midsole and outsole in the toe region. To counter this many manufacturers perform a "wrap-over" of the outsole onto the front of the toe box. This operation must be done by hand (Figure 5.17a). The leather on the front of the toe box is roughed, cement is applied to both parts and finally, after curing, a separate press is used to complete the bond (Figure 5.17b).

The last has now served its purpose and is removed from the shoe in an operation called springing (Figure 5.17c). Lasts are made with a hinge which effectively breaks it into two, allowing the shoe to be lifted off.

In the better factories each shoe is now carefully inspected. It is cleaned all the way around the featherline

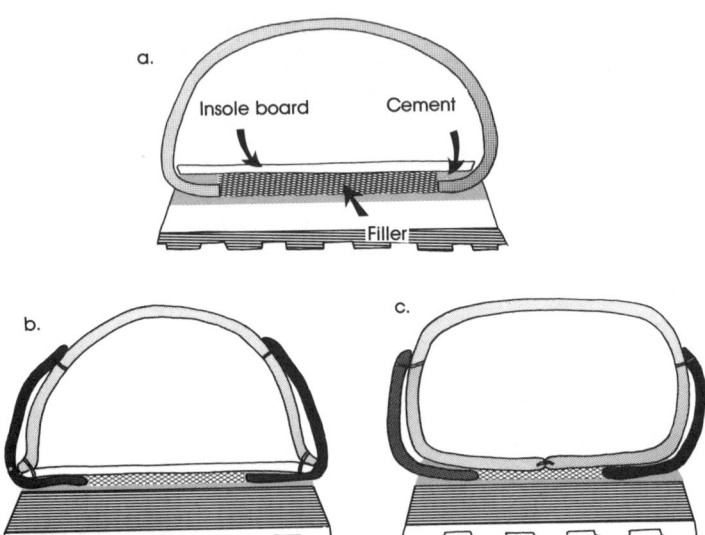

Fig. 5.16 Cross sections through the toe box of completed shoes made by a) cement lasting b) and c) slip lasting.

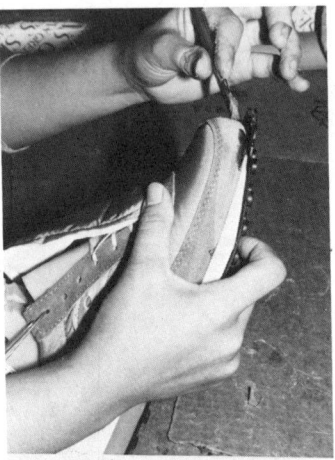 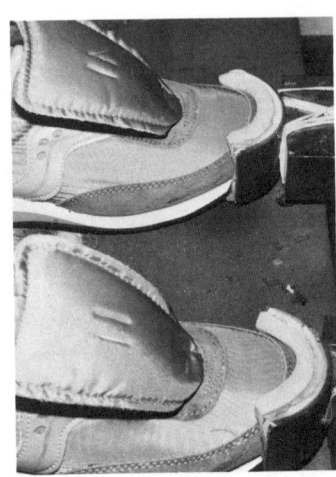

Fig. 5.17a (left) Extra care should be taken with the "wrapover" of the outsole on the toebox, since this is a point of frequent delamination. In this operation additional cement is applied by hand. Fig. 5.17b (right) The toe press insures a firm bond between the tip of the outsole and the upper.

to make sure no excess cement is left. The inspector also checks for major structural defects such as badly lasted shoes, poor bonds between midsole and upper, and stitching errors. Shoes that do not meet standards are rejected at this point.

Finally, the sockliner and arch cookie (if any) are cemented into the shoe (Figure 5.17d). At the last moment the laces are added and the shoes are boxed always with the left shoe underneath and the right one on top.

The Manufacturing Process—A Retrospective

And so the job is done. For better or for worse the shoes are boxed, shipped, and on their way to your feet.

The astonishing thing about shoemaking is the num-

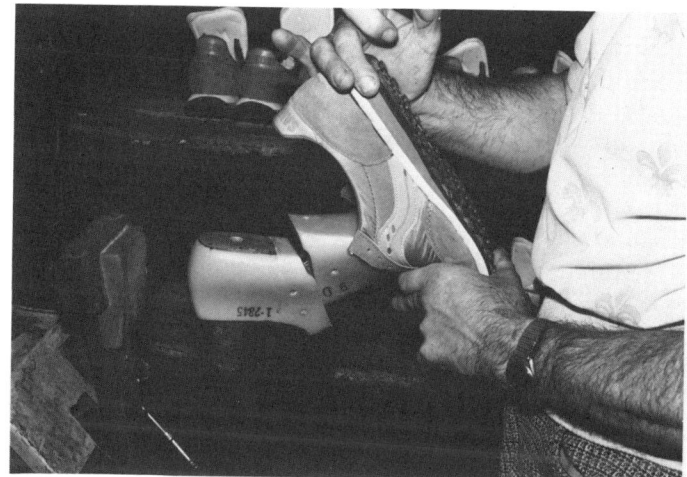

Fig. 5.17c The shoe and last finally part company in the operation called "springing the last."

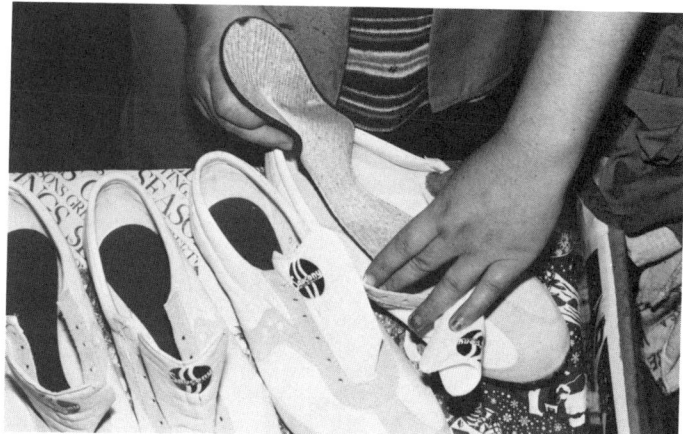

Fig. 5.17d The sockliner and arch cookie are cemented into the shoe.

ber of steps required to make a relatively simple object. At least twenty-five different people touch the running shoe at some point during its manufacture. In the end it is their attitude toward their work which determines how well our running shoes are made.

As in most manufacturing industries the philosophy of management is a critical determinant of quality. There is a marked contrast between different factories. In some it is hard to understand how the operator gets his hands out of the way quickly enough before the press comes crashing down for the next operation. In other factories the work seems more relaxed and the emphasis is on quality rather than quantity.

Running shoes which are returned because of manufacturing defects are bad news for everyone involved in the chain—the manufacturer, the retailer, and the runner. Sometimes a manufacturer has to compromise, knowing that more shoes could be squeezed out of the factory in a given day, but that quality would suffer. Considering the exacting and repetitive nature of the work, it is amazing that running shoes turn out as well as they do.

6

What Shoes Are Made Of — A Closer Look

Looking at a new running shoe is like looking at a new watch. It might look very good, but how will it work? Even if all the care in the world has been lavished on making the shoe it will fail if poor materials have been used.

We saw from the review of running shoe history that there have been tremendous improvements in shoes in the last twenty years. Certainly the design of running shoes has changed, but better materials have also been a critical factor in this progress.

In our look at materials used to make running shoes, we will examine some parts of the shoe with the help of a microscope. This will bring to life some crucial properties that cannot be seen with the naked eye.

UPPER MATERIALS—LEATHER

Very few running shoes now use leather for anything other than the accessories designed to reinforce and trim the upper of the shoe. This is something that has happened since the late 1960s when Tiger first introduced the nylon weave upper.

Although leather has fallen into disuse as far as running shoe manufacture is concerned, it does have some excellent properties which make it good footwear material. Most importantly, leather can adapt to the foot by a permanent change in its configuration—an impossibility with synthetic uppers. Also, it can both store perspiration and transmit water vapor from the foot to the outer air while preventing water from making the journey in the opposite direction. These factors are crucial for foot comfort.

Leather is also very strong under tension, it is easy to affix to other materials, will take color easily, and will resist abrasion.

Most of the leather in running shoes is taken from "splits." These are skins which have been divided into two or more layers to reduce the thickness. Thus, what seems like true suede (the flesh side of a skin) may actually be a "split."

Figure 6.1 is an electron micrograph of a piece of split leather taken from the wing tip of a running shoe. Split leather tends to fray much more than true leather and is a poor substitute for the real thing.

When skins are taken from the animal they must be cured or "tanned" to fix the protein in the skin and dissolve tissues that would be subject to bacterial breakdown.

Fig. 6.1 A scanning electron micrograph (SEM) of a piece of split leather from a Brooks Vantage Supreme upper. It is easy to imagine how the leather can stretch as the fibers pull past each other, and also how fraying can occur as the surface fibers are roughed up. (Norman Macmillan photo)

The type of processing affects both the properties of the finished product and its texture. Tanning agents for leather vary widely, but most common in the footwear industry are chromium salts and vegetable extracts. Part of the reason why few leather shoes are found in archaeological excavations is that the tanning process was not well done and the leather has decomposed.

WHAT SHOES ARE MADE OF—A CLOSER LOOK

The physical properties of leather depend both on what animal the skin comes from and where on the skin the part is cut. Figure 6.2 shows a cowhide with the strongest and stiffest regions shaded the darkest. There is an approximate six-fold difference in strength and stretch between the skin overlying the backbone (strongest) and that under the belly of the animal (weakest).

Some exotic animals have donated their hides to the feet of runners. For many years, kangaroo was the preferred skin for running shoes because of its lightness and strength. In 1973 Australia instituted a ban on the export of kangaroo skins. Although this has now been lifted the United States has its own importation ban still in effect. So the makers of running shoes had to make do with the more usual skins of calf, cow, kid, goat, sheep, and pig. Adi Dassler tried some unusual species including dog, shark, and badger skin, which were used for special shoes with undocumented success.

Why Synthetic Uppers Have Won the Day

Well, with so much going for it, why has leather fallen into disuse among running shoe manufacturers? Perhaps a major reason is that runners are not known for staying out of the rain, watching where they step, or looking after their shoes.

Although it possesses good elastic properties, leather, particularly when wet, is also quite plastic. It will

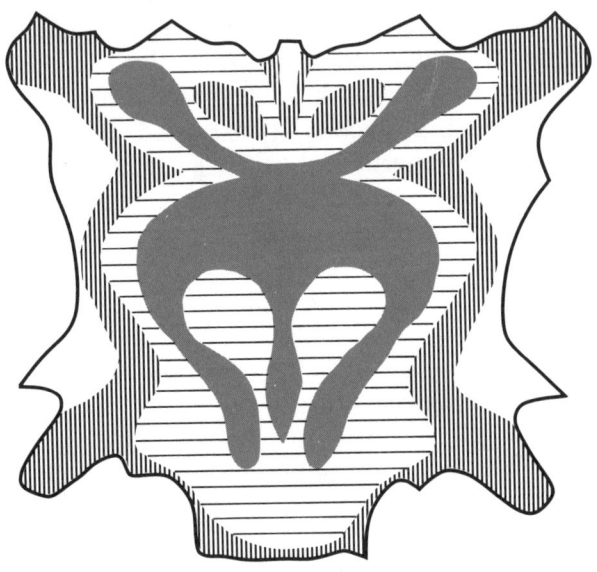

Fig. 6.2 A cowhide spread out and shaded to indicate the strongest and stiffest regions (dark) and the weakest and most stretchable areas (white).

stretch to a new length under stress and will not return to its initial length. Thus running in a wet shoe will stretch it in the direction of the largest forces. While some accommodation of the upper to the foot is an advantage in cases of unusually shaped feet, the kind of large deformations that occur in a running shoe can also be a positive disadvantage. Because the forces tending to stretch the upper are strong, permanent extension can occur, making the fit of the shoe sloppy.

Care of leather shoes is something many runners don't have time for. If your shoes get wet on a training run and they are the only pair you own, then you want them dry for the next run, which may be less than twelve hours away. Leather does not respond well to accelerated drying.

The solution to the problems with leather in running shoes was to try synthetic uppers. The footwear industry as a whole is wary of synthetics. Many early plastics were tried in footwear and their lack of permeability to water vapor was neither comfortable nor healthy for the foot. Even when materials which simulated leather were produced, they were not successful. DuPont lost an enormous amount of money on Corfam, originally hailed as the first of a new generation of "poromeric" materials that would revolutionize the footwear industry. At the time it was introduced leather was cheap, Corfam was expensive, and the conservatism of the shoe industry won the day. Adidas introduced Kangoran as "good news for kangaroos" but runners have not moved to this "synthetic leather" upper in great numbers.

Nylon Weave

Nylon taffeta is an upper material which is about evenly balanced in its pros and cons with respect to leather. Figure 6.3 shows a piece of taffeta taken from the upper of an Etonic Streetfighter. It is hard to be-

Fig. 6.3 Scanning electron micrograph (SEM) of nylon taffeta from a running shoe upper. The individual nylon filaments were first spun together and then the material was woven in this basket weave type of pattern. The spots of cement which held leather parts of the upper down are clearly visible. (Norman Macmillan photo)

lieve that your running shoe can look like a wicker basket, but it does.

Taffeta is a fine plain weave, smooth on both sides. Its major variables are the size of the threads making up the individual bundles, and the number of thread bundles going lengthwise (the warp) and widthwise (the weft).

A big advantage of nylon taffeta from a manufacturer's standpoint is its consistency. There is no problem about choosing which piece of the shoe should be made from which part of the material — each piece is as good as the next. Nylon weaves are by far the most popular materials used in the uppers of today's running shoes.

Nylon Mesh

The picture of nylon taffeta gives the impression that there is not much room for water to pass through. Certainly the material resists permanent deformation, and it is easily washed and dried, but "breathability" is not as good as it might be. The solution is to make the holes between adjacent strands bigger. A taffeta with fewer threads does not have enough resistance to abrasion or snagging, so the logical next step is to try nylon mesh.

Because a mesh is knitted rather than woven, it has an intrinsic strength which does not depend on the tightness of the weave. Two types of mesh taken from running shoes are shown in Figure 6.4.

Early meshes in running shoes were a disaster. They ran, tore, snagged, and ripped so much that many runners swore against them forever. But the supply houses who send the shoemakers their fabric went back to the drawing boards and came up with new methods of manufacture. Most of these early problems have now been overcome.

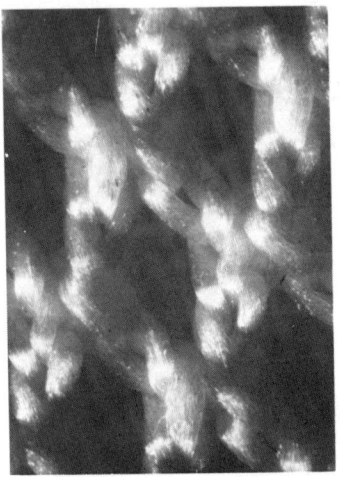

Fig. 6.4 SEM of two types of nylon mesh from running shoe uppers. (Norman Macmillian photo)

The Package

Look for a moment at the uppers of your running shoes. On the outside is the nylon weave or mesh. On the inside you can see a nylon or cotton lining. When magnified this lining looks like the picture in Figure 6.5, which is a loose-knit nylon tricot lining from an Etonic Streetfighter.

If you have an old pair of shoes, dig further and cut the upper. If not look at Figure 6.6 where the cut has been made. Notice that not only is there a lining on the

What Shoes Are Made Of—A Closer Look 127

Fig. 6.5 SEM of a loose trico kint lining from an Etonic Streetfighter. (Norman Macmillan photo)

inside and the nylon mesh or weave on the outside, but there is a layer of foam and possibly a layer of backing for the nylon. Thicker foam is used to make the tongue to insure good protection from irritation.

You are right if you think it would be a massive job to make what are effectively four separate shoes, one inside the other. The job of laminating all the layers—"combining" as it is known in the shoe trade—is done on the rolls of material before they come near a shoe factory.

The basic package for a nylon taffeta upper has three

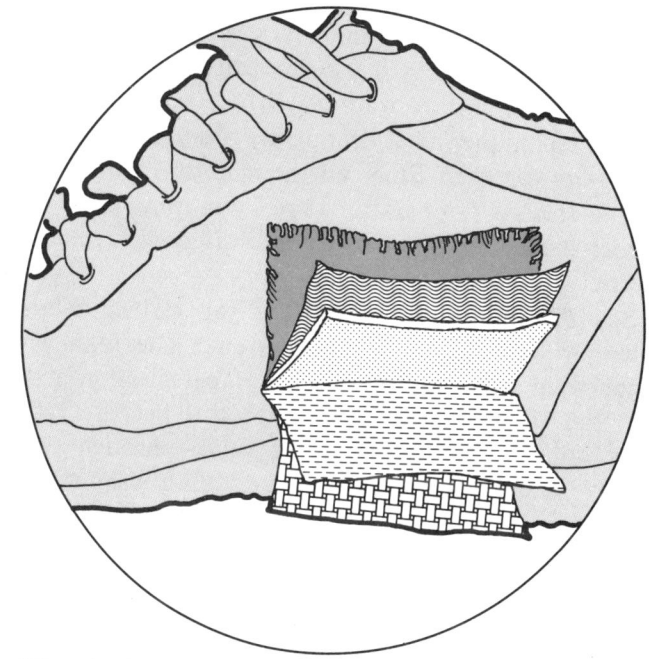

Fig. 6.6 A diagramatic representation of a four layer upper package. The nylon taffeta is backed by a cotton weave, and then a layer of foam is sandwiched between the backing and the lining of the shoe.

components: the taffeta, foam, and the tricot lining. As part of the solution to the durability problems of nylon mesh mentioned earlier, a backing layer of woven drill is sometimes included between the mesh and foam lining.

There are two techniques for laminating these layers. Cementing each layer to the next gives the most durable bond. But it also leaves the shoe stiff and tends to decrease permeability to water vapor.

The technique most frequently used is to "flame" the layers together. Since all the materials tend to melt with increased temperature, brief exposure to a flame during the combining process will effectively bond the layers.

So, industry's best substitute for leather requires three or four layers to nature's one! The foam layer is included both for absorption of perspiration and to give the shoe a comfortable feel. But because taffeta does not let too much water vapor through, water simply accumulates in the foam, adding weight to the shoe.

There are other materials which would seem to be good candidates for the uppers of running shoes, and we shall speculate about future trends in Chapter 8.

Customs Quirks

In closing out the discussion of uppers it is interesting to note that current customs regulations are doing as much as science and technology to influence what materials are used in them.

In an attempt to protect the domestic shoe industry, the Customs Service has established a quota for each country, specifying the number of shoes that can be brought into the country each year at low duty rates. Korea, for example, is allowed about twenty-three million pairs of athletic shoes for fiscal 1980-81. However, "quality shoes" are exempt from the quota. Quality in this case is defined as a shoe which is more than fifty percent leather on the outer surface of the upper. Careful measurement would reveal many imported running shoes that have just over fifty percent leather (by surface area) when all the trim, foxing, and other parts are counted. So we must thank Uncle Sam for the fact that leather has not completely gone from our running shoes.

MIDSOLE AND WEDGE MATERIALS

As we showed in Chapter 2, midsole and wedge construction is what has characterized the development of the running shoe in the last ten to fifteen years. Although initially made of sponge rubber, these components are now made almost exclusively from a class of materials with the rather awesome title of "polyolefin foams."

First, a little background. In the 1930s and '40s running shoes had leather soles and, in an attempt to provide better shock absorption, runners and shoemakers stuck on crepe rubber heels and soles. By the 1950s the leather soles had gone and natural sheet rubber formed the outsole layer. Sheet rubber is rather heavy and not particularly good at absorbing shock.

As early as 1920 attempts had been made to increase the shock absorbing properties of rubber by producing a rubber which had small bubbles of air encapsulated in it. This was called foam rubber and later became known as "microcellular rubber." The key element in the technique is a chemical blowing agent. When the temperature and other conditions are right, this agent reacts with other chemicals in the mixture and begins to produce gas. If the pressure in the vessel containing the mixture is kept high the gas cannot escape. As the compound cures, small bubbles of air are trapped within the material, making what is known as a closed cell foam. Even though these rubber foams were lighter and better shock absorbers than the sheet rubber used during the '50s, they were abandoned in favor of polymeric foams during the '70s.

Foams made from polymers are superior to rubber foams for a number of reasons. The overwhelming factor in regard to running shoes is lightness. The Monarch Rubber Company, which first introduced the foam called "solelite" in 1973, has made progress to the point where they have reduced the density of the material (and consequently its weight) by a factor of four, while actually improving its shock absorption characteristics.

Figure 6.7 is a microscopic picture of the surface piece of a compound called ethylene vinyl acetate (EVA), taken from the midsole of a Brooks Vantage. The closed air cells close to the surface of this material

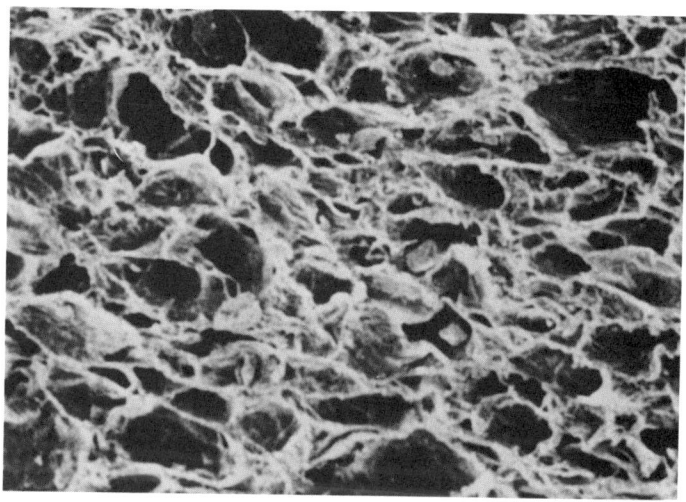

Fig. 6.7   SEM of a midsole from a Brooks Vantage. The cut used to slice the specimen off the shoe has destroyed many of the air cells which are usually sealed up. The material is classified as a closed cell foam. (Norman Macmillan photo)

have been ruptured during preparation, making the specimen look like a sponge. But a sponge is what is known as an open cell material, and is very different from the closed cell foams used in the wedge and midsoles of running shoes. Perhaps the best idea can be gained by looking ahead to Figure 6.10, which is a much lighter EVA used for sockliners. The basic structure is the same.

Closed cell foams absorb energy in two ways. First,

the walls of the air cells deform just like the springs in a car, and in deforming they absorb energy. Also, the small bubbles of air are compressed and they too act as shock absorbers.

Despite the widespread use of EVA foams in running shoes there are some basic questions which remain unanswered. One of the most important of these is their longterm durability. All foams take a certain amount of "set" as they adapt to continual stresses. But as the density of the material goes down in the quest for lighter running shoes, will the shock absorbing properties be maintained over the long term? If not, we shall be wearing running shoes that are at their peak for only the first five or ten miles of running. We will return to this topic in the chapter on shoe gerontology.

OUTSOLES

As we saw in the discussion of Spalding marathon shoes of the early 1900s, wear of the outsole has long been a problem for the manufacturers. Rubber has been the material of choice because it is both soft and durable. Also, since the early days of this century a massive technology of rubber used in the manufacture of car tires has been accumulating, much of which is directly applicable to shoemaking.

The basic unit in all natural and synthetic rubber is an organic hydrocarbon called isoprene. The degree to which the isoprene units are linked together in long

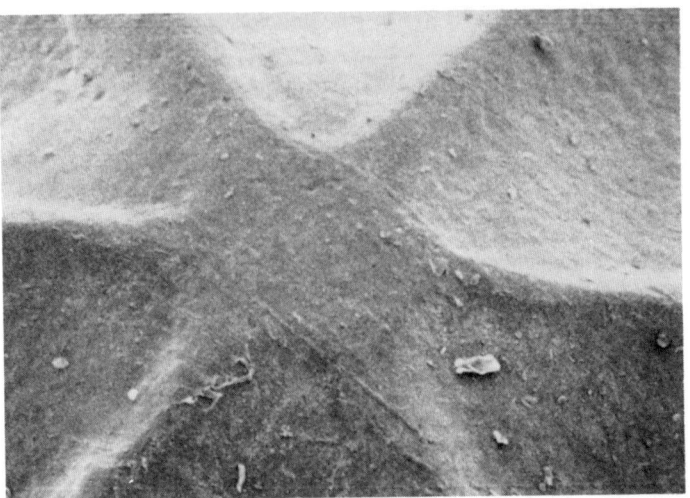

Fig. 6.8 SEM of a rubber outsole from an Etonic Streetfighter. (Norman Macmillan photo)

chains, and the type and quantity of other substances used in processing, give the wide range of mechanical properties available in different types of rubber.

At the level of magnification that has been useful for looking at uppers and midsoles, rubber outsoles will give up none of their secrets as shown in Figure 6.8. The specimen still looks like a continuous material with no visible substructure. The particles of rubber are extremely small and its structure can be better examined by x-ray than a standard microscope.

What gives rubber its strength and resistance to abrasion is the filler used during the final curing process. The rubber which performs best on abrasion tests has a highly structured carbon black as a filler, and this type of rubber is commonly used for running shoe outsoles.

In their search for lightness some shoe manufacturers have recently turned to an EVA compound for the outsole. There is, however, considerable debate about the abrasion properties of these soles. On all standard abrasion tests they do badly. On some runners they do even worse, wearing through in as little as 200 miles, but other runners seem able to get more miles from this type of outsole. These discrepancies highlight the wide variations there are among runners in the way their feet contact the ground. Some runners are hard on shoes and others are not. The process of foot strike is much more complex than we can presently explain.

Besides abrasion, the frictional and flex properties of outsoles are also important considerations. One of the big problems with polyurethane soles is that they offer very poor traction in wet conditions. As distinctive as the materials used in outsoles are the various tread patterns employed. A change in tread configuration can affect both shock absorption and traction. These factors will be discussed in Chapter 8.

INSOLE BOARD

All shoes which are cement lasted have an insole board which is a critical component of the lasting process. In many shoes this is the only piece of natural

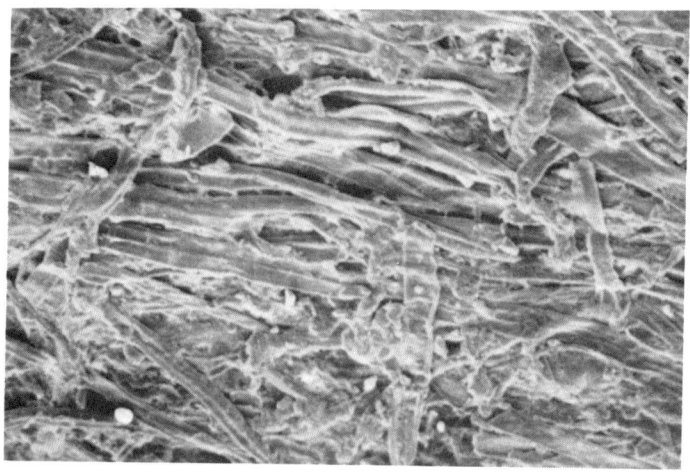

Fig. 6.9 SEM of a Texon fiber insole board. The cellulose fibers can be clearly seen. (Norman Macmillan photo)

material in the whole shoe. Figure 6.9 shows how the board is made of cellulose fibers imbedded in an elastomeric matrix which binds the fibers tightly together. In the better boards, various additives are included to inhibit bacterial and fungal growth and to give wet strength.

The insole board ends up living much of its life under water. Perspiration not passed through the shoe upper soaks through the sockliner and onto the insole board. Some of the poorer quality insole boards tend to shred under the combined action of moisture and continual stress.

The board must be a compromise between stability and flexibility. It should provide a rigid base for the shoe, without unduly restraining the movement of the foot once it is inside the shoe. Texon, one of the major manufacturers of insole boards, has made a board hinged at the ball of the foot to improve flexibility. Other manufacturers have made a series of cuts in the board, under the rearfoot and forefoot areas, to improve the response of the shoe to impact.

SOCKLINER

The sockliner, sometimes called the insole, sits between the foot and the insole board. Manufacturers have tried many substances in the search for a perfect interface. Because the sockliner is right next to the foot it has to perform a number of important functions. It must absorb perspiration, help in energy absorption at foot strike, and promote comfort in several ways.

First, since the insole board is flat, a good sockliner will mold to the shape of the foot, giving what is known as a conforming footbed. The Brooks soft support shown in Figure 6.10 is an example of this type of footbed, which is made from a closed cell EVA foam. As the picture shows there is much more air than material in this kind of insole.

Next, the sockliner should provide good friction between the foot and itself so that the foot does not

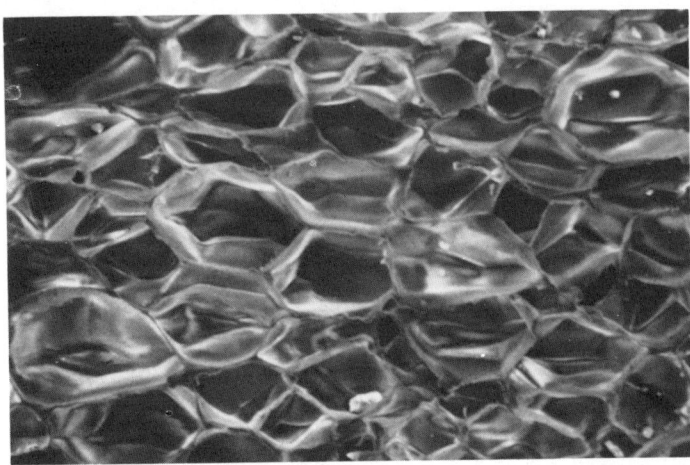

Fig. 6.10 SEM of a Brooks "Custom Contour" insert. The thin walls of the closed cells allow the unit to deform easily to take the shape of the foot. (Norman Macmillan photo)

slip about inside the shoe. Even better, it will allow a small amount of fore and aft movement of the foot to occur by rolling over itself in the manner shown in Figure 6.11. The Spenco insole has been found useful in this respect.

The two other sockliners which are magnified in Figure 6.12 show unusual surface features. The first is a terrycloth lining. Terrycloth is made by leaving large loops of material on the surface. This provides a greater surface for absorption of perspiration. The second picture is a brushed velour which generates a lot of

What Shoes Are Made Of—A Closer Look

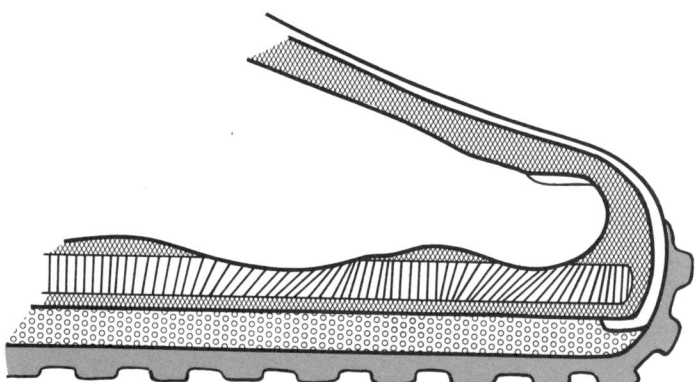

Fig. 6.11 An important function of the sockliner is to allow shearing movement to take place so that the foot can move slightly backward and forward without any chafing occuring on the undersurface of the foot. Too much movement though may cause blisters on the top of the foot which may rub on the upper.

Fig. 6.12a SEM of a velour sockliner. (Norman Macmillan photo)

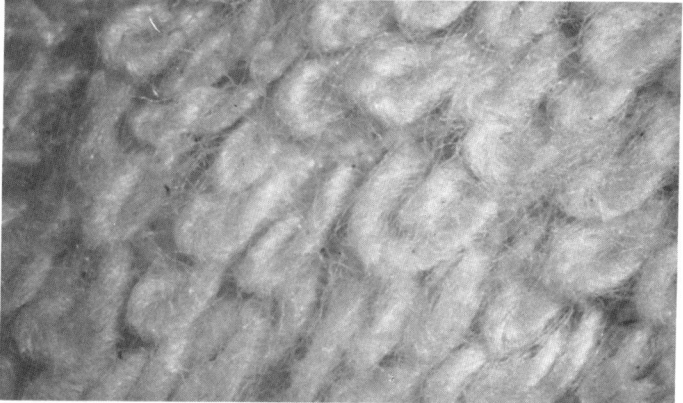

Fig. 6.12b A terrycloth sockliner where loops of yarn are left close to the foot surface for maximum absorption of perspiration. (Norman Macmillan photo)

friction. Some of the more unusual sockliners and insoles used in running shoes are considered in Chapter 8.

ARCH COOKIES

The topic of arch supports and inserts in shoes is a very controversial one and a complete chapter is devoted to a discussion of their pros and cons (see Chapter 12). Some runners routinely rip them out of new shoes. Others feel that they are always in the wrong place but endure them anyway, while others must replace them with some custom arch support device.

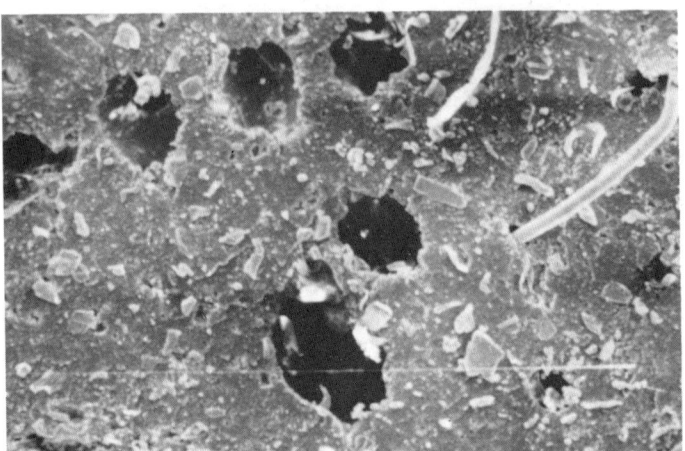

Fig. 6.13 SEM of a sponge rubber arch cookie from a KAEPA shoe. The density of this material is high as evidenced by the small number of air cells. (Norman Macmillan photo)

Arch cookies that come in running shoes are generally made of foam rubber. Figure 6.13 is a picture of typical arch cookie material taken from a Kaepa shoe. The magnification in this picture is the same as that for the soft support in Figure 6.10. It is clear that the arch cookie has much more rubber than it does air, in complete contrast to the soft support. The reason for this is that manufacturers feel that foam rubber will take less of a compression set during use. There are very few air cells; thus the buckling and compression of the cell walls cannot take place to the extent that it can in a less dense material.

It is unlikely that most of the arch cookies supplied with running shoes can do more than provide a feeling of tight fit in the arch area. If the arch needs additional support it will probably have to come from a device which is considerably stiffer.

HEEL COUNTERS

For many years Adidas and Puma were the only manufacturers who put heel counters into their running shoes. Now heel counters are universal, but they vary greatly in quality and physical properties.

Fiberboard is widely used, but it has the great disadvantage that it loses all of its stiffness after a few soakings in water. Various plastics have been tried and these stand up somewhat better than fiberboard.

To insure an adequate fit, many heel counters are molded during the lasting operation. They are coated with a thermoplastic material before insertion into the upper, and the rear part lasting machine (see Chapter 5) applies heat and compression to form them in the shape of the last. An example of this process is shown in Figure 6.14a.

Other counters are premolded to the required shape, and some have a large lip which fits between the upper and the insole board (Figure 6.14b).

Molded polyethylene counters have been used in other sports footwear but have not seen service in many running shoes. They are far superior to the

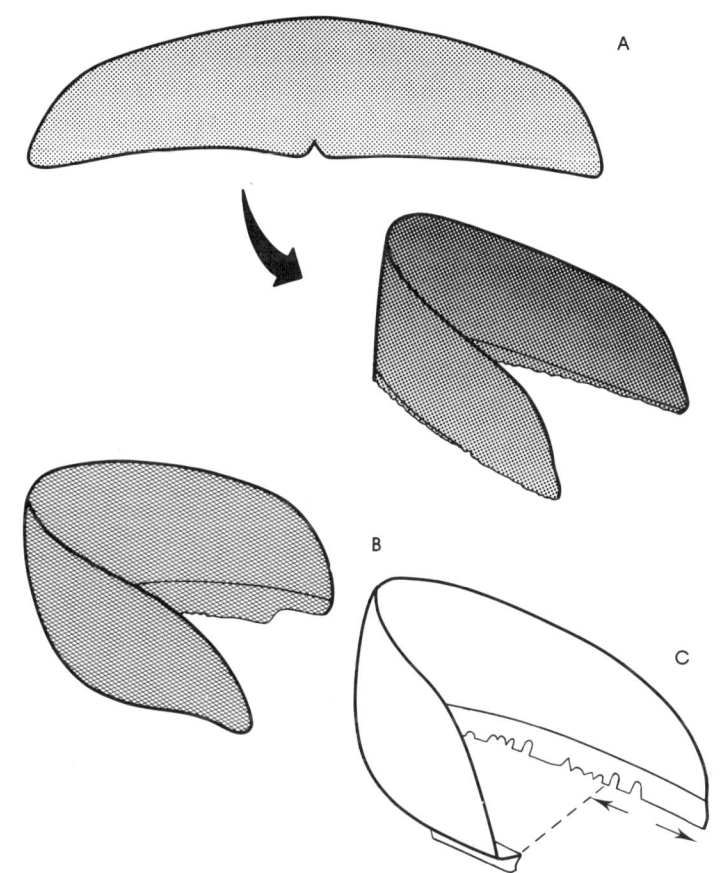

Fig. 6.14 Two types of heel counter. a) A flat band which is thermoplastic so that it takes the shape of the last when heated. b) Premolded polyethylene counters and c) one showing an extended medial (inside) border.

fiberboard counter in their longterm wear properties unless exposed to extremes of temperature. They can become brittle in the cold and pliable under hot conditions.

Since most runners need rearfoot control on the inside of the shoe, several manufacturers have lengthened and raised the height of the counter on the inside. This is shown in Figure 6.14c. While on the topic of size, one thing to watch out for is a small heel counter disguised by a large overlay of leather foxing. This foxing will be no help at all in rearfoot control. Occasionally the lip of the counter is "nail seated" for additional stability. We saw an example of this during our visit to the shoe factory in Chapter 5.

Considering the importance of the heel counter to shoe stability, and its relatively low cost, it is surprising that many manufacturers are still willing to cut a few cents off the cost of the shoe by using an inferior heel counter. One or two presses of the counter in a new shoe is often sufficient to reveal that it is not going to stand the test of time.

FINDING THE RIGHT MATERIAL

The runner has to face the problem of finding the right materials in running shoes. There is no taking a microscope or testing equipment along to the store to categorize and test materials used to build shoes.

The big problem is that visual examination will only

go so far. How can you tell a good EVA midsole from a bad one? Unfortunately you can't by just looking or poking with a finger. How do you know if a particular outsole will be durable? Again, you can't tell by looking.

Obviously, experience will help. If you have run in a certain shoe you will know if the materials withstood the particular kind of battering that your running style and habits inflicted. But even that is not foolproof. Manufacturers change the materials they use in a given shoe from year to year as things like price and availability fluctuate. All this implies the need for some form of testing which will provide you with information to guide your purchasing decision. We will now turn our attention to shoe testing and explain how it can help.

7

Shoe Testing and Shoe Surveys

I went to Penn State and asked the people who were rating shoes about balance and spring. Well, they didn't know what I was talking about. How can they rate shoes if they don't know even the most elementary things? They're not experts.

Arthur Lydiard
Coach

Arthur Lydiard lives by what he feels, and of course that's not a bad way to live. He felt that Peter Snell could win an Olympic medal and he did. He felt that he could turn the Finnish distance program around and he did. It's hard to argue with success. But there comes a time when feeling is not enough. Science has been the basis for the vast improvement in the quality of life that has occurred in the last century, and science cannot be based on feeling and subjectivity.

If balance and spring are important features of a running shoe, then let's try to measure them. English morphologist D'arcy Thompson once said that ". . .

when you cannot measure it your knowledge is of a meagre and unsatisfactory kind." Thompson represents the other end of the spectrum from Lydiard, and somewhere in the middle lies the truth.

When faced with the glut of running shoes on the market today, we have to call on measurement for help. Feelings about a shoe are certainly important, but the time for feelings is after test results have been used to select shoes for further consideration. At that point such subjective elements as fit and comfort enter into the picture, but the study of shoe test results is an essential precursor to an intelligent decision about which running shoe to purchase.

TESTING THE MATERIALS

The footwear industry is not known for its research and development. One veteran shoe manufacturer describes how, until recently, walking into a shoe factory with a tape measure was considered research.

One of the industry's prime concerns has been to minimize the number of shoes returned due to structural breakdown. In general, returned shoes mean lost money. The shoes can't be recycled and most of them can't be sold as seconds because they have already been used. So the majority of tests which the industry developed are designed to insure that materials will not show early signs of wear. An English organization called SATRA (Shoe and Allied Trades Research Association) has been instrumental in the development of test methods in this area.

SATRA's catalogue describes such items as "upper material flexing machines," "the finish rub fastness tester," and "the upper leather waterproofness tester." These and other devices subject the materials that shoes are made of to a hostile environment or rigorous stress. The evaluation is invariably visual and a pass/fail examination—"yes, the material cracked," "no the water didn't come through."

One of the few test machines of this nature that has found its way into the shoe factory is called a tensile tensor. This pulls the material apart (like a medieval rack) to measure the force and stretch until it tears into two pieces. Another machine frequently seen in shoe factories tests the strength of the bond of the sole to the upper.

CONSUMER TESTING

Testing of the final product by having consumers try it out has been a standard practice in the shoe industry for many years. The industry calls this "wear testing," but it should not be confused with tests which measure how quickly the outsole wears down. Consumer tests involve giving free shoes to athletes and trying to convince them to offer their opinions about the shoe in return. The psychological effect of getting free shoes can often influence the comments of the wearers in a positive direction. Unless the selection of subjects is carefully controlled the results can be biased in a number of ways.

Even under well-controlled conditions many of the comments received are often inadequate and inexact. "I like them," "Okay," "I didn't like them," are often the best responses the manufacturer can get.

This rather haphazard "testing" certainly has a place in the overall scheme of things, but it should not be considered a primary means of evaluating shoes. Rather, it should be a final confirmation that all of the research and development has resulted in something that makes sense for the foot and feels comfortable on the athlete.

SHOE TESTING

What matters most in a running shoe is that it protects the foot from injury and feels good for running. It is an additional bonus if the shoe looks nice, the leather foxing doesn't scuff badly, and the vinyl trim doesn't crack, but none of the tests we mentioned earlier measure features of the running shoe which relate to injury prevention.

In 1977 *Runner's World* magazine introduced five lab tests into their annual shoe survey. These were designed to provide answers to safety questions such as impact protection and flexibility. By 1980 this had been expanded to a total of eight tests which formed the basis for the complete shoe rating. Following *Runner's World*'s lead, several of the more progressive shoe manufacturers began to develop testing programs of their own. They realized that they could not simply sit back and produce the same models year after year. Other running publications also started testing programs. Shoe testing had clearly arrived to stay.

The Philosophy of Shoe Testing

It is as important for the runner to understand shoe tests as it is for someone buying a car to know about engine size, fuel economy, and transmission differences.

Like any measurement, the results of tests on running shoes can be used or misused. They provide a way to guide the runner through the shoe buying maze, but they can't eliminate the possibility of a completely wrong and uninformed choice.

The most important thing that shoe tests do is provide information concerning the performance of the shoes which cannot be obtained by simple observation. The results of the *Runner's World* tests have shown, for example, that the thickness of the midsole in a running shoe is a poor index of its ability to absorb shock. Without the test results runners may have felt that measuring the thickness of the shoe's midsole was a reasonable way to identify a shoe with the best shock absorption.

As we shall see shortly in our discussion of the different methods of measuring shock absorption, there are several ways to approach the testing of a running shoe. You can test the shoe itself under controlled lab conditions; or, while a subject is running you can test the effect of the shoe on the ground or try to measure some aspect of the runner's response to the shoe.

My own feeling, as described in the October 1979 issue of *Runner's World*, is that shoe testing should be a three-stage process. During stage one experiments are conducted using large groups of runners to gather data on the conditions the shoes will face in practice. This involves measuring the loads the shoe will bear, the amount of flexion it goes through, and such things as temperature gradients between the inside and outside of the shoe. The results of some biomechanical experiments of this nature were described in Chapter 4. The desired outcome of this stage is a set of design criteria for a good running shoe.

In stage two the runner is no longer included in the experiment. This phase involves digesting the information collected in stage one and devising ways of subjecting a running shoe to the actual conditions during running.

There are many reasons why it is best to test shoes without the runner inside. First, every step by the same runner has the potential to be different from the previous step. In an extensive shoe survey it may be necessary to test over 200 different pairs of shoes. Even if the test subject ran only one lap in each pair of shoes, this would involve running fifty miles for one test sequence. The influence that fatigue, fitting, and day-to-day aches and pains would have on test results would make the final results extremely questionable.

Second, runners change their styles over time, making a valid retest impossible. Because each runner is different it is extremely difficult for a test which includes the runner to be generalized and replicated by researchers in different locations. Finally, the terrain and climatic conditions under which the tests are conducted will also affect the result. Tests on consumer products must be repeatable if they are to have a wide application.

For all these reasons, laboratory testing can provide the best vehicle for generating performance data on running shoes, provided that the tests are valid and reliable simulations of the conditions which occur in running.

In stage three, all available shoes are subjected to the testing sequence under tightly controlled conditions. The important thing is that each shoe faces an identical sequence of tests, so that the results really do reflect the behavior of the shoe and not the influence of uncontrolled variables.

The runner is an essential component at both ends of this three-stage process. In the beginning, advanced technology is used on runners in motion to determine the exact requirements of the shoe. When the test process is over and the results have been analyzed the opinions and perceptions of the runner are sought and included in the equation. The runner must insure that shoes which scored well on the tests are satisfactory in the subjective areas that were not part of the testing sequence. A shoe that tests well but fits badly will not find favor among runners.

We will now look at some of the tests that are performed on running shoes and discuss their significance.

Tests of Shock Absorption

The shock absorbing qualities of running shoes have improved dramatically in the last ten years. We shall see in Chapter 13 that this has led to a considerable reduction in a number of injuries, especially in the forefoot area.

But the importance of protection from impact in running goes far beyond the foot. The foot is simply first in line to receive the jolt. The "earthquake" that happens every time the foot hits the ground has some effect on almost every joint in the body. The muscles crossing the joints try to modify and attenuate the shock waves. Some of the long bones of the leg, particularly the tibia and fibula, find the punishment hard to take. Every joint in the vertebral column has some reaction to the applied forces. So whatever the shoe can do to lessen the shock received by the body at foot strike will be helpful to the entire body.

What Kind of Impacts Can the Body Stand?

Although there has been a number of experiments which have measured forces at foot strike in running, almost nothing is known about the relationship of either level or duration of impact to injury. One of the main reasons for this is that gathering information on human tolerance is difficult, risky, and can be a procedure of doubtful integrity.

In the early days of biomechanical experiments volunteer studies were common. Men and women, generally in the armed forces, subjected themselves to a variety of hazardous environments simply for extra pay or benefits. The results to science were useful, but the effects on the subjects were sometimes damaging. From experiments such as these we know quite a lot about the effects of impact on the head, but we know very little about how the foot will respond to controlled impact conditions. Cadaver studies are likely to miss the point because the body is constantly repairing and rebuilding; take this property away and the situation is no longer realistic. Animal experiments might be useful, but so far few have been carried out.

At present the only evidence we have available on the effects of the repeated impacts in running is from runners with injury, and that is hardly the result of controlled experiment. So until we have better evidence we have to strive to get the best possible shock absorption from running shoes.

How Do Shoes Absorb Shock?

As we discovered in Chapter 4, the midsole and wedge are the primary shock absorbers, although the sockliner and the outsole configuration also help. The principal shock absorbing mechanism of the midsole and wedge is the deformation of the millions of air cell walls that are captured in the foam material. Each cell wall acts like the leaf of a car spring bending and buckling, and in doing so, converting energy to heat. Some of the energy is also stored as it is in a stretched elastic band. When the force is removed the cell walls can rebound, giving energy back to the runner if the conditions are right. This is analogous to a bouncing ball which does not "die" as it hits the ground but rebounds upward because some energy was stored.

How Can Shock Absorption Be Tested?

There are at least three ways to test the shock absorbing ability of the shoe. First, measuring devices can be put in the ground to record the force and pressure as the runner steps on them. Shoes with differing amounts of shock absorption should cause changes in these measurements. Next, one could try to measure the effects of different running shoes on the forces transmitted to the body. Lastly, the shoes can be subjected to impact similar to that of running, and measurements can be made to determine the amount of shock absorbed. All these means of testing have been tried, and we will talk briefly about each.

1. Measuring the Effect of the Shoe on the Ground. A force platform is commonly used in biomechanics research to measure the forces between foot and ground. Some of the data presented in Chapter 4 were collected using this device. Although the device is useful in collecting basic information on the pattern of forces during running, the force platform has not proven helpful at detecting the differences between shoes. We have used this technique at Penn State, and so have Dr. Barry Bates and his colleagues at the University of Oregon. The variability among runners tends to complicate the results. Also, the results of a force platform study depend not only on the shoe, but on what all the other parts of the body are doing. Even when we know that there are dramatic differences between the shock absorption of different shoes, they don't always show up on a force platform test.

2. Measuring the Effect of Footstrike on the Body. Another way to measure the shock absorbing properties of running shoes is to measure the forces transmitted to the leg bones. The most accurate way to do this would be to affix measuring devices directly to the bones of runners. Unfortunately since we are forced to take measurements on top of the skin, muscle, and other tissues overlying the bone, there is much information we lack.

The results of tests made on top of soft tissue, seeking data on bone, are open to considerable question until reliability and validity studies can be done. There have been one or two promising attempts in this direction. Scientists in England worked with volunteers who would allow small screws to be placed in the periosteum (or covering of the bone). These screws held small measuring devices which gave information about just what shock effects the bone was experiencing during walking in shoes.

3. Impacting running shoes with a machine. This method is used in the *Runner's World* testing program. Using the machine shown in Figure 7.1, a weighted shaft is dropped down onto selected parts of the shoe's rearfoot and forefoot. The exact locations of the parts of the shoe tested were determined by a series of experiments similar to those described in Chapter 4.

A measuring device called an accelerometer is mounted onto the head of the shaft, and as the shaft strikes the shoe it is slowed down and eventually forced back in the other direction. The way in which the shaft is slowed down will affect the output of the accelerometer. If the shaft was dropped on a steel plate the instrument would receive a very sudden shock and the reading would go out of range in the region of 200 G's (A G is a unit of acceleration equal to the acceleration due to gravity on earth). A running shoe will modify this to between nine and thirty G's depending on its

Fig. 7.1 The impact machine used in the *Runner's World* tests to measure the shock absorption of running shoes.

construction. In an impact test of this type the lower the score the better.

It is very important that the conditions of the impact test reproduce the conditions that occur in running. The foams used in the midsole and wedge of running shoes change their properties depending upon the circumstances of impact.

The impact test machine can also detect how far the shaft drives down into the shoe. This is important in that it is one aspect of rearfoot control. Obviously energy absorption must involve deformation, but the more the foot penetrates into the surface of the midsole, the less stable the support will be. Penetration values in the 1980 *Runner's World* survey varied from 4.8 to ten millimeters. So like most other properties we have tests for, there is a tremendous difference between apparently similar shoes. The ideal midsole material would have good shock absorption but could resist the tendency of the foot to sink down in the shoe.

Flexibility

It is almost a reflex action. You pick up a running shoe and the first thing you do is flex it across the ball. If it's easy to flex you probably nod your head approvingly. And most clinicians will agree with you. A shoe that is flexible across the ball seems less likely to lead to certain injuries than a stiff shoe. But just how flexible is too flexible? No one quite knows, so as with shock absorption, the current rule of thumb is the more flexibility the better.

Of course it's not just how flexible the shoe is when you try to bend it, but where it flexes that is important. If you put some running shoes between your hands and push them together, the shoe will bend exactly at the point where the wedge ends. This will not be too much use to the foot since it cannot bend in this region.

High-speed film studies have shown that the flexing motion of the running shoe is a complicated one. It is certainly not a hinge movement. It is as if there was a moveable hinge, the center of which rolls down the shoe during the support phase starting just ahead of the midfoot and progressing toward the toe. The maximum flexion occurs when the center of rotation is about forty percent of the shoe length from the toe.

The *Runner's World* flexibility test forces the shoe to bend at this spot and measures the force required to flex the shoe through a forty degree range. In the test (shown in Figure 7.2) the shoe is clamped down at the heel and toe with compressed air clamps. The upper is removed in the interests of a more reliable measurement. While the upper does contribute to flexibility, the overwhelming contribution is from the midsole, wedge, and outsole. As a cam pushes up the front of the shoe, small devices called strain gauges detect the amount of force needed to flex the shoe through the prescribed arc.

After a long series of preliminary flexes designed to get over the initial break-in period, the data collected by the strain gauges is digested by a computer. The

Shoe Testing and Shoe Surveys

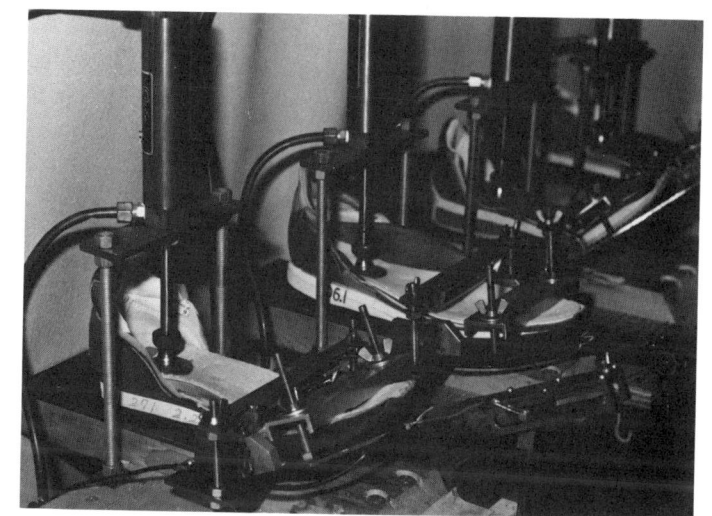

Fig. 7.2 The *Runner's World* flexibility test. The upper is cut off the shoe, which is then flexed through an angle of about 40°. The force needed to flex the shoe is measured with strain gauges.

results come rolling off the computer shortly afterwards in terms of the energy needed to flex the shoe. The more energy needed, the worse for your foot. The muscles of the foot and leg will have to apply force to bend the shoe during late support, and the bottom of the foot may suffer from extra stress leading to inflammation.

Our results have shown tremendous variety in flexibility among running shoes. Women's training flats, for example, span almost a four-fold range in test scores.

REARFOOT CONTROL

The first three to four hundredths of a second after touchdown is a critical time for the running foot and leg. In this brief instant the foot strikes, generally on the outside border of the shoe, and rolls to a flat position. Depending upon the alignment of the runner's body and the shoes worn the inward rolling motion will then either stop or continue. This motion of the subtalar joint is called pronation, and excessive pronation can exert a devastating influence throughout the leg, particularly on the knee joint.

Experimental studies referred to in Chapter 4 have shown that different shoes offer different levels of control of this important body motion. The prevention of excessive movement of the rearfoot has become known as rearfoot control.

Such control is an extremely complex phenomenon. It is a function of fit, midsole and wedge materials, the type of inshoe device used, and the way the rearfoot of the shoe is constructed. The *Runner's World* series has three separate tests which measure different elements of rearfoot control.

Heel Counter Stiffness

As we saw earlier all running shoes have a stiffener, called the heel counter, which is placed in a small pocket at the back. This counter plays an important role during the support phase, when there are forces which tend to drive the foot sideways off the platform of the shoe. Depending upon the style and skeletal alignment of the runner, this pull could be in either direction. Most often it is directed toward the midline of the body.

Both the size and stiffness of the heel counter will influence what kind of fight the heel counter puts up to keep the foot in place. The test called "heel counter stiffness" in the *Runner's World* series (Figure 7.3) measures the force required to deform the heel counter through a standard distance on the inside border of the shoe. A measuring probe is placed on the counter at a standard height and distance from the back of the shoe. After several initial movements into the counter the maximum opposing force that the counter can generate is measured. The more force needed to move the counter the better, since the foot will be held more firmly in place.

The results of this test display more variation among shoes from different manufacturers than almost any other feature. Some shoes offered almost ten times more resistance to deformation than others. The best counters are nestled between the insole board and the midsole, and provide a stiffness that will not show signs of aging. Considering the relatively low cost of good heel counters, it is surprising that some manufacturers use the counter as a place to save a few cents.

Fig. 7.3 The *Runner's World* heel counter stiffness test.

Rearfoot Stability

One of the properties that allows the foot to pronate is the compression of the midsole and wedge material in the rear of the shoe. While shoe designers were striving for good shock absorption, one way they achieved it was by using soft, highly compressible foams in the midsole and wedge. This certainly improved shock absorption but had a negative effect on the control of rearfoot motion.

The test for rearfoot stability (Figure 7.4) is designed to give an index of how well the shoe will resist the compression it receives during the early support phase of running. The shoe is mounted upside down and laced onto a metal footform. The outsole is then subjected to a compression force of 200 pounds. The compression platform is hinged as shown in the diagram, and an arm extends laterally on the inside border of the shoe. A mechanical hammer is automatically raised a standard distance and then dropped onto the arm. The process is repeated once a second. As the arm is deflected downward into the shoe a small measuring device detects the rotation. This information is fed into a computer which calculates the exact deflection that occurs. The greater the angle of deflection, the less control the shoe will offer.

Overall Rearfoot Control

The results from the three tests for penetration, heel counter stiffness, and rearfoot stability are included separately in the overall weighting process to give the shoe a final score in the *Runner's World* survey. To get an index of the rearfoot control properties, the results from the three tests can be combined statistically so

Fig. 7.4 The rearfoot stability test used in the *Runner's World* survey. This machine deforms the inside border of the shoe to estimate how well the shoe will resist excessive pronation during running.

that they each have equal importance in the final result. It is interesting to note that many of the shoes that do well on shock absorption do relatively poorly on rearfoot control. There is a tradeoff here which has a logical reason. Shock absorption is achieved by gradually slowing down a moving object, in this case the foot with the body attached. A soft and compressible material will therefore do well on shock absorption, but poorly on penetration and stability. Hopefully in the future ways can be found to eliminate the need to choose one property or the other.

Sole Wear Test

Sole wear is rarely considered as more than an economic factor when buying shoes. The better the sole wear, the longer it will be before you have to buy a new pair.

It is an economic consideration, but it is more. If the outsole of the shoe is badly worn two things can happen. First, the decreased thickness can mean reduced shock absorption. More importantly, excessive wear of the sole can radically change the alignment of the foot and leg during the early phase of contact with the ground. This can result in aches and pains and possible injury to the leg.

But the issue is by no means a simple one. Some wear may benefit the leg and foot. Steve Subotnick, in his book *Cures for Common Running Injuries,* says that he is beginning to think that building up the shoe with a filler (see Chapter 10) should be done very cautiously. He feels that "too much repair may reverse what the body is trying to achieve." Although this statement should be regarded as Steve thinking aloud, his point that certain wear patterns may be beneficial should be given consideration. This is related to my statement in Chapter 4 that for most of us running is not a back to front movement when viewed from the bottom of the shoe. The outside border of the shoe and not the back edge is first in line to receive pressure at initial contact. The soft "knife edge" of the lateral border of the shoe may not be an optimum design for the best transition between contact and mid-support. We may be seeing a different configuration on the lateral edge of the outsole in future years.

Runners wear out their shoes in different ways, and they also wear them out at different rates. Some runners will go completely through a sole in 300 miles, while for others the same outsole will last 1,000 miles. This is all related to the exact way in which the foot is planted on the ground. How much scuffing there is on approach and how much "shuffling" there is after foot placement all affect the type and rate of wear. If all landings were of the "helicopter" type very little wear would occur.

The most common location for outsole wear is the rear outside border of the shoe. This occurs during the scuffing phase as the foot moves in for placement. It is rather like scraping the shoe many times over a coarse abrasive surface, and that is exactly what the *Runner's World* sole wear test is designed to do.

The shoe is oriented in a typical landing position (Figure 7.5) on top of an abrasive belt, and loaded with a weight to enforce contact between shoe and belt. The belt is moved past the shoe for periods of thirty seconds. After each period the shoe is inspected to see if

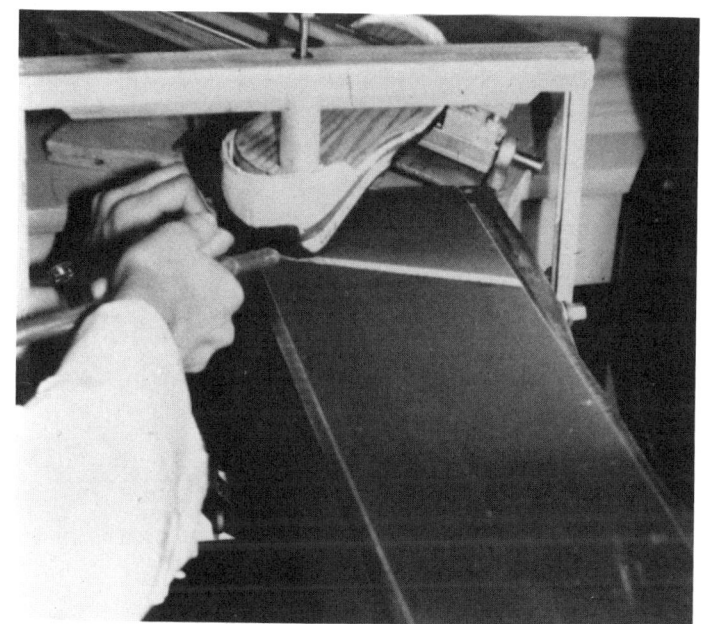

Fig. 7.5 The wear test used in the *Runner's World* survey.

the outsole has worn through to the midsole layer. The total time on the belt until this terminal wear condition is reached is the score in minutes given to the shoe. If after twenty wear periods (ten minutes) the sole is still going strong then the test is terminated.

The design of the tread pattern in the rearpart of the shoe will have a considerable effect on its performance on the road and on the wear test. Wear bars or plugs are used in many shoes to build up the area between the tread projections, to prolong the life of the outsole.

The test results provide a good guide to the comparative performance of shoes for a given runner. However, different individuals may show vastly differing wear rates. Midfoot and forefoot strikers will tend to wear the outsole more severely under the ball of the foot, in a region not currently tested in the *Runner's World* series, a fact that these runners should consider when using the wear test results for shoe selection.

There are other standard abrasion tests which test a small piece of outsole material rather than the complete shoe. The problem with these is that different manufacturers put the same material into different shoes which wear at very different rates. The tread design, the use of wear bars, and the exact configuration of the outsole all have an effect on the way a shoe will wear in practice. It is for this reason that the *Runner's World* test uses the finished product rather than a small specimen of material.

Traction

On a clean, dry surface most running shoes give good traction. You hardly ever feel unsure footing under good conditions. But running on a wet street is a different story. The water mobilizes any residue left on the surface of the road and the result is a slick and unstable interface.

The traction test in the *Runner's World* series reproduces these slick conditions in the laboratory using a James Machine (Figure 7.6). This is designed to provide an index of traction called the coefficient of friction. Only the front half of the sole is used in the traction test. The outsole is first lightly abraded to remove a compound used during manufacture to make the sole come out of a mold easily. The front part of the shoe is then attached to a metal block, placed on a smooth surface, and submerged in slightly soapy water. The arm of the machine begins by pressing vertically downwards. Under these conditions there are no forces acting which tend to cause slippage. But the arm gradually changes its orientation and actually pushes the specimen to try and make it slip. At some point the shoe can no longer resist the shearing force being applied.

You will notice a chart on the machine; this records the rapid transition when slip occurs. The chart has a scale which converts the information on where the slip occurred into the coefficient of friction which can be read directly off the chart. The higher the coefficient of friction, the better traction the shoe will provide.

Note that this test is measuring backwards slip. As we saw in Chapter 4 conditions for slip occur at both ends of the contact phase in running. At foot strike there is a tendency to slip forward, and in the later part of support there is a tendency to slip backwards.

Traction on an uneven surface is extremely difficult

Fig. 7.6 A modified James machine used in the *Runner's World* tests to measure the traction of the shoe under smooth, slick conditions.

to measure. The interaction of a tread pattern with a rough and broken surface gives different results every time a test is attempted. There is at present no satisfactory test method to measure traction under these conditions.

Permeability to Water

The ideal running shoe upper allows water vapor generated from perspiration to travel outside while it prevents water from getting into the shoe from outside. It is possible to achieve a certain balance in these apparently contradictory requirements, and tests have been devised to measure the transfer in both directions.

A new test for permeability to water vapor was included in the 1980 *Runner's World* survey on an experimental basis (see October 1980 *RW*). The test works by using the shoe upper to seal the top of a container of calcium chloride. This chemical is a desiccant which absorbs water. When the container is put into a controlled environment, different uppers allow different amounts of water to be drawn through and be absorbed in the desiccant. The test results show some shoe uppers to be very breatheable, while wearing others would be like sealing your feet in plastic bags. This test is obviously one which deserves a wider application.

As far as keeping water out, the United States Army had developed a machine (shown in Figure 7.7) in which the shoe is moved on a mechanical foot through a sequence of motions similar to those in walking. The whole process is carried out in a tank of water, and small sensors monitor the presence of water that seeps through the shoe. This test is obviously of importance for footwear designed to be used in wet or swampy conditions, and such data may also be of use to runners who anticipate running in foul weather.

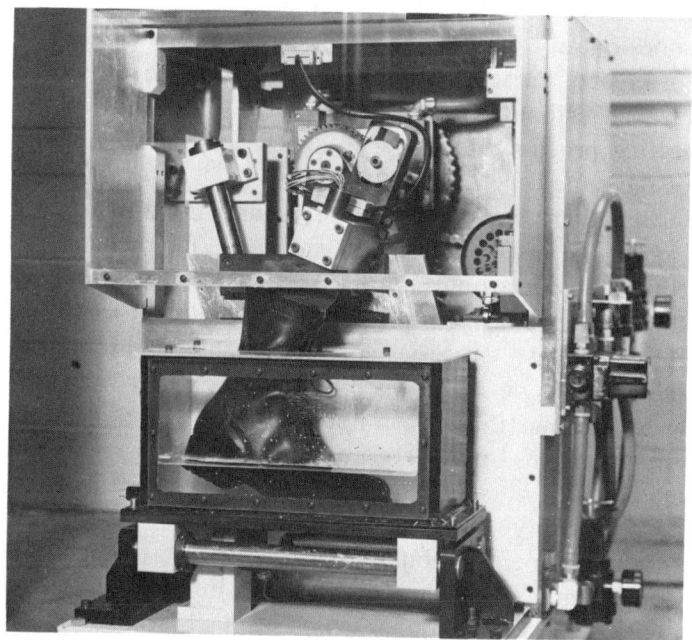

Fig. 7.7 A machine made for the United States Army designed to test the waterproof qualities of boots and shoes.

Testing Quality Control

Quality control is a difficult thing to test unless unlimited time and resources are available. It is quite feasible to test ten pairs of the same model running shoes on any of the tests described in this chapter. The difference in scores among the twenty shoes would give an estimate which incorporated the errors of the testing process with the real differences between shoes of the same type.

But there is a number of reasons why this method cannot be used. Cost is obviously a factor. Perhaps twenty shoes would not be needed but it is unlikely that fewer than ten would give reliable information. How are these ten shoes going to be chosen? Preferably they should be made on different days, and from different plants (if the manufacturer has more than one). All this makes for an extremely costly and time-consuming process.

Also, many features which fall under the heading of "quality control" would be very difficult to measure. For example, how do you atttach a number to one or two stitches on the upper which seem a bit loose? Many of these things, of which the user is the best judge, are mentioned in Chapter 14.

Tests on Old Shoes

One of the big limitations of shoe testing to date is that all information published has reported on new shoes. The tests determine the properties of the shoes as they are lifted out of the box. It is very important that the same methodology be used on shoes which are in various stages of their life. The best situation would be a controlled study on the same group of shoes being worn by runners who are in a well-controlled training program. Some preliminary results of tests on old shoes are described in Chapter 10.

Rating the Shoes

When all the test results are in, some decision has to be made on the way the scores are combined. My own mailbag has been heavily weighted by letters asking why simply adding up the scores on various tests does not constitute the final ratings. There are two reasons why this "cross-country" scoring is not used.

First, all the tests are not of equal importance. Rearfoot control and impact response are more important to most runners than, for example, traction. Next, the positional ranking is not an adequate representation of the performance of the shoe on a test. If, for example, the top three shoes scored 10.0, 16.0, and 16.1 on an impact test, the first shoe is clearly in a class of its own and should receive more overall benefit from the six point gap between it and the nearest shoe. Also, shoes two and three are almost identical in performance with only 0.1 separating them, so they should take almost similar scores in the overall ranking.

To compute the overall scores in the 1980 *Runner's World* tests, the results of each test were replaced by a number representing where the shoe scored in relation to the mean of all shoes in the test. In statistical terms this is known as a Z score. What is important about Z scores is that they can be added together in a way raw scores cannot.

After all the test results were converted into Z scores, they were multiplied by a weighting coefficient, which scaled the score by a factor incorporating the importance of the test. In the 1980 *Runner's World* shoe survey, the weights were as follows:

Rearfoot Impact	20
Flexibility	20
Shoe Weight	20
Forefoot Impact	15
Sole Wear	10
Traction	10
Penetration	5
Heel Counter Stiffness	5
Rearfoot Stability	5

That is a total of 15 points for factors which influence rearfoot control.

Finally, all the weighted Z scores were totaled and overall listings generated. Lines were then drawn at various points in the overall listing to separate the shoes into the various star categories with the five star shoes the cream of the crop in terms of overall performance.

The weighting of the various tests is a subject of continuing debate within the running community. As new evidence becomes available showing the importance of different tests the weighting factors may be moved up or down. New factors will be added to the sequence and these will be given appropriate weights. For example, in the 1981 *Runner's World* survey (published in the October 1980 issue) the weighting value for traction was dropped from ten to five and a total of twenty was ascribed to tests measuring rearfoot control.

It is possible for a runner with a mathematical bent and a calculator or home computer to decide on his own set of weighting factors for the various tests and generate his own list of top shoes. The effort would be considerable. Easier ways of using the *Runner's World* shoe issue together with your own input are outlined in Chapter 14.

Manufacturers and Testing

In the ten years or so that running shoe surveys have been in existence there has been gradual movement among shoe manufacturers toward the position that testing should be an integral part of the research and development effort. Over the years shoe surveys have been a hotly debated issue that polarized people rather quickly. Some manufacturers were very positive about the testing process and tried hard to improve their product year by year. Others reacted aggressively against it, employing media campaigns, the skillful use of innuendo, as well as threats of violence and physical abuse against those involved in the testing process.

All too often the attitude toward testing was based on how a particular company's shoes did in a given year. For example, a manufacturer whose shoes were consistently at the bottom of most of the ratings circulated letters to dealers talking of the "pseudoscientific mumbo jumbo" used in the shoe surveys. The sales manager of another manufacturer who had been top-rated one year but slipped slightly the next wrote to his dealers claiming exaggerated durability results for his product which he later agreed were simply misleading. Occasionally a manufacturer will bring out a new shoe in October with the deliberate intent of having it on the market for twelve months before any test data is available to runners.

Shoe surveys bring out the best and worst in shoe manufacturers. They have stimulated some to build their own machines, develop their own research labs, and strive in every way possible to improve their product. Others simply turn their back and long for the days when the tape measure was the only instrument of research and testing.

While there is general acceptance of shoe testing as essential, there is an ongoing debate over the specifics of various testing protocols. But the important thing is that lines of communication are open, and each side is benefiting from the experience of the other.

The Retailer's Attitude

Shoe surveys get mixed reviews from retailers. Some use the survey carefully and point out the strong or weak features of a particular shoe to their customers. They find it an aid to an informed sale, and since many customers will walk in with the October issue of *Runner's World* under their arm, they know they are dealing with people who have done their homework.

Other retailers feel that the survey takes away their prerogative of recommending a given shoe to a given customer. Part of the problem is not with the tests themselves but with the way in which some customers use the results. The true story of a man trying to convince his wife to buy a shoe that hurt because it was a five-star shoe about sums up the problem. We will return to this topic again shortly.

The retailer's biggest problem is not with the mechanics of the survey but with the problem of inventory and availability. If a store has a quantity of shoes that performed poorly on the shoe survey then they will tie up capital and be difficult to move. On the other hand, if retailers have problems getting a supply of shoes that have done well on the tests then they may be turning customers away.

How the Runners Feel

When talking to runners there is a stronger consensus about shoe surveys than from the manufacturers or retailers. Runners are not faced with a business rationale but with the complicated task of finding a good shoe in the wealth of apparently similar models.

What shoe surveys do for the runner is to sift the wheat from the chaff in a manner which is not feasible for most individuals to do. How many shoes does the average runner own in a year? Probably three pairs at the most. So if runners can receive some guidance which will help them choose their three pairs from the other 100 types available, they are likely to be thankful.

Many runners also realize what a positive stimulus shoe testing and shoe ratings have been to the improvement of the running shoe. Marty Liquori, both a superb athlete and a businessman with more than a passing interest in selling shoes (see Chapter 16), puts it this way: "The amount of research has increased substantially since the ratings began. The ratings have made the shoes better. As a fifteen to twenty mile a day runner, they have made it more enjoyable for me." One has only to look at the way the basketball shoe has remained unchanged for the last thirty years to realize just how much running shoes have benefited from being in the spotlight.

The runner is also helped because shoes, even if they have the same name, often change from year to year. Manufacturers will use a different material or process and so change the performance of a shoe without changing its name. For runners, shoe testing put them on a more even footing with the manufacturer. Advertisements are no longer the only source of information about how a shoe performs.

How to Use Shoe Test Data

The tendency when looking at any ranking system is to reach for the top and ignore all other contenders. This is why *Runner's World* abandoned the one through thirty ranking in 1978 in favor of grouping the better shoes by levels.

But even within a particular grouping it is important to realize that each shoe has a character of its own which must be matched to your needs. Chapter 14 gives a complete explanation of how to buy a shoe, and includes a detailed discussion of how the shoe survey can help you find the right shoe.

The most important thing you can do with the shoe survey is take the time to dig beneath the overall ranking to find the strengths and weaknesses of the various shoes. Remember, there is a best shoe for you but not one that is best for everyone. Read the survey intelligently and it will be a tremendous help; use it carelessly and you might end up disappointed in your purchase.

Are Standards a Reality?

When methods of testing a product become available there is often a push to establish a standard. Several groups are currently trying to develop standards so that running shoes can bear the label "approved by this or that standards association." Whether this will ever happen and if it will benefit the runner are open questions.

The reason for doubt is that establishing a standard that everyone will agree to is necessarily long and complicated. All available methods of testing a property in the shoe must be examined, and then all objections to a particular method that has been chosen must be examined for their validity. Finally the test method must give similar results when used by different investigators.

The question of the usefulness of a standard is a more vexing one. Most consumer standards are usually of the pass/fail variety. The product either meets the standard or it does not. However, it seems to me that a running shoe requires a different approach to testing than most other consumer products. A hair dryer is either safe or unsafe, but no such statement can be made about a running shoe because it has the potential to respond differently to each user. If a line is drawn to represent the boundary between safe and unsafe shoes, it is likely to be useless in distinguishing the good from the mediocre.

Some segments of the running shoe industry are in favor of such standards for a number of reasons. First, standards will provide a certain degree of protection from product liability lawsuits. If a judge or jury can be told that a product met a particular standard they will look less favorably on a complaint against the product. Lawsuits attempting to implicate the design of a running shoe in certain injuries have been rare so far, but they can be expected to increase in the future.

Secondly, the establishment of "a middle of the road" standard will give some manufacturers of "middle of the road" shoes a certain respectability. Their shoes will for once be put in the same category as the top shoes. One may excel and one may be mediocre, but they both meet the standard.

Overall the push for standards is a positive force. It provides a forum where the industry, the academics, and the runners can sit down together and air their views about shoe design and testing. A pass/fail measurement will be useful in removing the really poor shoes from further consideration, but it is unlikely that this type of standard will help the serious runner in his or her search for a superior shoe.

8

Gimmicks or Greatness?

"Every new feature in running shoes should be considered guilty until proven innocent."
—Joe Henderson

There is a hidden literature on running shoes that most runners will never read. The source is the United States Patent Office and the language is dull, legalistic, and repetitive. The documents are full of seventy-five-word sentences, with every other word being "plurality," "substantially," or "relatively." Dull though the reading may be, the ideas contained in these documents are both a chronicle of innovations that have influenced the development of running shoes and an archive of crackpot inventions which never stood a chance.

There is something about footwear that attracts more than its share of inventors. Exactly how many patents have been filed in the last fifty years is difficult to estimate because the patent office is in a state of disarray. Computerized record-keeping is something that has not yet reached this bureaucratic backwater, and with al-

158 GIMMICKS OR GREATNESS?

most five million patents to catch up on, it is unlikely that there will be a comprehensive access system.

Mixed in among the unknown inventors from Anytown, U.S.A. is a liberal sprinkling of disclosures by Adi Dassler, Armin Dassler, Bill Bowerman, Stan James, and the like. Some ideas bear the sign of clear genius while others read like *Mad* magazine.

The two patents in Figure 8.1 and 8.2 show the extremes of the spectrum. Figure 8.1 shows Bowerman's patent No. 4,098,011 for a waffle sole incorporating wear bars, which have been a feature of the LDV for some time. Patent number 4,030,213 (Figure 8.2) was granted to one Alexander Daswick of West Pasadena, California for a highly unlikely invention: ". . . relating to certain novel and valuable improvements in sporting shoes used for running or jogging."

Although some inventions are developed by the shoe companies themselves, many are purchased by a company after a persistent inventor tries one shoe factory after another until the idea is bought. Such was the case with Nike's air shoe, the Tailwind. Inventor Frank Rudi tried several manufacturers for more than three years before Nike was finally hooked.

The major shoe companies are asked to see many different ideas in the course of a year and sometimes they simply do not recognize a good one when they see it. This happened with the split vamp shoe. The inventor, Tom Adams, got fed up with refusals and decided to start his own shoe company.

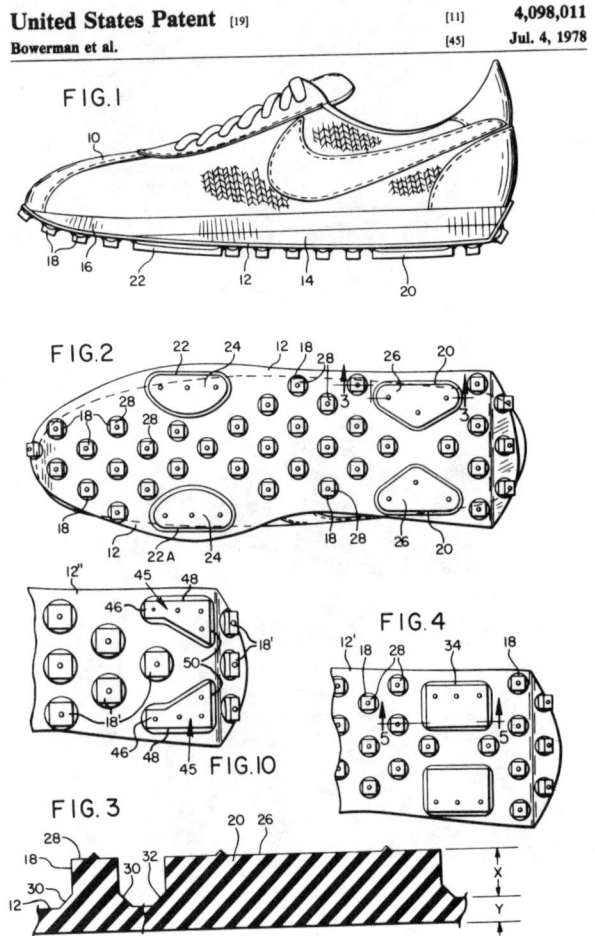

Fig. 8.1 The original drawings from a patent granted to Bill Bowerman incorporating wear bars into a waffle sole.

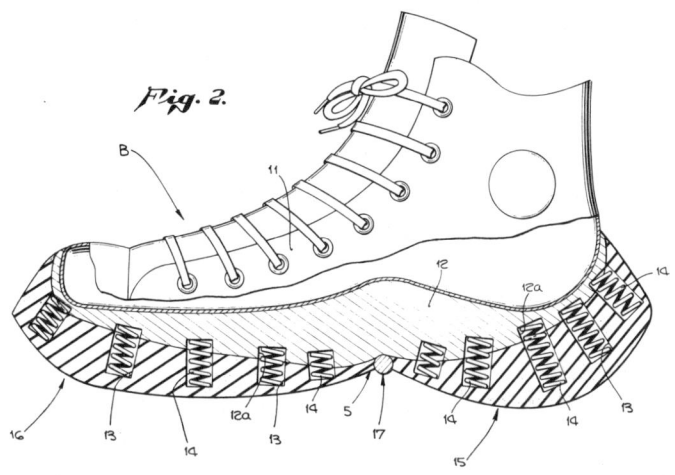

Fig. 8.2 A patent granted to Alexander Daswick describing a running shoe with springs and a single hinge point in the midfoot. Not the most likely to succeed idea of the decade!

HOW TO TREAT NEW IDEAS IN SHOES

To the runner, the importance of knowing about one invention or another is transcended by the general question: Are these special features just gimmicks, or a sign of true greatness in a shoe?

It would be an impossible task for some laboratory to devise tests for every new feature that is introduced into the running shoe market. As fast as they began to work on one idea ten more would be knocking on the door

Gimmicks or Greatness? 159

for evaluation. So when it comes to evaluating new concepts the runner is left to his or her own devices in a field where truth in advertising is sometimes pushed to very liberal limits.

When you see a new feature advertised how should you respond? Should you dash out and buy it, believing what the manufacturer says in the advertisement, or should you step back and wait awhile, think a little? My feeling is really summed up by Joe Henderson's quote which forms the start of this chapter. New ideas should be treated with healthy skepticism, until it is clear that they really are a useful innovation and not just an eye-catching gimmick designed to sell more shoes. The reason for this conservative stance is that the borderline between running in pain and running pain-free is a knife edge—an edge whose subtlety we cannot at the moment approach by measurement. Trying a new feature in a shoe can be a very risky process if it means committing yourself to the shoe for more than a short training run. Every slight change in your footwear is an invitation to potential pain or injury. This is because the shoe can cause alignment changes in the lower extremity which generate forces that your legs are not accustomed to.

As we emphasized in Chapter 7, there is no such thing as the best shoe for all runners. This is even more relevant to special features in a shoe, which may be great for some people but positively harmful to others. Suppose, for example, a shoe with good forefoot but minimal rearfoot cushioning was introduced. This might prove tremendous for a forefoot striker running a level race because of the weight saved. But it would be disastrous for a runner who first contacts the ground further back on the foot.

Where Do Innovations Come From?

Before we turn to an examination of product ideas you can find in the marketplace let's look for a moment at the process of generating new ideas. Many new concepts, as we mentioned earlier, simply "walk in" off the street. People whom shoe companies have never heard of arrive with an idea the inventor feels will revolutionize the running shoe.

Most companies will not even look at an idea until the inventor has applied for a patent. They have been burned too many times by lawsuits claiming that ideas have been stolen or plagiarized. The old adage that "there's nothing new under the sun" holds true about ninety percent of the time in the shoe industry. Most "new" ideas are simply re-inventions of concepts tried previously.

But what about the shoe companies as actors rather than reactors? There are four categories that I use to classify the way shoe manufacturers come up with new ideas of their own. They range from good to bad to ugly.

GRADING THE RESEARCH: A For Advanced

Very few shoe companies have research facilities of their own. Most have one or two test machines to make sure that the materials they receive from suppliers are of uniform quality, but this can hardly be classified as research. So the most progressive companies sponsor research projects at private or university laboratories which are equipped to measure the effects of a particular feature on the runner. This might involve a test designed to see if cushioning materials are in the right places, or if a device designed to improve rearfoot control really works. The project can be very specific—is this feature good or bad? Or it might be diffuse—can you find a way to give our running shoe better rearfoot stability?

Regardless of how the goal is defined, this approach rates A for advanced. It is A-plus if the company has their own lab, since this demonstrates that they have committed themselves to improving their product through careful research. Any research process costs time and money, the two things most shoe companies don't want to spend.

B for Better than Average

In this category, the company decides that they cannot afford to spend money on research but neither can they be without expert opinion. So they engage the services of a technical advisor or group of experts to serve as an advisory panel. These individuals might be podiatrists, orthopedists, biomechanists, coaches, or athletes. They function both as sounding boards and sources for new ideas.

This process is characterized by an absence of hard evidence but the presence of informed opinion. It rates a B for better than average, but it must be remembered that the resulting shoe is built on the basis of ideas which are not substantiated by experimentation. Experts, almost by definition, always disagree with each other and the final product will be very dependent on the ability and particular bias of the people involved.

C for Caution

The third approach to new ideas is based purely on the need to be different. The shoe company probably has an ambitious marketing manager who realizes that there are a lot of shoes out there. A distinction is sought which will make the shoe stand out from others in the marketplace. There is probably the underlying hope that the feature will be beneficial to some runners, but what matters is being different at all costs. If it takes a heel wedge that is higher, wider, and longer than any other shoe, then so be it. The key is having what the trade calls "good cosmetics"—something that stands out. This route to innovation is rated C for the caution needed in approaching the shoe which is produced at the end of the line. You must realize that the "design team" in this case might be an individual with an M.B.A. who has never run a step. It might also be someone who is an avid runner and a good thinker. There is no certainty, so caution is the word.

D for Dangerous

The last category of "innovators" would be better described as copiers. The approach here is to survey the market for the most distinctive differences and to incorporate them into a production shoe, making small changes to satisfy patent protection as necessary. This rates D for Dangerous since the maker has ignored everything but the dollar sign. They have most likely incorporated changes they do not fully understand, have not attempted to research, and whose effects on runners they don't particularly care about.

THE RUNNER AS GUINEA PIG

So how do you tell which companies fit into which categories? Until runners start demanding more justification of new ideas from the manufacturers there are, unfortunately, very few hard facts to use in evaluating special features of running shoes. The industry is completely unregulated and it is entirely possible for an innovation to be dreamed up one week and in production the next, even though the idea may turn out to be harmful.

In many cases, the manufacturer's idea of research may include you—the unsuspecting purchaser of one of the first batch of new shoes. By putting down your money you might have paid for the privilege of becoming a guinea pig.

The only recourse runners have is to complain, loudly

and frequently, if they feel they have been exploited by a new idea that was simply being tried as a test. Most companies are responsive to their mail and often use ideas from runners to modify their product.

The hope for the long term is that less conscientious manufacturers will either graduate to a sound research program or stick to producing standard shoes. There are some signs that more companies are willing to invest some of their profits in research. Ten years ago, this would have been thought unnecessary; what mattered most was cosmetics. Manufacturers know that runners are a sophisticated consumer group, but they also know that they can be lured to pay more for the promise of a safer or faster shoe. We must hope that the future will bring fewer unfulfilled promises than the past.

The rest of this chapter is devoted to five areas of innovation, grouped by the part of the shoe where the feature is found. Different lacing methods are also included although many of these can be put into practice on any shoe. Many of the novel features of running shoes will simply be described in this chapter without a pro or con statement being made. This is an honestly "open verdict" since the effectiveness of most of the features has not been subjected to scientific scrutiny.

OUTSOLE FEATURES

While nubs, ripples, and waffles are now common on the outsoles of running shoes, it is still hard for the runner to decide what configurations of the outsole are really useful. When the tread pattern has the manufacturer's name or trademark you can usually figure that the design is cosmetic.

I have to admit to being mystified by the current dominance of waffle soles in shoes that are specifically designed for road running. I'd bet that Bill Bowerman, the man who started it all, is more than a little surprised himself. Waffles were originally conceived by Bowerman as a substitute for track spikes, but soon gained wider acceptance (see Figure 8.1). They are a natural for cross-country, where adverse conditions under foot will be helped by the added traction, but for road running, what is the big advantage? Waffle-soled shoes do not have such good outsole wear properties as a full-surface outsole made from the same material. So this is an advantage for resolers and the shoe trade only. It is interesting to note in Figure 8.1 that the concept of a forefoot wear bar was also covered in the original patent, but so far as I know this feature has not been included in production running shoes.

When waffles first appeared, Dr. Stan James reported that several runners with knee pain found relief in waffle-soled shoes. This was no doubt due to the lower resistance to twisting which waffles offer. When the foot is planted with full weight, a waffle does not make such a rigid connection between the foot and the ground. Some twisting can occur without any slip at the interface, since the twisting is done by the waffles themselves.

Also, there is no denying that waffle outsoles contribute to better shock absorption. How much better will depend on the composition of the midsole. One pair of worn shoes was resoled with a waffle outsole, and then the new waffles were mercilessly ground off on a sanding machine. Although this wear was more severe than normal it resulted in a twenty percent decrease in shock absorption. The contribution in a new shoe will be considerably less than this.

Cantilevers

The purpose of the designs in Figure 8.3a and 8.3b is clear; both are intended to act as springs. You might think they have a lot in common despite the difference in size. Osaga (Figure 8.3a) and Puma (Figure 8.3b) think so too, and are currently engaged in legal wrangling to establish who owns the idea. This concept of building more shock absorption into the outsole is an intriguing one. Taken one step further, the stiffness of the springs could be varied by reinforcing the sole in a transverse direction with a suitable material. Different body weights could be accommodated and regions of the shoe could vary in stiffness.

Non-Uniform Outsoles

There are many good reasons for making different parts of the outsole in different configurations. In the simplest case we could consider the shoe to be in two parts as far as friction is concerned. If we land on the heel the rear part of the tread should prevent forward slip. And if propulsion occurs when pressure is distributed in the front part then this should halt backward slip. Although this is an oversimplified view of ground contact, it illustrates the point.

As we saw in Chapter 4, different parts of the shoe experience different forces, which suggests that materials with a range of physical properties could be used in various regions of the outsole. A few shoes like this exist, but there are also shoes which are simply different colors in different regions. The latter deserve to be ignored so that the runner can inform the manufacturer that his intelligence has been underrated.

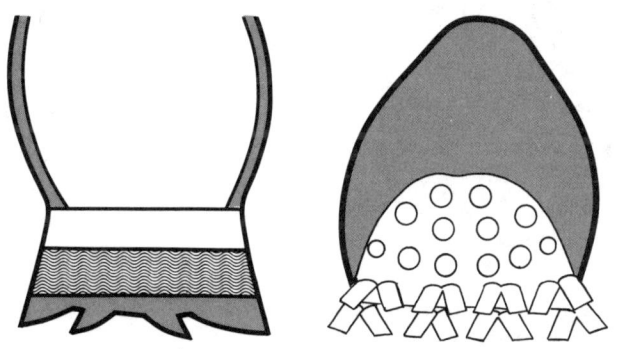

Fig. 8.3a The Osaga Cantilever. b The Puma Federbein Cantilever.

The shoe shown in Figure 8.3c is an Adidas SL 80, featuring rubber which is more abrasion resistant in the lighter shaded regions. A similar concept was used in the design of the Pony outsole (Figure 8.3d) which has a sawtooth pattern under the front inside border to provide better traction.

Replaceable Wear Plugs

A new idea introduced in 1980 by Stride Rite are replaceable plugs at points of high sole wear (Figure 8.3e). The main part of the outsole is injection-molded polyurethane, and in the early models six holes about one-quarter inch deep and three-quarters inch in diameter were left in the molded sole unit at the locations shown. SBR (styrene butadene rubber) plugs to fill the holes are supplied with the new shoes together with a few extras. The idea is that the plugs can be replaced before the surrounding outside begins to wear away.

It is a promising idea which will take some experimenting to get right. In early models the plugs projected above the outsole surface, making the effect rather like running on cleats. The prospect of losing a plug and unbalancing the contact area must also be faced. These problems can no doubt be solved and we shall probably see more shoes with "user replaceable" parts in the future.

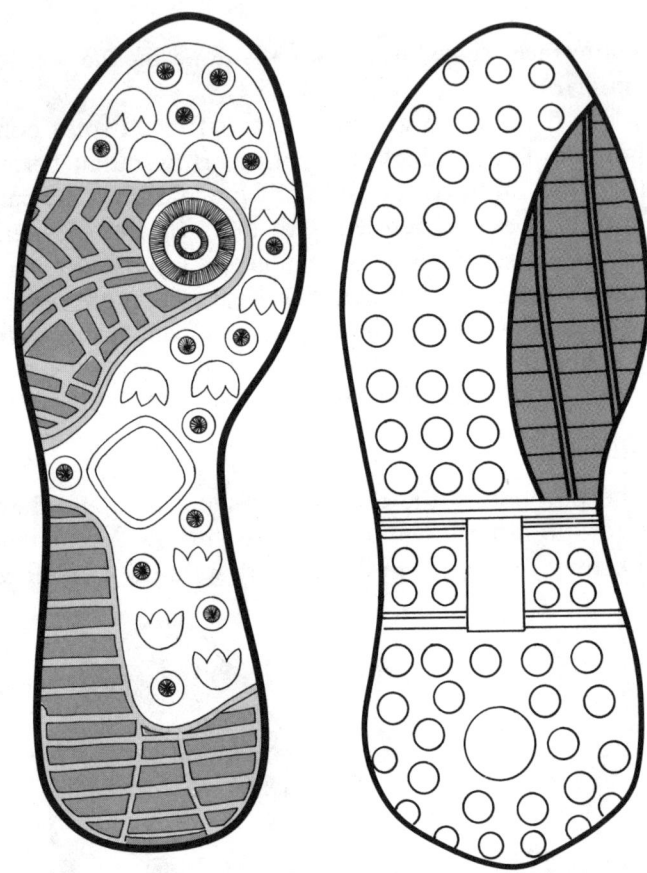

Fig. 8.3c-d The composite outsole of an Adidas SL 80. Different tread designs in regions of a Pony running shoe.

Different Soles for Different Surfaces

One of the best reasons for having several pairs of running shoes is that different surfaces will call for different traction and cushioning. An extreme example is the outsole of the Adidas Falcon (Figure 8.3f) which was described in patent No. 4,130,947 by Francis Denu. The outsole is like a winter tire tread; it will probably give better traction under muddy conditions than most other designs if it can be prevented from clogging. One of the problems with deep indentations is that they collect mud which can increase fatigue on a long, wet run.

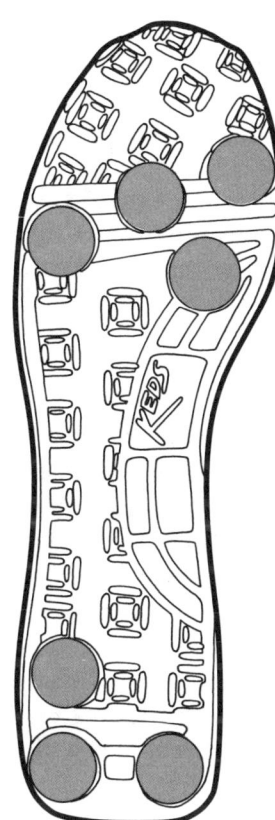
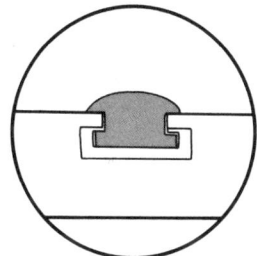

Fig. 8.3e A novel idea from Stride-Rite incorporating replaceable wear plugs (inset) into high-wear regions.

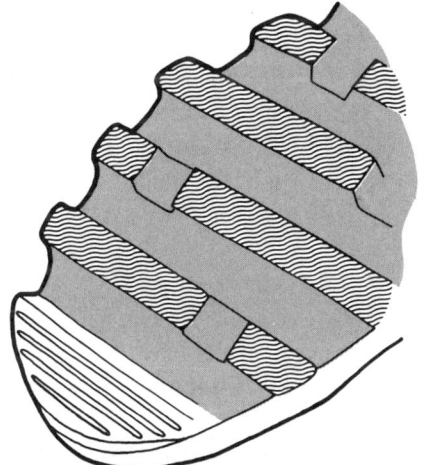

Fig. 8.3f The "winter-tire" tread of an Adidas Falcon.

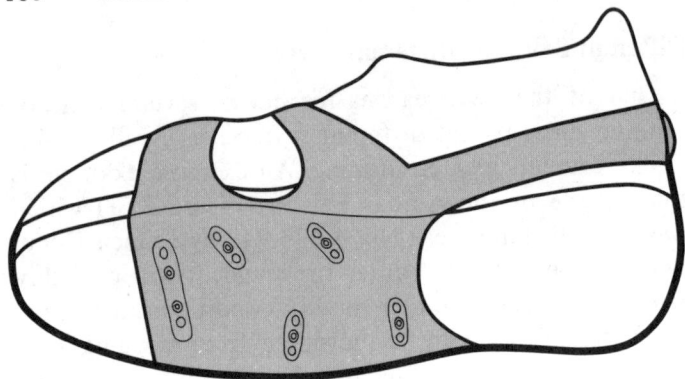

Fig. 8.3g   A snap-on device for traction on ice called "Surefoot."

An attempt to make shoes adaptable to ice is shown in Figure 8.3g. The snap-on device called Surefoot is reminiscent of the crampons often strapped to the boots of winter climbers to give them added traction on ice and snow. The Surefoot has small diameter spikes with carbide tips to penetrate ice, and larger metal cleats about one inch wide and one-sixteenth inch thick for looser terrain.

On uniformly soft terrain these accessories seem to work well, but over concrete or blacktop they tend to give somewhat of a negative heel because the cleats, which are all under the forepart of the shoe, cannot penetrate.

Running on wet pavement calls for special attention to outsole design and composition. Traction tests show that although most shoes give good traction under dry conditions, they separate rapidly into good and bad in wet, slick environments. But it's not just the outsole design that matters; the material used in the outsole has the largest influence. Large and complex tread patterns are fine for rough surfaces where there is a chance they will get added grip, but on smooth surfaces it is the interaction between surfaces at the microscopic level that makes the difference. Some indentations are certainly needed to clear excess water from the surface, but from then on traction is in the hands of the rubber chemist.

Backward Projections

One feature which probably started as a "trial balloon" was an extension of the outsole beyond the heel, tried by Adidas first in the Formula One shoe in 1977 (Figure 8.3h). This was called a spoiler and never really became popular. The theory is difficult to fathom, but what it appears to do is cause a footslapping effect in a rearfoot striker. This is possibly because contact is made slightly earlier than normal, unless the runner raises the foot slightly during the late stages of the swing phase.

MIDSOLE AND WEDGE FEATURES

Compared to other sports footwear, running shoes have made vast progress in the last decade. But one would still have to characterize the running shoe as a

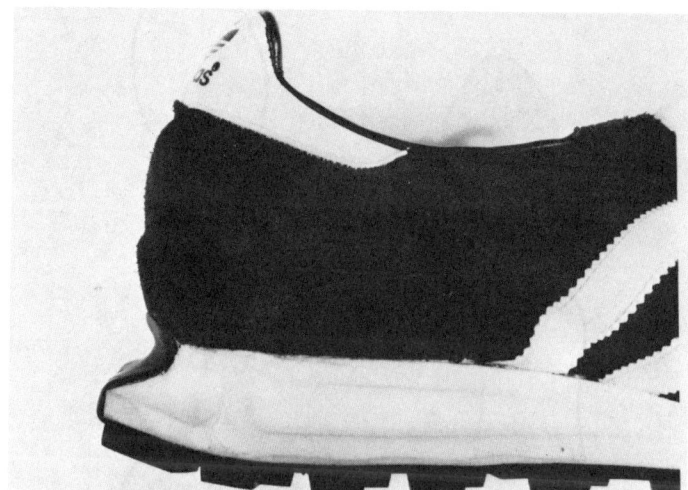

Fig. 8.3h The rearward projection of the Adidas Formula I.

relatively low technology item when the possibilities for improvements are considered. Nowhere does this possibility exist more than in the midsole and wedge. This is the very heart of the running shoe, and it is a major determinant of the most important properties of a shoe—energy absorption, flexibility, and control, among others. So far the experiments in design of this area have been fairly conservative.

Lateral Flare

First introduced in 1975, this feature has become standard in ninety percent of the shoes on the market. The midsole starts out wide at the base and gradually tapers up toward the featherline. The original goal was to improve lateral stability, to prevent the side-to-side rolling of the foot during the support phase. In 1975 Nike reasoned that if some flare added stability then more flare would add more stability. The result was the LD 1000, which had almost a one inch difference in total width at the outsole and featherline. The rest is history; see the conversation with Stan James in Chapter 16. It was quickly discovered that use of the shoe was highly correlated with lateral knee pain in runners.

This is a good example of a feature that can help some runners and harm others. The exact reason why excessive lateral flare causes knee pain is difficult to pinpoint, but is probably a combination of rapid changes in foot orientation immediately following contact, and too much restriction of normal movements which occur during support.

There is no reason that the flare should be symmetrical on the inside and outside border of the shoe. A good argument could be made for reducing the outer flare because the most resistance to an inward rolling motion is needed on the inside. This modification is shown by the dotted line in Figure 8.4a. The exception would be for runners who are habitual ankle sprainers, because turning the ankle over on the outside is by far the most common type of sprain.

On occasion, flare is used in a shoe which is already very narrow at the outsole level. This can undercut the platform on which the foot rests and make the shoe very unstable. The counter soon deteriorates as the foot "overflows" the back of the shoe. If the runner does not have a balanced gait this construction will result in the foot literally falling off the inside or outside edge early in the shoe's life.

Mixed Material Midsoles

The biggest area for potential developments in the midsole and wedge is in the use of materials with different mechanical properties for areas with different tasks to perform. Such construction is a relatively simple matter with injection molding techniques where finely defined edges can be made. One of the few current uses of this is the midsole unit from Tred 2, shown in Figure 8.4b. The construction, which Tred 2 calls the "Double D," incorporates a rearfoot section (dark in Figure 8.4b) which is harder than the forepart. Their idea is that a rearfoot striker will benefit from the firmer rearpart (in terms of rearfoot control) while the forepart will be more flexible thanks to the softer material.

My own version of this design would locate the areas of high pressure within the shoe by the techniques mentioned in Chapter 4 and build these regions, in both back and front, with a firm but shock absorbent ma-

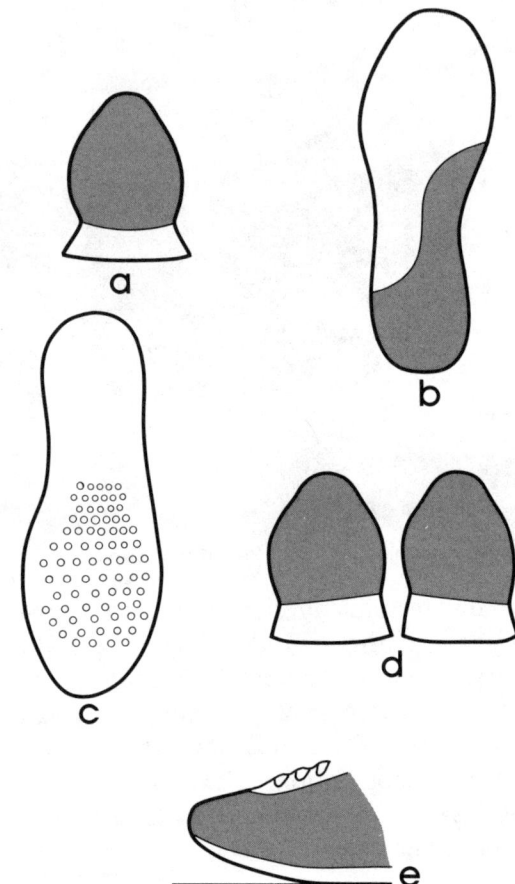

Fig. 8.4 Midsole and wedge features a) Lateral flare on a running shoe. b) The dual density midsole of the Tred 2 "double d" shoe. c) A perforated midsole from a Brooks Vantage. d) The varus wedge concept in some Brooks shoes. e) Toe spring.

terial. The rest could be modified according to the specific demands made upon different regions.

But Tred 2 has certainly led the way in showing that a midsole does not have to be a single homogeneous sheet. The midsole in Figure 8.4c looks as though it's been taken over by tunneling insects. In fact, this design attempts to avoid the apparently inverse relationship between shock absorption and flexibility.

Generally, the more flexible the shoe the worse it will do on forefoot shock absorption tests. But experiments have shown that small holes in the forepart of the midsole can improve flexibility with only minor changes in shock absorption. The technique was first introduced by Brooks in their Vantage Supreme in 1978 and has since been used by other manufacturers in both the forefoot and rearpart. The weight saved by this process is negligible and is not a factor in the design.

The Varus Wedge Explained

There is often confusion about what a varus wedge really is. This is because the word varus is not clearly understood, and because the side-to-side varus wedge is confused with the normal front-to-back heel wedge in a running shoe (see Figure 5.1).

The varus wedge, as Figure 8.4d shows, is designed so that the platform where the foot is placed is higher on the inside of the shoe than the outside. This is accomplished by tapering the midsole so that it is thicker on the inside border. The effect is like standing on the crown of the road. Both feet are on the side of a hill which has its apex in the midline of the body.

The idea behind the varus wedge is this. For two reasons the foot tends to pronate beyond the neutral position during the early stance phase. First, the whole lower extremity has the functional varus (discussed in Chapter 5) which occurs because the foot is placed underneath the body during the support phase. Second, one of the most common dynamic alignment problems in running is excessive pronation during the early contact with the ground. The varus wedge is designed to reduce the pronation occurring for both of these reasons.

Exactly how the varus wedge works is shown in Figure 8.5. On the left side of the figure you see the leg of our anatomical model, introduced in Chapter 3, in a position of functional varus during the support phase. Notice what has happened to the subtalar joint, which is the joint between the talus and rearfoot. It has had to pronate so that the inside edge of the foot could touch the ground.

Now, you will recall that varus means "turning in" toward the midline of the body, and on the right side of Figure 8.5 a wedge has been inserted under the rearfoot. This turns the rearfoot in toward the midline of the body. That's why it's called a varus wedge. The effect of the wedge has been to bring the subtalar joint

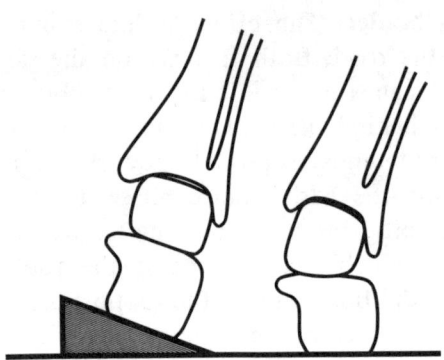

Fig. 8.5 The rationale behind the varus wedge. Since the leg is under the midline of the body during the support phase, the buildup under the inside border of the shoe will keep the foot in a neutral position during contact.

back into a neutral position; the rearfoot and leg are now in alignment.

The varus wedge is not a new idea to footwear. It has been used by specialists for many years as a correction for excessive pronation. It was even suggested, in a classic book written by Dickson and Diveley in 1939, as a feature that should be included in "a properly constructed basketball shoe." But it was new in running shoes when the Brooks company introduced it in their 1978 line on the advice of podiatrist Steve Subotnick.

For most runners the varus wedge will be a positive feature. For others it is something that should be approached with caution. You may be one of those rare runners who run on the outside edge of their shoes throughout the stance phase (see Figure 4.7). If so a varus wedge will make you fall off the outside of your shoe, and may increase the risk of both inversion sprains of the ankle and knee pain. If you do pronate excessively you may require more or less than the normal four degrees which the Brooks shoes have.

Some podiatrists feel that a correction built into a shoe verges on a "treatment" and that a varus wedge should be prescribed on a custom basis by a doctor. But despite the risks of putting a shoe with a varus wedge on a runner for whom it is unsuitable, there have been few bad reports from runners. A leaflet is enclosed with the shoes describing the initial period that may be needed to get used to the new alignment. If you find that a varus wedge shoe is causing pain then you should stop using the shoe.

Toe Spring

When shoe bottoms were made from rigid material such as wood, the only way to make them walkable was to turn up the forepart so that even though normal forefoot flexion could not occur a toe-off situation was possible. The raising of the forepart of the shoe out of the ground plane is known as toe spring.

In recent years the shoe manufacturers have begun to introduce toe spring in greater amounts each year (Figure 8.4e). The thinking is that the running stride will be more efficient since there will be a natural rocking forward onto the forepart of the shoe. As far as I know the evidence for this supposedly "more efficient toe-off" does not exist except in the minds of manufacturers and inventors. There has not been one experiment to my knowledge in which this feature has been tested in any quantitative way.

It seems likely that excessive toe spring could lead to problems of the plantar surface of the foot. I would like to see the trend toward greater toe spring stopped until we understand the process a little better. Excessive toe spring can occur during manufacture if the shoe is not lasted correctly, and the consumer should watch out for this by standing the shoe on a flat surface before making a purchase. If it seems that the toe is turned up excessively then don't buy it.

LACING MODIFICATIONS

The vamp (or upper) and lacing systems are critically important elements of the running shoe. Some people have the feet and the running style which will fit any kind of shoe. For others the type of upper and lacing will make the difference between a useful shoe and a shoe that is a failure.

Lacing does much more than close the shoe. In a properly constructed shoe it allows the upper to apply uniform pressure over the forefoot. If width sizes are not available, a good lacing system can also compensate for a shoe which might otherwise be too narrow. There is a large number of lacing methods and we shall examine some of them here.

The Split Vamp

A feature of the Kaepa shoe shown in Figure 8.6a is described under United States patent number 3,546,796. The vamp is in two parts so that the forefoot can be laced to one tension and closed. The part of the vamp over the instep is then laced separately. This system can accommodate considerable differences in foot size. The initial patent disclosure stresses the use of the shoe for someone with a "high instep." In this

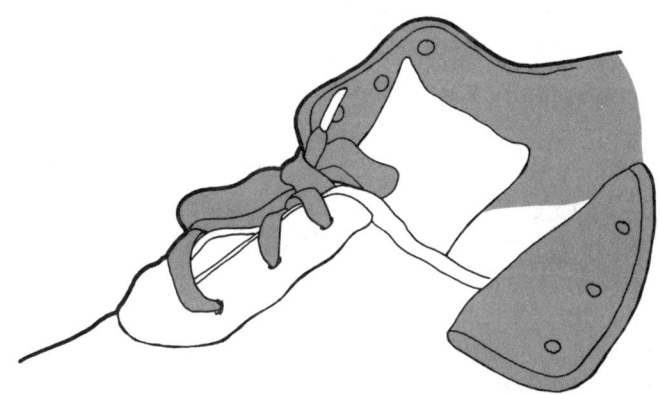

Fig. 8.6a The Kaepa shoe, which has a split vamp with separate laces for the forefoot and midfoot regions.

172 GIMMICKS OR GREATNESS?

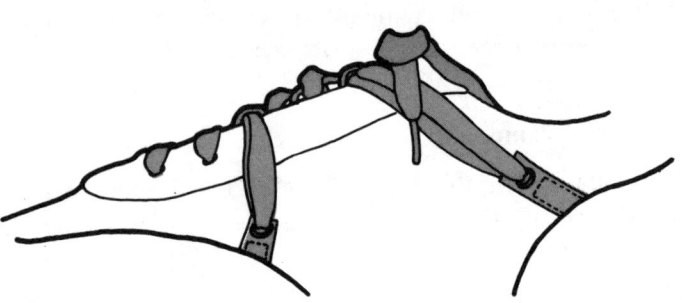

Fig. 8.6b Tabs in the rearfoot and forefoot designed to increase control of the foot.

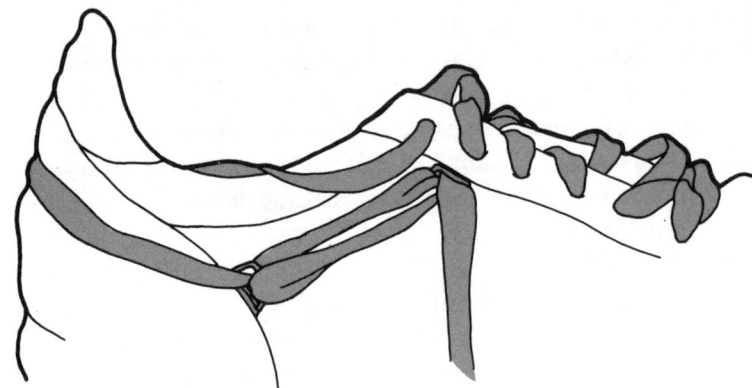

Fig. 8.6c A separate lace around the rearfoot—a feature of the Etonic Stabilizer.

type of foot, the front part of the vamp can be tightened over the forefoot while the separate back vamp can be fixed at a wider spacing. This presents new options for people with hard-to-fit feet.

Supplementary Lacing Systems

This is another new-but-old idea. Look back at Figure 2.14 where you see a picture (taken in 1904) of one of England's most versatile runners, Alfred Shrubb, who had just broken the British four-mile record on grass. Notice that Shrubb's right shoe had a strap which came up over the instep. Other photos show Shrubb with this strap on his left shoe, and still others with straps on both. This may be because at this time in England races were held along straight courses and both clockwise and counterclockwise on tracks. The picture from a Spalding catalog of 1894 (Figure 8.7) shows the shoe he was probably wearing.

Baseball shoes have traditionally had leather "outside collar ties." Early soccer boots always had a loop on back of the heel to thread the long laces through, which were then tied underneath the sole. Recent developments in added lacing are shown in Figure 8.6b. The shoe shown is a composite of the Brooks Hugger GT and a Saucony TC 84, while Figure 8.6c is an Etonic Stabilizer.

The Brooks and Etonic shoes attempt to provide a firmer link between the rear part of the shoe and the foot. By tensioning the upper in the rearfoot it seems likely that improved rearfoot control would result, although no experiments have yet been performed to show if this is true. The Saucony shoe has forefoot strapping which offers the possibility of better forefoot control; this may be important for a runner whose foot continually seems to be falling off the edge of the shoe due to a misalignment in the forefoot.

Note that the additional anchor points are not just attached to upper material. They are almost always joined to a "leather stay" which is part of the foxing and provides a firm support for the side wall of the shoe.

It has been claimed that the three Adidas stripes and other markings evolved into trademarks after initially being designed for the same function as these lacing systems. The idea was that the stripes joined the throat to the featherline, providing much more support for the foot than the upper alone. This explanation is supported by photographs of early Dassler brothers shoes shown in Chapter 2. Considering the variety of nonsupportive materials used for the stripes, swooshes, and stars on logos today, the feature seems to have become cosmetic despite its original purpose.

Nonaligned Eyelet Holes

Introduced on the Nike Bermuda in 1979, this method (shown in Figure 8.6d) features alternate lacing holes which are either high on the vamp in the usual position or approximately one centimeter lower toward the foxing. The lower holes are reinforced by a leather strip attached to the foxing.

The idea is to give both better fit and more forefoot support via the direct link to the midsole. Some runners with narrow feet have used only the single row of lower holes in an attempt to draw the sides of the throat even closer together.

Speed Lacing

In a standard lacing pattern there is a large amount of friction between the lace and individual eyelet holes. This can lead to loosening as the movement of the foot allows equalization of forces between various parts of the throat.

With speed lacing, shown in Figure 8.6e, the friction is considerably reduced by avoiding contact between the lace and a leather or suede leather throat. Contact instead is between the lace and a plastic or polyethylene 'D' ring. Force applied to the end of the lace causes tension at all points on the throat. This type of lacing is also much less likely to loosen during use if the initial tension is good.

As the name implies, speed lacing is much quicker to get in and out of. It is friction between the lace and throat that slows down this process. In shoes with speed lacing it is important to look for a well-padded tongue,

174 GIMMICKS OR GREATNESS?

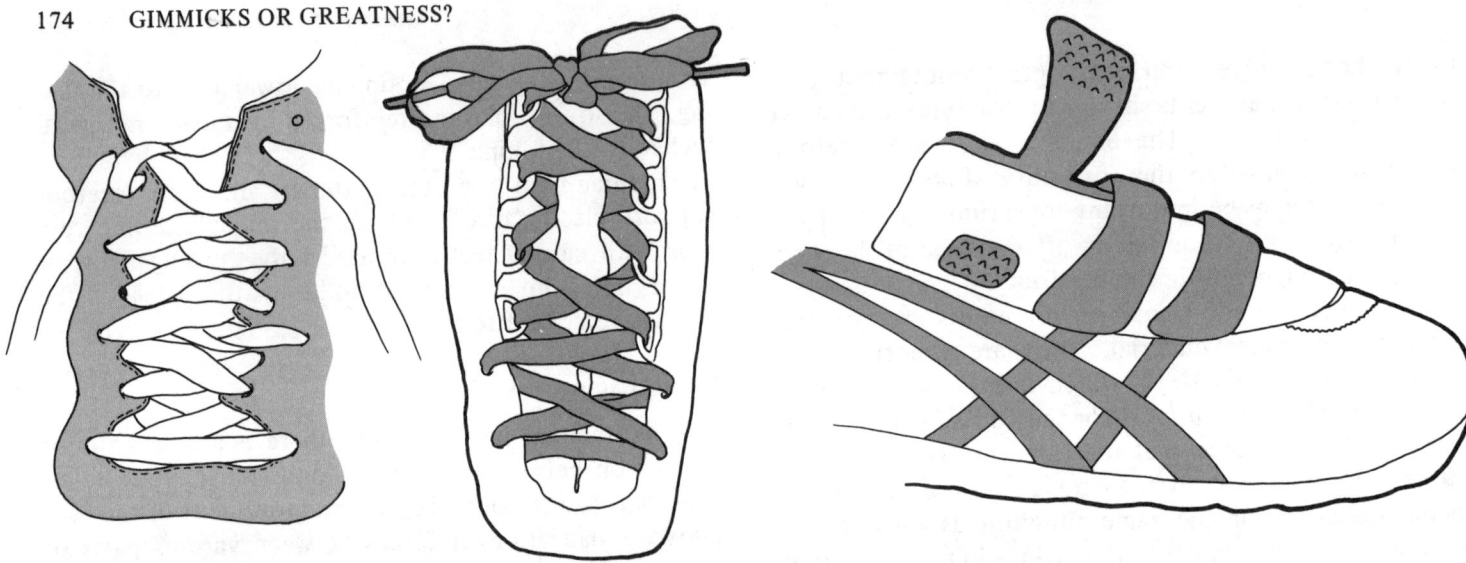

Fig. 8.6d-e Nonaligned lace holes on the Nike Bermuda. Speed lacing of the top four holes, designed for quicker entry and exit as well as more even pressure distribution.

Fig. 8.6f Velcro closing.

so that the plastic rings will not cause pressure problems on the foot's upper surface.

Velcro Closure

A promising feature introduced in the early seventies by Puma, then dropped suddenly, was a Velcro closing (Figure 8.6f). Velcro consists of a matrix of tiny nylon hooks on one end of the link and a diffuse anchor layer, which holds the hooks, on the other. The strength of this type of closure seems entirely adequate for the job but what has hindered wider use is its cost; Velcro closure costs about three times the standard lacing pattern. ASICS Tiger and Mizuno have one or two shoes with this type of closure in their domestic lines, but these have not been imported yet into the United States.

Novel Lacing Techniques

Before leaving the topic of lacing, some mention of the different ways that the laces can be tied seems appropriate. John Thornton, an English expert on shoes and shoemaking, described ten ways to lace a shoe in a trade publication in 1963. Some were merely cosmetic

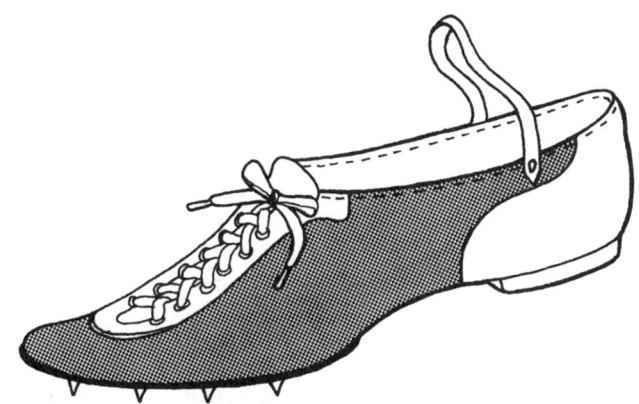

Fig. 8.7 A Spalding shoe from 1894, with an instep band designed to keep the shoe from slipping off the heel in muddy terrain.

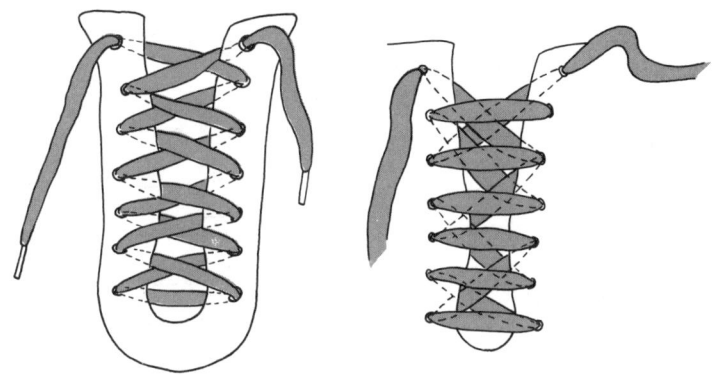

Fig. 8.8a-b Conventional diagonal or chevron lacing pattern. Conventional parallel lacing.

variations, but the most applicable of his methods, together with one or two others, are shown in Figure 8.8.

Running shoes are characterized by a long "U" throat or a "lace-to-the-toes" throat, while most casual shoes only lace up over the instep. Lacing is very important to the runner. Each time the foot contacts the ground, there is a force equal to about half the runner's body weight which makes the foot slip forward. The friction between outsole and ground is generally high, so the platform of the shoe stays fixed. The foot, however, if the closing of the upper is not adequate, will move forward. Then the toes and toenails will suffer and the top part of the foot will become irritated.

Most running shoes have seven pairs of eyelets along the stays which make up the throat. Some have six pairs. The older New Balance shoes (320, 305) have only four pairs of eyelets. This was possible because the shoes came in width sizes, and accommodation to a wider or narrower foot could be achieved in construction of the vamp.

The odd or even number of eyelets does influence the way in which closure can be made. Figures 8.8a and b show the traditional diagonal or chevron pattern lacing, and parallel lacing. The problem of laces creating undue pressure on the top of insteps has been generally avoided in modern running shoes by the use of well-padded tongues and flat cotton laces. If there is

GIMMICKS OR GREATNESS?

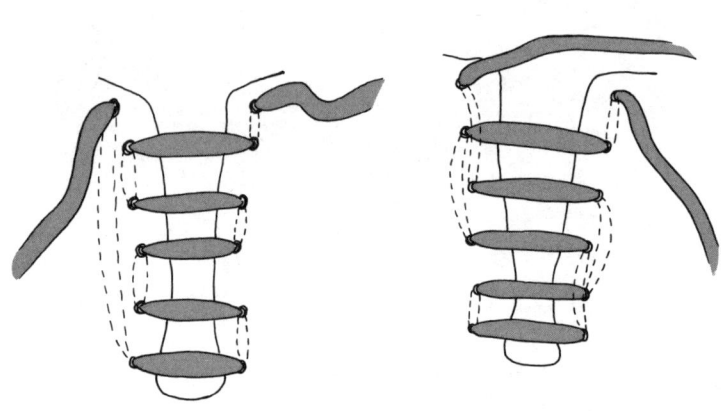

Fig. 8.8c-d Two additional techniques for parallel lacing offering different pressure distributions.

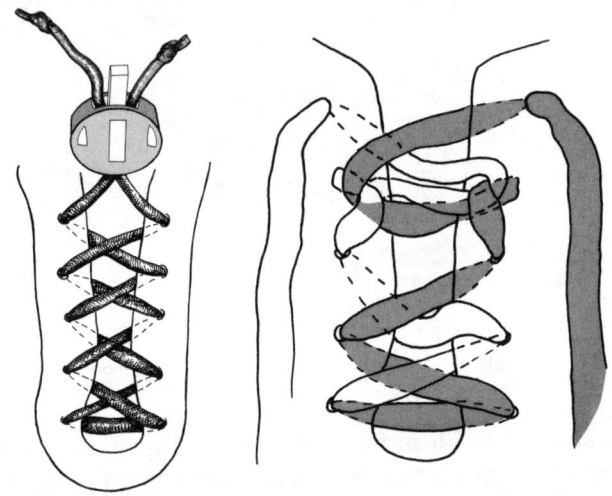

Fig. 8.8e-f A toggle designed for rapid closure. A means of equalizing the pressure at the top of the throat by making loops with one side of the lace and passing the other side through it.

still a pressure problem, one of the parallel techniques shown in Figures 8.8c and 8.8d could be employed.

Various lacing methods have been used to eliminate the tying of a bow. They are not likely to be of use to the runner since the shoe would amost certainly loosen. An alternative currently being tried with elastic laces uses a sliding toggle closing (Figure 8.8e) similar to that used on backpacks.

Tom Adams, the inventor of the Kaepa shoe, and Don Marron, a Syracuse podiatrist, both recommend the system shown in Figure 8.8f which essentially creates speed lacing out of a conventional throat. The pressure created by the cross lacing on two parts of the stay gives a definite feeling of greater support. This lacing is much more effective on a vamp with a smaller number of eyelets.

AIR SHOES

When air shoes first appeared they were hailed by many as the shoes of the future. Early designs have left some runners shouting for more and others shouting no more. Why is it that air has fascinated inventors over a long period of time? Well, it's light and cheap, but more importantly it can exhibit a wide range of mechanical properties by changing its pressure and by restricting its flow between different chambers. This creates the possibility of accommodating different body weights and foot types. A further possibility is that an enclosed capsule of air can store and return energy during the contact phase.

A number of problems have prevented air shoes from becoming more popular. Air is remarkably difficult to encapsulate without leakage. Many of the plastics which are easily molded will eventually release their air if there is a pressure gradient over a long period of time. Traumatic puncture is also possible with some designs. Once the air is encapsulated it is both expensive and difficult to build this capsule into a midsole with the desired mechanical properties. It is much easier to cut out a single piece of material such as EVA than to build a container which will restrain a column of air.

The properties of encapsulated air are also temperature dependent, so when the shoe warms up on a run it will offer a different stiffness to the foot. It will also be different during hot and cold weather. A major problem is that controlling the flow of air among various parts of the shoe requires more know-how than is currently available. Biomechanics has not yet provided information on how the pressure changes in various regions of the sole during ground contact. Once this is known the design of air shoes will be much easier.

There are three basic choices in an air shoe. First, how many chambers will there be, and where will they be placed? Second, what type of connection will there be between chambers, and will these incorporate valves with velocity dependent flow rates? Third, what pressure will the air or other gas be under.

There are four types of air shoes currently being marketed or developed which solve these problems in different ways. We shall look at each in turn.

As Figure 8.9a shows, the design patented by Karhu is simply a circular gap in the midsole. The original patent allows for multiple chambers under the heel and

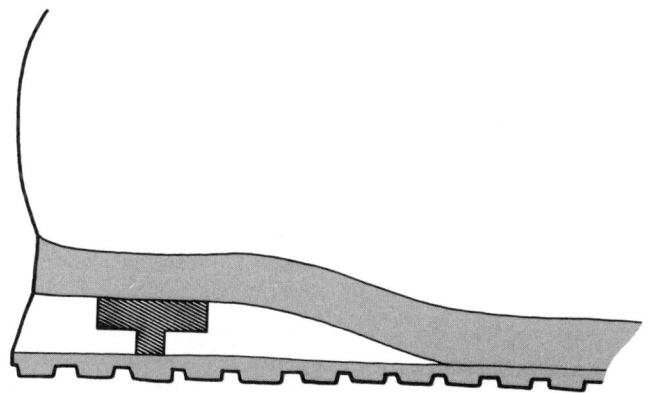

Fig. 8.9a Chambers of air at atmospheric pressure in a design patented by Karhu in 1978.

arch, as well as the circulation of air, displaced around the chamber, via valves and tubes. To date these features have not been built into a production model. One would think it would be relatively easy to puncture the air cavity by piercing the thin outsole, although the manufacturers tell me they have never seen this happen. The intent of the invention as described in the patent documents is not simply to improve shock absorption, but also ". . . to provide a shoe construction that is capable of supporting the foot while adapting the shoe to feet of different shapes. . . .".

We shall discuss in the next section some more effective ways of adapting the shoe to the foot without the need to perforate the midsole.

Aroused by the classic advertisements from Nike some six months before it was available, runners were clamoring to buy the shoe called the Tailwind when it appeared, despite the fact that it was the first training shoe to break the fifty dollar price barrier. The construction of this shoe is shown in Figure 8.9b. A series of polyurethane tubes is imbedded in an injection molded midsole. Only the two outside tubes are connected and all contain freon gas pressurized to about three atmospheres. Present versions of the shoe have no device to control the flow of air along the length of the shoe. The midsole is shaped to give a heel/forefoot height differential, and there is a stabilizing bar under the heel to provide some rearfoot stability.

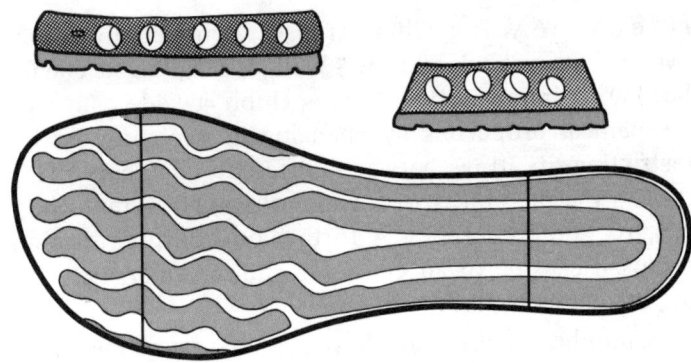

Fig. 8.9b Sections along and across the midsole of the Nike Tailwind. The plastic tubes contain pressurized Freon gas.

Early versions of the Tailwind ran to mixed reviews. Some runners, particularly those who had suffered foot and leg injuries, found that the shoe allowed them to continue training when other shoes would not. The 1980 *Runner's World* survey showed why, as the shoe trounced its competition in forefoot impact properties by a staggering eighteen percent and came in near the top in rearfoot impact.

However, the tests also showed where runners were having problems. The Tailwind ranked sixty-seven out of eighty-five entries in rearfoot control. The midsole material used was simply too mushy to give the support that many runners needed.

An intriguing new facet to the story was added by an experiment conducted for Nike by Dr. Ned Fredericks at the University of Montana. In a controlled laboratory study Fredericks found that a group of eleven runners were, on average, almost three percent more efficient when running in Tailwinds as opposed to another Nike shoe, the LDV. This increased efficiency is presumably due to improved return of stored energy from the midsole. We shall return to this topic in Chapter 11.

As I have stated already, it is my feeling that the most important feature in a training shoe is its capacity to protect the foot. Improved efficiency is certainly an added bonus but it is probably the last factor in line as a basis for choice.

In short, the 1979 Tailwind was not a great shoe. However, if increased efficiency, good impact response, and rearfoot control can be combined into a single shoe it will be a major advance. It should be recalled that the Tailwind was a first generation shoe; subsequent models can be expected to consolidate the strengths and improve upon its weaknesses.

The device shown in Figure 8.9c resembles an air mattress in the shape of a shoe insert. There is some doubt at the time of writing as to whether Pony or Brooks owns the rights to this device. The current design, which is still being tested by both companies, has transverse air pockets which are inflated to the desired pressure by a pump. The valve is at the side of the shoe. Individual chambers are connected by openings which can incorporate valves to control the flow of air. When

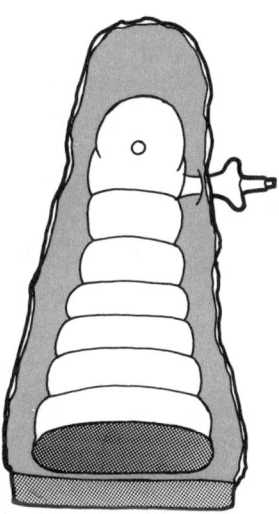

Fig. 8.9c   An in-shoe air mattress-type device tested by Brooks in 1979.

there is pressure under the rearfoot the chamber in that region can slowly empty to provide a cushion.

Predictably, an early problem was that the device lost air over a period of running. That has been improved in later models. The important aspect of this air shoe is that it opens up the prospect of adjustable air pressure for different individuals and different surfaces. Although research is still required to identify optimum combinations of pressure, running style, body weight, and running surfaces, the future is bright if technical and materials problems can be overcome.

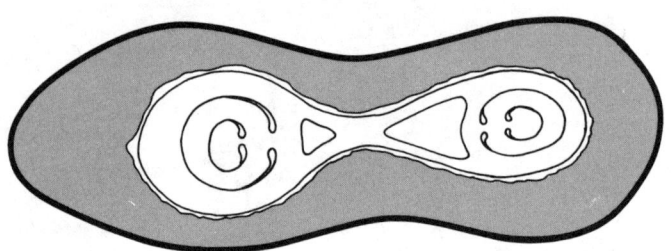

Fig. 8.9d A further prototype from Brooks with sealed compartments of pressurized air set into the midsole.

The device shown in Figure 8.9d is in some ways similar to the Tailwind. Rather than mold the air insert into an injected midsole, Brooks, who owns this design, sculpted part of the normal foam midsole away to make room for what is basically an air cushioned heel seat and metatarsal pad with interconnecting tubes.

It is too early to judge this design, but runners can figure that one way or another, manufacturers seem determined that there is air in their future.

SOCKLINERS AND SPECIAL INSERTS

Almost every running shoe is built on a last with a flat bottom, but the underside of your foot is far from flat. What lies on top of the insole board is therefore very important as far as matching the foot to the shoe.

Ski boot makers solved this problem a long time ago by providing stores with a mold which will customize the inside of the boot in the store. But the problem in a running shoe is very different. In skiing the foot is held absolutely rigid, while in running there is a tremendous amount of foot movement. So imprisoning the foot in a rigidly molded container will not succeed in the running shoe.

A number of manufacturers have put a device inside their shoes which, after a few miles of running, will customize the footbed to the wearer's foot. The Brooks "soft support" was the first such device introduced into the Vantage in 1977. (A microscopic picture of this insert was shown earlier in Chapter 5.) In the forefoot the soft support is about seven millimeters thick, under the heel about five millimeters, and more than one centimeter thick under the arch. The whole unit is covered with a piece of terrycloth (Fig. 8.10a).

Within fifty miles this unit will have taken a pressure set. It becomes paper thin over areas of high pressure, but retains its body under low pressure. Thus it becomes a conforming footbed.

Nike used a similar approach in their Liberator with a "permafoam" insole. It is more dense and thinner than the soft support. This means that there will be less room for adaptation but also less change in overall dimensions.

Besides the sockliners that are in new shoes, a variety of products which you can buy as supplementary inserts is available. One such product, called the Foam-Gard

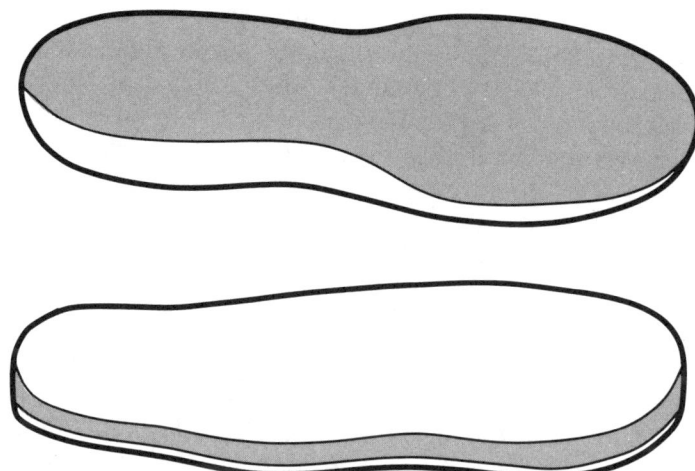

Fig. 8.10a-b The custom contour device from Brooks (see Figure 6.10). The two-component "Footbed" by Foamguard.

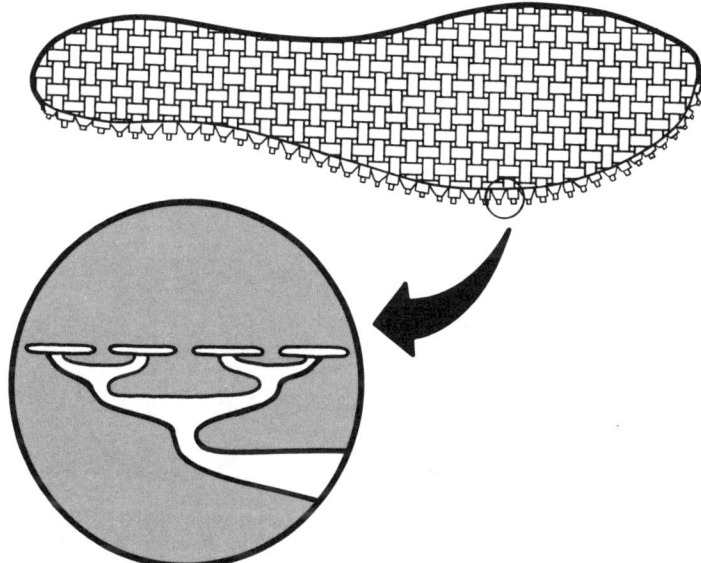

Fig. 8.10c The Bostonian "Pacer" unit built from Hytrel, which features a nesting of cantilevers of increasing size toward the base.

"footbed," is shown in Figure 8.10b. This is a sandwich of two foams with different properties. One is designed to take the shape of the foot permanently, while the other rebounds between runs so that it maintains a certain amount of shock absorption.

An intriguing insert called the "Pacer," developed by the Bostonian Company, is shown in Figure 8.10c. At the time of writing this is only used in some Japanese running shoes. The main property of this insert is that it has two degrees of firmness. It yields easily to a small object such as the underside of a toe, but is firm to pressure from a larger area. You can see exactly how it works in the inset to the figure. Localized pressure causes one of the small beams to bend. If all four pads on one arm have equal pressure, then the large beam will not bend because it is much stiffer. The properties also seem very stable with time, since the unit is made by the injection molding of a plastic called Hytrel. The beauty of this design is that the mechanical properties can be modi-

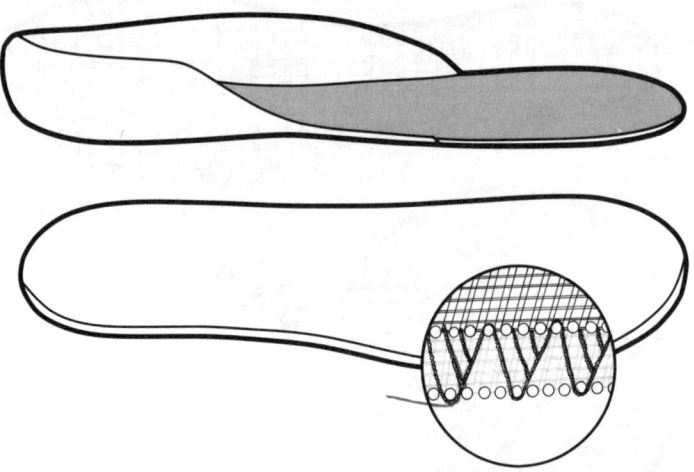

Fig. 8.10d-e The "suophas"—single unit one piece heel and arch support—used in Etonic shoes. The "Profoot" sockliner designed to enhance air circulation under the foot.

fied at will, and they can vary in different parts of the insole. As more research is done to determine the optimum size of the pads, their spacing, and the size of the beams, this design should lead to important improvements in foot comfort.

The insert used in Etonic shoes has received a lot of attention. Designed by podiatrist Rob Roy McGregor, it has two parts. The basic sock is one-eighth inch foam rubber covered with a cotton drill. Underneath the rear-part of the sockliner, extending upward around the inside of the shoe, is a heel cup (Figure 8.10d) which thickens considerably in the long inside arch. Etonic calls this device a "suophas"—an acronym for "single unit one piece heel and arch support." It takes some compression set during the early life of the shoe, but provides the heel with a considerably better fit.

Another interesting insert is the "profoot," shown in Figure 8.10e. This is made of a product called Therma-flex K which, as you see from the magnified section of the figure, is like a series of small bridges which support the foot. Because of the open weave design, air can circulate under the foot, which is not possible in most other designs. So the possibilities are a layer of warm air in winter or cool air in the summer. For cooling to occur air must be able to circulate or it will simply heat up to foot temperature.

The topic of inserts which provide additional support to the arches is dealt with separately in Chapter 12.

WHAT WILL THE FUTURE BRING?

While this chapter has presented a broad selection of design innovations currently available in shoes, it also seems like a good place to speculate on what we might see in the future. Starting with uppers, we have to realize that there are hundreds of materials which have not yet been tried in running shoes. To date, uppers have been either leather, nylon, or a blend of the two.

The three- or four-part sandwich which we now see in an upper is probably unnecessary since a thin film of strong material would do the job. It may be that uppers in the future will be made by spraying a compound over the top of thin supports which affix the bottom of the shoe.

In racing shoes it may be feasible to do away completely with the upper. Patent No. 4,107,857, issued to Gerard Devlin and shown in Figure 8.11, seems quite close to the idea of a skeletal shoe that Bruce Tulloh, the barefoot English runner, had dreamed of (see Chapter 16). As long as the bottom is firmly held on, the upper is not really necessary under good conditions.

It is probably in the midsole where the greatest advances are going to occur. The single most important development will likely be the production of "tuned shoes." These are specifically designed for the physical and biomechanical characteristics of an individual runner. This will first happen for the elite athletes, and the spinoff may be shoes for people with a given body weight and running style. This will allow shock absorption and energy return to be maximized.

Another likely direction is a component shoe kit which will allow runners, under the supervision of a qualified technician, to put together the right combination in the shoe store. Adidas has made a start in this direction with the shoe shown in Figure 8.12, which they call the L.A. Trainer. The plugs through the mid-

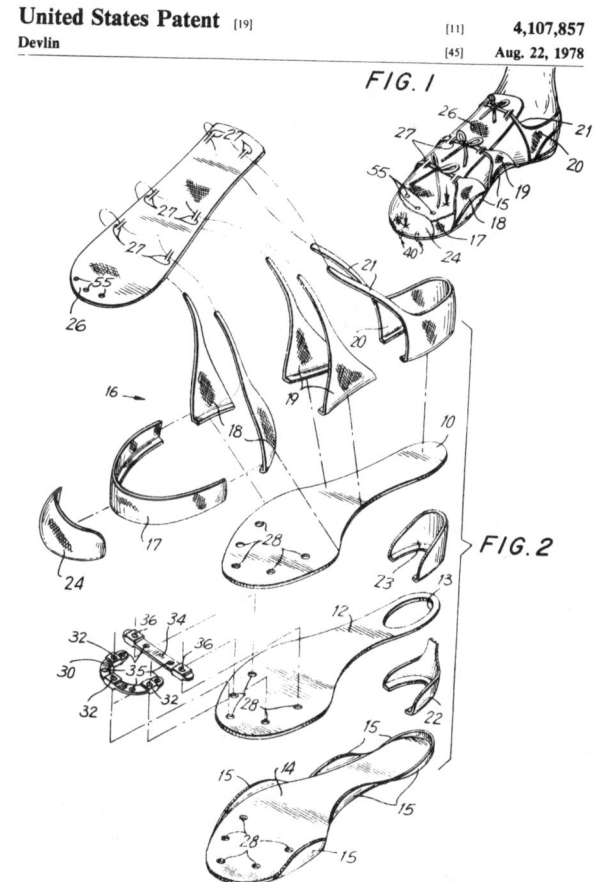

Fig. 8.11 A patent for a "skeletal shoe" which may become a familiar design for racing shoes in the future.

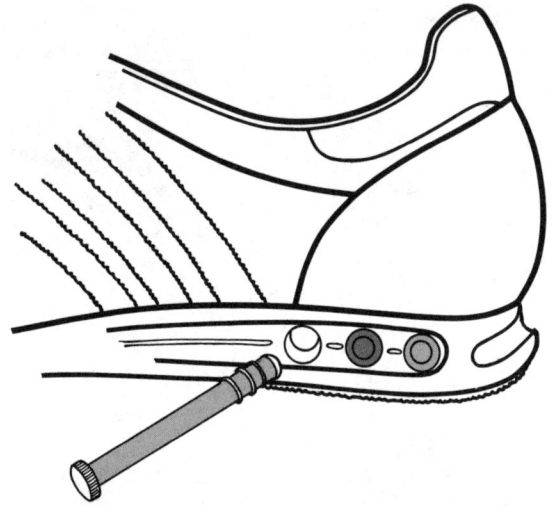

Fig. 8.12 The Adidas L.A. Trainer with removable plugs to change the stiffness of the midsole.

sole are supplied in three different hardness values and also can be left out completely. A large number of combinations of midsole responses are therefore possible. A light runner might use two of the softer plugs while a heavy runner would choose three of the stiffest plugs to give improved rearfoot control. A more elaborate example of the kit idea might provide several varus or valgus corrections in the rearfoot and forefoot together with different thicknesses of midsole or wedge materials. Width and length variations between the left and right feet could easily be accommodated, and some form of molding the footbed would customize the interface for the individual. This composite approach is the only way to provide for individual requirements while avoiding a massive inventory of shoes. The most difficult thing is to determine the exact requirements for each runner. This point is given further attention below and in Chapter 14.

We will probably see manufacturers supplying more than just one pair of sockliners in the future. This is particularly true for devices which contribute considerably to shock absorption but change their properties within the course of 100 miles or so. Memory foams will make their mark in the next few years, and we shall see more serious attempts to make the inside of the shoe conform to the foot.

Outsoles with interchangeable components will also become more widespread. The replaceable wearplug that we saw earlier in the Keds shoe will probably evolve into designs in which whole sections of the sole can be interchanged for running under different conditions. The adjustable shoe will probably become a reality. Part of the tuning process mentioned earlier will be an adjustment for the surface and speed of running. Air midsoles offer considerable possibilities in this respect. It will also be within reach to adapt to warm, cold, and wet weather using an adjustable component system.

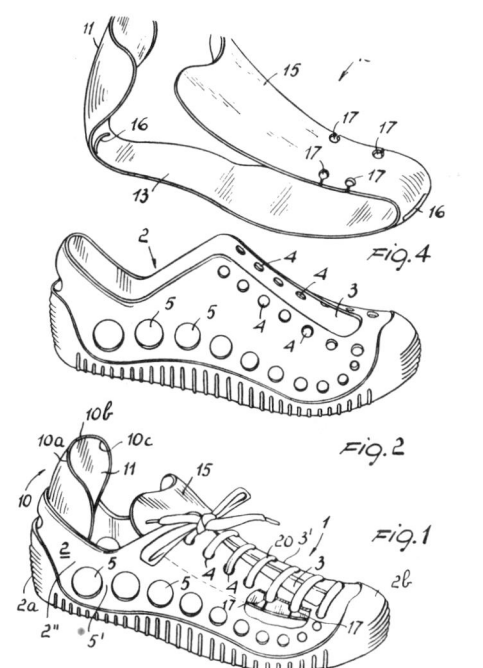

Fig. 8.13 1979 U.S. patent granted to Frank Vaccari for a component shoe—an idea which may find application in running shoes.

Some of the ideas shown in Figure 8.13, which is a patent granted to Frank Vaccari, could be adapted to these goals.

Finally, there has to be a better way to close shoes than laces. Our distant ancestors, who were chasing down now-extinct relatives of the bison, tied their shoes to their feet in much the same way as we do today. Manufacturers seem slow or unwilling to experiment with different types of closure.

Running Style Centers

Part of the problem in customizing shoes on the basis of running style is that the runner has to know something about his or her style. Very few individuals have access to the facilities of a biomechanics laboratory. But I believe we will see the growth of centers which will allow runners to learn the subtleties of their style, foot type, and foot size in a way that we can now only dream of. Runners today only get professional help when they are injured, but in my opinion we should encourage the trend toward preventative approaches in sports medicine. Much of the equipment needed to analyze a runner's motion is the same as that used in a sophisticated orthopedic clinic, rehabilitation center, or biomechanics laboratory. Most of these facilities are lying idle at least twelve hours per day so they could be used, particularly in the major cities, to provide this service. Such analysis will of course cost money, but it would be an expenditure comparable to and as important as a major medical examination. The results would be a better equipped and informed running population.

9

Fit and Comfort

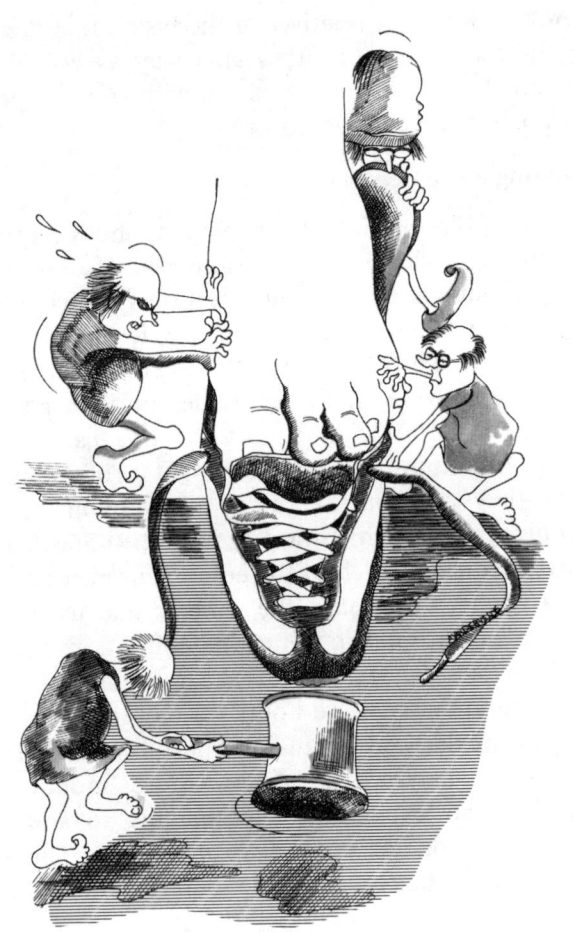

"Gentlemen: I received the shoes you sent me and they are fine. For ten years my feet hurt me. The last couple of years my feet have been so tender and sore that I couldn't even sleep with my husband. After wearing your Nordstrom's shoes for only two months, I find that now I can sleep with anyone."
—Letter from satisfied customer to Nordstrom's of Seattle

Factors such as impact response and flexibility, which can be measured directly, are the easy things to assess. Running a finger down a table of results in the shoe survey will tell you whether a particular shoe has the desired characteristics. If the test results are bad then you probably need look no further at that shoe. But if the shoe's test performance is good, then the difficult part begins.

Fit and comfort are features that no shoe survey is ever going to be able to measure successfully. Fit is an individual matter because all feet are different, even the left and right feet of the same person. Comfort is subjective, again because of individual differences in temperature regulation, sweat rates, soft tissue distribution, and other factors.

Because comfort and fit are difficult if not impossible to measure, it is important for the runner to have as complete an understanding as possible of the factors which influence these important properties of a shoe.

FIT

A good starting point for fit is to consider how the shoe has the shape it does. The last is the form over which the upper is pulled during manufacture. It was discussed in Chapter 5 but the subtleties of last construction and the implications for the fit of the shoe will be examined here.

It is important to realize that the last is shaped like the shoe, not like the foot. Before they are parted in the manufacturing process, the shoe will fit the last as if the upper had been molded onto the last. The most critical determinants of fit are therefore already built into the last, so our journey in search of fit leads to the last maker.

Although Roman lasts from the first century A.D. have been found in England, last makers in America trace their origins back to the second voyage of the Mayflower. A shoemaker named Thomas Beard and his journeyman Isaac Rickman landed near Salem, Massachusetts in 1629. The story goes that these early "cobblers" or "cordwainers" did not bring any lasts with them. I find this a little unlikely, but the record does describe how they "whittled . . . lasts from maple or hard wood with spoke shave and drawknife."

As we can see in Figure 9.1 the process has hardly become modernized in the intervening three and a half centuries. Here we see a model maker at work on his bench and the ingredients are still the same — a skilled pair of hands and a good piece of wood.

In a small room in Braintree, Massachusetts, John Lacerda and Bob Albert perpetuate the craft of Isaac Rickman not twenty-five miles, as the crow flies, from the place where he practiced it back in 1629. It is one of the last bastions of true craftsmanship left in the sprawling shoe industry. These two men are model makers and they work for Jones and Vining, a company that was making lasts at the turn of the century. They are responsible for a large proportion of the lasts used to build running shoes in the United States. It is very likely that, at one time or another, you have put your foot inside a shoe for which they built the last.

The question I kept asking the model makers was, where is the data that describes the shape of the lasts? The answer was always that "what we have to go by are the models." The last maker rarely, if ever, starts

FIT AND COMFORT

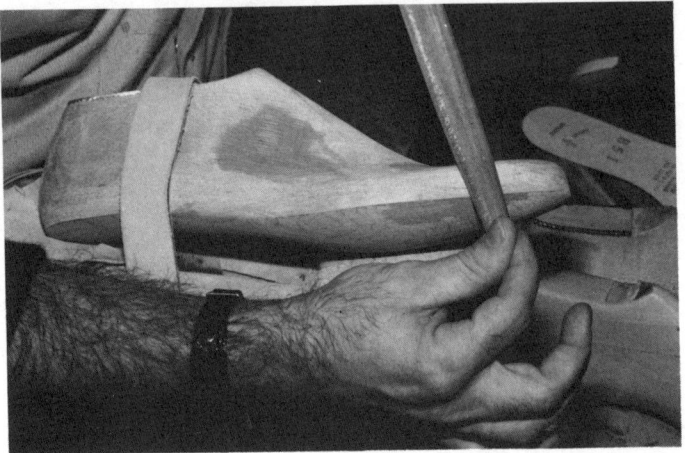

Fig. 9.1 A model maker shaping a piece of rock maple, which will form the basis for a production run of lasts.

from scratch. There will always be something that went before to use as a starting point. In fact there have been some extensive measurements on feet as we shall see shortly, but these have had little impact on the last maker.

Changing Lasts

Running shoe lasts are not as strongly influenced by fashion as dress shoe lasts. In the latter it is not uncommon for a last maker to receive a request from a company to leave the back part the same and change the toe. Last year's square toe might have gone out of fashion and now a round toe is all the rage. This kind of change is simply cosmetic and should not affect the rear two-thirds of the last.

Changing the last is not something the running shoe manufacturer will do without good reason. First, changing lasts is a very expensive proposition. Each pair of lasts costs about thirteen dollars, and a major manufacturer will own perhaps five thousand pairs of lasts for each of its models. Even the slightest change would mean an outlay of $65,000. A second reason is that customers buy a particular kind of shoe because they know it fits them well. Changing lasts might mean losing customers.

How Lasts Are Made

When a manufacturer decides to make a new running shoe they will meet with a model maker to talk about how the new shoe will be made. The discussion will usually center around an existing last which is to be "a little wider in the forepart" or "a little higher in the heel," "a bit more inflared," and so on. The manufacturer will state how the shoe will be made — slip lasted or cement lasted — and will describe the thickness of the sockliner he proposes to put inside the shoe. He will also have an outline of the shoe bottom. With this meager information as a start, the model maker will go to work. His aim will be to produce a wooden model of the last, probably a men's size nine or a women's seven in D width. Starting with a previous shoe model he will make a rough likeness, fashioned from a piece of rock maple now mostly brought in from Canada. In extreme cases, he might make a mold of a shoe he wants to copy out of dental plaster, and glue it to the front of an existing last.

Although the end product is a complex three-dimensional shape which does not have a single straight line on it, the model maker has only six measurements to guide him. These values (shown in Figure 9.2) are derived as follows. First the points marked one, two, three, and four are defined on the last. Although their exact location seems arbitrary to an unskilled observer, the model maker will quickly locate and name them (in order one through four) as the vamp, instep, ball break, and heel points.

The first five measurements are taken all the way around the last between these points and are called:

A — Ball Girth
B — Waist Girth
C — Instep Girth
D — Long Heel Girth
E — Short Heel Girth

The final measurement, F, is an overall heel-to-toe measurement on the last which shoemakers call the stick length.

Tables that list the approximate values of these

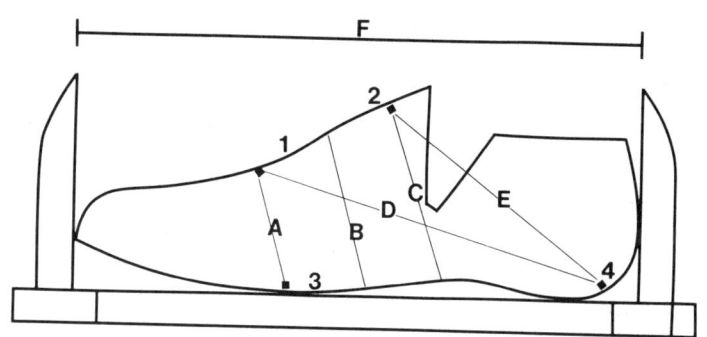

Fig. 9.2 The six measurements used by a model maker to insure that the dimensions of the shoe conform to the required foot size.

measurements for each shoe size are standard equipment in the model shop. (Where the measurements come from and how they change with size is something we shall discuss shortly.)

The model maker shapes and files, sands, and smooths until the measurements match and the model "looks right." Looking right, of course, is where the subjective elements come in. Within the basic six measurements there is an infinity of possible shapes. The way the model is shaped will critically affect the way the shoe will fit.

What is clearly more important than the six pieces of information on paper are the years of practical experience that the model maker possesses and the hundreds of years of experience incorporated into the lasts which

Fit and Comfort

exist today. To a scientist the process is unacceptably subjective. But most of the time it works.

When the last maker is happy that the shape is right, he will carefully insert nails completely around the abrupt junction between the top and bottom of the model. This line is called the featherline, and will be the point where the upper and bottom meet in the finished shoe. The nails are then filed down so that a piece of card, cut out in the exact shape of the footbed, fits on the model. This card is called the last bottom paper.

The next step is to put this handmade model onto a copy lathe which can produce either replicas of the model or generate additional models which are scaled up or down in size or width (Figure 9.3). A complete size run is made of the model and then a plastic version, on which shoes are actually made, is produced. In making the plastic lasts a hinge is added to "break" the last so it can be removed from the finished shoe, and a hole in the top, called a thimble, is made. This allows the last to be positioned in the various snoe machines.

The Pattern Maker

When the design of the last is finalized, another craftsman called the pattern maker moves into action. His job is to come up with the exact shape of the various pieces of material which will comprise the upper of the shoe. The first stage in this process will usually be to

Fig. 9.3 The handmade model is placed on the left side of this copy lathe, which then generates an exact replica of the same or different size.

sew a "skin" onto the last—a tightly-fitting layer of material which can be sliced off according to the way the shoe will be made. The pattern maker will then make careful drawings of these parts, adding extra space for seams and a lasting allowance. His drawings will be used in the manufacture of cutting dies for the finished product (Figure 5.7a).

Computer Invasion

It is unlikely that model making for lasts and patterns will stand the onslaught of high technology. Al-

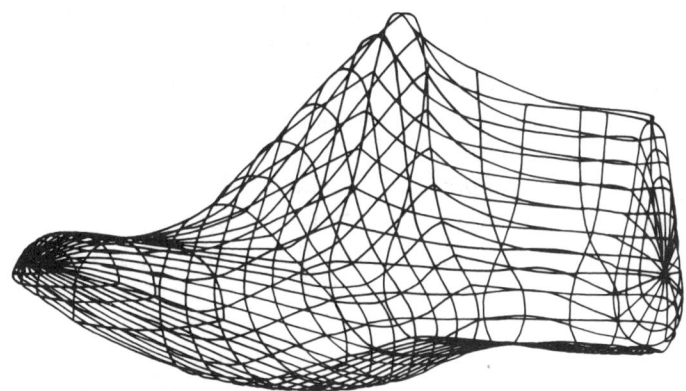

Fig. 9.4 A three-dimensional last pattern drawn by a graphic computer. Technology is edging the craftsman out of his place of prominence.

ready, plans are afoot to replace the craftsman at his bench by a computer designer at a video terminal. Figure 9.4 is a computer reproduction of a last generated not by a model maker but by a mathematician. If change is needed the designer will modify the pattern using an interactive program, and a computer controlled machine tool will quickly make the model. How simple it once was!

Shape and Size Variation

Having seen the process of lastmaking, we begin to see why it is possible for running shoes of the same size made by different manufacturers to fit differently. In Figure 9.5, last bottom papers from training flats made by four different companies are shown. All are nominally men's size nine, but there are obvious differences in length, width, and shape. Actually there is a three-eighths inch difference in overall length which is greater than one full size. The width difference in the ball of the foot also varies by over one-quarter of an inch. This diagram is very good evidence for not buying running shoes on the basis of size alone.

The most striking feature of Figure 9.5 is not the size but the shape differences. On some of the bottoms (such as Inset A) the last is straight and it is hard to tell left from right, a feature sometimes called a vector last. Others (for example Inset B) show an exaggerated inward curve, known variously as a spike, banana, curved, racing, or as we shall call it, an inflared last.

Two lines have been drawn on each shape. All four shoes have been positioned so that the rearpart midline lies along the same thick line (Figure 9.5). The thin line on each outline is sometimes called the axis of the shoe and joins the centers of the heel and toe. The angle between the two lines is a measure of how much the shoe curves or flares toward the inside. In the two extreme examples shown (inset in Figure 9.5), these angles are three degrees for the straight last shoe and ten degrees for the inflared shoe.

The straight last is something of an historical remnant making a comeback. Of the thousands of Roman

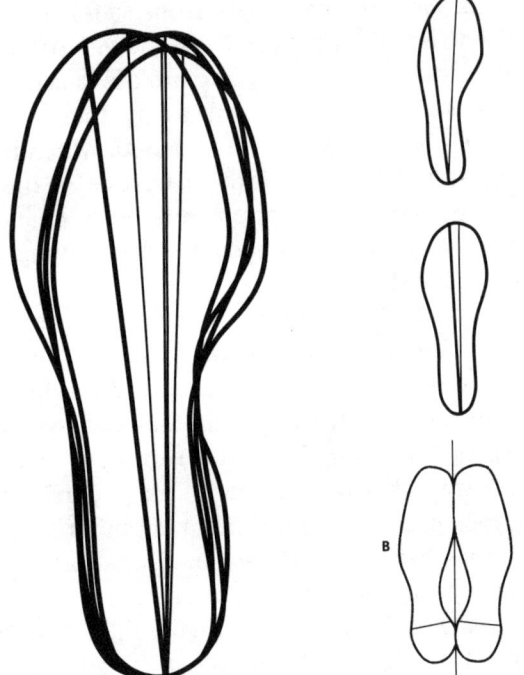

Fig. 9.5 A tracing of last bottom papers from four size 9 running shoes made by different manufacturers. The thick line is the midline of the rearpart of the shoes which have been superimposed. The thin lines join the midpoints of heel and toe. Notice the differences in length and width and the wide range of inflare. The outlines of the two extremes of inflare and straight shoes are shown inset. B) Shape suggested by Meyer (1860).

shoes seen by British expert John Thornton, all were clearly distinguishable as either for the right or left foot. But, as with so many good Roman ideas, the Middle Ages had a way of forgetting this sensible approach to shoemaking. Thus as late as 1900, identical left and right shoes were being made.

In the nineteenth century foot problems were widespread, much more so than today. In 1860, the German anatomist Herman Meyer wrote a classic book called *Why the Shoe Pinches*. He chastised those who were "sufficiently foolish voluntarily to sacrifice comfort, health, and beauty to an absurd fashion." Meyer noted that although a shoemaker might make several measurements on the foot, "... of all the measurements he takes, none have a decided influence on the shape of the sole." And of course the situation has not changed today. Meyer also observed that the straight lasted shoes simply didn't fit the curved shape of the foot, and suggested the "radical" shift to an inflared shape. Shown in figure 9.5b.

Dr. Stan James (see Chapter 16) believes that there is no evidence that the foot actually turns in, the way proponents of the inflared last would have us believe. James' view is that if the foot does have this curvature, it may have developed from wearing shoes with an inflared last from early childhood. Straight lasts of today are not the same as the old "one shoe for left and right" styles. They do have a slight inflare as Figure 9.5 shows.

Footprint or Foot Outline

My own opinion is that part of the discrepancy results from confusion between the shape of a footprint and the shape of a foot outline. In Figure 9.7 is a

Fit and Comfort

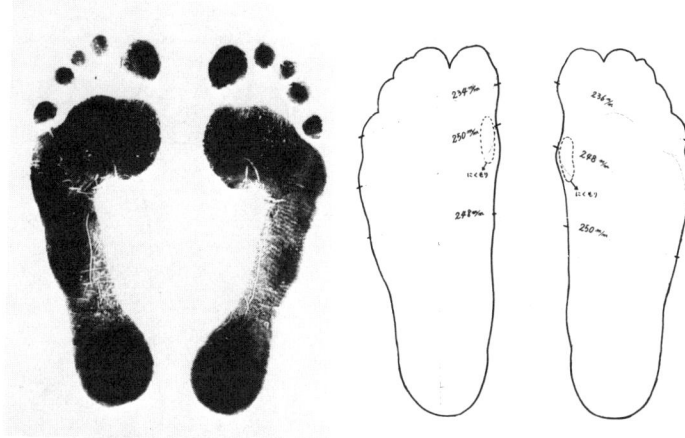

Fig. 9.7 (left) The footprints of marathoner Bill Rodgers. Compare this print with the outline in Figure 9.8 (right), an outline of Bill Rodgers' feet made by the technicians of the Tiger Shoe Company. (Courtesy ASICS Tiger)

famous pair of footprints. They belong to Bill Rodgers. In Figure 9.8 an outline made of Rodgers' feet by the technicians at ASICS Tiger Company is shown. If you compare the print and outline with the last bottoms in Figure 9.5, it will be clear that the print resembles an inflared shoe, while the outline resembles the straight last.

So what does the foot want? The print, of course, represents the weight-bearing surface of the foot. The discrepancy between print and outline is that areas of the foot such as the long inside arch (which on Rodgers' feet do not touch the ground) are given floor space. It seems likely that a straight lasted shoe will not give a foot like Rodgers' as much support as an inflared last.

But the variety of foot types is overwhelming. Neither the straight nor inflared last will fit all. The process simply has to be trial and error. Let's take a look at some experimental data on foot shape and size that will reinforce this point of view.

Measurements of Feet

In 1945 the United States Army became concerned about the relationship between the shape and size of the boots they were issuing to soldiers, and the shape and size of the soldiers' feet. They commissioned one of the most extensive studies of foot dimensions that has ever been conducted. Twenty-seven dimensions on both feet of 6,775 men are reported in what has become known as the Fort Knox Report; the data makes fascinating reading. The six dimensions used by the last maker are reported, but so is much more: the curvature of the heel and toes, information on foot flare, the height of the toes, arch height, and lateral foot contour.

The data base is a tremendous resource for shoe manufacturers but it has slowly drifted from awareness, and I doubt that one in twenty shoemakers has a copy in their factory.

Perhaps the most important finding from this massive survey is contained in the following stodgy "Army-ese" conclusion:

"... (to make a new single last to fit all men) may not prove possible since it is evident that consistent or orderly schemes of dimensional inter-relationships applicable to all, or even a majority of men, probably do not exist."

More simply put, some people have short fat feet, and others long thin feet. Not a particularly stunning conclusion from a major study, but rather than just make the observation, the army charted the variations. What is most interesting are shape differences. If all feet were simply bigger or smaller versions of the same model, shoemaking would be simple. A part of the range of foot shapes revealed by the study is shown in Figure 9.9. Notice that these figures have been adjusted as if all the feet were the same size.

The flare data is interesting because it shows that there is a range from outflare to inflare, reinforcing the statements made earlier about wide variability. The tremendous range of toe curvatures, heel contours, and forefoot-toe joint angles show the impossible task that the designer faces who must make one shoe to fit all. It also highlights the need for you to try shoes made by different manufacturers because some brands will fit you very well, others poorly.

The Left Foot Might Be Bigger Than the Right

The Fort Knox study found differences between the right and left feet of the same person, but concluded that there were no systematic differences that

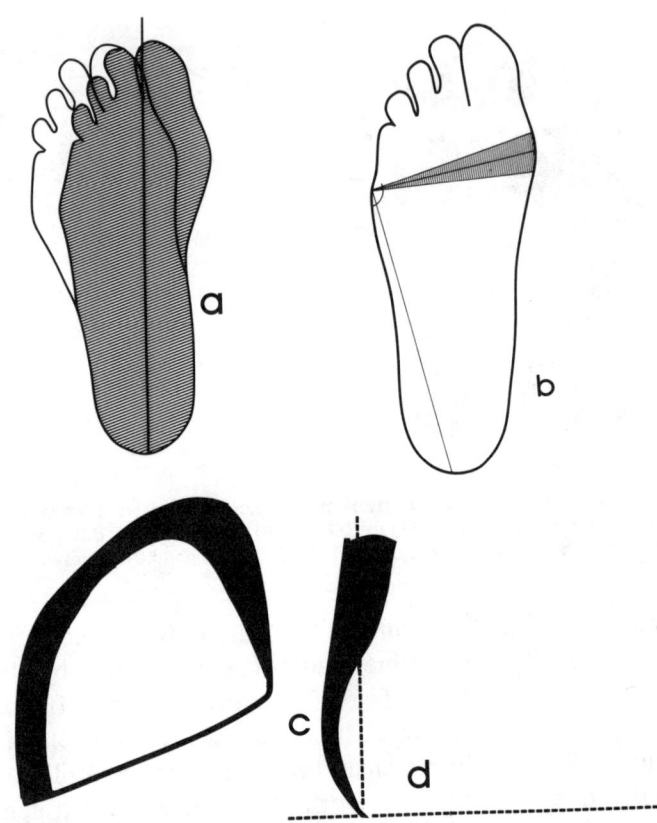

Fig. 9.9   Foot shapes measured in the Fort Knox study conducted by the United States Army. a) The range of inflare-outflare that describes ninety-five percent of the population. b) The range of orientations of the line linking the joints of the first and fifth toes. c) The range of toe curvatures. d) The range of heel curvatures.

held for all subjects. In a more recent study Dr. Alan Spencer of the Ohio College of Podiatric Medicine has concluded that there are, at least in his sample, consistent differences between left and right feet. On average the left feet of Spencer's subjects were significantly longer than their right.

The explanation for this is that the majority of people are right side dominant and thus the left leg becomes the supporting leg in such activities as kicking or stepping up and down. The larger forces exerted on the left leg may cause the ligaments and muscles of the foot to lengthen.

If this finding is confirmed it is pretty important for the shoe buyer. Shoemakers *always* put the right shoe on top in the shoe box. It is supposed to look better than the left. So if you do have a larger left foot and you only try on the right shoe because it's first out of the box, you could be in trouble. If the right shoe just fits, the chances are the left will be too short. The moral is obvious. Always try both shoes.

SHOE SIZES

The stories surrounding the origins of shoe sizes are many and varied. The English system is said to have had its origin in 1324, when Edward II wrote into law the rather questionable standard that three average-sized barley corns placed end to end would equal one inch. If we suppose that the longest foot was thirteen inches (thirty-nine barley corns) and each size smaller than "size thirteen" was one barley corn less (size twelve would be thirty-eight barley corns, or twelve and two-thirds inches) we are very close to the present sizing system.

The single size we use today is a combination of two measurements: the length of the shoe, and its width across the ball of the foot. The length unit between sizes is one-third of an inch.

From this simple beginning, things become complicated. Where do the sizes start? Well, size zero in English sizes is exactly four inches. Thirteen sizes later (that's at eight and one-third inches long) the children's sizes end, and this becomes the starting point for men's sizes. So a size one man's shoe is eight and two-thirds inches long. A size two is nine inches long, and so on. Confused? There's more to come.

American grades (the industry term for a size increment) are the same but the starting point slipped a little. So size zero (American) is actually at three and eleven-twelfths inches. Each American size is therefore one-twelfth of an inch smaller than its United Kingdom equivalent. This is why you may find European shoes such as Adidas and Puma are slightly looser at a given size, since these are graded according to the English system.

American women's sizes stretch the imagination even further because they do not have an exact match in the men's sizes, although the length increment is still one-third of an inch per size. A size zero woman's shoe is seven and three-quarters inches long, so women's shoes lag almost two sizes behind the same number men's size.

The French sizes (sometimes called Paris Points) are slightly more rational; they do have one continuous range. The unit this time is two-thirds of a centimeter per size with size zero starting at zero centimeters.

Figure 9.10 wipes away all the numbers and sets the various size systems on a grid together with scales of inches and centimeters. Remember that the size is the stick length of the shoe (see Figure 9.2) and not the size of your foot. The configuration of your toes, together with the shape of the toe box and the amount of inflare of the shoe that you are trying on, will determine exactly which size of a particular shoe you will need.

What Width Sizes Mean

The simplest way to consider width sizing is not in terms of widths but in terms of girth, i.e., the distance around the forepart of the foot at its widest point. (This is equivalent to the ball girth measurement on the last—see Figure 9.2.) Between widths of

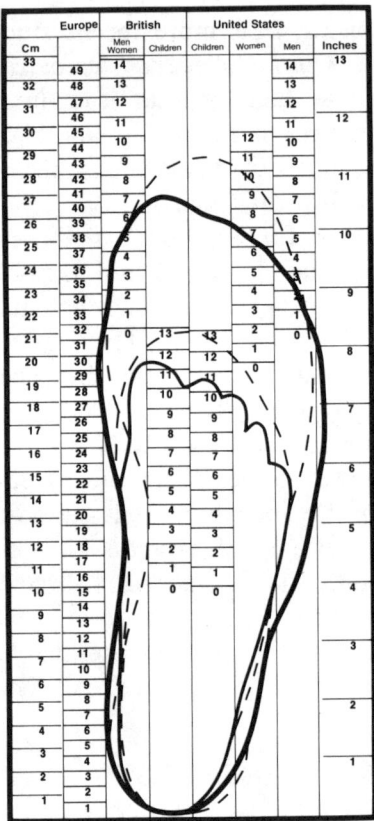

Fig. 9.10   A size chart showing the length in inches and centimeters of American, European, and British shoe sizes. Superimposed on the chart are the outlines of a man's foot fitted by a size 9 shoe and a child's foot fitted by a size 13 shoe. Notice that the foot outline is outside the shoe outline, and that the size is a measurement of the shoe length, not the foot length.

the same size, this dimension will increase by one-quarter inch. The shoemaker and last maker call their widths by name. Ironically Albert, usually thought of as "fat Albert," is the name for the narrow "A" width. The AAA is called Three Albert, and then we move through Benny, Charlie, David, and Eddie for the B, C, D, and E widths. Each of these represents one-quarter inch difference in the ball circumference. The standard width, the D, will also increase by one-quarter inch as the length size increases. Both trends are shown in Figure 9.11. Notice how the ball girth of sizes 7EE, 8E, 9D, 10C, and 11B will all be the same.

Unfortunately, very few manufacturers make a range of width sizes. Not because it wouldn't be good for the runner—it would. The big drawback is inventory for both retailers and manufacturer. Neither are disposed to triple the amount of money they have tied up in stock.

For people with exceptionally wide or narrow feet this means that their choice of shoes is limited to one or two brands. This is unfortunate because they may have to compromise on other important features. The only alternative is to choose a shoe with special lacing to accommodate a wider range of width sizes than the usual U throat. A number of these designs is described in Chapter 8. However this is only a partial solution because different lacing systems will do nothing to increase the weight-bearing area of the footbed. The only

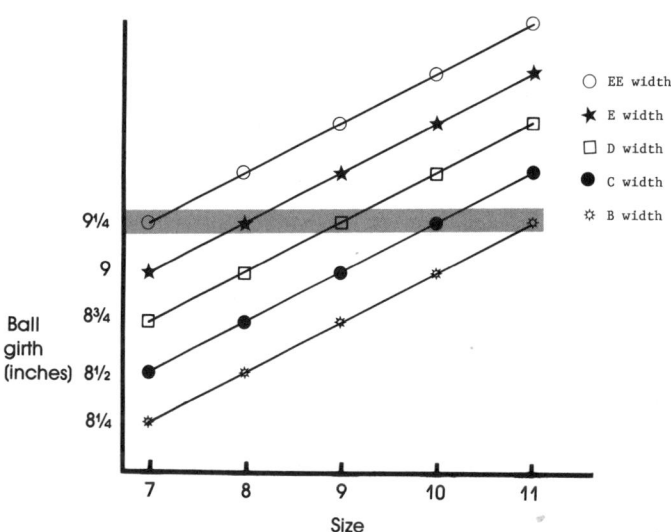

Fig. 9.11 The ball girth of various sizes and widths. In a given size the increment of width is one fourth inch. The step up of one size in lengths also involves a one fourth inch increase in ball girth, so that sizes 7EE, 8E, 9D, 10C, and 11B all have the same width as shown by the shaded box. (Adapted from *Manual of Shoemaking* by C. and J. Clarke)

solution is to keep bothering your favorite manufacturer until they start producing width sized shoes.

How Do You Find Your Length and Girth?

How can all these numbers be translated into a shoe size and width that will fit you? The most likely encounter you will have with these numbers is with a measuring device like the Brannock unit shown in Figure 9.12.

This measures foot length, width, and a quantity called arch length. Remember that all of the measurements mentioned so far in this chapter refer to the last or the shoe, while measuring devices like the Brannock measure the foot. So there must be some allowance built into the instrument.

In the Brannock the length allowance is about three-quarters of an inch. A men's size nine foot on the Brannock would be ten and a half inches long. But we can see from Figure 9.10 that a size nine shoe is actually eleven and a quarter inches long. So built into the Brannock is the idea that the foot should be three-quarters of an inch smaller than the stick length. For this reason the measurement of foot length should be taken as a first guess at shoe size, to be confirmed by trial and error. Similar allowances are built into the width measurement.

The maker of the Brannock recommends that arch length, which is the distance between the heel and ball of the foot, also be used to determine the correct size. Unfortunately, if the heel to ball distance suggests a longer shoe, most runners would find the added space in front of the toe a problem. There are so many shape variations in the foot and shoe which will affect fit that

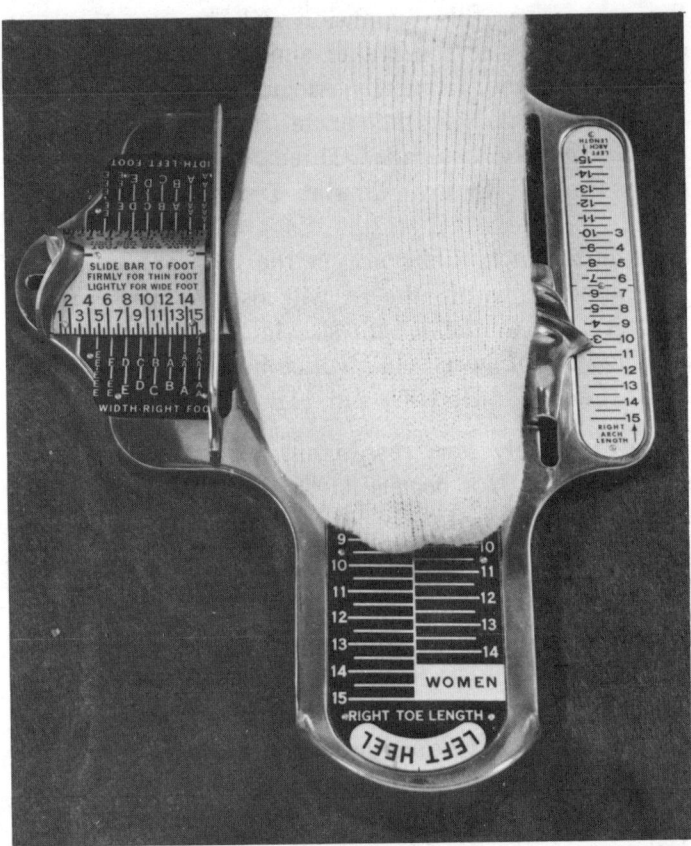

Fig. 9.12 The Brannock measuring device used in many stores to estimate length and width sizes. Although foot length and breadth are measured, the scale reads in terms of shoe size.

the best way is to try on shoes of various sizes from various manufacturers.

You know what approximate size you take, but as we saw in Figure 9.5 that size shoe may vary considerably in its actual dimensions depending upon who makes it.

Heel Fitting

With so much emphasis on length and ball girth for shoe sizing, it is easy to forget that fitting is also important in the rearpart. Unfortunately, there is no running shoe presently made with varying heel widths, although Puma apparently has plans for such a design.

A good fit in the heel is critically important because too much rearfoot movement can cause pain and injury. I have never yet heard a runner complain that their shoe is too narrow in the heel, so it is a fair guess that many are too wide.

Part of the problem of rearfoot fit is that the bottom of the heel bone is covered by a thick layer of soft tissue. What it does or should do under weight bearing in running no one quite knows. Podiatrist Dick Schuster believes that the layers of padding form a doughnut under the heel and function as a protective ring.

The only shoe manufacturer to include some heel spacing as standard equipment is Etonic. The insert designed by podiatrist Rob Roy McGregor forms a compressible heel seat all around the rearfoot. Coach Arthur Lydiard believes that the heel should fit into the shoe like an egg in an egg cup, and the design of the Lydiard shoes have a concavity to reflect this view.

If the heel is too wide a heel cup is the only solution. We shall describe several types in Chapter 12.

Are There Standard Ways to Fit a Shoe?

Believe it or not, the acronym "ANSI/ASTM F539-78" refers to a standard practice for fitting athletic footwear. This is tucked away in the archives of the American Society for Testing and Materials. Besides telling which way to hold up the Brannock device, the standard is not really too helpful. It suggests that the toes should "never touch the end of the toe box." An admirable sentiment, but as stated, it does not exclude putting a size eleven shoe on a size eight foot. It suggests "a little extra leather over the tops of the toes but not too much." But how much is a little, and how much is too much?

It may hearten you to know that there is a human link in the chain from last to shoe box. Every running shoe company has a person on staff who is their "standard size" individual. It may be a machinist, janitor, or the president of the company, but if a new shoe which should fit this person's size does not fit well, they will go back to the drawing board and make some changes until it does fit. Little wonder that shoes from each company fit a bit differently, since their "standard size" people will all be slightly different.

All of this goes to show that it doesn't make sense to specify what fit is. Fit is as individual as a fingerprint, and the only satisfactory way to find it is to try many shoes and listen to your feet.

Changes in Foot Size

We have talked so far as if the dimensions of feet were as fixed as the dimensions of lasts. But feet do change their shape over a period of years and, somewhat surprisingly, over the course of a single day.

It is critically important that children's feet are not restricted in their normal growth patterns by shoes which fit poorly. Recent studies at the University of Michigan show that there is a fairly steady increase in foot length between the ages of four and eleven. The average rate of growth during these years is approximately one-third of an inch per year. This is an intriguing coincidence with the increment in shoe sizes, which is also one-third of an inch. The correspondence is accidental; sizes were not designed with growth in mind, and indeed growth patterns have changed dramatically over the years while sizes have stayed the same. Theoretically, a child following the mean growth rate should need a shoe one-half size bigger every six months. Data from the same study show an increase in ball width of about one tenth of an inch per year. Growth slows down between the age of eleven and after puberty, apart from the spurt associated with adolescence. It has to. Otherwise the mean foot length would be about twelve inches by age twenty, and the Fort Knox data show a mean value of ten and six-tenths inches for adult males.

Changes With Exercise

We often forget that some of the dimensions of our body change in the course of a day. A gradual decrease in height occurs, and it is not uncommon for a person to be half an inch shorter just before bedtime than they were first thing in the morning. Most of this is due to compression of the intervertebral joints by gravity and inertial forces.

The foot responds to the stress of standing, walking, and running by getting bigger, not smaller. Very few experiments have charted what happens to the foot during running, but we do know from the preliminary experiments of Muller-Limroth and Diebschlag in West Germany that approximately five percent increases in foot volume occur in one hour of barefoot standing. The increases occur because extracellular fluids tend to pool in the foot, a process known as edema. Foot volume will be greatest after a hard day on the feet.

Exactly what changes occur during a training run or a marathon nobody quite knows. But there are certain to be big individual differences, and there are probably runners who can feel their shoes getting tight during a run.

Foot length and girth will also depend on the amount of force being exerted on the ground. As we have seen in Chapter 5, this can be three times body weight or more at each foot strike, and in the absence of any good data, we must assume that changes in foot length are considerable.

One thing, then, is certain. The worst thing you could do as far as trying on new shoes is concerned would be to go to a shoe store at 8:00 a.m. and try the shoe on only while sitting down. Under these conditions your foot will be at its smallest, shortest, and narrowest.

Changes in Shoe Volume

We also should not ignore the fact that as a shoe is used, it will change its length, width, and volume, and that this change is invariably in the direction of an increase in all three values. Chapter 10 will examine the aging process of a running shoe in more detail.

It is sufficient to mention now that just like changes in the foot there will be both short- and long-term changes in the shoe. Many manufacturers are putting sockliners into their shoes to take a "compression set" within the first few miles of running. Therefore your foot may feel as if there is too much pressure against the upper when you first put it on, but the room will appear after the shoe is "run in."

Longer term dimensional changes will be more marked in shoes with leather uppers than in nylon. Nylon taffeta is very resistant to permanent changes, which can be both good and bad. Leather uppers will mold to the shape of the foot, but this molding may make the shoes oversize quickly, particularly if much wet weather running is done.

Unusual Fit Problems

Apes, monkeys, and Greek statues invariably have second toes which are longer than the first. The English anatomist T.S. Ellis found great comfort in the fact that most of his countrymen had feet which were distinguishable from the apes. He remarked that "... my own impression is that in England the great toe is generally more prominent and I am glad to think it is so."

Runners think of themselves as cursed if their "digital formula" is not "one longer than two longer than three, etc.," counting the big toe as one. In particular the long second toe (or short first toe) has been implicated in a number of running related problems. The runner in Figure 9.13 has an unusual problem with fitting the left foot. It is not an optical illusion; he really does have six

202   FIT AND COMFORT

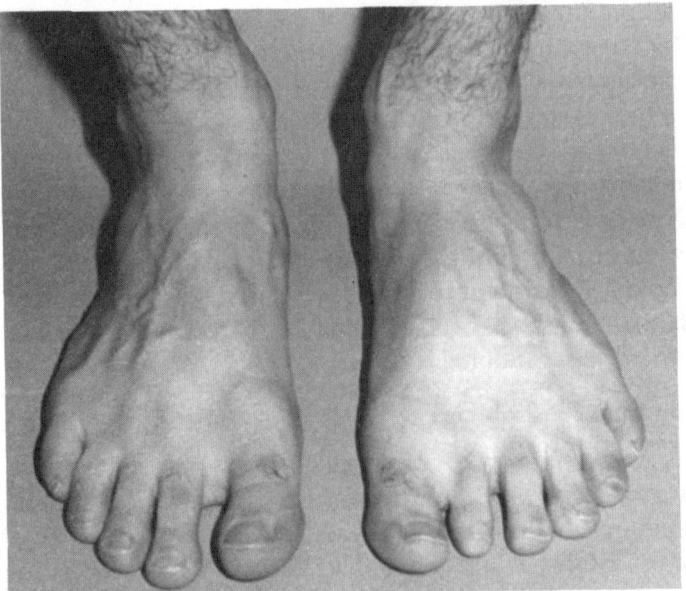

Fig. 9.13   A person with special width requirements in a running shoe. The left foot has six complete toes while the right foot has five.

complete toes which make the left foot considerably wider than the right. Although "polydactylism," having more than twenty fingers and toes, is unusual, it does highlight the fact that the left and right feet can be very different.

Besides the possible clinical consequences of different toe and metatarsal lengths, a good fit in the toe box goes beyond simple considerations of length. It will be dependent upon matching your own toe contour with a suitable toe box shape. Shoe length is defined as the distance between the heel and the longest toe, but as we saw in Figure 9.9, toe contour can vary considerably in feet of the same length. There are still some running shoes available for people with arrowfeet—a mythical foot type in which the middle toe is longest. I was foolish enough to wear such a pair in a ten mile race recently and still have a number of black toes as a consequence.

Molding to the Shape of the Foot

Look back at the outline of Bill Rodgers' feet in Figure 9.8. You will notice that the shoe technicians have drawn elipses over both first metatarsophalangeal joints. These represent slight abnormalities, and are in the position where bunions form. Any raised areas such as these will provide additional problems for a good fitting shoe. Many such problems are pressure related and will only be made worse by ignoring them.

The answer, if custom shoes are not possible, is to buy either a leather shoe or a shoe with a leather forepart. As we shall describe shortly, leather is able to undergo what is known as a plastic or permanent deformation under the influence of a continually applied force. This accommodation to the foot will never occur with a nylon upper. If you are looking for accommodation to your foot, beware of shoes that have a leather forepart sewn onto a nylon upper. The nylon will not allow the leather to mold to your foot.

Even under conditions which will not cause permanent deformations, leather uppers will stretch more than nylon. This property is known as the compliance of the material. Taffeta will usually have the same compliance along the length and breadth of the shoe. Meshes often stretch differently depending on the angle of pull, and leathers will stretch differently depending on which part of the animal they came from.

Custom Fitting

The custom shoemaking trade has all but died, both for sports and everyday footwear. In the early days, Spalding would make custom running shoes for ten percent above the regular price. To order custom shoes you would send an outline of your foot, together with three of the standard last measurements and an ankle girth. The instructions are shown in Figure 9.14, reproduced from an 1896 catalog of the Spalding Company.

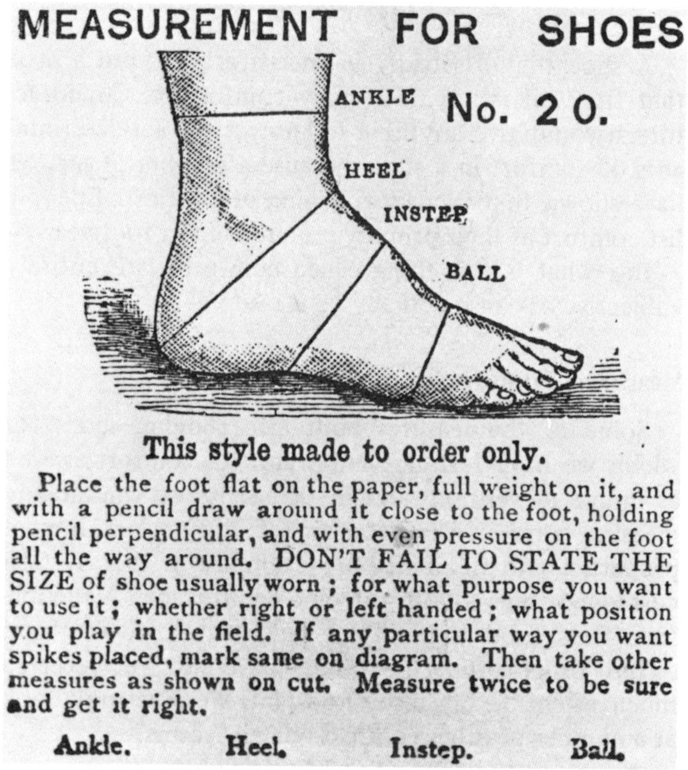

Many of today's elite athletes go through the process of having their feet measured and traced, but most shoe companies will understandably try first to match the athlete's measurements to one of their standard lasts. If the fit problems are so severe that the athlete cannot get a good fit from a standard shoe then a custom last will be made. But the process is expensive and represents a real commitment to the runner.

MEASUREMENT FOR SHOES No. 20.

This style made to order only.

Place the foot flat on the paper, full weight on it, and with a pencil draw around it close to the foot, holding pencil perpendicular, and with even pressure on the foot all the way around. DON'T FAIL TO STATE THE SIZE of shoe usually worn; for what purpose you want to use it; whether right or left handed; what position you play in the field. If any particular way you want spikes placed, mark same on diagram. Then take other measures as shown on cut. Measure twice to be sure and get it right.

Ankle.   Heel.   Instep.   Ball.

Fig. 9.14 Instructions for ordering custom shoes given in the Spalding Catalog of 1894. (Courtesy of International Sports and Games Research Collection, University of Nortre Dame)

COMFORT

A shoe that fits badly is uncomfortable, but a shoe that fits well is not necessarily comfortable. Manufacturers would give anything to know the exact determinants of comfort in a shoe, because a number of surveys have shown that an overwhelming proportion of people list comfort as their primary requirement in footwear.

But what is this thing called comfort? Is it entirely subjective or can it actually be measured?

Measuring Comfort

Some of the features built into running shoes for which we have tests are important for comfort as well as injury prevention, and in that sense we can already measure some of the determinants of comfort. Impact properties and flexibility are examples of this. A well cushioned shoe is both safe and comfortable. A flexible shoe feels good and will not cause trauma to the foot.

But other properties which have not yet received much attention are also important. We must now look at a number of other comfort-related factors.

There has been only one serious attempt to measure comfort in footwear. In 1974, French scientist J.P. Boulanger and his colleagues at the Leather Technical Center in Lyon, France, performed an experiment in which 198 subjects were given three pairs of street shoes. The subjects wore these shoes in rotation for a period of five months, in both hot and cold weather. They were questioned once a week on their reactions to the various shoes.

Meantime, scientists in the lab were busy trying to measure the characteristics which the subjects thought important for comfort.

From a multiple choice format, the subjects named six factors as most important in shoe comfort:

1. Fit
2. Minimize perspiration
3. Good thermal insulation
4. Sole flexibility
5. Upper flexibility
6. Protection against the elements

As you see, fit jumped right to the top of the list. Preferences might be very different in a running shoe, and unfortunately no comparable data exist. But the responses from the French study do give us some insight into the variables of the comfort equation.

The Microclimate of the Foot

The second preference in the French survey, that the shoe should minimize perspiration, takes us into a new area which is sometimes called the microclimate of the foot. For shoe manufacturers this comes down to "weather forecasting" for the air between the foot and the shoe.

The foot experiences the highs and lows of temperature and humidity variation on the surface of the body.

It is a lot like Chicago—cold in winter and humid in summer. Because the foot is further from the heart than any other part of the body, by the time blood arrives there it has already cooled considerably.

Although the core temperature of the body varies only slightly with large changes in the temperature of the environment, the foot is not so lucky. For example, at an air temperature of sixty-eight degrees, the surface temperature of the foot at rest without clothes may be hovering at around seventy-two degrees, while the core temperature is close to ninety-eight degrees. Clearly, cold feet are more than just a figure of speech. Comfort under cold conditions therefore means the ability to provide thermal insulation while at the same time not restricting blood flow to the feet. Keeping water out of the shoe is an important part of this function.

In the opposite environment, the shoe has a very different task to perform. During exercise in hot weather the foot temperature becomes elevated and the relative humidity of the air in the shoe rises sharply. The material used to make the upper of the shoe and the sock will drastically affect both temperature and humidity, and these two factors are both perceived by the wearer as indications of comfort.

Heat Exchange

Heat can be lost or gained by four distinct mechanisms: conduction, radiation, convection, and vaporization.

When conduction occurs heat flows directly through a conductor. For example, the pressure-bearing area of the foot is in contact with the sockliner and, through the various layers, with the road surface. In running shoes, the K factor (thermal conductivity) is fairly low, so that not too much heat is lost or gained this way unless the temperature of the road is extreme (for example running on desert roads or snow).

Radiation involves heat exchange between two objects of different temperatures, regardless of what separates them. The skin is a good radiator, but the foot covered by a running shoe will not lose a great deal of heat by radiation.

Convection requires a flow of air, and it is the air which acts as the carrier of heat from one object to another. Since the foot is so carefully covered up by the shoe, not much air movement takes place. Some authors have speculated that there is a pumping action of air out of the shoe with each stride. Indeed some patents have been filed to incorporate channels to allow this movement to occur. In general though, convective cooling of the foot is probably minimal.

Evaporation and Temperature Regulation

So that leaves us with vaporization or evaporation as the major mechanisms which the foot uses for controlling its climatic conditions.

Human beings have a delicate mechanism to use evaporation to control their body temperature. When water evaporates from the surface of the body, cooling of the skin occurs as heat from the body is used to change the state of the water from liquid to gas. Since more than sixty percent of the body weight is water, there is obviously a ready supply to use for cooling purposes.

The palms of the hands and the soles of the feet are unique from a number of points of view when sweating is considered. First, their sweat glands are arranged in very orderly fashion along the ridges of the skin surface. Such a clear pattern is absent from the rest of the body. Second, the hands and feet together with the axilla (armpit) are areas where sweating will occur in response to psychological stresses—from fear to extreme concentration. Last, and most important from our point of view, is the fact that the density of sweat glands on the soles of the feet is greater than any other area of the body. One researcher estimates that there are more than 600 sweat glands per square centimeter on the sole of the foot (although some think the number is as low as 200). This means that there are almost 100,000 sweat glands on the bottom of each foot and perhaps 50,000 on the rest of the foot surface.

For evaporation to occur, certain conditions have to be met. One of the most important is that the covering of the skin—in this case the upper of the running shoe—should allow water vapor to pass freely through. A rubber upper on a shoe, for example, will not allow such movement and is termed non-permeable to water vapor. Perspiration will simply accumulate in the shoe.

Obviously, one easy way to make any material permeable to water vapor is to punch holes in it. But this is unacceptable from the standpoint of waterproofing from the outside in. Water could move freely in both directions.

Upper materials vary greatly in their permeability. Leather uppers of street shoes have been shown to be at least three times more permeable to water vapor than some synthetic uppers. To my knowledge, tests on uppers commonly used in running shoes have not been published. The results will depend not only on the upper material itself and how it is woven or knitted, but also on the various linings used (see Chapter 6).

Saturated Socks

To find out a little more about socks, I bought five pair made of different materials. The dry weights varied by more than twenty-five grams (approximately one ounce). The cotton socks were the lightest at thirty grams, while the half wool and half nylon were the heaviest at fifty-eight grams.

After weighing, all five pair were thoroughly soaked in water and then hung until they stopped dripping. The amounts of water that each sock retained at this point, which I arbitrarily called saturation, are shown in Figure 9.15.

The results show almost a five-fold range in the quantity of water that the best and worst sock can absorb. Of course, not too many runners run in wool socks, and if they do, it is for different reasons. When wool is wet it does not collapse completely as some of the other fabrics do, and so the pockets of trapped air give added insulation from the cold even when wet. As mentioned earlier, the socks had different dry weights. Looked at in this way, wool socks take up sixty percent of their own weight, while the cotton, orlon, and wick socks took up almost two and a half times their weight in water.

How Much Do Runners' Feet Sweat?

I have not been able to locate any data in the scientific literature describing climatic conditions inside the running shoe. The closest thing available is information obtained by Dr. Wilfried Diebschlag from the Institute for Work Physiology in Munich, West Germany.

During a one hour walk on the treadmill at about three miles an hour, one of his subject's foot temperature rose by more than fifteen degrees Fahrenheit, and the number of active sweat glands rose from an initial eighteen to a final eighty-three per square centimeter.

Now no one ever won a marathon at three miles per hour, so I decided to collect some simple values on two runners to give some idea of the amounts of perspiration involved.

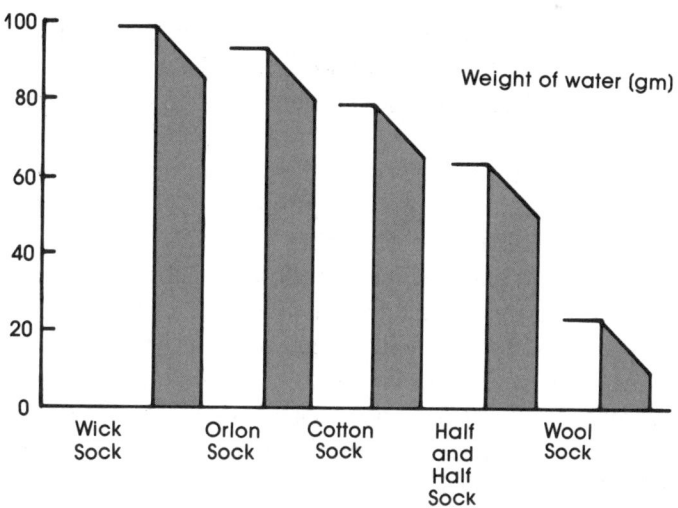

Fig. 9.15 The weight of water needed to saturate five different kinds of socks completely. The higher the bar on the graph the more water absorbed, and the longer it would take before the foot felt that it was swimming in perspiration. a) Wick socks. (60% orlon, 25% cotton, 10% nylon, 5% misc., see Figure 9.16) b) Orlon socks. (90% orlon, 10% nylon) c) Cotton socks. (80% cotton, 20% nylon) d) Half and half socks. (45% wool, 55% nylon) e) Wool socks. (85% wool, 15% cotton)

The Odd Shoe Run

On a day when the air temperature (inside) was sixty-six degrees, and the relative humidity a very dry thirty-four percent, two volunteers ran 10.3 miles in one hour on an indoor tartan track.

To give each foot different conditions, I had them wear a shoe with a nylon upper on the left foot and a leather upper on the right. (Both shoes were Brooks

Villanovas). To further add to their discomfort, the left sock was eighty-five percent wool and the right sock a "wick" sock. Shoes and socks were weighed before and after the run.

Any experiment with two subjects is doomed to failure and this one was no exception. The two subjects showed very different responses. The heavier runner collected thirty grams of perspiration in his leather shoe, and twelve grams in the nylon shoe. The other runner only accumulated about five grams in each shoe.

Now what we are seeing in these weights is the perspiration that didn't get away. There is no way of knowing from such a simple test how much water vapor passed through the barrier of the shoe upper. The ambient air humidity was very low, a condition which would facilitate evaporation. Also the assumption that perspiration would be the same from both feet under potentially different temperature environments is questionable.

One of the properties of leather that synthetics have had a hard time duplicating is its ability to store water. It seems that the runner who carried eighteen grams more perspiration in the leather shoe was experiencing this retention.

Weighing the socks produced much more consistent data. The increases in weight were eleven, twelve, thirteen, and fourteen grams for a mean increase of twelve and a half grams. Socks are often little more than an afterthought with runners, but they have the power to modify the properties of the shoe considerably.

Sock Talk

One of the few experiments with different types of socks again came from the Institute of Work Physiology in Munich. The experiment involved measuring the temperature and humidity inside the shoes of eight subjects during a seven hour day which involved three mph walking, periods of quiet work, and rest.

Even though a wide variety of natural and synthetic socks was used no significant differences were found among any of them as far as temperature and humidity is concerned.

We must remember that these tests were relatively low level tasks when compared to distance running, and I don't think the results can be generalized to running, particularly under hot and humid conditions.

Part of the comfort "feeling" of socks is their ability to remove moisture from the surface of the skin—even if evaporation to the outside air is not possible. So how much water will the socks themselves hold and how do they remove water from the skin surface?

It's interesting to look at how much water the socks can hold in relation to the weight of the socks taken from two runners who ran the ten-mile time trial. We should recall that only about two-thirds of the surface area of the sock is inside the shoe, so it would give us a more realistic figure if we multiply the amounts shown in Figure 9.15 by two-thirds. This gives values for the amounts of water needed to saturate the socks which vary from fourteen grams for the wool sock to sixty-three grams for the wick sock.

Since the wool socks gained a total of twelve grams during the one hour run, they were probably near the point where they could hold no more water, while the wick sock had a long way to go before it would reach saturation. We should also note that perspiration will not accumulate in uniform amounts over the whole foot, but will probably be greatest under the toes and long arch; these areas may reach saturation first. We should emphasize again that the one hour run was conducted under very favorable climatic conditions, and the only thing certain about perspiration on a hot, humid day is that it would be considerably more.

Comfort vs. Pressure

An adequate definition of one aspect of comfort in running shoes would be "minimum pressure on any part of the foot." In the upper, this will be sensed first as a part of the feeling of fit when the shoe is tried on.

But running puts tremendous demands on the shoe's upper. From the biomechanical evidence presented in Chapter 4 we can think about the first half of the support phase this way: your shoe is firmly planted on the ground and your foot is being pulled forward with a force equal to about half your body weight. The toes and forefoot are being driven into the toe box which, even if it is wide and high, will be under pressure at this time. If the material is compliant, the upper will stretch while the pressure is on and return to its original position when allowed to do so.

This brings us back to the way in which uppers stretch. Clearly an important aspect of breaking shoes in is stretching the uppers permanently where the foot needs more space. Leather will stretch much more than nylon taffeta under an identical force. The behavior of nylon mesh will vary considerably depending on the knit pattern used. But controlled stretch of the upper will be felt as a kind of dynamic comfort. It may be necessary to go with a slightly larger nylon taffeta shoe to allow for movement of the foot which cannot be compensated for by stretch.

No one has ever actually measured the force and pressure environment between the foot and the upper. So we really don't know how well the materials in use at the moment are suited to the task. This is yet another uncharted area in shoe science.

Pressure on the Sole of the Foot

Look inside a new running shoe, not just at the surface, but also under the sockliner. You will see that the surface is as flat as a board. In fact it probably will be a board—the insole board. All running shoes are made on a flat last. Even slip-lasted shoes which do not have the insole board are flat. But the bottoms of most feet are far from being flat. So why do manufacturers make flat shoes? Because it is easy. Many higher priced street and dress shoes are made on lasts which look exactly like the bottom of the foot. Bostonian, for example, still builds their men's formal line on a last with a shaped bottom.

But the manufacturing process for a contoured sole is time consuming. Traditionally pieces of wet leather were hammered onto the last, beaten into the shape they would take when the water evaporated.

Comfort Through the Sockliner

With flat-lasted running shoes the norm, manufacturers have tried several methods to restore the comfort that a contoured footbed offered. Most of these attempts have involved the sockliner or insert, which is the covering for the flat insole board.

It should be pointed out that sockliners can not only give the footbed a true shape, but also play an important role in shock absorption. Some preliminary experiments at Penn State have shown that different sockliners can add as much as twenty percent to shock absorption when both shoe and sockliner are new. In many sockliners this contribution will fade as compression occurs. But while it lasts it will make the shoe feel more comfortable. During the early life of a thick sockliner the shoe may also feel tight, since the manufacturer may have left the upper the same dimensions as a shoe which has a regular insert.

Sockliners which adjust to the shape of the foot are often called memory foams. Nike's Permafoam, Brooks' Custom Contour Insole, and FoamGard's Footbed are all variations on the memory theme. The first two mold permanently to the shape of the foot, while the Footbed has two layers—one which is intended to spring back after use, and the other to take the shape of the foot permanently.

It is early, but in time the memory foam approach will probably be more successful than making shoes on a contoured last. The memory impression is of your own foot, and not an average shape. How much support the memory foams actually give after a few long runs is a debatable point; no one has yet found a way to measure it inside the shoe. A sensible approach is to have several pairs of memory inserts. Wear them in your regular street shoes and have them ready to exchange with those in your running shoes when they seem to have gone too thin.

Further research is certain to give us more comfortable footbeds. Until then, despite some unproven assertions, there is little doubt that most of the memory units available are a step up from a flat board inside the shoe.

Fit and Comfort 211

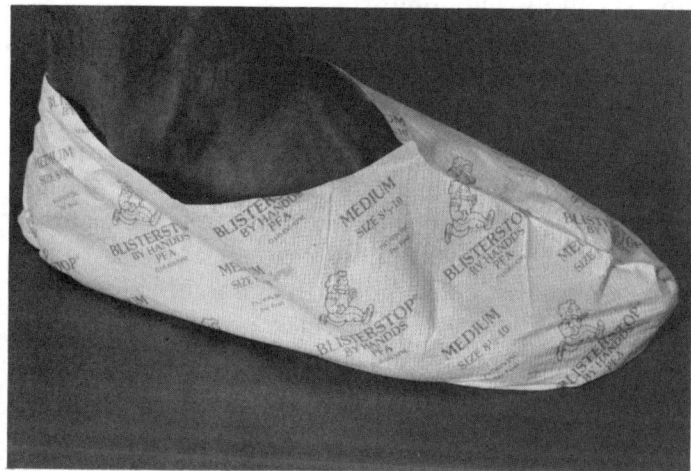

Fig. 9.16 Blisterstop—a paperlike undersock advertised as a means of preventing blisters.

Avoiding Friction

There are areas of runner's folklore that we have left out of the comfort equation so far. Seams in the toe of both socks and shoes are something that most runners avoid. They cause blisters and chafing, and many runners lubricate their toes and feet to avoid trouble. A new way to eliminate blisters is a product called Blisterstop shown in Figure 9.16. This is like a paper sock which is worn underneath the regular sock. It is too soon to tell, but initial reports are encouraging. More traditional remedies include the use of moleskin over tender spots.

Friction from movement between foot and shoe is a barrier to comfort, particularly on the sole. One well-known attempt to combat this blister generating problem is to use a sockliner which allows the foot to move slightly without sliding. The material must be capable of a lot of shear strain; its top and bottom surfaces should be able to move in opposite directions. This will let the foot move forward without sliding.

But the line between enough movement and too much is very thin. As the foot eases forward it will tend to rub on the upper; so while the sole is being spared the top may suffer.

Insoles which get slippery when wet will heighten the blister problem. The foot will slide and, although the sole is lubricated, the upper is not and trauma to the toes and instep may result.

Comfort and Hygiene

Keeping a shoe comfortable requires some care from the runner. Good foot hygiene goes hand in hand with comfort. The optimum environment for the growth of bacteria and fungi is warm, damp, and dark, which pretty accurately describes the conditions inside a running shoe. As we have seen from the "odd shoe run" a considerable amount of perspiration will accumulate in the shoes and socks during running, probably regardless of the type of uppers worn.

space, is particularly vulnerable to infection and should receive special attention. The spaces should be dried individually, making sure that the powder covers the area well. If the spaces close up, small pieces of cotton wool can be used.

Athlete's foot is a fungal infection which can also be encouraged by poor hygiene. Dr. Joseph M. Greenberg is a dermatologist who saw more than his share of foot infections during a tour of duty with the American army in Vietnam. He saw the effects on feet that had been damp for long periods of time, and had some success in reducing infection by painting the feet with a solution of glutaraldehyde. This substance tends to inhibit perspiration, keeping the feet drier and healthier.

Closing Out Fit and Comfort

We have shown in this chapter that there are critical ingredients without which a shoe will simply not feel good. Some of these, like last dimensions and permeability to water vapor, can be measured, but many cannot. The key to a comfortable shoe is still the intelligent use of trial and error. Progress in material technology in the next decade should allow us to obtain significantly better fit and comfort from our running shoes. The custom shoemaker may well be displaced by the creative chemist in the quest for better fit and more comfort.

10

Shoe Gerontology

College students are always on the lookout for a few extra dollars to help them through the week. So when the following advertisement appeared in our college newspaper, students appeared in droves:

MONEY FOR OLD SHOES

Give your old running shoes to science and get $3.00 a pair for them.

As well as overwhelming, the response was worrisome. As the pictures in the following pages will show, some of the shoes had been used far beyond the limits of safety. They had been worn until they were falling apart, until they had no outsoles, holes in the uppers, midsoles that were rock hard, and counters that were completely shredded.

Old shoes do not keep their secrets well. They reveal a wealth of information, not only about the reluctance of their owners to spend money on new shoes, but also on the running styles and habits of those owners. This information can be extremely useful to both the wearers and their physicians. We discuss in Chapter 14 how to "debrief" your old shoes before setting out to buy a new pair. The wear patterns can show you how you approach the ground at foot strike, and they reveal any unusual side-to-side forces that you are exerting during contact. Many doctors insist that running patients bring along their old shoes to an examination so that clinical observations of running patterns can be confirmed by empirical evidence of shoe wear.

But this chapter is not designed to tell you how to sit back and watch your shoes take a beating. We shall look at wear patterns that occur, but we shall also look at such questions as shoe care, resoling, and how to tell when enough is enough and throw your old shoes away. Let's start by looking at wear patterns in four major regions of the shoe: the outsole, the upper, the midsole, and the rearpart.

OUTSOLE WEAR

Most runners check the wear of the outsole to determine when to buy a new pair of shoes. This is not an entirely foolproof procedure. The major areas of outsole wear are shown in Figure 10.1a, in which the density of shading represents the frequency of wear. By far the most common feature of outsole wear is a grinding off of the rear outside border, typified by the shoes in Figure 10.1b, which have been taken far beyond reason-

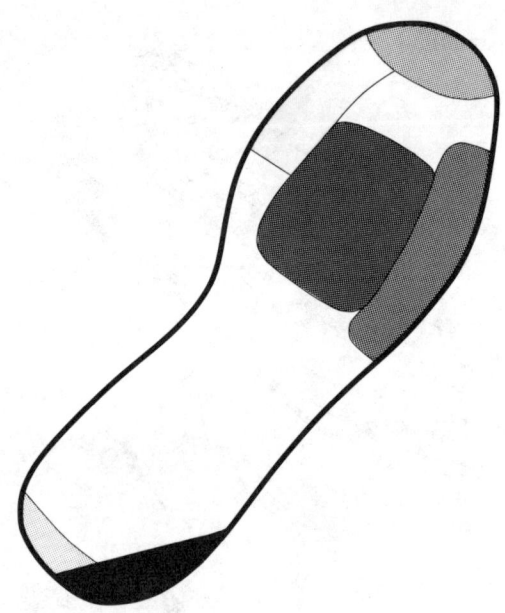

Fig. 10.1a The major areas of outsole wear, shaded from dark to light in approximate grading of normal wear (darkest areas wear most).

able limits of wear. Not only has the runner worn through the outsole, but also right through the wedge and into the midsole. This pattern, typical of a rearfoot striker, occurs when the foot first contacts the ground

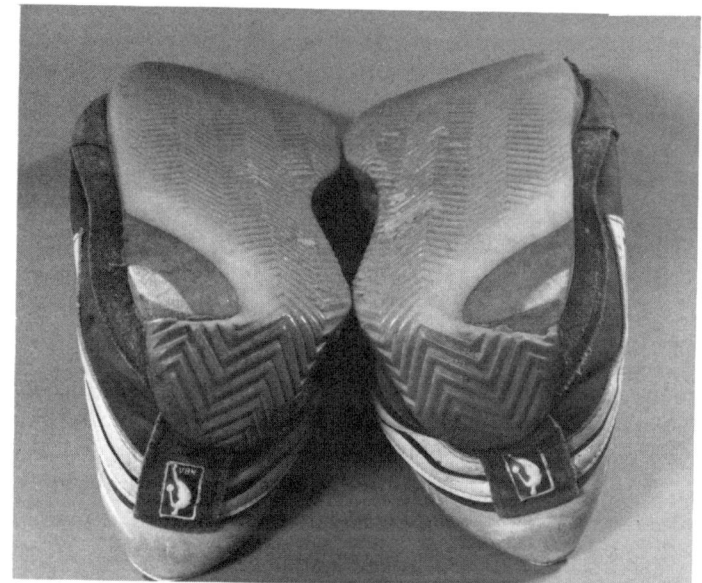

Fig. 10.1b The classical wear pattern, taken too far. The outside border of each shoe is completely worn down through the wedge to the midsole.

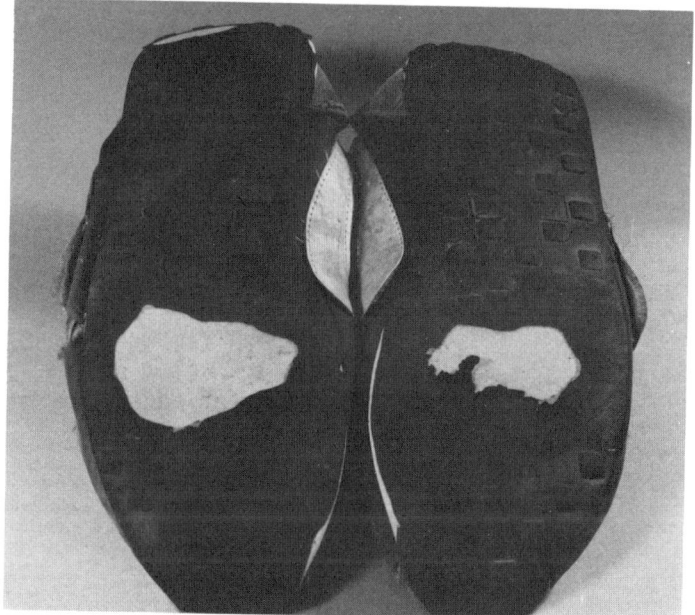

Fig. 10.1c A forefoot wear pattern in which the outsole has been completely worn away.

and relative movement occurs between the shoe and the ground. Even if the runner is a midfoot or forefoot striker their shoes will show this wear pattern if they do an appreciable amount of downhill running.

Wear under the ball of the foot is also extremely common. This occurs not because of large forces but because most people move the foot while it is "planted" on the ground during the support phase. This movement is usually a twisting outward as the pelvis moves forward to achieve adequate stride length. The shoes shown in Figure 10.1c have also been worn far beyond their safe limit. The outsole has been completely worn away, and already sections of the midsole have been ground away.

A runner who is a midfoot or forefoot striker often shows a unique wear pattern. The owner of the shoes

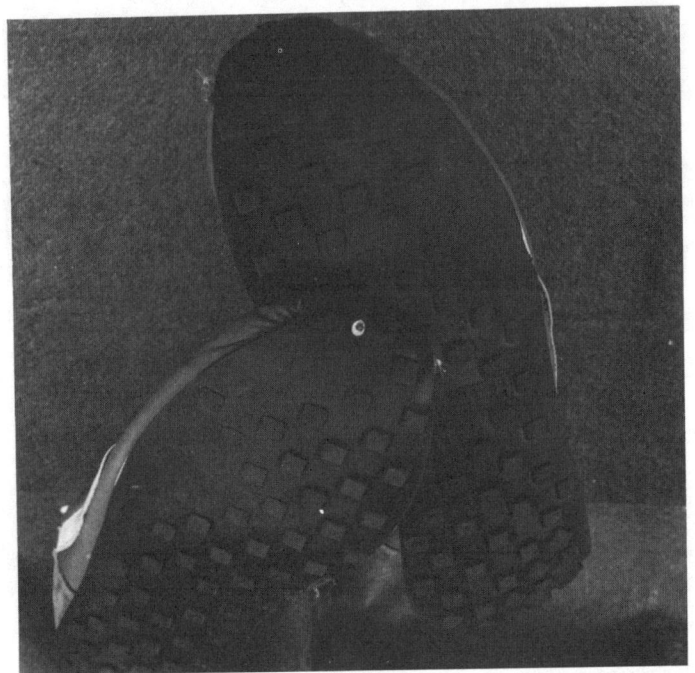

Fig. 10.1d The wear pattern of a forefoot striker. The waffle nubs in the rear part of the shoe are prominent while those in the forefoot have almost disappeared.

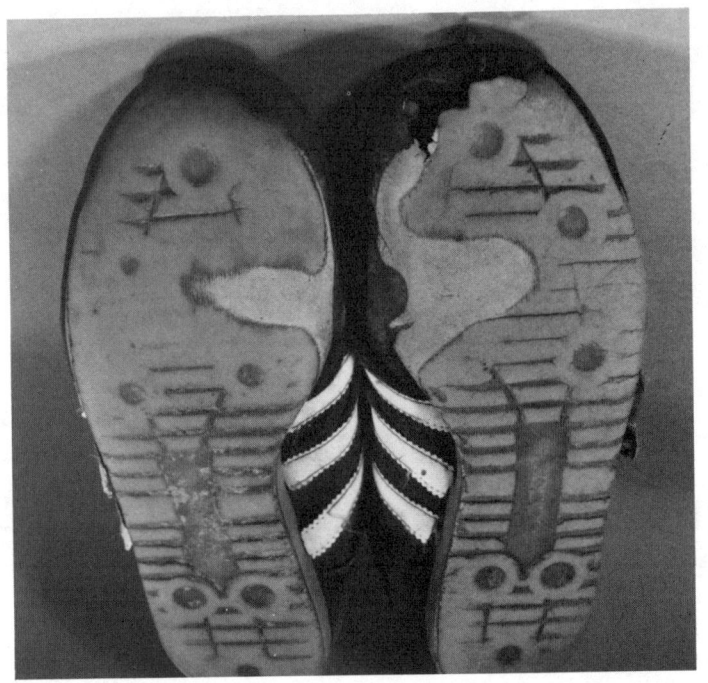

Fig. 10.1e An unusual pattern showing most wear under the inside border of the forefoot. These shoes also show a wearing down of the outsole in the toe region.

shown in Figure 10.1d is a forefoot striker who is also considerably pigeon-toed. It is intriguing to see the waffles on the back still in good shape, while the forward outer edges of both shoes have been completely shaved away. This kind of wear can make the shoe uncomfortable as each small stone begins to be felt. The possibility of stone bruises becomes greater.

Outsole wear in the toe often occurs if the runner's feet drag on toe-off. This wear pattern can accelerate the breakdown of the bond between the midsole and

Shoe Gerontology 217

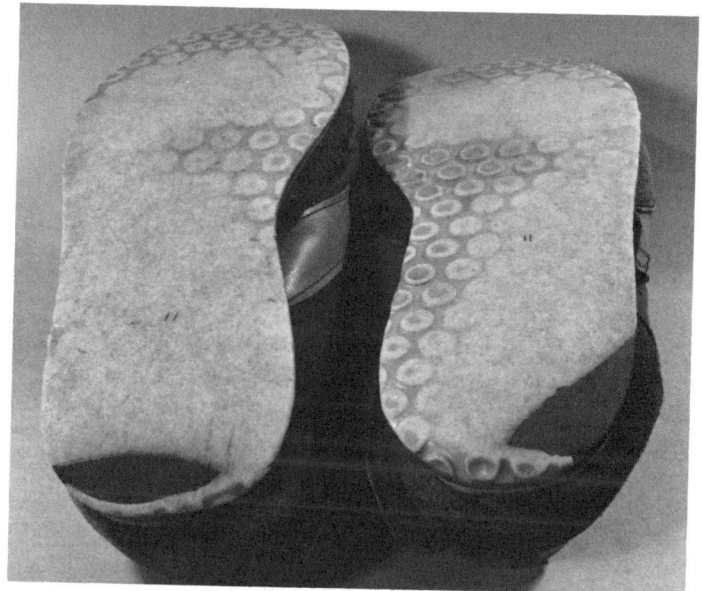

Fig. 10.1f A telltale pattern of asymmetrical wear between left and right shoes.

Fig. 10.1g Outsoles that became brittle and cracked under the ball of the foot.

the outsole as shown in Figure 10.1e. Shoes in which the outsole is wrapped over the front of the toebox help this problem considerably.

It is frequently possible to see asymmetrical wear patterns on the right and left shoes which are reflections of skeletal asymmetries or dynamic imbalances in running. The shoes in Figure 10.1f show that the right foot makes contact with the ground on its rear border, which is an extremely unusual pattern of contact in running. The left foot shows the typical diagonal wear similar to Figure 10.1b.

Unusual wear patterns are occasionally seen, such as that in Figure 10.1e. This runner had a considerable amount of forefoot valgus (see Chapter 4), and made first contact with the ground on the inside border of each foot, resulting in this wear pattern. Another unusual problem is seen in Figure 10.1g where the sole

218 SHOE GERONTOLOGY

was so brittle that it cracked under the ball of the foot in both left and right shoes.

What To Do About Sole Wear

If sole wear is allowed to go to the extremes shown in Figure 10.1b, there is little doubt that it can become harmful. When the foot finally does become flat, it turns over a knife edge caused by the worn area; this causes rapid motion at a number of joints in the foot and leg.

Several methods are available to build up worn areas on the sole. One which has waned in popularity in recent years is the use of a hot glue gun. Sticks of glue are fed into the electrically heated gun and smoothed out over the worn surface. A more convenient form of repair is the Shoe-Goo approach, in which a solution is squeezed from a tube onto the outsole (Figure 10.2a). A piece of scotch tape around the edge of the region can act as a mold and the compound will set overnight. Bostik, who make the glue gun pellets, and the manufacturers of Shoe Goo both abruptly rejected inquiries about the exact composition of their products and are clearly interested in keeping runners in the dark.

While both of the gluing methods provide a temporary fix, the "Eternal Sole" and the "Wedgee-Patch" attempt a more permanent solution. In these techniques (Figure 10.2b) a small piece of hard elastomer is embedded into the worn surface. This is much more

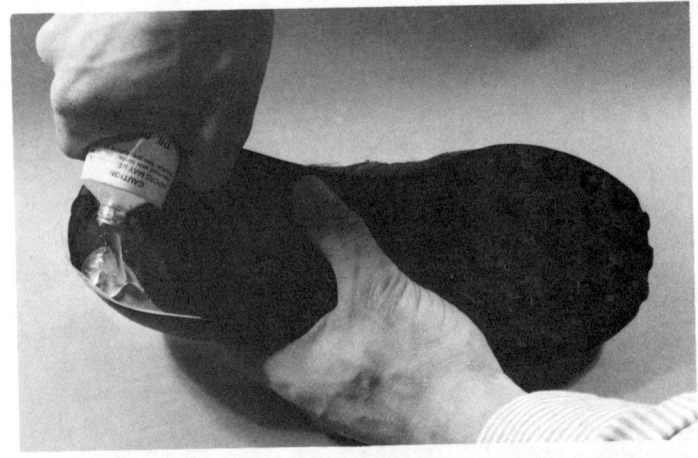

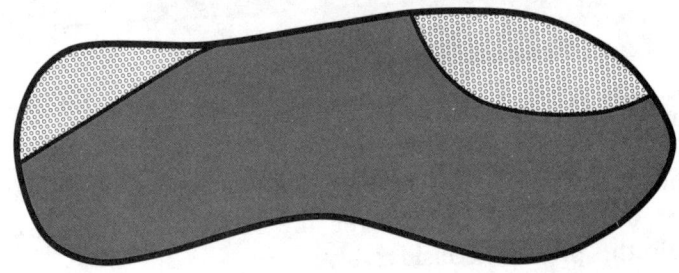

Fig. 10.2 Two solutions to sole wear. a) "Shoe goo" is spread into the worn rearfoot area outlined by a piece of scotch tape to provide a mold. b) A piece of hard elastomeric material is shaped and cemented into the worn regions.

abrasion resistant than the original rubber or a glue, but it is also difficult to use under the ball of the foot, and may be slippery in wet conditions.

The new Stride Rite shoes described in Chapter 8 offer a novel possibility for repairing worn outsoles. This design features replaceable wear plugs which the user can change as they wear down. I would not be surprised if this technique was employed by other manufacturers in the future.

The final cure for a worn sole is to have the shoe completely resoled. This costs about forty percent of the price of a new pair, and so it is vital that the rest of the shoe is in good condition before this alternative is chosen. It is of particular importance that the cushioning properties of the midsole and wedge have not deteriorated enough to cause worry that they are inadequate. We shall return to this topic shortly.

UPPER WEAR

Often the first part to break down on the upper is the company logo, which is made of vinyl. The days are long gone when the stripes, swooshes, or stars on the side of the shoe did anything functional. So this damage is not really cause for concern.

Leather and nylon show distinctly different wear patterns. Despite their many advantages, nylon uppers also have the disadvantage of inferior wear. If a shoe with a

Fig. 10.3 a) A SEM of torn nylon taffeta uppers.

nylon upper is scuffed or rubbed the nylon filaments may break easily and rip over a large area. The result, shown in magnified form in Figure 10.3a, is a tangle of broken fibers which is often the beginning of the end. A tear in a mesh upper is potentially even more serious than in nylon weave. The mesh is knitted, and may unravel or run in exactly the same way as a woolen sweater or a pair of nylons. The results can be catastrophic, as shown in Figure 10.3b.

Sometimes wear will occur in specific regions. The shoes in Figure 10.3c were not well fitted to the length

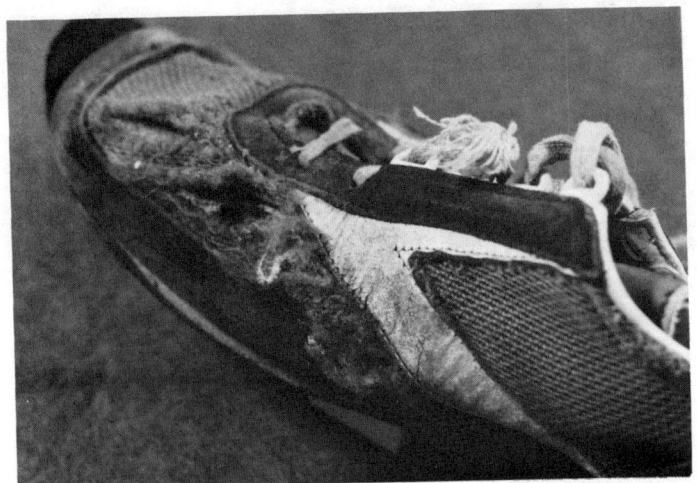

Fig. 10.3b A badly worn nylon mesh upper.

Fig. 10.3c Toenail holes, often caused by wearing shoes that have a toe box that is too low for a particular foot. A dab of shoe goo was used to repair the damage.

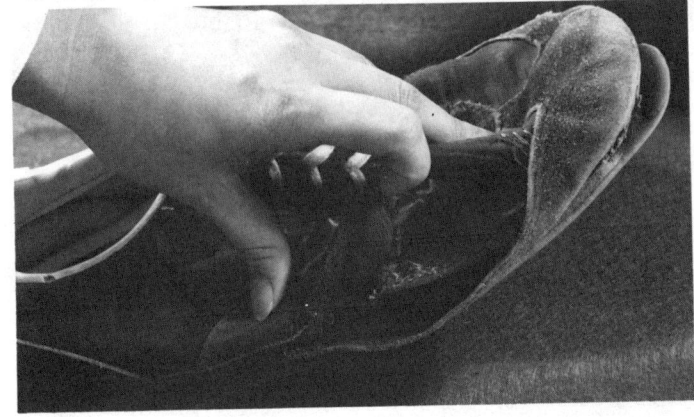

Fig. 10.3d A separation of the nylon upper and leather foxing.

or height of the runner's foot. The toenails on both second toes poked a hole through the upper. As you see from the photograph, the runner managed to halt the process by squeezing a blob of glue over the area.

Another common problem is rotting or tearing of the stitching which secures the various leather trimmings to the upper. These leather sections usually have more than a cosmetic function. They strengthen the shoe, particularly against lateral forces. If their breakdown is not prevented, the upper may pull loose from its bond between the insole board and the midsole, as shown in Figure 10.3d.

Fig. 10.3e Excessive wear caused by an unusual foot strike pattern and a lack of leather reinforcement.

Fig. 10.3f Deformed leather uppers from feet crying out for wider shoes.

If there is no leather trim around the border of the shoe with a nylon upper, excessive wear can occur. The amazing wear patterns shown in Figure 10.3e were caused by a runner whose foot had considerable forefoot varus (see Chapter 4 for definition). The effect was such that he actually scraped the ground with the outside border of the upper. The fact that he continued using the shoe until the hole was large enough to slip an egg through speaks volumes about the pay of graduate students.

We mentioned that one of the big differences between nylon and leather uppers is in their ability to take the shape of the foot. Nylon will not stretch permanently, while leather, particularly if helped along by heat or moisture, will expand and set in a new position. This is illustrated dramatically in Figure 10.3f, which shows feet crying out for more space. Besides needing a wider shoe, this runner's style created side-to-side forces which pushed his foot sideways, off the shoe. The leather responded by taking the stretch and leaving the foot overhanging the sole.

Leather uppers need more care than their nylon counterparts. If leather is put through wet and dry cycles without any special attention, it gets stiff, brittle, and wrinkled. This is shown in Figure 10.3g, where we see a permanent change in configuration. This shoe

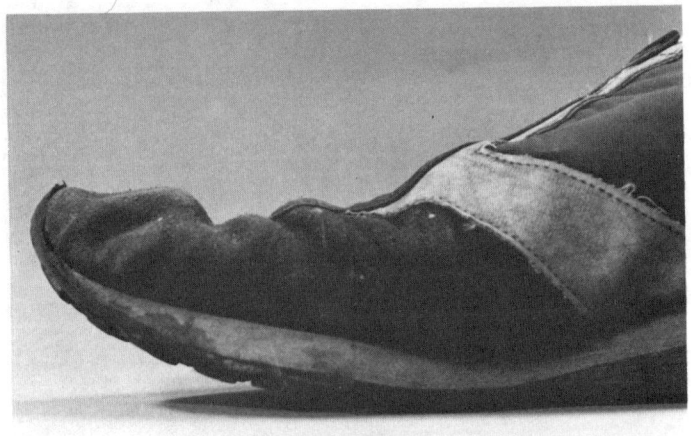

Fig. 10.3g Stiff and brittle folds in a leather upper caused by poor care.

would be uncomfortable and did in fact crack along the featherline.

Care of Uppers

Nylon uppers are almost maintenance free unless they start to snag or rip. I know very few runners who have patched their nylon uppers successfully. If stitching is attempted, it should be done with a blunt rounded needle so that more nylon filaments are not damaged in the repair.

Trying to stop mesh uppers from ripping with glue is usually successful, but this stiffens the area, sometimes to the point of discomfort. Special shampoos are sold for nylon uppers, but soap and water will do just as well. Although the uppers will not be harmed by a hot air dryer, the midsole will. Running shoes should *never* be put into a hot air dryer. A shoe drying rack is marketed in some European countries, but I have not seen this in America.

There is a number of ways to care for leather uppers. One of the best is still the remedy used by Jock Semple fifty years ago to soften his marathon shoes. Rubbing neatsfoot oil into the shoe keeps the upper from becoming hard and dry. It is available at most shoe stores. Rapid drying should be avoided for wet leather shoes, and don't wear them right after they have been drenched. Not only does this lead to blue feet due to lack of color fastness in the leather, but may permanently stretch the shoes until they are too big.

MIDSOLE AND WEDGE WEAR

Aging of the midsole and wedge is potentially the most serious wear in a running shoe. What makes it sinister is the fact that the shoe may have lost a great deal of its cushioning properties long before the upper or outsole show visible signs of damage. I say "may have" because we don't have final answers to these questions, but there are some worrisome indications.

Twenty-eight shoes were chosen at random from

those collected in our "old shoe buyback." The estimated mileage on these shoes varied from 400 to 2,000 and they showed very different amounts and characteristics of wear. We put the shoes through the same tests that new shoes take in the *Runner's World* survey. Although we didn't test the specific shoes before and after they were worn, we did know how that brand tested when new on the previous year's *Runner's World* test.

On the impact test described in Chapter 7, the old shoes performed an average of eleven percent worse than the new in the rearfoot, while the shock absorption of the forefoot decreased by nearly forty percent. These values are averages; individual shoes showed larger discrepancies. The worst shoe in the batch showed a drop of seventy percent in the forefoot and forty percent in the rearfoot. These were very different shoes when tested than they were the moment they were lifted out of the box.

The question obviously needs more study. Was the decline steady, or did the shock absorption suddenly plummet after a certain number of miles? Do some shoes deteriorate more than others, and are there visible clues a runner can watch for?

The last question can at least be answered partially without further study. The EVA foams used in the midsole harden with age. Unfortunately hardness does not correlate directly with shock absorption even when the shoe is new. But if the foam gets harder, you can be

Fig. 10.4a A test of the hardness of a midsole using a Durometer. Wear and weathering increases the hardness of the material.

sure that some cushioning ability has been lost. There is a test of hardness which quantifies the "fingernail test" you can do yourself. The device shown in Figure 10.4a is being used on a well broken in shoe. Where the new shoe would register from thirty to thirty-five, the meter is reading double this value. The shock absorption had

Fig. 10.4b Shrinkage of the midsole and wedge by overheating has resulted in the delamination of midsole and outsole. Putting shoes in a hot air dryer or leaving them in the trunk of a car on a hot day can cause this to happen.

Fig. 10.4c Permanent deformation of the midsole in the ball region has caused excessive toespring in this shoe.

probably deteriorated long before this hardened condition was reached. So if your own shoes have very hard midsoles, you are overdue for a new pair.

Another regression seen in the midsole is shrinkage, which most often occurs through carelessness. The shoe in Figure 10.4b was left in the back of a car during a series of extremely hot days. Both the midsole and wedge shrunk about a quarter inch in all directions, probably hastening the delamination of the outsole. A partial shrinkage in the ball area can cause the toe to turn up like a banana (Figure 10.4c). The same thing happens when a shoe is put into a hot air clothes dryer. Most midsole materials cannot tolerate temperatures above 160 degrees Fahrenheit, without changing their structure and mechanical properties. Shoes put in the dryer are ruined.

A very critical aspect of midsole and wedge wear is compression set or thinning of the sandwich on the

Fig. 10.4 Cracks forming between the midsole and wedge layers during aging.

Fig. 10.4 e A breakdown of the bond between the insole board and the midsole.

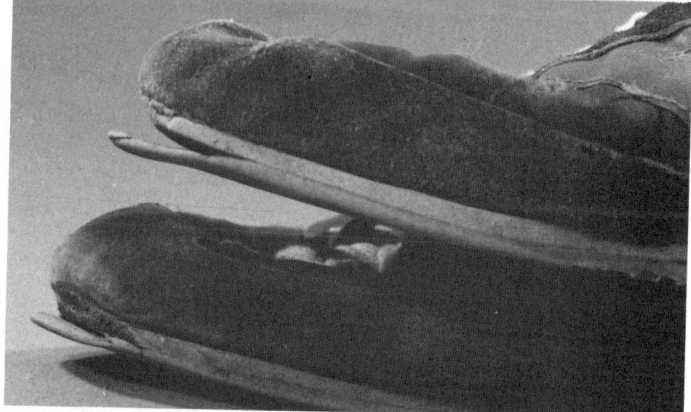

Fig. 10.4 f Shredding of the midsole in the toe region.

inside or outside border of the shoe. We will discuss this in the next section since it is particularly apparent from the back of the shoe.

Other telltale signs of wear include cracks between the midsole and wedge layers (Figure 10.4d), a breakdown of the bond between the midsole and the lasting board (Figure 10.4e), and occasional shredding of the material by abrasion, particularly in the toe region (Figure 10.4f).

What To Do About Midsole Wear

There are two options for a midsole that shows wear. You can either throw the shoe away or try to rejuvenate it with a new outsole. Although some repair people will replace everything below the upper, the cost of replacement rapidly approaches the price of a new shoe.

To see what resoling would do for the shock absorption of a worn shoe, we resoled four of our battered shoes, two with a waffle type outsole and two with a standard herringbone pattern. We impact tested them before and after resoling. The waffles were slightly more successful at restoring some shock absorption to the shoes. Overall the rearfoot registered a five percent return in shock absorption, while the forefoot showed a marked improvement, regaining over half its lost cushioning. Clearly, resoling does more than just make up for lost traction. The outsole is a factor in shock absorption by the shoe. But it can never restore the shoe to its former glory; once the midsole has deteriorated, it cannot be revived. Unless the midsole is unquestionably in good condition, it is a safer bet to buy new shoes.

WEAR IN THE REAR OF THE SHOE

The back of the shoe takes a hard beating, and soon begins to show the signs of wear. In particular the heel counters are a weak part of many good shoes. A poor fiberboard counter will cease to function effectively the first time it gets wet. Even the best counters do not hold up over time, and new thinking by shoe manufacturers is needed to give the rearfoot better long-term control. Most heel counters become "mushy," and are little better than thin cardboard. They fail to keep the foot in place, and with each foot strike the foot breaks the shoe down a little more, enabling increased lateral movement to occur.

Eventually, the whole rear of the shoe takes a "set" in one direction or another. If the runner tends to pronate, the rearpart of the left and right shoes form an arrowhead pointing inward (Figure 10.5a). The shoes of a runner who stays on the outside of the foot during the support phase will lean away from each other (Figure 10.5b).

This leads to further complications. The midsole and wedge are subjected to uneven compressive forces under either the inside or outside border, depending upon the runner. Because these pressures are greater than they would normally be, the materials are slowly reduced in thickness. You can see this clearly in Figure 10.5c, which is the result of cutting the back two inches off a worn shoe. The darker material (the wedge) is about twenty percent thicker on the outside.

All this tends to exaggerate the skeletal alignment problem. This particular runner tended to roll off the inside of the shoe; by lowering the inside border, this

Shoe Gerontology 227

Fig. 10.5a Shoes leaning toward the midline, indicating a runner who pronates excessively on both sides.

Fig. 10.5b Shoes leaning outward. This runner tended to fall off the shoes on the outside border.

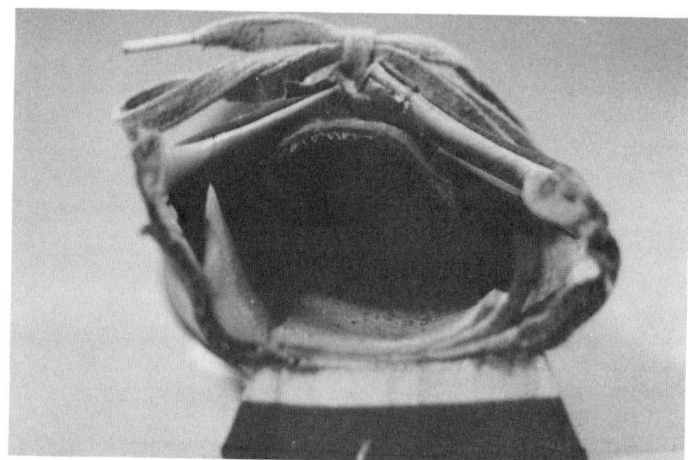

Fig. 10.5c A cross cut through a right shoe that had taken a compression set on the inside border. The wedge (dark material) is about twenty percent thicker on the outside border.

tendency is encouraged. The material has actually molded itself into a valgus wedge which is the reverse of what this runner needs. Compressive set is not limited to the rearpart and can occur along the whole length of the shoe.

Even heel counters which are molded from such compounds as polyethylene can deteriorate. Those shown in Figure 10.5d have become brittle, broken into many parts, and are ineffective in providing rearfoot control.

If the platform in the rearfoot is extremely narrow, the counter does not stand much chance of success.

228 SHOE GERONTOLOGY

Fig. 10.5d The heel counter pocket of this shoe has been sliced open to show the shattered heel counter. The material was initially firm but too brittle to last.

Fig. 10.5e The heel counters in this shoe have expanded on both sides so that they overhang the midsole platform, which was too narrow to give adequate support.

Fig. 10.5f This wraparound of the outsole onto the heel is a configuration that adds to the stability of the rearpart of the shoe.

The shoes in Figure 10.5e belonged to a runner with a fairly neutral alignment during the support phase. The rearparts did not end up tilting, but simply "overflowed" the shoe on both inside and outside borders because of the narrow width.

One benefit of the high sole wrap-around at the heel is the stabilizing effect it can have on the rearpart. The shoes in Figure 10.5f have quite soft heel counters, which have shown signs of wear similar to some specimens we have discussed. But even after an estimated 1,000 miles, the rearpart of the shoes remains firm and vertical because of the strong bond between the wraparound of the rubber outsole and the back of the shoe. This feature, although common a few years ago, has almost disappeared. Some manufacturer would do well to introduce this construction again.

Solutions to Rear Part Breakdown

There are no really good solutions to the wear problems we have just described. Heel counters are not replaceable, because as we saw in Chapter 5, most are incorporated into the back of the shoe before the lasting operation. Many counters also have a flap which is cemented between the insole board and the sole. A heel cup (see Chapter 12) may provide some stability, but the chances are that it will not have too much inside the shoe to restrain its movement. The only long term solution is for runners to pressure shoe manufacturers into finding alternatives to those materials currently in use. What is needed is a material which will stand up to hard wear, but not be so stiff when new that it causes pain.

The lack of repair possibilities highlights the importance of choosing quality in the first place. You should buy a shoe which is well-rated on the stiffness test in the *Runner's World* survey and one that has a counter which you think can go the distance.

Once midsole or wedge compression of the kind shown in Figure 10.5c occurs, the shoes should be discarded. A total height difference between inside and outside borders of approximately three millimeters should be considered critical. This is enough to give the shoe a three degree tilt which will change the alignment of the whole leg. Running with this sort of encouragement to an alignment problem can end in an overuse injury (see Chapter 13). In the next few years, as ultralightweight foams are incorporated into running shoes, it is going to be very important to make sure that rapid and permanent deformation of materials does not occur. Otherwise, we may end up with light, but very dangerous, running shoes. If this is planned obsolescence by shoemakers, then runners will have to let their voices be heard against it.

WEAR INSIDE THE SHOE

The environment inside the shoe is in many ways more hostile than that on the outside. Whereas the outside usually has to withstand little more than mud and water, those 150,000 sweat glands on the foot are busy producing a variety of substances bent on breaking down the inside of the shoe.

How well they succeed depends to a large extent on the quality of the insole board (in a cement lasted shoe, see Chapter 5). If the shoemaker has used a low-grade board to save a few pennies, when you lift the sockliner in a well-used shoe there will be a tangled mass which looks like old blotting paper. A better board will retain its dimensions and integrity.

Sockliners which are not designed to take a form fit to the foot will occasionally tear, particularly under the forefoot. If both the sockliner and insole board have worn badly, then the foot is left in direct contact with the midsole. Since the insole board is no longer there to distribute the pressure. the shape of the foot begins to form a pressure set in the midsole. This can become uncomfortable as the toes slide in and out of the depressions in the midsole.

The lining inside the shoe is a much less substantial material than the upper itself. Lining is usually a loose knit cotton or polyester which can rip or tear. If the ripped lining rolls up and forms ridges inside the shoe it can lead to blisters.

Fixes for Wear Inside the Shoe

Drastic breakdown of the insole board can be repaired, but it is best to entrust the job to a shoe repair person. There are many materials that will serve the purpose—leather, reconstituted leather, or an exact duplicate of the original, if it is available. It is worth having the job done only if the rest of the shoe is in at least fair condition.

I believe that new shoes should come with a spare set of sockliners. Because the sockliner is a component of the shock absorbing system, which is easily replaceable, it makes eminent sense to replace it often. Since not one manufacturer agrees with this idea, you are left to choose from those sold in running shoe stores as extras. Several types are discussed in Chapter 9, and you would do well to buy a pair when you get your new shoes.

Improving With Age

As running shoes age, some of their properties actually improve! Many of the shoes in our "old shoe study" showed markedly better scores on flexibility, rearfoot stability, and penetration. Part of this is simply the process of breaking the shoe in. During the first few weeks of wear, the various materials are softened and some of the initial stretching that takes place is positive.

But the improvements in stability and penetration are the other side of losses in cushioning. As the midsole material hardens it does offer better rearfoot control, but at the expense of shock absorption.

Accelerating the Wear

Doing anything but running is going to accelerate the wear patterns we have described. Walking might be the only exception, but that too will cause additional wear. The worst thing you can do though, both for your shoes and yourself, is to play a sport, like tennis or basketball, which involves both stopping and starting and a lot of lateral movement. Running shoes offer very little stability for side-to-side motion. They don't need it in the sport for which they were intended, and such motions can destroy a running shoe in a hurry. Playing these sports in running shoes can also make such traumas as ankle sprains more likely to occur.

The other side of the coin is that when a pair of shoes is no longer any good for running, they can be worn around the yard or for some similar purpose. This can sometimes soften the blow of having to set the shoes aside from running because they will be useful for a good length of time.

THE ECONOMICS OF IT ALL

I have seen enough battered shoes to realize that most runners don't like to spend money. Runners just become emotionally attached to their old shoes.

But the economics of wearing shoes until they fall off your feet do not make good sense. Suppose you pay thirty-five dollars for a pair of shoes that you use for 500 miles. Your sport has cost you seven cents a mile. Now let's presume you decide to ignore the warning signs, and try to squeeze another 500 miles out of the shoes. This would lower the overall cost to three and a half cents a mile. But we have seen that aging shoes may deteriorate considerably in their protective qualities. Thus these additional 500 miles carry with them the risk of getting injured. This may involve a visit to the doctor, X-rays, and so on, which could easily exceed the cost of three new pairs of shoes. For most runners, the economic argument is superfluous, because the harsher penalty is being forced to stop running.

Putting an exact mileage limit on a pair of shoes is difficult. It will depend on the usual mixture of running style, habits, temperature conditions, shoe care, and other factors. More research is needed to see what changes accompany various wear histories. For some people the limit may be as low as 500 miles while others may manage 1,000 miles or more in a shoe without substantial risk.

If 500 miles does not sound very far, think of it as almost a quarter of a million impacts to each shoe, and then remember that as the shoe deteriorates in its ability to cushion these impacts, the next 250,000 will be felt a little bit more with each step. Then go out and buy yourself a new pair of running shoes while the feeling lasts. If you only remember one thing from this chapter, it should be this: your running shoes may have lost at least a quarter of their protective qualities before any obvious signs of wear occur. So don't wait until the shoes are literally falling off your feet before you get another pair.

11

Racing Flats

There is nothing quite like putting on a pair of racing flats to convince you that you can qualify for the Olympics. But most runners have lingering doubts. They know there are psychological benefits to wearing racing shoes. But when there is one mile done and more than twenty-five to go they wonder if the lack of protection will begin to offset the mental lift. In this chapter we will look at evidence which might be used to decide if the change to racing shoes is worthwhile.

What Does an Average Shoe Weigh?

The decision to change from training to racing shoes is usually motivated by a desire to save weight. Looking at the results of the 1980 *Runner's World* survey shows us exactly what savings are achieved.

The average women's training and racing flats weighed 258 grams (9.1 ounces) and 188 grams (6.6 ounces) per shoe, respectively. The corresponding men's values were 320 grams (11.3 ounces) and 235 grams (8.3 ounces), respectively. The values quoted are for size 7 (women's) and size 9 (men's).

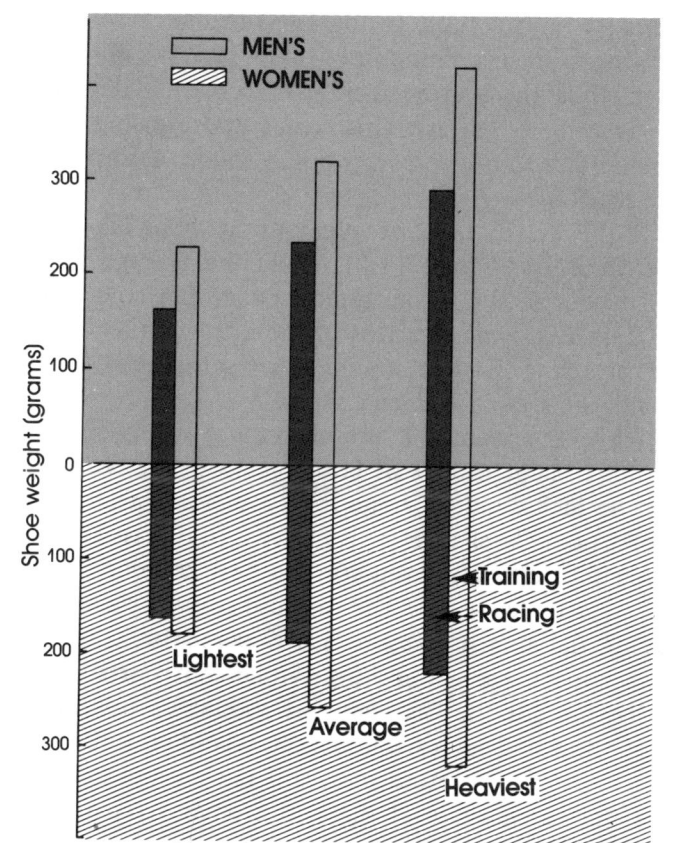

Fig. 11.1 The weights, in grams, of men's (above the zero line) and women's (below the zero line) training and racing flats in the 1980 *Runner's World* survey. The lightest, average, and heaviest shoes are shown in each category.

In addition to the mean values we should look at the extremes. These values, shown in Figure 11.1, indicate ranges of over 193 grams (6.8 ounces) and 116 grams (4 ounces) in men's training and racing flats, respectively. For women's shoes the ranges are 142 grams (5 ounces) and 60 grams (2.1 ounces), respectively.

Are the Weight Differences Significant?

When all the arithmetic is done, men changing from the average training flat to the average racing flat will save about 85 grams (3 ounces) per shoe, and women will save 70 grams (2.6 ounces). Is this saving significant?

There have been several experiments which have attempted to provide answers to this question. The most recent study was conducted at the University of California at Davis by Mike Catlin and Rudy Dressendorfer. These researchers had seven marathoners of varying abilities (2:18 to 5:03) run on a treadmill on two separate occasions. Different shoes were worn for each session. The subjects wore racing flats weighing 260 grams per shoe, and training flats which weighed 435 grams each. The average response to the total weight increase of approximately 350 grams was an elevated oxygen uptake of approximately three and a third percent when wearing the heavier shoe.

We should note the possibility that other factors such as midsole composition helped to decrease the energy cost in the racing shoes. But let's say that it was all due to weight. This suggests the rough rule that a saving of one percent in energy cost is achieved for every 100 grams of total (left plus right) shoe weight saved.

Now, a good argument can be made that reduction in oxygen cost translates directly into faster speeds. The apparently small energy saving achieved with racing shoes is of potentially great significance to the marathon runner. In the 1978 Boston Marathon Bill Rodgers beat Jeff Wells by two seconds with a winning time of 2:11. This is a margin of about one-fiftieth of one percent. If the theory is carried to the limit it predicts that each of Wells' shoes need only have been one gram (less than one-twentieth of an ounce) lighter to have made him the winner.

So it seems that racing shoes give the runner an advantage because of their reduced weight, providing all other factors are equal. But this is where the warning comes: all other factors are not equal.

Shock Absorption

Racing flats have traditionally been skeletal. When taken to extremes, the shoe is made with no midsole. All the forefoot has to protect it is the insole board and outsole. Every pebble can be felt, and a burning deep inside the forefoot is common to many who wear racing flats.

These deficiencies are reflected in poor scores on the standard impact tests. In the 1980 *Runner's World* survey the average training flat scored 12.7 G's in the rearfoot while the average racing flat scored 14.1 G's (the lower score is better). This means that a racing flat offers about fourteen percent less shock absorption in the rearfoot.

If this is not bad enough, look at what happens in the forefoot (Figure 11.2). While the average training flat scores 18.0 G's, the typical racing flat comes home at 23.8 G's. This is a loss of more than thirty percent by changing from a training to racing shoe. Similar trends are seen in women's shoes.

While the average is useful because it represents the trends in large groups of both types of shoes you might not be lucky enough to go from average to average. The worst possible change is also shown in Figure 11.2. The impact results are given for the best training flat and the worst racing flat. The rearfoot impact score of the racing flat increases by over 100 percent and the forefoot impact is an astonishing 440 percent worse.

To present the case fairly it should be pointed out that the worst men's training flat would rank fifth from the bottom in forefoot impact if it were put in the racing flat category. And the best women's racing flat in forefoot impact would rank in the top twenty in the training category for women's shoes.

But the worst case is a warning to the runner who is in search of nothing but lightness. The sudden change

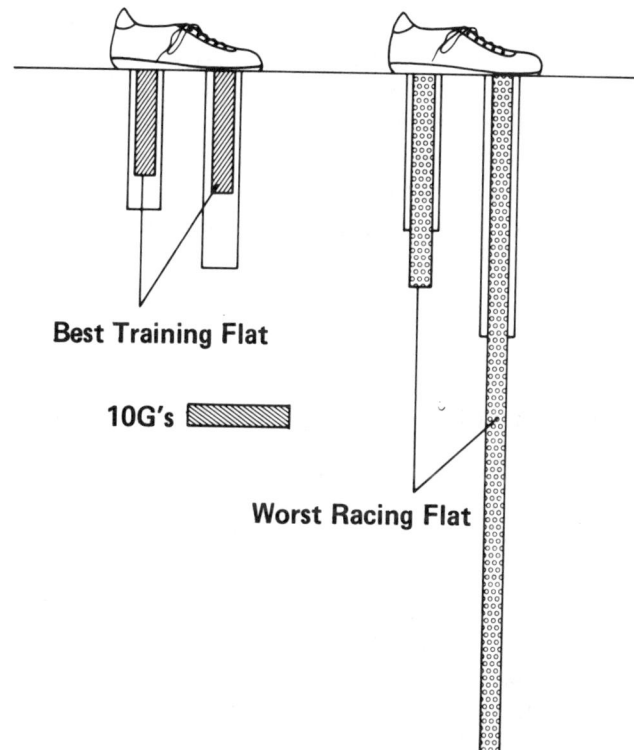

Fig. 11.2 Shock absorption in training flats (left) and racing flats (right). The bigger the bar under the foot, the larger the shock your foot would feel at foot strike. Changing from the best training flat (shaded left) to the worst racing flat (shaded right) would involve over a 400% decrement in forefoot protection. The average values for the two types of shoes measured in the 1980 *Runner's World* survey are shown by the unshaded bars.

from the protection offered by a good training shoe to the complete lack of protection in the worst racing shoe would be a traumatic event for the foot, indeed for the whole body, and would most likely lead to injury.

Rearfoot Control

It is a mistake to say that rearfoot control is not an important feature of a racing flat. Considering that road races are mostly between ten and forty-two kilometers, it is clear that they are equal to or longer than most training runs.

In the 1980 *Runner's World* survey the mean racing flats were characterized by slightly less rearfoot stability, less stiffness in the heel counter, and slightly less penetration in the rearfoot than the average training flat. Although the heel counters used in racing shoes are clearly inferior, the other two changes are relatively small. The inference is that the two groups do not differ markedly on rearfoot control.

An additional factor is that the width of the racing shoe in the rearpart is generally less than the corresponding width of a training flat; this is likely to affect its rearfoot properties.

Flexibility

Flexibility is one area where the runner is paid back for some of the deficiencies of the racing flat. Every racing flat tested in the 1980 survey would have finished in the top thirty of men's training flats. The average flexibility for racing flats was almost twice as good as that for training flats. These differences are understandable when one considers the lack of material in the forepart of many racing flats.

While most experts would agree that flexibility in the ball of the foot is extremely desirable, this also brings with it an increased flexibility about the long axis of the shoe. Many people contend that this leads to a less stable platform for the foot during segments of the support phase.

Traction

Traction is important in a racing shoe, particularly under wet conditions. The introduction of traction tests into the *Runner's World* series uncovered the interesting fact that there are dramatic differences between shoes in the traction they provide. On a dry surface almost all shoes will provide slip-free running, but under wet conditions there is about a two and a half times difference between the best and the worst.

A survey of traction results for training and racing flats shows that the range is about the same in both groups, with the mean values identical. To find a good shoe for wet weather racing, a careful examination of the traction results in the October issue of *Runner's World* is needed.

Sometimes it may prove impossible to find a shoe which has all of the desirable characteristics *and* good traction. The solution for someone who is serious about racing would be to get a pair of their favorite racing flats resoled with an outsole material that offered good traction under wet conditions.

In the world of auto racing it is common to have different tires for wet and dry conditions because traction is such an important component of good performance. In competitive road racing this factor is equally important and it's one that has been overlooked in the past.

Wear in Racing Flats

When the Law family made shoes for Roger Bannister's attempt on the mile record in 1953 they were guaranteed to last—for one race. And for runners at the top of the ladder there is little need for shoes to endure any longer. The shoes are usually free, and as long as they perform well during the race their purpose has been fulfilled.

But for most of us economics comes into play. Despite their skeletal nature racing flats are at least as expensive as training flats, so they represent a large investment. The outsole wear tests from the *Runner's World* series are not comparable between racing and training flats. If racing flats were subjected to the same treatment as training flats they would probably all wear through very early. This is because the outsoles of racing flats are considerably thinner than their training flat counterparts. So the outsole wear test was modified to provide less severe conditions for the racing flats.

Racing flats simply do not wear well on the outsole. They are not designed to and they don't.

Construction Differences

Shoe designers seem to let their hair down on racing flats. As mentioned in Chapter 9, another name for the inflared last is the speed last; this sometimes seems to mean the more inflare, the more speed—which is an entirely false proposition. The results of this kind of thinking are seen in Figure 11.3 which shows a racing flat with an extremely inflared design. Most racing flats have an inflared design, but if your foot is not suited to this shape you will find it uncomfortable and possibly damaging.

To save weight, the area of the sole underneath the long inside arch is sometimes shaved away as shown in Figure 11.4. This construction puts even more stress on the long arch of the foot, and cannot be supported as a reasonable trade-off for a few grams reduction in weight.

Since many of the racing flats do not have a substantial midsole, there is generally less height difference between the footbed in the forefoot and rearfoot regions. For a runner who has been working out in a training shoe with a considerable height differential, this can

Fig. 11.3 The insole board of a racing shoe. The arrows show the excessive inflare and the narrow width in the midfoot region.

lead to problems. The ankle joint will have become acclimatized to moving through a smaller range due to the elevated heel in the training shoe. When the racing flat is worn with its lower heel lift, the first body part to complain will probably be the Achilles tendon which is being forced through a larger range of motion than normal. At the first signs of Achilles problems in racing flats, the runner should be prepared to return to training flats. A more sensible approach to the transition would be to reduce the height differential progressively, since training flats with a range of forefoot to rearfoot height differences can be found.

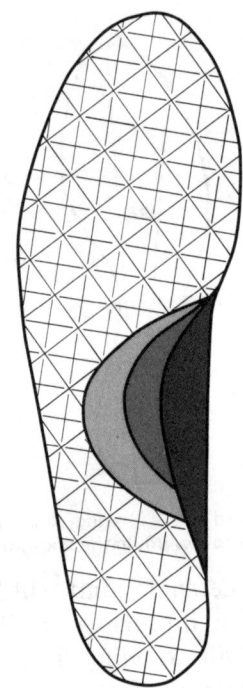

Fig. 11.4 A racing flat that is shaved underneath the arch as a weight saving measure.

Is the Pattern of Movement Different?

Besides the question of weight, it is sometimes argued that a different shoe is needed for racing because of differences in the biomechanics of running during training and racing. This argument is flawed on two counts.

First, I don't believe that many long distance runners, particularly marathoners, run substantially faster in races than they do in training. Since few runners train at or beyond the marathon distance, their training runs are at reduced distances, which usually implies increased speed. Also, interval training is becoming more popular among marathon runners, and in this case the training pace will be much faster than a marathon pace.

A second objection to the argument is that if we find a runner who races faster than his or her training pace, it's likely that the increased speed will place greater demands on the forefoot of the shoe; this is just the place where racing flats are weak. A shoe truly designed to provide the forefoot with protection during speed running would need increased, not reduced, cushioning in the forefoot region.

Weighing the Evidence

It is now time to summarize the evidence for and against racing flats. So far we have taken a shotgun approach, looking at the various measurable properties of training and racing flats. In my view the evidence is conclusive. The average runner should stick with training flats for both racing and training. The elite athletes are a special case and I shall reserve comments about this group until Chapter 15.

By the average runner I mean anyone who runs a marathon in more than two hours and thirty minutes.

Now that might not sound very average to you, but there is a reason for choosing such a respectable marathon time. For runners who are not on the fringe of national competition, the most important thing is that they can continue to run. In my view weight has been exaggerated as an important factor in running shoes. A small drop in weight can easily be negated by an injury caused by a light shoe with inadequate cushioning. If you can reduce the weight of the shoe without reducing protection, fine. But we have seen that the disadvantages of racing shoes seem to outweigh the advantages.

Let's summarize. Racing flats have lighter weight, better flexibility, and rearfoot control approximately equal to training flats. But on the negative side they have, in general, poorer rearfoot and forefoot impact, inferior sole wear characteristics, are often excessively flared, have a different heel/forefoot height relationship than training shoes, and are normally more expensive. It should be pointed out that the weight of training shoes is dropping rapidly year by year. The heaviest components are the midsole and outsole, and these are the parts which materials science is doing most to improve.

There are some people who should stay completely away from racing shoes. Runners who are habitually injured, particularly those who have had stress fractures and injuries to the forefoot, should not even consider giving up the protection that their training shoes offer. Heavier runners should also steer clear of racing shoes, particularly those at the lower end of the scale which will simply not offer them the protection or performance they need.

An Unpopular Verdict

I am aware that coming out against racing flats will be unpopular with a number of groups. Obviously shoe manufacturers would be happy if we needed a different pair for every surface, for every speed, and perhaps for every day of the week. It would help sales tremendously. Also, many runners will be unwilling to give up the psychological lift they feel when wearing shoes that weigh less than their regular training shoes.

If you are not prepared to accept this and are determined to wear racing flats, there are several things you should do. First, look very carefully at the tests on racing flats in the October issue of *Runner's World*. Choose a shoe which combines good performance with its light weight. Look carefully at the properties which are important to you; Chapter 14 will guide you through this process.

Next, make sure you try the shoes out before you race in them—preferably when you are planning workouts at a race pace. The line here is a fine one. Training in racing flats on a long-term basis can hardly be supported. But if there is a substantial difference in design between the racing shoe and your regular training shoe, you must give the body time to adapt before the all-out effort of a long race.

Some experts also believe that the pattern of limb movements is different in lighter shoes. If this is true then a new learning process may be required; this is a further argument for doing some workouts at race pace in racing flats. Also the shoes must be broken in and any sore spots on the feet identified.

Lastly, be aware that you are taking a calculated risk by wearing some of the lesser racing flats, and as with any risk, look at the probabilities before you make a move. Consider your injury history, the length of the race, your recent training level, and the properties of the racing flats you have. If the risks outweigh the benefits then lace up your old training flats and look elsewhere for that slight advantage.

12

Inserts, Arch Supports, and Orthotics

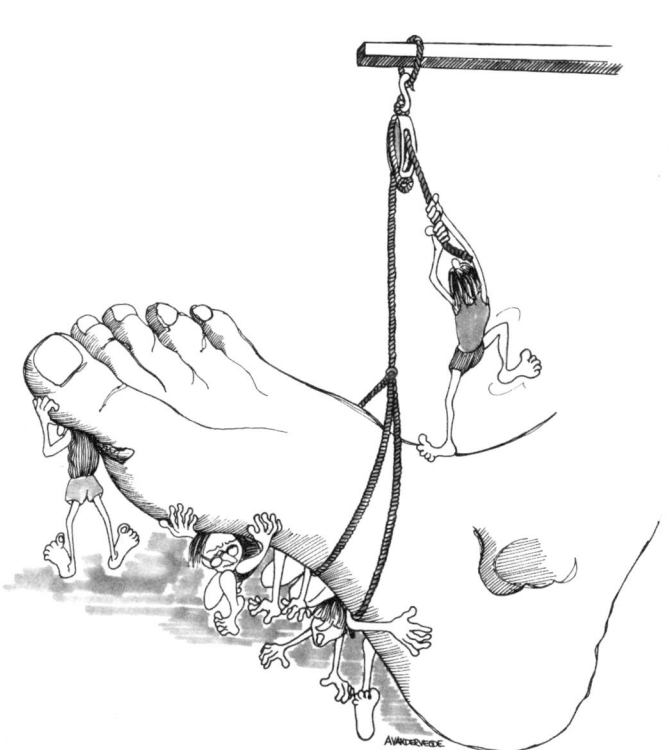

Over the years the public has placed arch supports and other shoe inserts in the same category as hair restorers, muscle building systems, and cures for rheumatism. This "medicine show" sentiment is well expressed by the advertisement in Figure 12.1 from a 1901 copy of *Physical Culture*. The advertisement for arch supports claims a positive relief and cure for flat feet.

Claims, counterclaims, and promises of miraculous cures have not slowed with the passage of time. Open any copy of a running magazine and you will be promised one or all of the following: for $9.95, "gives you the edge against running injuries, specially designed to control torque, the biomechanical twisting . . ."; for $12.00, "a varus heel post (approximately five degrees) . . . arch height molded from an average height arch . . . will improve your running performance and may alleviate the discomfort of shin splints, arch sprain, heel spur . . . engineered for the average."; for $15.95, "a non-prescription orthotic specifically designed to con-

242 INSERTS, ARCH SUPPORTS, AND ORTHOTICS

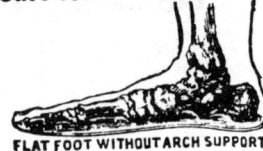

Fig. 12.1 An advertisement that appeared in a 1901 copy of *Physical Culture Magazine.*

trol pronation of the ankle."; for $59.95, "an 'orthotic' every bit the equal of those supplied by the foot doctor."

All these devices can be obtained without anyone (qualified or otherwise) ever looking at your foot or leg to determine what the cause of your particular problem might be.

Division Among Doctors

Members of the medical profession are sharply divided on the ethics of selling devices over the counter which make a radical change in the alignment of the foot or leg.

Some, like George Sheehan and Rob Roy McGregor, feel that runners should be able to tinker with their own limb mechanics as much as they please (see Chapter 16). "I think there should be a level at which we can do it ourselves and only involve the doctor as a last resort," is how Sheehan describes his feelings. When asked if a runner should be able to purchase over-the-counter help, McGregor's response was, "Of course he should—absolutely and totally!" Podiatrist John Pagliano also believes in runners' self-help. "Not only will you be saving yourself the expense of visiting the doctor initially, you may be preventing serious injuries that could require more costly treatment down the road."

Other people are more conservative, and also make distinctions among the various types of devices. Podiatrist Lloyd Smith puts it this way: "It may be acceptable for a runner to use a soft, over-the-counter device for a minor problem if the person knows their foot type. They should definitely not use the device for more than two weeks if it does not seem to be working. I am strongly against anyone using the hard-shell devices that are bought over the counter."

Sheldon Langer, president of the company that produces "Sporthotics" (see Chapter 16), which are made-to-order orthotics prescribed by the runner's doctor, is more outspoken than most. "Most of the people who purchase over-the-counter and mail order devices are, to a large extent, being cheated."

This division of opinion among experts leaves the runner in a ponderous position. It seems to me that there are two important questions to ask if the dilemma is to be resolved. First, does the average runner have the knowledge to help himself or herself? And second, can any damage be done by self-help intervention which turns out to be wrong?

On the question of self-knowledge, I think the answer generally has to be no. Runners cannot see themselves running, or measure the misalignment they may have in parts of the lower extremity during the support phase. Certain simple observations can be made, and we shall discuss these in Chapter 14. But the task of detecting subtle alignment problems is difficult enough for a physician with his trained eye or a scientist with his array of measuring equipment. The runner certainly knows where it hurts, but why it hurts is often a very different matter. That pain on the outside of the knee, for example, could come from a number of imbalances in the leg, foot, or shoe which may take qualified personnel some time to identify.

Whether or not runners can hurt themselves by tinkering with self-help devices is more of an open question. Many runners have gone through trial and error cycles and hit on the right solution. But the reverse has also happened. Runners have brought on other injuries by a piece of do-it-yourself podiatry that turned out to be just the opposite of what they needed.

Surveying the Over-the-Counter Field

Since there is support on both sides of the issue, we will divide our look at "in-the-shoe devices" into two parts. First, we will cover the more common over-the-counter and mail order devices, and then discuss how a podiatrist or orthopedist can make a custom product suited to the runner's foot and particular structural dynamics.

Advertising has so misused various words which used to have a precise meaning that classification is sometimes difficult. I will divide the over-the-counter devices into four categories.

1. Heel Cups and Heel Pads
2. Arch Supports
3. Do-It-Yourself Pads
4. "Morthotics"—an acronym I have coined for "*m*ail *o*rder *o*r*thotics*" which do not involve direct medical input in their prescription.

This discussion is not concerned with the flat "sockliner" insert that was covered in Chapter 8. Sockliners do little more than change the height of the footbed equally over the entire shoe. Most of the devices discussed here either cover just part of the shoe, such as the heel, or attempt to change the orientation of part of the foot, as in arch supports which raise the inside border.

Heel Cups and Heel Pads

Most heel pads are sold with the express purpose of providing cushioning for the heel. Thus it is a little surprising that, to my knowledge, there is no direct evidence of the cushioning properties of any in-shoe devices. In this section we will simply describe the devices and speculate as to how they might work. It should be noted that women may find heel cups particularly beneficial because many of the "scaled" down men's shoes are too wide in the heel.

Figure 12.2 shows some of the more popular products. The two heel cups differ slightly in their function. The M-F is a noncompressible, thin cup which will add no more than two or three millimeters to heel height and fit. The Tuli's cup will raise the heel more than half a centimeter. Both of these will do two things besides absorbing shock. They will make the fit of the shoe more snug in the heel. In addition, they will raise the heel. A simple heel lift has often been described as a "podiatrist's panacea" because this is so often successful in relieving foot and leg pains. In particular, Achilles tendonitis can frequently be eased by adding a lift in the heel. The pads shown in Figure 12.2 are a good first line of defense against heel pain.

The Spenco heel cushion, at seven millimeters, is thicker than the regular Spenco insert. The Scholl device is very thin at three millimeters, while the "Cameltrotter" has a unique fluid-filled coil that sits underneath the heel bone. If you find heel pads helpful, you should pay particular attention to changes in their thickness over time, and be prepared to buy a new pair if they seem to have compressed too much. Also, it is a good idea to wear a pad or cup in both shoes even if only one needs it. Wearing one pad will cause an ap-

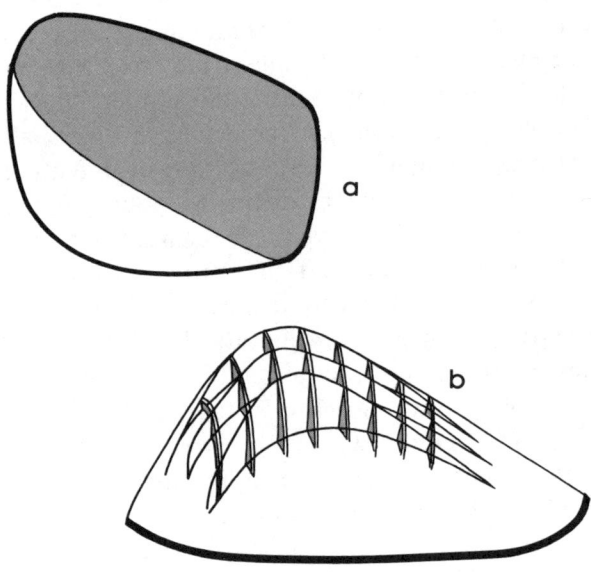

Fig. 12.2 Heel pad and cups (a) The M-F cup, (b) Tuli

Inserts, Arch Supports, and Orthotics 245

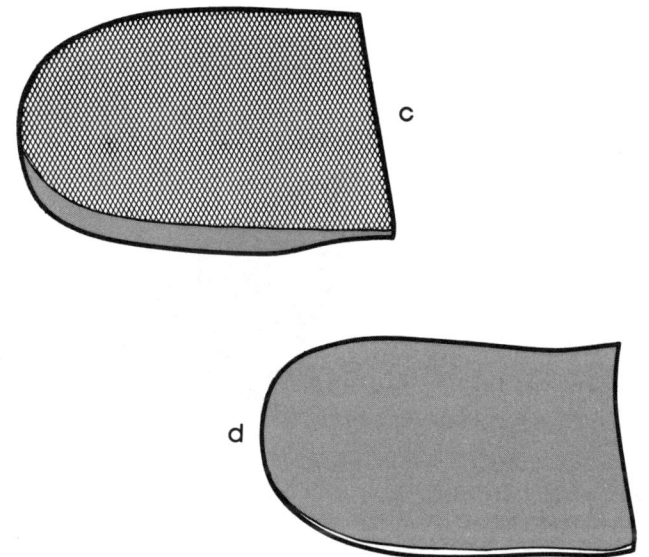

Fig. 12.2(cont.) Heel pad and cups (c) The Spenco heel pad, (d) Dr. Scholl pad.

parent short leg which, unless you really have a limb length discrepancy, could lead to problems.

Arch Cookies and Supports

Most shoes come with a bump in the inside arch area, which has become known to runners as the arch "cookie." Most arch cookies are just about useless in supporting the arch for a number of reasons. First, they will generally be in the wrong place, since they are prepared for an average foot which doesn't exist. Second, they do not have enough firmness to give any significant support to the long arch, even though they are generally made of foam rubber, which will not take as much of a compression set as the polymeric foams. Third, they are not long enough to cover the whole arch, which really extends from the heel to the metatarsal heads. Runners should tear arch cookies out of their shoes if they don't feel right, without worrying that this is going to devalue their substantial investment.

A variety of supports can be purchased to fit inside the running shoe. The Dr. Scholl 610 Arch Support, shown in Figure 12.3a, is slightly more substantial, but it is still sponge rubber with a covering of leather. This combination is unlikely to provide a great deal of resistance to the kind of compression it will experience during running.

A firmer arch support is sold by Spenco under the name of "Orthotic Arch Support" (Figure 12.3b). It is included here because the part under the heel does not attempt to tilt the heel toward the outside, as the "morthotics" in the next section do. It is made from a fairly rigid plastic covered with a layer of Spenco. The device is rather large, and will have trouble fitting in narrower running shoes.

Although most of the supports are designed for the long, inside arch of the foot, some are intended for the transverse or metatarsal arch. An example is shown in Figure 12.3c, which the manufacturer claims will pro-

246 INSERTS, ARCH SUPPORTS, AND ORTHOTICS

vide "moderate" support to the metatarsal arch, whatever "moderate" might mean.

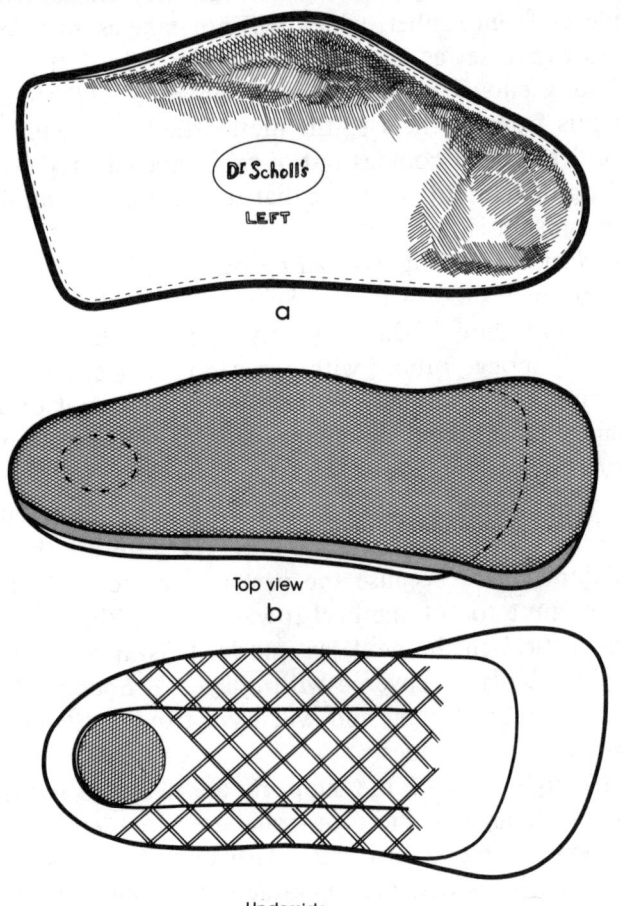

Fig. 12.3 Arch supports (a) Dr. Scholl 610, (b) Spenco Orthotic Arch support, and (c) Metatarsal arch support.

Do-It-Yourself Devices

A few examples of "cut and paste" supports are shown in Figure 12.4. These are typical of what your orthopedist or podiatrist might provide as a stopgap measure to tide you over a temporary discomfort, or as a prelude to custom-made orthotics.

The materials most often used are quarter-inch felt or moleskin (with an adhesive on one side), Spenco, or other insoles. The device on the left foot in the diagram has a feature to give added heel protection, and an extension underneath the big toe, known as Morton's Extension. On the right shoe, felt wedges have been placed

Inserts, Arch Supports, and Orthotics   247

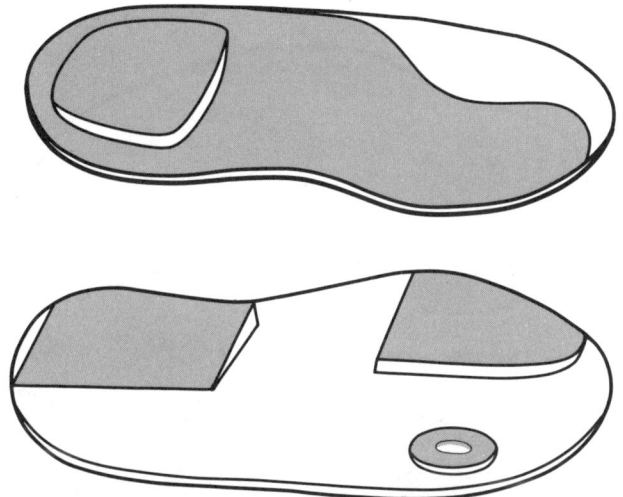

Fig. 12.4 Do-it-yourself podiatry. Layers of adhesive-backed ¼-inch felt stuck to an insole to acheive various corrections.

on the inside borders under the heel and big toe, and a felt "donut" has been put under a metatarsal head to keep a surface wound free of abrasion.

It is not of course suggested that these features all be incorporated at the same time (unless you have some very unique foot problems). More details on finding the design for your needs can be found in *The Foot Book*, by Harry Hlavac, D.P.M.

Morthotics—Mail Order Orthotics

It can be argued that the commercial devices we have considered so far are relatively benign, since all they do is give more or less support to the long arch and provide a lift for the heel. But "morthotics" are completely different, because they seek to alter the alignment of the runner's lower extremity, and we shall learn in Chapter 13 that alignment is a critical factor in running injury.

Almost without exception, morthotics attempt to give the rearfoot a varus correction of between four and eight degrees. (See Chapter 8 for an explanation of varus correction.) The thinking behind this is as follows: the most common alignment problem in runners shows up as excessive pronation at the subtalar joint. Notice that I say "shows up as": we have seen that subtalar joint pronation might be compensation for a problem elsewhere in the foot or leg.

So, the makers of these devices look for a number which might represent an "average" amount of structural variation at the subtalar joint. This angle is built into the device, which tries to hold the foot in its neutral position during the stance phase.

Notice that the same correction is given to both feet, and in most of the devices the same correction is provided for all runners. Now if you have the "average" amount of structural variation, this will be fine. But I am not aware of studies which give details on the average amount of excessive pronation during running, or what the usual differences are between the left and right sides. Furthermore, a correction prescribed by a

248 INSERTS, ARCH SUPPORTS, AND ORTHOTICS

physician does not depend on the amount of foot deformity only. The structure of the leg is also important, and the integrity of the foot—its tightness or looseness—may dictate different correction for the same apparent structural abnormality. Over-the-counter devices cannot incorporate this sophistication. Devices such as Dr. Robert's Rearfoot Controls, the Runski, Arch-Ease, and Dr. Scholl's Runner's Wedge are typical over-the-counter morthotics.

The Runski (Figure 12.5a) is a flexible device with a heel post which tends to tilt the foot upwards on the inside border at about a five degree angle. There is a bulge on the front, said to be a metatarsal arch support, which I personally find very uncomfortable.

"Arch Ease" is different from the others, mostly because it is about four times more expensive. The company sends an "impression kit" for the runner to make an impression of the shape and size of his or her foot. What happens next is unclear. Samples of "Arch Ease" that I have seen (Figure 12.5b) do not seem to have a custom molded shape, and there is no apparent correction; just a bulge under the long inside arch. The "runner's wedge" (Figure 12.5c) offers a marginal varus tilt for the foot, with minor support for the long inside arch.

Play Carefully By Ear

My feeling is that runners should be extremely cau-

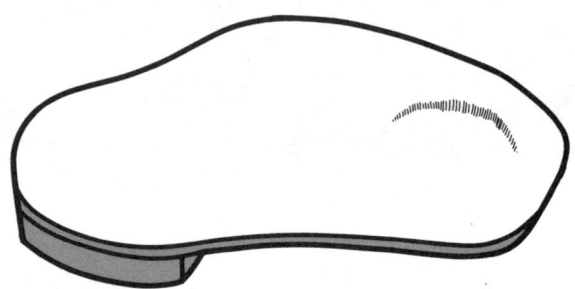

Fig. 12.5a Over-the-counter orthotics—Runski

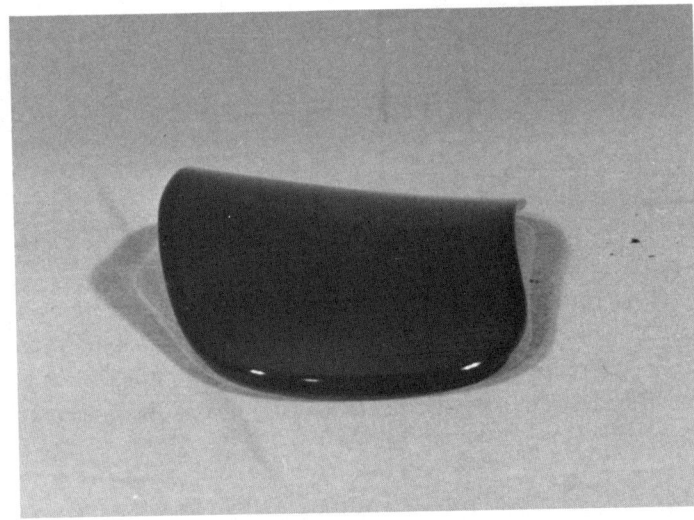

Fig. 12.5b Over-the-counter orthotics—Arch Ease

Inserts, Arch Supports, and Orthotics

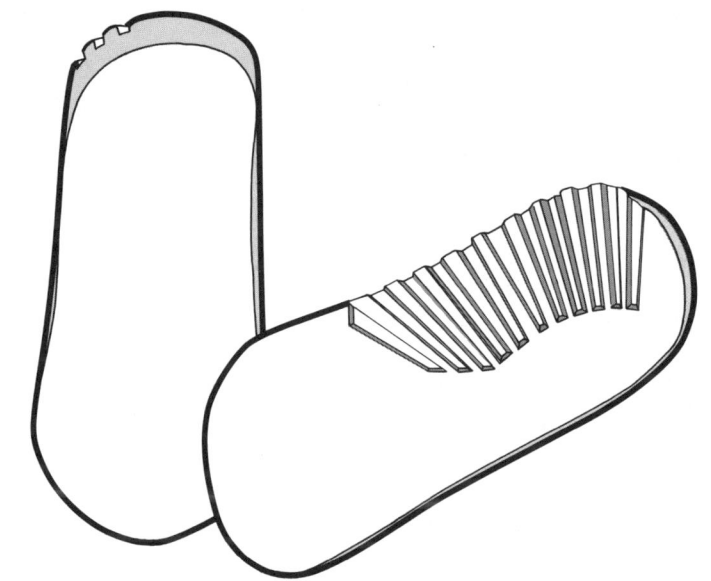

Fig. 12.5c Over-the-counter orthotics—Runner's Wedge

tious about changing the alignment of the foot or leg joints. As I have said repeatedly, the pattern of joint movement in the lower extremity during running is so incredibly complex that what might appear to be insignificant changes can have major effects. It may be that one of these morthotics will relieve some bothersome symptoms, but the byword should be *caution*; listen closely to your body for danger signs. Some of these "stock" devices are also becoming extremely ex-

pensive. It would probably be worthwhile to spend money on an office visit to a podiatrist or orthopedist who would at least inform you of the nature of your problem, and what might be the most appropriate correction.

If you do buy one of the devices, there are some things you should keep in mind. Be certain that you have the insert for the left foot in the left shoe and that it is the right way up. This may sound rather basic, but an error here could cause major problems. Second, if there are signs of other leg or foot problems which persist after a trial period with the device, stop using it immediately and seek professional advice.

On to Orthotics

Arthur Lydiard has been quoted as saying that people in the United States wear orthotics because of our "terrible American shoes." I think he is wrong. Orthotics have become widespread because people's bodies are not built in perfect alignment, and perhaps because they were not designed to take the incredible beating that distance running imposes.

Leg or foot alignment problems may be perfectly benign for walking or performing the tasks of daily life. But running five times a week without correction may cause some part of the chain to break down.

We have been pretty clear so far about what is not an

orthotic. So now we must define what an orthotic is. The word is derived from the Greek "orthos," meaning straight or correct. An orthotic, then, is literally a device which straightens anything from a deformed spinal column to a joint in a flaccid limb which has no muscles to control its movement. As an in-shoe device for runners, a broader definition of an orthotic is usually given. An orthotic changes the orientation of certain parts of the foot and leg with respect to each other or the ground during the support phase of running. It is important to appreciate that orthotic devices are designed for the dynamic control of the foot and leg. During running, the joints of the lower extremity go through movements entirely different from those which occur during standing and walking, and therefore require different control

Typical Problems Requiring Orthotic Correction

Although this is not intended to be a complete review of orthotic control, we will mention one or two of the more straightforward difficulties which respond to orthotic intervention. The first, shown in Figure 12.6a, is forefoot varus. This means that when the rearfoot is in its neutral position during stance, the inside border of the forefoot is raised from the ground. The correction, shown below the drawing of the foot, is a wedge, higher on the inside, placed under the forefoot. This brings the ground up to meet the raised part of the forefoot. In this case, the rearfoot would not change alignment.

The subject represented in Figures 12.6b and 12.6c has two problems. First, examination revealed that the left leg was shorter than the right. The correction for this rather common problem would be an orthotic which raises the heel off the ground, and makes no attempt to tilt it from side to side. On the right side, the rearfoot is pronated abnormally during stance. This calls for a varus correction, shown in the diagram, with an inclination to correct the misalignment caused by the deformity. The goal would be to hold the heel in its tilted, neutral position, with the inside higher than the outside; this would prevent it from going into an excessively pronated position. Note that only one of these problems would have been corrected by a typical "morthotic."

Who Needs an Orthotic?

There is a runner in every club, who, despite having no injuries or problems, can't wait to get orthotics because he or she will then be a "real runner." Going to your doctor with a running injury and asking for an orthotic is like going to the hospital with a stomach ache and demanding an appendectomy. Orthotic control is just one weapon that your doctor has at his disposal against running injury. It may be that your particular problem would not benefit from an orthotic.

When searching for help for your injury, it is im-

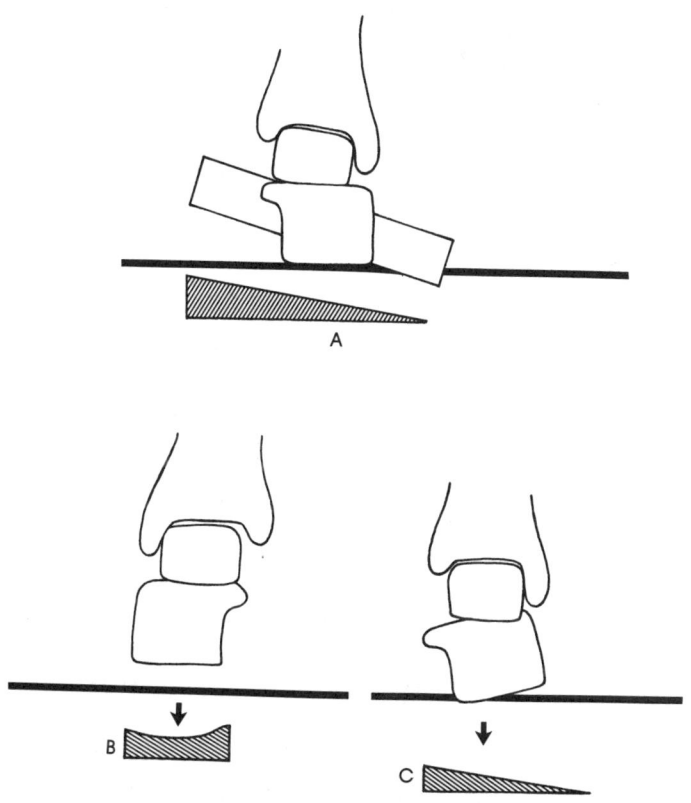

Fig. 12.6 Three conditions requiring orthotic correction. (a) Forefoot varus in a right foot seen from behind, corrected by a forefoot wedge higher under the inside border. (b) A short leg, corrected by a neutral heel post, and (c) Excessive pronation in the right foot seen from behind, corrected by a rearfoot wedge higher under the inside border.

portant to realize that there are some people in every profession who are better at their job than others. We all know there are good and bad politicians, so why is it so shocking that some doctors are better than others? Part of the skill of getting healed is going to the right person in the first place.

Doctors who treat runners frequently and are trained in the biomechanics of foot and leg function will have their eyes open wider to running injuries than those who don't. If a doctor is interested in runners' problems, it's likely that he will have joined a professional association concerned with the treatment of sports injuries. The two major organizations are The American Orthopedic Society for Sports Medicine and the American Academy of Podiatric Sports Medicine. Both groups maintain registers of members, which are a good place to start when looking for medical help.

What to Expect of an Office Visit

There are several ways to tell whether you can have confidence in the person who is looking at your injury. What you can typically expect is that the doctor will first take a detailed history, including your running habits, past injuries, the surfaces you run on, mileage, and more. He or she will probably ask to see your running shoes, and should do a complete examination of your lower extremities, which will include measuring the alignment of foot and leg joints and checking leg lengths. The exam may also include X-rays of the lower extremity, probably in a weight-bearing position.

It is crucial that the doctor ask to see you walk, or preferably, run. More and more practitioners of sports medicine have a treadmill in their office, and are able to look at patterns of movement which actually cause the problem. Visual analysis is difficult; in the future it is likely that film, videotape, or some other means will be used to make accurate and permanent records of your movement.

It is important from the start to establish a dialogue on both a professional and business footing. You should be aware of what the doctor thinks is wrong, and what it will take to correct the problem. The question of fee schedules should be discussed openly so that there are no unpleasant surprises at the end of a time-consuming treatment program. You should realize that diagnosis is something of a trial and error process, and response to treatment varies greatly among runners. It will thus be impossible for the doctor to give you a cast iron figure for the whole process at the first examination.

It is also good to remember that the doctor is contributing his time, expertise, overhead costs, the cost of X-rays and casting, lab fees, and more, before he gets to the point of making a profit. There are unscrupulous doctors who have trouble seeing past the dollar signs when they look at a runner's leg. But they are a minority whose reputation has spread far and wide, and they deserve the disdain they get from runners. The problem of excessive costs has probably also been exaggerated by a few runners who a) did not talk about cost before their treatment started, b) were not aware of the time and effort involved in treatment, and c) may have been unsuccessful in finding a solution to their injury problems.

Types of Orthotics

There is a variety of orthotic devices which might be prescribed for you. The most basic categories are usually called soft and hard. Although not everyone agrees with these labels, they are fairly descriptive of the products. Sometimes the doctor will offer the runner a choice of devices to be used, but usually the doctor's personal preference together with the needs of the patient will prevail.

The soft orthotics are sometimes labelled "accommodative" devices since they will undergo some molding to the foot. They are generally made of a blend of leather, cork, or "Plastozote" and can often be made right in the doctor's office.

Many doctors use nothing but these soft devices and claim great success. Others feel that the forces involved in running will cause too much accommodation, changing the correction built into the device.

The hard devices are the most common; they are usually made of a semi-rigid shell which has a variety of accessories attached to suit a particular problem. Since runners only see the end product when they receive their orthotics, we are going to take a more detailed look at the prescription and manufacturing process for hard orthotics.

If You Need an Orthotic, What Then?

While you are lying on the couch, with your feet off the ground, your doctor will make a negative cast of your foot (shown in Figure 12.7). First, plaster of Paris splints are carefully wrapped around the non-weight-bearing foot, until they form a snug "slipper" over the entire plantar surface. The cast will also extend upwards to just below the ankle joint.

Now comes the critical part. While the cast is setting, the doctor will apply pressure underneath the base of the little toe, while positioning the foot so that the subtalar joint is in a neutral position. This is important because the objective of the process is to allow the subtalar joint to function close to its neutral position. The orthotic will make any corrections required to let that happen.

Just before the cast becomes part of you forever, the doctor will pinch the skin on top of your foot, pulling it away from the sides of the cast, and finally slip the cast off. The finished cast will have, inside it, a smooth replica of the contour of the foot in its neutral position. Some doctors will make a weight-bearing cast on the

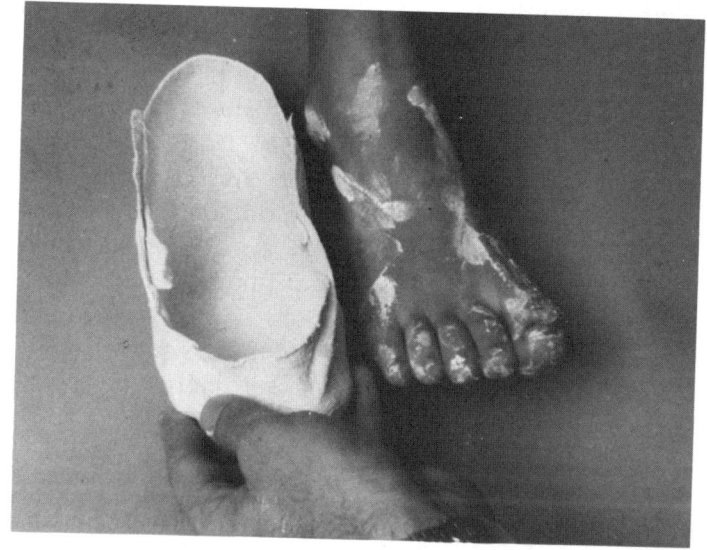

Fig. 12.7 Preparation of a negative cast. The finished cast will be sent to an orthotics laboratory with a description of the doctor's findings and measurements during the examination. (Courtesy of Langer Laboratories)

theory that under these conditions the foot will be closer to its shape during running. Others feel that while bearing weight it is difficult to determine the precise alignment of the leg and foot. How ever it was made, the finished cast will be left to dry for a day or so, and then mailed to the laboratory where the orthotic will be made. It will be accompanied by the results of the physical examination and the doctor's evaluation of what you require.

254   INSERTS, ARCH SUPPORTS, AND ORTHOTICS

What Happens in the Lab?

When the casts arrive at the orthotic lab, they are seen first by a trained evaluator (Figure 12.8). The relationship between the forefoot and rearfoot are measured and marked, and the results are compared with the information supplied by the doctor. The casts in Figure 12.8b, for example, show a marked and asymmetrical rearfoot varus (turning in) on both sides which will require a different correction. If there is any discrepancy between what the evaluator finds and what the doctor requested, good labs will call the doctor to discuss the situation.

Next a positive "foot model" is made by pouring liquid plaster of Paris into the negative cast (Figure 12.8c). The top is then ground until it is level, and the cast is marked on the bottom to show the area that the orthotic shell is required to cover. The positive foot cast is placed under a vacuum molding device (Figure 12.8e) and a sheet of roughly shaped thermoplastic material is placed on top of it. When pressure and heat are applied, a shell is formed which is an exact replica of the runner's foot (Figure 12.8f and g). According to the particular requirements of the runner, the rearfoot and forefoot posts are then added (Figure 12.8h).

Next comes the all-important stage (Figure 12.8i) at which the posts are ground down to meet the exact specifications for the correction required. If care is not

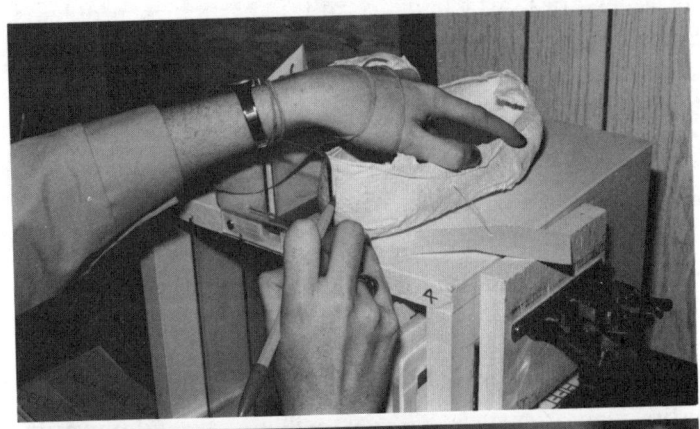

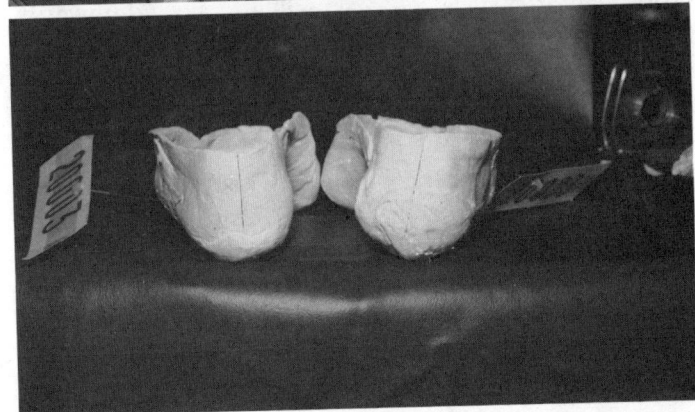

Fig. 12.8 (a, top) The cast is evaluated and marked in the orthotic lab. The doctor's findings and measurements on the casts are evaluated to determine the type and extent of correction required. (b, bottom) These casts show a marked and asymmetrical rearfoot varus which requires different correction on left and right sides.

Inserts, Arch Supports, and Orthotics

taken here, the device may under- or over-correct, leading to unsatisfactory results.

Some labs then put plastic screws through the rearfoot post onto the base of the shell. This helps to prevent excessive compression of the post material. The finishing touches (Figure 12.8k) involve adding some shock absorbent material between the post and the forepart of the device, putting a plastic covering on top of the posts, smoothing and finishing the edges, and finally, covering the surface with a vinyl lining.

The final device, then, is a carefully engineered composite of the parts shown in an exploded view in Figure 12.9.

What to Expect From Your Orthotics

When you get your orthotic devices back from the doctor, you should ask for thorough instructions on how they should be used. Don't expect that they will be comfortable the first time you wear them. The joints of your feet and legs have been going through their possibly abnormal movements many thousands of times, and any change is likely to feel strange at first. Most podiatrists suggest that you get to know your orthotics gradually. The worst thing you could do, for example, would be to go out and run a marathon the first day you got them. Build up slowly, using the orthotics for progressively increasing parts of your workout on successive days.

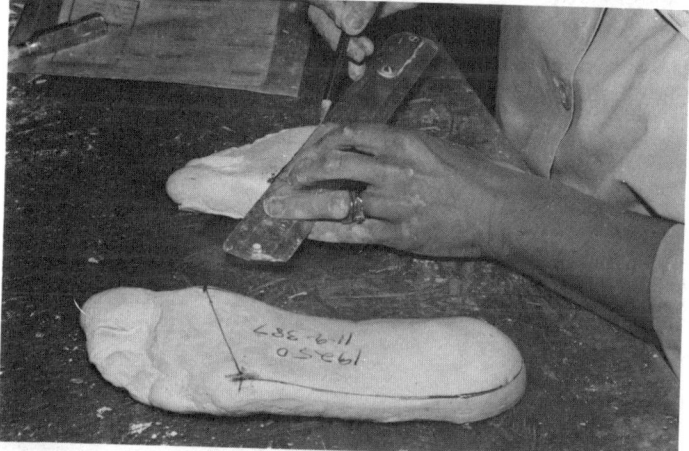

Fig. 12.8 (c, top) A positive "foot model" is made by pouring Plaster of Paris into the negative cast. (d, bottom) After leveling the top surface the cast is marked to define the area the orthotic shell is required to cover.

256 INSERTS, ARCH SUPPORTS, AND ORTHOTICS

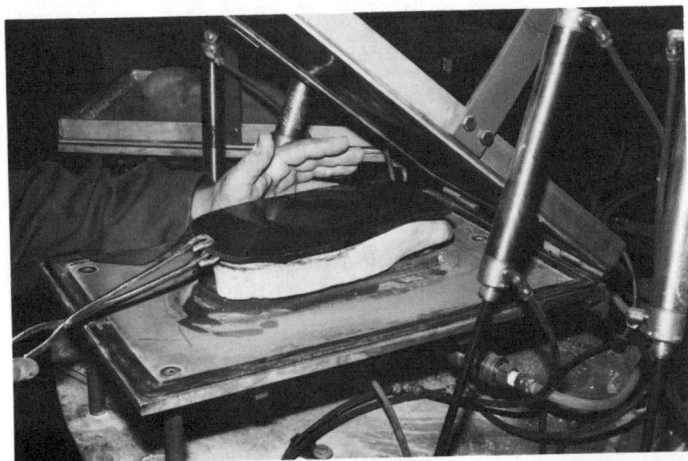

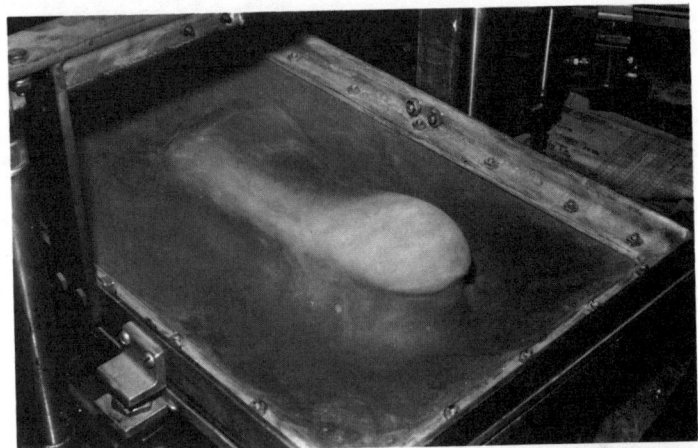

Fig. 12.8 (e, f, and g) The cast is placed under a vacuum molding device and a sheet of roughly shaped thermoplastic material is placed over it. When the pressure and heat are applied, a shell is formed which is an exact replica of the runner's foot.

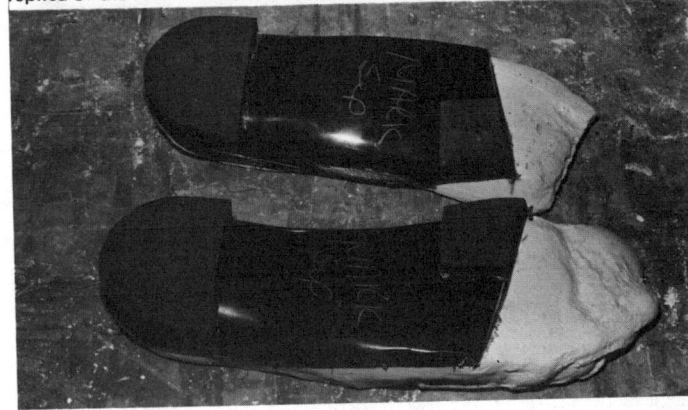

Inserts, Arch Supports, and Orthotics

Fig. 12.8 (h. bottom right, page 256) According to the requirements of the runner, the rearfoot, and forefoot posts are added. (i. top left, page 257) In the all-important stage, the posts are ground to meet the exact specifications for the amount of correction required.

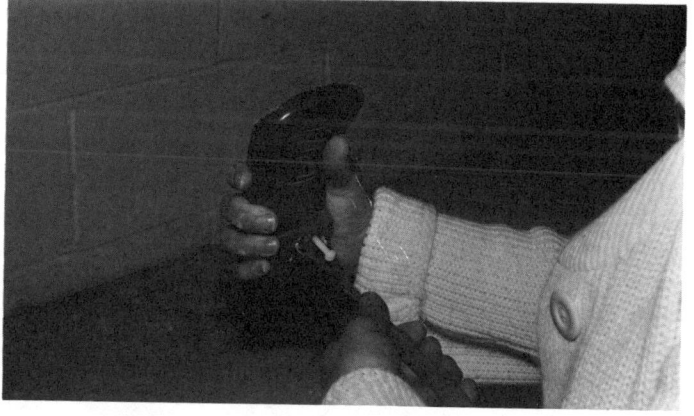

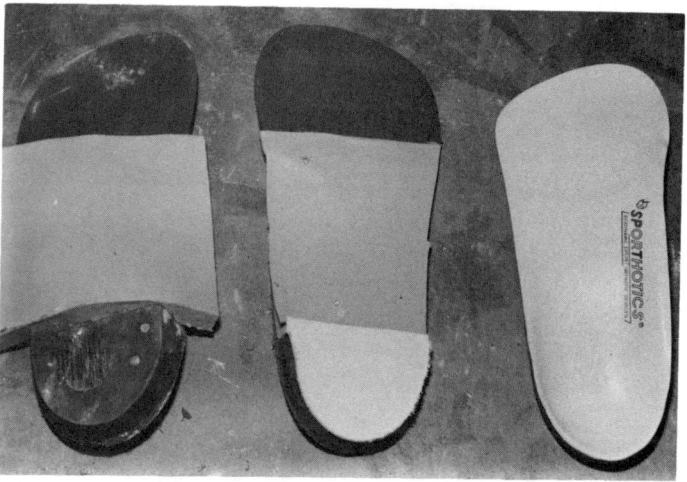

Fig. 12.8 (j. bottom left, page 257) Nylon screws are inserted between the shell and the bottom of the rearfoot post to prevent compression of the post. (k. above) The finishing touches. A shock absorbent material under the arch, a plastic covering for the posts, finishing of the edges, and a covering for the surface of the shell.

Shoes for Orthotic Wearers

The choice of a shoe for an orthotic wearer requires an extra consideration. Some shoes simply don't have enough room to hold both your foot and orthotic. It may be necessary to buy a shoe which is deep enough to accommodate both.

Whatever shoe you use, one requirement is to rip out

258 INSERTS, ARCH SUPPORTS, AND ORTHOTICS

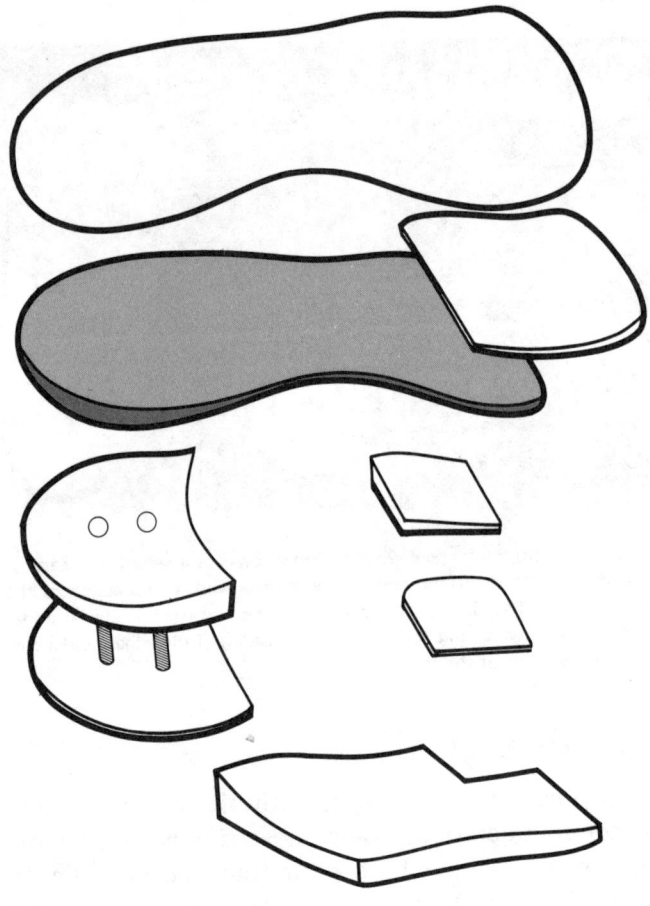

Fig. 12.9 An exploded view of a completed orthotic.

all the bits and pieces that the manufacturer puts inside, until the insole board is showing. If the orthotic only extends to the head of the metatarsals (as most do), then leaving in the front part of the sockliner will do no harm. But the correction built into your orthotic assumes that the orthotic will be resting on a flat surface. If your shoes are no longer flat under the orthotic, you should buy a new pair.

It is not advisable to wear shoes with a varus wedge with your orthotic unless the doctor took this into account when prescribing the correction. Also, make absolutely sure that you have the left orthotic in the left shoe.

You may find that orthotics are hard on the rearpart of your shoes. In particular, if the shoe does not have a good heel counter, the lateral pressure from the orthotic will tend to break down the counter and make it bulge outwards. If this is happening you should make sure your next pair of shoes has a better counter. Watch particularly for signs of the orthotic digging into the board or midsole of the shoe, under the forefoot or rearfoot posts. If this happens the correction will again be inappropriate, and the inside surface of the shoe should be built up until it is level again.

Follow Up

It is unlikely that the relationship with your doctor will end when you walk away from the office. There is considerable room for subjectivity in the whole process of orthotic prescription, and some fine tuning may be required. There will definitely be a period of adaptation, but initial aches and pains should begin to disappear within three or four weeks of cautious running. If, after this time, problems still persist, you should go back to your doctor and talk it over. Quality orthotics are guaranteed not to break for a specified period; if breakage does occur, that is another reason to go back.

Wear and tear of any in-shoe device will occur because of repeated stresses. Most manufacturers will duplicate a prescription at a considerably reduced cost when a replacement is required. Although there has been no experimental verification, many people feel that eventually the orthotic will cause a change in muscle balance and possibly joint alignment. If this happens, the amount of correction will need to be changed.

Do Orthotics Work?

Most clinicians have had a remarkable degree of success treating runners' injuries with orthotics. But like any treatment, they are not going to be successful all the time. They will sometimes require alteration if the initial correction proves inadequate. But if the doctor is competent, if the lab does a good job, and the runner is sensible in his or her approach to orthotic use, the treatment has a good chance of working. There are unfortunately too many runners who have a pair of

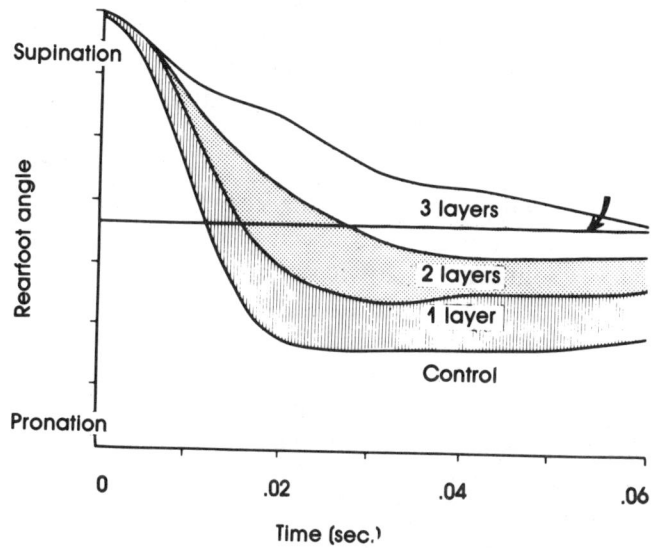

Fig. 12.10 Changes in the patterns of rearfoot motion in a group of runners as simple felt pad orthotics of progressively increasing thickness were placed along the inside border of their shoes. The arrow points to the neutral position and by the time three layers are in place, the movement barely approaches neutral showing that pronation has been reduced.

orthotics sitting permanently in a drawer because one of these three has not happened.

Certainly measurable changes result from orthotic intervention. Figure 12.10 shows the results of some of our own studies at Penn State with simple orthotics designed to correct excessive pronation. The diagram shows mean results attained by four runners who used progressively higher felt wedges on the inside of the shoe. The reduction of rearfoot motion with increased height of the orthotic is clear from the diagram.

The most frequently heard complaint about orthotics is that they sometimes correct one problem and create another. For example, a runner may get relief from knee pain, but soon finds that running leads to low back pain. In these cases the only recourse is to go back to the doctor for a solution which will not create secondary problems.

Orthotics have been used with consistent success in the treatment of running injuries. Their use has been nurtured by a better understanding of the mechanics of running and a realization that the surgeon's knife is a last resort which is better avoided. Overall, orthotics rate as one of the best things that have happened to injured runners in a long while.

13

Can Shoes Prevent Injury?

Running has filled doctors' offices with an unusual group of people—people who are in the best of health. An injury which is disabling for a runner might pass unnoticed in a sedentary person. But for the runner an injury serious enough to halt training is a crushing blow. This is true for all ages and levels of ability.

As the popularity of running has grown, there has been a gradual increase in our understanding of these new "diseases of the healthy." The last decade has seen the blossoming of sports medicine together with improved running shoes and radical changes in training patterns. In this chapter we shall try to untangle the injury picture and speculate on the part that running shoes play.

Join the Marines—See the Hospital

What worse way to start running than to join the Marines? They offer you a crash program in fitness training together with gentle encouragement to succeed, and it's all done in a pair of high-top boots.

In 1975 Dr. Carolyn Bensel monitored 879 young men who had decided to join the Marines. Mostly she followed them to sick call visits. Thirty-seven percent attended sick call for lower extremity problems during the ten-week boot camp.

The resulting data is an interesting lesson in how beginning runners might get injured if they go off the deep end. Let's look at the ten most common injuries suffered by the Marines. The percentages shown in Table 13.1 are expressed as occurrence of injury in all recruits. So a third of all recruits got blisters; eleven percent endured heel problems, and so on.

TABLE 13.1
Lower Extremity Injuries to Marine Recruits During Ten Weeks of Basic Training

Rank	Injury	Incidence
1.	Blisters	33.6%
2.	Heel Problems	11.2%
3.	Lace Irritations	12.1%
4.	Stress Fracture (incl. susp. stress)	6.4%
5.	Nail Problems	4.2%
6.	Ankle Sprains	4.1%
7.	Acute Inflammation	3.4%
8.	Callus	3.4%
9.	Tendonitis	3.0%
10.	Athlete's Foot	1.7%

Remember of course that the Marine recruits didn't just run. They marched, hit the dirt, climbed ladders, and did all the things required to produce a Marine.

Injuries such as blisters, lace irritation, nail problems, and inflammation are probably related to the fit of the boots. These injuries are typical of beginning runners who are adjusting to their shoes or perhaps have a shoe that did not fit well.

Now it is important to look at the pattern of activity which these recruits followed. The first three weeks consisted of short, intensive exercise; physical conditioning and drilling is how the Marines describe it. Thirty-four percent of all sick calls were in these first three weeks. The focus switched to rifle and infantry training in week four.

It is almost certain that the unyielding nature and poor impact response of the army boots were a cause of many injuries. Graduate student Richard Demoya, himself a West Point graduate, tested several army boots on the standard tests of impact and flexibility which are used in the *Runner's World* test sequence. He found that the average army boot is almost fifty percent worse in rearfoot shock absorption, 100 percent less flexible, and more than 200 percent less shock absorbent in the forefoot than an average training flat.

So as far as the Marines are concerned there is little doubt that wearing running shoes would have prevented many injuries if combined with a more rational approach to fitness training. But experienced runners run for more than ten weeks. They run longer than two miles. We would expect to see different patterns of injuries. Let's investigate and see if we do.

Injuries to Runners—Where Does the Data Come From?

The Marine study by Dr. Bensel and her colleagues is about as closely-controlled a study of the effects of exercise on the foot and leg as possible. Can you imagine the legal problems if almost 900 runners were shut up in a compound in California for ten weeks, issued different kinds of running shoes, and put through a grueling running program, accompanied by motivation which bordered on harassment? There would be lawsuits and mutiny. The one positive result would be excellent data on injuries. Known as epidemiological data by doctors and scientists, this information traces injury back to such causes as training patterns and footwear.

The closest we might come would be a controlled study of varsity track and cross-country teams. Unfortunately such studies do not exist. Control is the key, and that is where the military wins out. It is important to know exactly when runners exercise, how much, what their diet was, what surfaces they ran on. The study should also have experimental groups receiving different "treatments." For example one group might run on roads with racing flats, another on trails in training flats, and so on; a control group that did nothing would also be helpful.

The lack of such data is one of the biggest barriers to improved injury prevention, both in training and footwear design. Everyone connected with the sport and the medical profession should try to encourage the collection of better information in this area.

In the absence of such studies there are two ways to find out about injury. The first is through self-reporting; the runner answers a questionnaire about habits and injuries. The second is by an outpatient survey. Larger clinics in metropolitan areas see hundreds of runners a year. Patients fill in sheets, similar to self-reports, from which accurate diagnoses are possible.

Both methods have their advantages and disadvantages. If a self-report study has a large random sample, one can derive data on the incidence of running injury (e.g., one in three runners get back pain) because the forms come back from healthy runners as well as injured ones. The problem with self-reporting systems is that they depend on the respondent to make an accurate report of their injury, and many respondents may not have sufficient knowledge or may have a mistaken idea about their condition.

The problem with outpatient data is that it only includes injured runners. While it can be depended upon for an accurate estimate of the distribution of injuries within a group of runners, it cannot predict incidence rates.

For all their respective problems, these two techniques have made available the only data we have. What I have tried to do is to follow a chronological course. As shoes and training styles have changed, so have the injuries. The injury statistics provide important evidence of the effect of these changes on the runner's health.

1971: The First Runner's World Injury Survey

When the booklet "All About Distance Running Shoes" came out in 1971, it carried a page of results from a questionnaire which did not concern shoes directly. The runners were asked to "list type and duration of any major foot and leg injuries you've suffered (those requiring a complete layoff from running)." More than 800 athletes responded to the question. In so doing they provided the first documentary evidence that running might do other things to the body besides increase aerobic capacity.

This publication also probably marks the birth of the now infamous runner's knee. The results of the survey, given in Table 13.2, showed that almost seventeen percent of all runners surveyed had suffered from a knee problem of some sort. Close behind were Achilles tendonitis and shin splints. These three conditions, taken together, were experienced by forty-two percent of respondents. (Note that some runners appear in all three categories.)

TABLE 13.2

A Survey of the Ten Most Common Injuries Among 800 Runners Chosen at Random by Runner's World in 1971

Rank	Injury	Incidence
1.	Knee	17.9%
2.	Achilles	14.0%
3.	Shin Splints	10.6%
4.	Arch Injuries	6.9%
5.	Ankle Injuries	6.4%
6.	Metatarsal Fractures	4.9%
7.	Stone Bruises	4.4%
8.	Calf Pulls	3.6%
9.	Heel Bone Damage	3.0%
10.	Hip (General)	2.6%

The injuries described by runners as arch injuries (probably including plantar fasciitis and ankle injuries including sprains) as well as metatarsal stress fractures had five to seven percent of runners reporting occurrence.

No Help From the Doctor

Back in 1971 it was a hard thing for runners to accept that their sport caused injury. But it was even harder to realize that their doctor was not much help in overcoming the injury. They almost always got the same advice: rest and stop running.

At the start of the decade, sports medicine was just beginning. The medical profession was being jolted by the "aerobics revolution" but special clinics for runners or other athletes were few and far between. In the spring of 1970, *Runner's World* magazine had recruited a running physician named George Sheehan to field readers' questions concerning their medical problems. In "All About Distance Running Shoes," in 1971, Dr. Sheehan ventured a few suggestions on why the injuries were occurring. But by the time the second *Runner's World* injury survey was published in "Shoes for Runners" in 1973, two years of seeing a multitude of problems but few answers had galvanized Sheehan's prose into the earthy, honest, and irreverent statements that have endeared him to runners. The following is a sample of 1973 vintage Sheehan:

> "At the present time the medical profession's batting average against runners' occupational hazards is close to zero. When the cause is unknown, prevention is unknown. Treatment comes down to attack on the symptoms, and not the cause. A glance at the record will bear this out.
> *Heel Spur Syndrome:* Cause unknown. Prevention unknown. Treatment: symptomatic (which means rest, painkillers, cortisone shots, or surgery).
> *Achilles Tendonitis:* Cause unknown. Prevention unknown. Treatment symptomatic.
> *Stress Fractures:* Cause unknown. Prevention unknown. Treatment: symptomatic.
> *Shin Splints:* Cause unknown. Prevention unknown. Treatment: symptomatic.
> *Runner's Knee (Chondromalacia):* Cause unknown. Prevention unknown. Treatment: symptomatic.
> *Etc., Etc.. Etc.*
> Sports medicine has been a case of the blind leading the blind. An uninformed patient population is being treated by doctors who don't know the cause of their ailments."

But through "encouragement" such as this and other developments, sports medicine achieved a considerably stronger position during the decade.

1973: More of the Same

The 1973 survey in "Shoes For Runners" revealed that the bad news from 1971 could get worse. Significant injuries reported in the population of 1600 runners surveyed numbered 1680. How? Many runners reported more than one significant injury. In fact, two out of three had experienced an injury "serious enough to require an interruption of running for at least one week, medical treatment, and a prolonged recovery period."

The actual injuries suffered (see following page for Table 13.3) were about the same as those reported in 1971. This time the sample was larger, leading supposedly to more reliable data. The knee again topped the list. It is hard to detect what changes are really "significant" from one self-reported survey to the next. Some fluctuation is expected due to sampling error. But it was hard to ignore the six percent increase in Achilles tendonitis and the troubling fact that knee injuries were on the increase—even if the change would not satisfy a statistician.

TABLE 13.3
The Top Ten Injuries and Their Incidence in the 1973 Runner's World Survey

Rank	Injury	Incidence
1.	Knee	22.5%
2.	Achilles Tendon	20.3%
3.	Shin Splints	9.9%
4.	Forefoot	7.2%
5.	Heel	7.2%
6.	Ankles	7.0%
7.	Arch	7.0%
8.	Calf	6.8%
9.	Hamstring	4.6%
10.	Hip	3.7%

A Pattern Emerges

The injury data, and Dr. Sheehan's hard line on his medical colleagues, caused quite a few waves. Slowly, a pattern of running injuries began to emerge. As we look back to the studies mentioned so far, the following rules seem to apply:

1. Runners suffer from different injuries than Marine recruits in training.
2. Runners' injuries don't usually occur in the feet. The majority are from the ankle upwards.
3. By 1973 runners were running more miles in training than ever before.
4. The shoes used by runners in the 1971-73 period were lacking in what we now believe to be important protective characteristics.

The contrast between injuries in the road runners and Marines was startling. Marine training caused extremely few knee injuries, but something about prolonged running was clearly leading to problems for the knees of about a quarter of the runners out there.

The lack of direct foot injuries was also paradoxical. Certainly injuries were caused by contact between foot and road. But it was the way in which the foot responded to impact which led to trauma in other parts of the leg.

The questions of increased mileage and footwear could not, and indeed cannot today, be separated. It is just not possible to say with assurance what percentage of injuries is due to one or the other. But two things were clear. High mileages had come to stay and running shoes had to change. Many of the 1971-73 shoes were heavy, thin under the forepart, lacking in shock absorption, and provided a relatively small differential in height between heel and forefoot. For example, the second most popular shoe among runners in the 1971 report was the Adidas Olympia. A single size eight shoe weighed twelve and a quarter ounces. The sole was gum rubber with no midsole or wedge. The shoe looked very much like a leather all-court shoe of today.

The changes introduced by Tiger during this time had, as we saw in Chapter 2, a profound influence on the design of running shoes. By 1973 the Olympia was down in eighth place and stood out for "showing the effects of age and a changing market." Nylon uppers were now more common. Most of the shoes had a heel wedge, although many were still inadequate in the forefoot. So shoes were changing, but what would happen to injuries?

Podiatry Takes One Step Back, and One Forward

Few orthopedists in the early 1970s had the time or inclination to look at legs and feet which hurt but showed no overt signs of significant trauma. A well-known physician commented, "The study of the bones and muscles of the foot during medical training is often presented in an uninteresting and confusing manner with no correlation to function."

And it turns out that function was the key. Instead of taking a step forward to examine the patient, what was needed was a step back to look at the way the lower extremity was put together.

So while orthopedics stepped forward to examine, X-ray, and cast broken limbs, podiatry began preaching about alignment in runners with no evidence of broken bones. And by stepping back, they made a real advance in the treatment of running injuries.

People like Drs. Steve Subotnick, Rob Roy McGregor, John Pagliano, Harry Hlavac, and Dick Schuster were able to keep runners on the road by using orthotics to correct misalignment. It was still a matter of visiting the battlefield to treat the wounded. But more of the wounded were being returned to combat. If there is one thing a runner cannot tolerate, it is inactivity; and now there were alternatives to rest and giving up running.

Overuse Syndrome

The search for the causative factor in many running injuries focused increasingly on "over-distance." Somewhere along the way, the term *overuse syndrome* was coined to describe injuries that seemed to occur because the legs were simply undergoing more repeated impacts in a brief period of time than they were realistically designed to take. The Marines didn't get knee problems, Achilles tendonitis, and shin splints because they didn't run far or often enough.

Will all runners who try to run a certain number of miles a week succumb to one or another of such injuries? Not necessarily, but a certain percentage will be likely to. These will be individuals with one of the alignment problems described in Chapter 3.

The combination of misalignment in some part of the lower extremity with over-distance is a formula for overuse injury. The problem is that alignment has to be defined, as does over-distance. While there are ranges of normality for both, the critical point for either will be different for each individual. The solution is to correct the misalignment and/or reduce the mileage.

Of these two potential solutions distance runners chose the first, and the sports podiatry profession blossomed in the mid-1970s by prescribing orthotics to correct a variety of structural problems. But the mileage mania went on and is still with us. Most runners think that more mileage in training equals faster times in competition. Most physicians treating runners see more miles as meaning more overuse injuries. As Dr. Bill Clancy was to write in 1976, "(Runners) who average more than 100 miles per week become an orthopedist's nightmare."

1974-1976: First Report from the Clinic

At a meeting in early 1977, Dr. Stan James and his colleagues, Drs. Barry Bates and Louis Osternig, presented data collected from 180 runners who had visited Dr. James's office in the preceding two years, bringing with them 232 separate injuries. This is the first running injury data that we have presented which includes information obtained from a physical examination of the runners.

While standing, only twenty-two percent of the runners had what was classified as "neutral rearfoot alignment" (see Chapter 3 for definition). Fifty-eight percent showed pronation during stance. (No examination of the alignment during running was made.) Thus the connection between alignment and injury was given further support. The five injuries which led the pack in Dr. James's patients are shown in Table 13.4.

TABLE 13.4
Five Most Common Injuries Reported by Drs. Stan James, Bates, and Osternig in 1977

1. Knee Pain	29%
2. Shin Splints	13%
3. Achilles Tendonitis	11%
4. Plantar Fasciitis	7%
5. Stress Fractures	6%

Remember that *all* the runners seen by Dr. James were injured. So it is not true to say that this study showed that twenty-nine percent of runners had knee pain. What it showed was that during the period studied twenty-nine percent of the injuries seen were knee injuries. The treatments offered were headed by rest, orthotics, reduced mileage, and shoe change or modification. Only later came the use of drugs or surgery.

A third *Runner's World* injury survey in 1977 showed little change from the two earlier ones. Two out of three runners were still getting injured each year, and the injuries were about the same as those in the 1973 survey.

Into the 1980s

In the last three years of the 1970s, I have seen data from tests on hundreds of running shoes come rolling off our laboratory computer. It is my firm impression that shoes have improved tremendously since about 1977 onwards. If it is true that shoes can help prevent injury, then improvement in shoe design should be reflected in the reduction of certain categories of injuries. We therefore complete our look at available injury statistics with a set of previously unpublished data made available by Dr. Lloyd Smith.

Dr. Smith practices podiatry in Newton, Massachusetts, a suburb of Boston in the heart of runners country. He has looked at the feet of the winner of the Boston Marathon in both 1935 (the great Johnny A. Kelley, shown in Figure 13.1) and 1979 (who else but Bill Rodgers). In his private practice, and at the Runners Clinic of St. Elizabeth's Hospital, Dr. Smith and his colleagues, Drs. Dianne English and John McGillicuddy, have gathered histories and diagnoses on 974 runners in 1978 and 1979.

This data base provides the best update currently available on running injuries. It is also unique in that

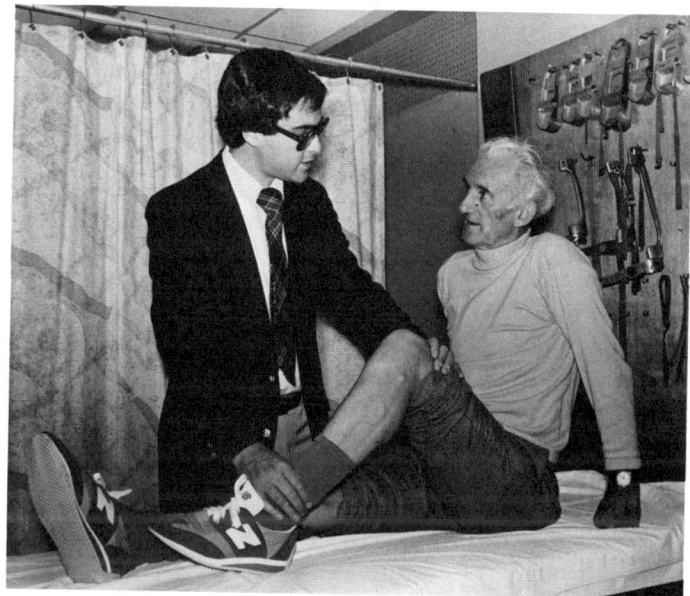

Fig. 13.1 Dr. Lloyd Smith examines the knee of Johnny Kelley, who will run his fiftieth Boston Marathon in 1981.

patients at the Runners Clinic are seen by a treatment team including podiatrists, orthopedists, and athletic trainers. Each team member brings his background to bear on diagnosis and treatment.

The most frequent injuries in this group are shown in Table 13.5 (see following page), where we see a new entry in the top three and one or two notable declines. The catagories listed accounted for a massive ninety

TABLE 13.5
Diagnosis of Injury Among 974 Runners in the St. Elizabeth's Hospital Series

Rank	Injury	
1.	Knee Pain*	30.5%
2.	Heel Spur Syndrome	13.5%
3.	Shin Splints**	10.9%
4.	Muscle Pulls	8%
5.	Achilles Tendonitis**	6%
6.	Stress Fracture (Tibia, Fibula)	5%
7.	Post Tibial Tendonitis**	6%
8.	Ankle Sprains	4.5%
9.	Low Back Pain	3.2%
10.	Peroneal Tendonitis**	3%

*Further breakdown of knee injuries:

Peripatellar Pain	23.3%
Lateral Knee Pain	5.6%
Other Knee	1.7%

**All tendonitis together totals 27%

percent of all injuries, although fifty-five distinct diagnoses were reported in the sample.

The diagnoses have been grouped in Table 13.5 to facilitate comparison with the other studies. We should comment on some special features of this data before moving on to a retrospective of a decade of running injuries.

Special Features of the St. Elizabeth's Data

In this sample knee injuries form nearly a third of all injuries to runners, confirming trends from earlier studies. But moving into second place is the heel spur syndrome. This does not mean that each of these 132 unfortunate runners had a clearly defined pathological bone growth jutting forward from the underside of the heel bone (see Figure 3.7). A syndrome is a collection of symptoms; in this case that may mean that the runner was suffering from inflammation of one or more of the plantar fascia, the covering of the heel bone (periostitis), or a bursa (one of the body's lubricating and spacing mechanisms).

The sudden prominence of heel spur syndrome is no doubt partly due to terminology. Dr. Smith and his colleagues have been more cautious in labeling. Rather than stating firmly that the injury is plantar fascitis or heel spur or periostitis, they have utilized a collective label; the resulting category is larger than the component parts. It is possible that what some of the early *Runner's World* respondents called arch pain and stone bruises would have fallen into this category. The rise of this syndrome to an unhappy position of prominence must be kept in mind in the future to determine whether it is a real trend or an artifact of classification.

The "shin splint" category in the St. Elizabeth's data

needs special attention. In a survey such as the 1971 *Runner's World* study, all leg pain between the ankle and knee was probably reported as shin splints. By contrast Dr. Smith has reserved the term to mean inflammation of the tendon of the tibialis anterior muscle (see Chapter 3). The two other categories, posterior tibial tendonitis and stress fractures, would probably have fallen into the "shin splint" basket in previous studies.

If tendonitis in all muscles is made a single group, it adds up to an astonishing twenty-seven percent of all injuries. This is true despite the fact that the incidence of Achilles tendonitis is lower than in any previous study.

Changes in Injury Patterns in a Decade

There are two major questions we must now ask concerning the statistics on injury that have been presented in this chapter. Are runners getting injured more or less than they were ten years ago? And looking at just the injured runners, are the type of injuries the same as they were ten years ago?

Let's take the "more or less" question first. The 1971 survey does not, unfortunately, give the number of injured runners out of the total sample, but in 1973, two out of three runners reported an injury serious enough to seek medical attention. In 1977 the figure was the same. So for the record, the percentage of runners getting injured did not change appreciably in the four years between surveys. But since the number of runners rose dramatically, we are looking at many more injuries. Let's not forget the fact that each of us has a sixty-six percent chance of getting injured during our year of running. This sport of ours, that has so many cardiovascular and psychological benefits, brings with it a better than even chance of injury.

We will now attempt an analysis of the differences between the injuries runners were reporting in 1971, and those seen in the clinic in 1979. It must be made clear at the outset that such a comparison is fraught with danger. The 1971 data is from a self-report study while the 1979 data is from a patient survey. All of the runners in the 1979 study were injured, while only some were in the 1971 study. (Adjustments have been made to the 1971 data to make the two comparable.) Sports medicine has enjoyed tremendous growth between the two studies; diagnosis is certainly more informed in 1980 than in 1970. Both studies are relatively small and thus subject to the ravages of sampling error.

Despite these limitations the comparison is worth doing, because the data is the best we have. It spans almost a decade of running, a decade in which running shoes came out of the dark ages and training methods were revolutionized. Let's at least call it informed speculation which will be confirmed or refuted in the coming years.

Figure 13.2 shows how patterns of injury have

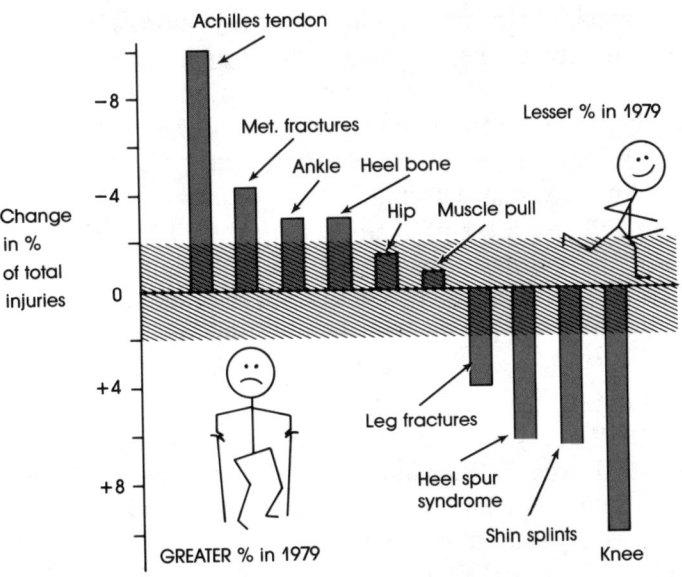

Fig. 13.2 Changes in the distribution of injury patterns in the last decade. Achilles tendon injuries have become scarcer, but knee injuries now form a much greater percentage of the total than they did ten years ago.

changed. Any box that rises above the line is good news. In the shaded region the increments cannot be considered to reflect a concrete shift one way or the other, so we call this the region of no change. Boxes falling below the shaded area stand for injuries that have increased in relative frequency during the period.

The Good News

Four classes of injuries show improvement according to our (somewhat arbitrary) criterion of greater than two percent change. The most notable of this group is Achilles tendonitis, which shows a dramatic ten percent drop. There is good reason to think that this is due, at least in part, to design improvements in running shoes. Training flats all have a height difference between forefoot and heel of at least half an inch, whereas many shoes in 1971 had no differential whatsoever. Besides providing good rearfoot impact qualities, the "wedge" in the shoe is shortening the distance through which the Achilles tendon has to move. By doing that the chances for irritation and inflammation are reduced.

The next category shows changes which I personally find very gratifying. One of the early inferences of our Penn State group was that manufacturers were ignoring the role of the forepart of the shoe in protection of the foot. Our experiments, described in Chapter 4, had shown clearly that for some people the forefoot region is more important than the rearfoot, and that for all runners it has a critical role to play.

Well, the manufacturers responded and so did the injury statistics. Metatarsal stress fractures can be blamed almost entirely on poor forefoot cushioning; this category declined 4.2 percent in the ten-year period.

Ankle injuries improved by three percent, but this category is so nebulous that ascribing reasons for this change is extremely difficult. "Heel bone damage," a category in the 1971 study, is something that has all but disappeared in 1979. In the absence of better information, we can assume that this was the type of damage experienced by the Marine recruits—bruising and stress fractures of the heel. Both of these have benefited by the superior rearfoot impact response of today's shoes. Of course for rearfoot strikers, the improved absorption of energy at touchdown is something that will benefit the whole body. I would anticipate that the drastic improvement in rearfoot impact response has been important in facilitating the high training mileages that have now become commonplace. We must add a note of caution here. Some of the injuries classified as heel bone damage in 1971 may have shown up in the heel spur syndrome category in the 1979 data.

The Same News

Muscle pulls and hip injuries have occurred with roughly the same relative frequency over the decade. The number of muscle pulls is quite large, accounting for about one in twelve running injuries. Awareness of the importance of stretching before and after workouts as a preventative measure has grown, and it is thus surprising that this has not reduced the number of muscle pulls. Hip injuries were and are fairly uncommon, hovering at approximately one in forty injuries over the ten-year span.

The Bad News

Four categories show considerable increases: leg fractures, heel spur syndrome, shin splints, and most of all, knee injuries. The increase in leg fractures, predominantly stress fractures of the fibula and tibia, can most likely be attributed to improved diagnostic methods. The survey from St. Elizabeth's Hospital includes some runners whose X-rays were negative; subsequent bone scans revealed the presence of stress fractures (see example in Chapter 3). The stress fractures would have been previously lumped into the thin splint category.

Nobody really knows why stress fractures of these long bones occur. Certainly they are an overuse injury—the biological equivalent of fatigue fractures in airplanes that we have heard so much about. But exactly what combination of footwear, lower extremity alignment, and training habits would reduce the likelihood of stress fractures is an open question. Common sense dictates that better protection from foot strike impacts, softer surfaces, and less mileage will help, but by how much no one knows.

The knee injuries give genuine cause for worry. Again there is no substantial understanding of cause and effect, so we are forced to speculate. The combination of poor skeletal alignment and high mileage is going to play its part in knee injuries. We also have to examine the proposition, however unpalatable, that shoes, far from preventing injuries, have been partly responsible for them.

Let's look more closely at the thirty percent of Dr. Smith's patients who suffered knee pain. They were divided as follows: twenty-three percent peripatellar pain, five and a half percent lateral knee pain, and the remainder distributed among three other categories. One of the structural problems some clinicians associate with peripatellar pain is excessive pronation; one of the properties of a shoe which helps prevent this is rearfoot control.

If a shoe has a very compressible midsole and wedge, it is not going to control the rearfoot well. In making a shoe which has very good rearfoot impact properties it is possible that one of the side effects has been inferior rearfoot control. As excessive pronation occurs unrestrained, the knee is subjected to greater forces in a direction it is not well designed to accept.

I stress again that this is only a theory. But it is a plausible one, and runners with knee injuries should buy a shoe which combines good rearfoot control with at least acceptable scores on other important properties.

If we accept the term shin splints to mean the same thing in 1971 and 1979, we would conclude that there had been no change—10.6 percent in 1971 and 10.9 percent in 1979. But as we discussed earlier, a truer comparison is to measure shin splints in 1971 against the combined categories of shin splints and posterior tibial tendonitis in 1979. This shows an increase of over six percent, which may be conservative. Perhaps stress fractures of the tibia and fibula, which form five percent of the injuries, should also be included. But the conservative figure has been taken for this comparison.

Explaining the increase in shin splint injuries is a difficult task. Running fast on hard surfaces is often implicated in some of the complaints, but the real causes of these complex and diverse injuries are not well understood.

The increase in problems on the underside of the foot, such as arch injuries, plantar fasciitis, and other members of the heel spur syndrome is curious. It may be, as we mentioned earlier, that this is not a real increase but simply a result of reclassification. You can see from Figure 13.2 that if stone bruises are considered heel injuries, and are added in together with heel bone damage to the heel spur syndrome category, this would help to balance out the increase in the heel spur syndrome. But for purposes of discussion let's assume that this category of injuries has increased in the last ten years.

Various authorities ascribe injuries included in the heel spur syndrome to inflexible shoes, tight calf muscles, lack of or too much heel raise in the shoe, poor arch support, excessive pronation, plain overuse—in short, just about everything. When different experts offer so many explanations it is a good bet that we are a long way from understanding the real cause. Lloyd Smith describes this group of injuries as "one of the most frustrating to treat" because response to different treatments is unpredictable.

My own feeling about support of the arch is that conventional arch cookies are just about useless (I expand on this in Chapter 12). It may well be that the drastic punishment to which a high mileage runner subjects the foot requires a more substantial, customized device to ward off plantar injury. Many clinicians find that custom-made orthotics are the best treatment of this intractible problem.

Shoes Can Cause Injury

If shoes can prevent injury, then the converse must also be true—that shoes can cause injury. The first week or two in a new pair of shoes is absolutely critical, and the runner's senses should be particularly heightened to the messages his body is sending. If a pain or injury occurs during this period, there is a good chance it has been caused by the change in footwear. Don't be tempted to change a shoe in which you have been running injury-free, simply because one manufacturer or another has got a "better looking" shoe on the market. "If it works, don't fix it" is a good guideline when thinking about changing shoe types.

Summing Up on Injury

Runners get injured—and often! That much is clear. Not the traumatic injuries that players in contact sports experience, but a peculiar variety of overuse injuries is the lot of the runner.

The combination of a limb which is out of alignment, and training mileage which is extravagant is lethal where such injuries are concerned. Even though the foot may be the cause of many of the injuries, it is able itself to escape injury most of the time. The great majority of running injuries are between the ankle and the knee.

Comparing changes in patterns of injury over the last decade is difficult. We know that shoes have improved, but we also know that distances and intensity have increased. Since the injury rate has stayed about the same to the best of our knowledge, it seems reasonable that running shoes have been preventing injuries. If people were running today's mileages in yesterday's shoes, there is no question that injury rates would be much higher.

But the injury patterns have definitely changed. It is clear that saving the knee must be the primary goal of shoe design in the next decade. Somehow we must find a way to allow runners to run reasonable mileages without suffering the disabling knee injuries which are at almost epidemic proportions at the moment.

There are two major barriers to progress. First, the whole process of injury prevention by changing shoe design is incredibly subtle. After four years of fairly intensive work on running and running shoes, I continue to be disappointed at how far I personally am from understanding the interaction between shoe design and running injury. Shoes can have their effect at a level of subtlety which is well beyond our current measurement systems. A small pad under the medial side of the heel, a slight change in the flare of the midsole and wedge, a different pattern on the outsole; all these may either cause or cure a particular injury, and our methods of measurement are inadequate to detect these small but very significant changes.

The second barrier is the lag time between new developments in shoes and the effects upon injury statistics. There is no question that wrong turns have been taken in the past, and will continue in the future. Some features introduced into shoes have actually made injuries worse, while some have caused significant improvement. Until we get controlled experimentation with careful follow-up, the lag between ideas and results will continue to confound the injury picture.

14

How to Buy a Running Shoe

"Buying a running shoe used to be easy when Runner's World *told you what was the number one shoe."*
—A Pennsylvania marathoner (who prefers to remain anonymous)

"What *is* the best running shoe?" This is probably the most frequently asked question at running forums around the country. But it is a question which has no answer. This is analogous to asking, what is the best prescription drug? Many more questions need to be asked and answered before a rational response can be given. What complaint is the drug for? Does the intended recipient have any allergies? How long has he or she had the problem? Do they suffer from other illnesses which might contraindicate certain prescriptions?

The parallel to buying shoes is quite close. If the question is rephrased to "What is the best running shoe for me?" then it does have an answer. Finding the right shoe requires asking the right questions of yourself, doing the right things before going to the shoe store, doing the right things in the store, and being on your guard during the first week or so of running. This chapter will help you find the right type of shoe—if you are prepared to do a little work in looking. I will present a ten-point plan to guide you through the shoe buying maze. Six of the stages must be completed before you go near the store. This emphasizes that the whole process should be a carefully planned campaign. Buying a pair of shoes on impulse is the worst thing you could do.

THE TEN-POINT PLAN—A SYNOPSIS

We start from the premise that there is no one shoe that is best for all runners. This has been said many times but in my view it can't be repeated often enough. As I have shown, there is an infinity of running styles, foot types, movement patterns, and training habits, all of which demand different features in a shoe. The speaker in our opening quote was looking for an easy way out; the business of choosing the right shoe has become extremely complex.

In 1967 the first survey in *Distance Running News* (the parent of *Runner's World*) found fifteen running shoes in all categories to describe for its readers. As podiatrist Steve Subotnick recalls, "Recommending shoes was pretty easy in the early days. There were a couple of good brands of shoes and a lot of bad brands. Now the whole thing is more complex." The 1980 *Runner's World* survey tested 178 models from more than thirty manufacturers. With this kind of choice there is no survival for the consumer without a well formulated plan of attack.

A summary of the ten-point plan is shown in Table 14.1. Take a brief look through it so you can get an idea of the approach suggested. You will notice that the first five points call for self-analysis of different aspects of your body, shoes, and running habits. As you are led through the various questions under each of these points, specific features of a shoe will be suggested or rejected in view of your particular needs. Most of the questions appear again in summary form in the shoe search charts (Table 14.2). When you have read the first five points, go to these charts and answer the questions as best as you can.

Gradually a composite of the kind of shoe you need will emerge. When the shoe search charts are completed, the next step is to summarize the properties you should look for. Table 14.3 will be useful here because it has an entry for each region and property of the shoe. Fill out the summary chart with the features assembled on the search chart.

Now comes the critical step. You must match the properties suggested by the summary chart to shoes which have the features you need and want. Don't try to identify a single shoe because it might feel terrible on

TABLE 14.1

A Ten Point Plan to Find the Right Running Shoe

POINT 1	Look at your old shoes.
POINT 2	Look at your feet and legs.
POINT 3	Consider your injury history.
POINT 4	Consider your running style.
POINT 5	Consider your running habits.
POINT 6	Summarize your needs and match them with a group of shoes using the October issue of *Runner's World*.
POINT 7	Find a good running shoe store.
POINT 8	Do the right things, ask the right questions in the store.
POINT 9	Be tough on quality control before you buy.
POINT 10	Be on your guard for the first few weeks.

your foot. Choose four or five shoes, preferably made by different manufacturers, which seem to fit your needs. To do this effectively you will need a copy of the October issue of *Runner's World* magazine.

Every October *Runner's World* publishes detailed test results of all available running shoes. Other magazines put out shoe surveys and information, but I do believe that the *Runner's World* survey gives the best available data. Certainly it is the most comprehensive. Of course, I am biased because I am responsible for the lab tests performed for *Runner's World*. In the 1980 survey eight separate tests were performed on 178 different types of running shoes; this will probably increase in future years. If you are not sure about the individual tests, look back at Chapter 7 where the details of most of them are given.

One thing to realize about the top groups of shoes is that they have their strengths and weaknesses. The best way to use the survey is first to scan the overall rankings to identify which are the good performers. Then look at the tests which have been done, and find shoes that do well on the tests which investigate properties most important to you.

How to Use the Shoe Search Chart

Go through the five areas of concern which are addressed on this chart. These are:

POINT 1	Examine your old shoes.
POINT 2	Look at your feet, legs, and body weight.
POINT 3	Consider your injury history.
POINT 4	Consider your running style.
POINT 5	Consider your running habits.

As you encounter each topic, check the boxes which apply to you. Read the text under each point for more details. When you are through, go to the Summary Chart (Table 14.3) which will help you compile your answers in a form which will lead to a definition of the features you need in a running shoe.

TABLE 14.2 SHOE SEARCH CHART

POINT 1 Examine Your Old Shoes

OBSERVATION	INFERENCE	CHECK IF APPLICABLE
1.1 Heel Counters:		
Turn inwards	You probably pronate excessively. Rearfoot control is important. Could try varus wedge.	_____
Turn outwards	May have rigid foot type. Avoid varus wedge. Look for a good heel counter but other rearfoot control properties not critical.	_____
Generally battered	Look for better heel counter in your next shoe.	_____
1.2 Uppers:		
Leather uppers badly stretched	May need a wider shoe, but leather may be essential to give your foot the space it needs.	_____
Hole above the big toe	Needs a higher toe box.	_____
Uppers in bad condition	Your running style and habits are hard on the shoe. Avoid mesh uppers. Go with well made nylon weave (taffeta).	_____
1.3 Midsole and Wedge:		
Hard and brittle	You waited too long before buying a new pair of shoes. Plan to run less miles in the next pair.	_____
Uneven compression on inside and outside edges	You need a more substantial material in the midsole and wedge. May have to sacrifice shoe weight.	_____
1.4 Outsole:		
Rear outside corner badly worn	Probably a rearfoot striker. Make sure new shoe scores well on rearfoot impact and sole wear tests.	_____
Front outside edge badly worn	Probably mid or forefoot striker. Forefoot impact is important and good wear characteristics under ball (note—not measured by _Runner's World_ wear test)	_____

OBSERVATION	INFERENCE	CHECK IF APPLICABLE
Right-left shoes wear differently	May suggest leg length discrepancy or dynamic asymmetry in style.	_____

1.5 Fit and Comfort:

Often had black toenails	Need higher toe box.	_____
Numb toes during run	Need wider shoe.	_____
Pressure points in forefoot	Leather upper may help.	_____

POINT 2 Look at Your Feet, Legs, and Body Weight

2.1 Foot type:

Normal foot	No worries on this score.	
Rigid high arch	Problem foot. Good impact properties essential. Shoe must allow motion so poor rearfoot control could be a positive feature. Also get a flexible shoe. You may need additional heel lift and professional attention.	_____
Flexible high arch	Still look for good shock absorption.	_____
Flexible flat foot	Needs all the support it can get. Good rearfoot control. Supportive upper. Try varus wedge. May need professional help.	_____
You wear an orthotic	See special needs for orthotic wearers in Chapter 12.	_____

2.2 Rearfoot Alignment:

Rearfoot valgus	Pronate in standing, probably even more extreme in running. Rearfoot control important. Try varus wedge.	
Rearfoot varus	Avoid varus wedge.	_____
Rearfoot-forefoot imbalance	May need professional help if severe.	_____

2.3 Foot size and shape:

Unusual "bumps" on foot	Leather uppers will adapt to unusual shape.	_____

HOW TO BUY A RUNNING SHOE

	CHECK IF APPLICABLE

OBSERVATION — **INFERENCE**

Left and right feet are different lengths or widths. — Fit larger foot. Lacing pattern which will take up slack on smaller foot important. In extreme cases may need to buy 2 pair to get 1.

2.4 Leg alignment:
- Bow legged — Varus wedge OK — both may need professional help.
- Knock knee'd — Avoid large flare

2.5 Body weight:
- Male over 170 lbs.
- Female over 140 lbs. — Avoid racing flats.

POINT 3 Consider Your Injury History

3.1 Knee Injuries: Rearfoot control important. Avoid excessive lateral flare.

3.2 Heel Spur Syndrome: Look for good rearfoot impact, good rearfoot control, good flexibility, but good torsional stiffness. May need heel pad.

3.3 Shin Splints: Good impact properties are important and good rearfoot control. Make sure your training habits are sound.

3.4 Stress Fractures: Impact properties are important as well as flexibility for "march" fracture.

3.5 Achilles Tendon problems: Good heel raise. Low penetration into shoe (part of rearfoot control).

3.6 Ankle Sprains: As low heel as Achilles will allow. Avoid varus wedge if inersion sprain.

POINT 4 Consider Your Running Style

4.1 Point of first contact with ground:

Rearpart of shoe — Both rearfoot and forefoot impact properties are important. Also rearpart wear should be good.

Middle or forepart of shoe — Forefoot impact properties are particularly important. Also good wear in region under ball.

OBSERVATION	INFERENCE	CHECK IF APPLICABLE
4.2 Foot motion during mid-support:		
Stay on outside border	Avoid varus wedge. Look for good heel counters—firm midsole.	_____
Tend to flick heel toward midline	Will lead to excessive wear under ball of foot. Look for good forepart wear but waffles may be necessary to alleviate leg pain despite their poor wear properties.	_____

POINT 5 Consider Your Running Habits

5.1 Running Surface:		
Road running	Good impact properties essential.	_____
Wet roads	Traction important particularly for racing.	_____
Trails and uneven surface	Good tread pattern, good rearfoot control.	_____
5.2 Competition:		
Average runner	Probably do not need racing flats (see Chapter 11).	_____
Elite runner	See comments in Chapter 15.	_____
5.3 Environment:		
Hot and humid	Breathability (permeability to water vapor) is important. Broad mesh with thin permeable lining would be good. Air circulating insert an advantage.	_____
Cold weather	Get waterproof uppers with no vents. May also need additional insert to insulate foot from cold sole.	_____

NOTE: All injuries may need professional help if you are constantly running in pain.

How to Use the Summary Chart

Fill out this chart after you have completed the shoe search chart. Each time you have put a check against an item on the shoe search chart, make an entry here under the appropriate heading. Repeat the entry each time the same feature is recommended so that emphasis will build up in areas which are important to you. Write in any specific comments that cannot be conveyed by a checkmark.

For example, if good rearfoot impact properties have been suggested on the basis of both your running style and injury history, then you should put two check marks against rearfoot impact. If you need a higher toebox then write this into the appropriate line.

When the chart is complete, you should have a fairly complete picture of what properties you need to look for in a running shoe.

You can then begin to identify a group of shoes with these characteristics by looking at test results in the October issue of *Runner's World* and trying on shoes in the store.

TABLE 14.3 SUMMARY CHART

FEATURE	RECOMMENDATION (Write in specific requirement or check a feature you need the shoe to perform well on. Enter a cross by a feature you should avoid.)
Shoe Size, Width, and Shape	
Properties Tested by *Runner's World*	
Weight	
Rearfoot Impact	
Forefoot Impact	
Flexibility	
Rearfoot Control	
Sole Wear	
Traction	

Upper _____

Outsole _____

Toe Box _____

Heel Counter _____

Lacing System _____

Midsole and Wedge Configuration (heel height, etc.) _____

Special Features (Varus Wedge, Lateral Flare, etc.) _____

Features you would like but don't necessarily need (conforming footbed, etc.) _____

Price _____

Extras (heel cups, inserts, etc.) _____

Special Requirements (room to fit orthotic, etc.) _____

At all costs resist buying a shoe when all you know is that it is well rated by *Runner's World*. You owe it to yourself to inject your own personal characteristics into the decision, and that's what this chapter will help you to do. Most likely your requirements will lead you to a shoe which is well regarded, but start with your own needs rather than a shoe's reputation.

The next job is to find a good store in which to examine the shoes on your list. I will have some guidance about this. Once inside the store there are some definite do's and don'ts which I will list together with some questions you might ask the clerk. This is also the time to think about extras like heel cups and sockliners which might help the shoe fit and feel better.

When you walk out with the shoes under your arm or on your feet the game is not over. The first few miles will be critical for your adaptation to the shoe and for guarding against early and unwarranted breakdown in the shoe.

If you think all this sounds like a long process, you are right. But the decision is a tremendously important one. Most people spend a maximum of ten minutes in the store when they are buying running shoes. Ten minutes is a hopelessly inadequate time in which to assess the many relevant factors. So the most important thing is what you do before you ever go near the store. Don't buy on impulse, but be prepared to do a little research on your own. The time you spend will be worthwhile because it will lead to a more informed choice.

So there is the general strategy. Let's now get down to the specifics.

POINT NUMBER ONE
LOOK AT YOUR OLD SHOES

When astronauts return from a long voyage in space they spend several days in "debriefing." The purpose of this procedure is to elicit information about their experiences which is not recorded except in their own memories. Before you throw away your worn out running shoes, you should spend a few minutes debriefing them, because they hold a lot of secrets about your needs in a running shoe.

We discussed shoe wear in Chapter 10, and it might help to refer back to the information there before examining your shoes. We will be discussing the photographs in Chapter 10 throughout this first section. If you are a beginning runner this step will have no relevance to you, so you should move on to point number two.

Heel Counters

First, stand the shoes up side by side on the edge of a flat surface and look at the backs of the heel counters. If the counters are leaning inwards or outwards, your particular style of running has put a greater strain on the counter than it could handle. The most usual direction will be inwards (Figure 10.5a) which means that you probably overpronate. If this is the case you should look for a shoe with good rearfoot control.

If your heels are slanting outwards (Figure 10.5b), your style or body structure makes you very susceptible to ankle sprains, because you are running on the outside of your feet. You probably have a rigid foot which does not adapt well to the conditions encountered during support. You should avoid shoes with a varus wedge. They will tilt your feet even further out, and this will make you more likely to sprain your ankle. There will also be the possibility of foot or leg pain.

In either case, if the counter is badly deformed, has cracked, or is very soft, make sure you choose a shoe which scores well on the *Runner's World* stiffness test. This is a direct measure of the firmness of the heel counter.

The Uppers

While the shoes are on a flat surface, turn them around and look at them from the front. What you are looking for are clues as to whether the width of the shoe at the ball and the height at the toe box were adequate. If the shoes have a leather toe box, they may have deformed in the directions in which your foot applied force. If they were nylon, the constant force together with abrasion may have caused the uppers to rip away from the sole in the ball area.

Figure 10.3f is a good example of feet crying out for wider shoes. Both sides are overhanging the sole area. This shoe is painful just to look at, and its owner should definitely get a wider shoe next time around. This may be difficult because only one or two manufacturers make running shoes in width sizing. Remember too that European brands tend to be narrower than an American shoe.

Recall from Chapter 9 that there is virtually no standardization of sizing in the industry; if shoes from one manufacturer proved too narrow or too wide you should look to another brand for your next pair. The variation between makers will probably work to your advantage.

If leather uppers have been badly deformed it may be time to try nylon, which, as we noted, will not take a permanent deformation. But such a change, may also mean that your feet need the extra room provided by the leather which has been stretched. If you have any unusual anatomical features on your foot then a leather upper is a must. Be wary of shoes which have a leather upper sewn onto a nylon taffeta. The nylon will not allow the leather to take the shape of your foot.

If your uppers are in relatively good condition, even though other parts of the shoe are badly worn, you have no need to look further. The same or similar uppers will make a good repeat purchase. But some runners are very hard indeed on uppers. If you are one of these you should steer clear of nylon mesh uppers, which are not as durable as nylon taffeta or weave.

Leather, of course, is the most durable if you are prepared to take care of the shoes and don't mind the extra weight they will bring. Look for a shoe with strong, well-stitched uppers; the best have double stitching at major stress points. If you buy a nylon shoe make sure it is reinforced with leather all around the featherline (the junction of the upper and bottom). This will relieve some of the wear on the nylon.

Midsole and Wedge

Take a good look at the midsole and wedge of your old shoes. If they've become hard and brittle you are overdue for a new pair. The shock absorbing properties of such shoes may have deteriorated considerably. Look further at the heel and ball areas to see if the material has taken more of a compression set on one side than another. (Remember that in a shoe designed to have a varus wedge the inside edge of the midsole will be thicker to begin with.)

If the shoe has thinned noticeably on one side, make sure you find a more dense and resistant midsole and wedge in any future shoe. This may mean going to slightly heavier shoes; in an effort to cut down the shoe weight, many manufacturers have reduced the density of the midsole and wedge. This may have compromised the properties of some lighter shoes.

The Outsole

Wear patterns on the outsole are indicators of both running style and shoe quality. Shoes don't wear out where the most pressure is, they wear out where the most motion occurs between the shoe and the ground. Noting outsole wear will be helpful in choosing the cushioning properties you need.

If you are a rearfoot striker it is likely that the back outside edge of the shoe will be worn off diagonally (Figure 10.1b) much more than the forepart. If this is the case you should look for a shoe with good rearfoot impact properties and sole wear. If you are buying a shoe with a waffle sole, make sure it has a built-up area or wear bar on the part that you wear down.

If the wear is mostly on the front outside (Figure 10.1d), you're probably a midfoot or a forefoot striker. You should bear in mind that conventional tests like those used by *Runner's World* only measure the resistance of the rearfoot to wear. A wear bar or plug is generally placed in this area, and so the score may not correlate with what you will experience as a forefoot runner. In particular, waffles will wear down faster than a homogeneous sole. This may be so extreme for a forefoot striker that after a few hundred miles the rest of the shoe will be in perfectly good condition, but the outsole useless. This makes good outsole properties very important from an economic standpoint. Hopefully manufacturers will soon devise outsoles which retard wear under the forepart as they now do for the rearpart. (See Chapter 8 for some new ideas on this.)

Fit and Comfort

Before tossing or bronzing your old shoes, ask yourself about fit and comfort. Did you get blisters? Were your toes ever numb after a run, or did you get black toenails? Look at the good points as well as the bad. If the shoes gave you many miles of injury-free running, you may need look no further. If you have found a shoe that fits well, at least keep it in mind as you look through the remaining questions.

POINT NUMBER TWO—LOOK AT YOUR FEET, LEGS, AND WEIGHT

Foot types were discussed in Chapter 3, and it's now time to translate your knowledge of anatomy into a prescription for a shoe. A good way to get an initial idea of your foot type is to look at your footprint.

First try to determine the characteristics of the long arches of your foot. Wet your foot and then walk across a dark, smooth surface so that a clear impression is left. Compare the print with those in Figure 14.1. If yours looks like the normal example, then you probably have a wide range of shoes at your disposal.

The people who should pay the most attention to the results of this simple test are those whose print differs considerably from the normal. A high-arched foot needs special care.

There are different types of high arches, but the major distinction is between the rigid and flexible. A rigid foot will have a limited range of motion in both flexion and extension, but particularly in supination and pronation. The difficulty with the rigid high-arch is that it cannot act as a shock absorber the way the normal foot can. This condition calls for a shoe with good performance on impact tests above all other criteria.

Strangely enough the runner with a rigid high-arch foot may be better off in a shoe with poor rearfoot control. This is because the foot already has tremen-

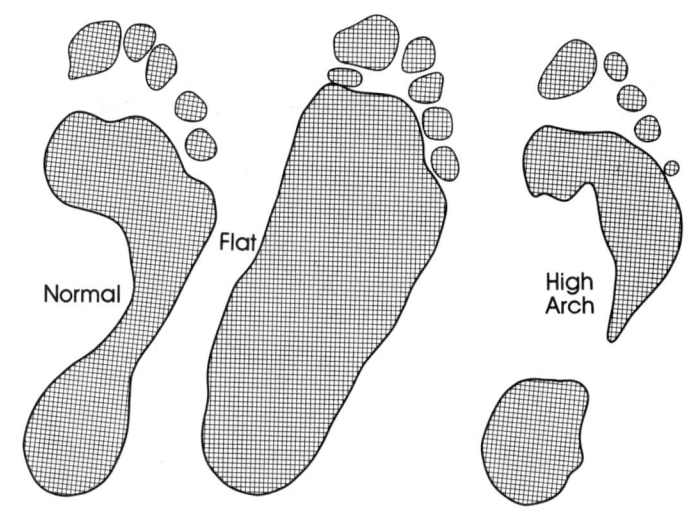

Fig. 14.1 Footprints from normal, flat, and high arched feet.

dous restrictions built in. A shoe which provides a lot of lateral stability may be harmful since it will not allow the foot and leg to compensate for the lack of internal motion in the foot. So impact is important, but rearfoot control can be compromised.

Most important for the rigid high-arch foot is to allow motion and not to control it. Foot specialists have varied opinions about runners with this foot type. Rob Roy McGregor thinks they should take up swimming, whereas Steve Subotnick prefers to take a file and get rid of the flared heels on the runners' shoes.

A flexible high-arch foot poses less of a problem. However it does have vast areas which are unsupported, and so all other factors being equal, the foot will be subjected to higher pressures during running. The conventional arch supports built into a new shoe will do next to nothing to help this foot. So if you have this foot type you should look for an additional insert which will take the shape of the foot and provide support. Even for the flexible high-arch foot good shock absorbing properties are important, so this should be high on the list of important criteria.

One more high-arch foot needs to be mentioned. This is the so-called equinus deformity, where the forefoot is 'dropped' in relation to the rearfoot, even when pressure is applied in an attempt to move it back up. Together with the other features mentioned, this foot will need a shoe which has a large height differential between the forefoot and the rearfoot. In some cases an additional pad will be needed to provide the necessary heel height.

Flat Feet

The flat foot may need considerable help or none at all. This type of foot has given up the fight against pronatory forces, and has taken a resting position in which the long inside arch has fallen or disappeared, and the rearfoot is in a pronated position. This may be due either to a congenital deformity, to history of poor footwear, or to some muscle imbalance. Again, there are rigid and flexible flat feet; in this case the flexible type is more likely to cause problems.

The general treatment for the flatfooted person will be support for the fallen medial arch and perhaps exercises to correct any muscular weakness. For flatfooted runners an orthotic is frequently needed: the flat foot needs all the support it can get.

Translating this into the properties of a running shoe, a straight-lasted shoe will often be recommended. Very few flat feet show an inflared forefoot, and a shoe with a large inflare may create even further problems. A shoe should be chosen in which the upper is strengthened in the arch area by an arch bandage, or a saddle which joins the welt and the lacing stay. If an orthotic is to be worn, you should make sure that there is sufficient room for the device and that the heel counter is strong enough to keep the device in place (see Chapter 12). Rearfoot control is very important to the mobile flat foot. The shoe must provide resistance against the pronatory forces, so rearfoot control should be a high priority for the flatfooted runner.

Rearfoot and Forefoot Alignment

We move now to more subtle variations in anatomy which have their part to say in what shoe should be worn. These are the alignments of the rearfoot and forefoot which were discussed in Chapter 3. You may want to look back to refresh your memory.

If you have a rearfoot valgus, where a line drawn upwards through the center of the heel bone tends to point towards the midline of the body, then a varus wedge may be worth a try. If your static position is rearfoot varus, where the upward line through the rearfoot points away from the body, you should stay away from shoes with varus corrections.

If there are substantial imbalances between your forefoot and rearfoot it is likely that you will need some professional help in customizing the inside of your shoe. Certain alignment problems may be compensated at various levels in the leg and foot; if this is the case you will also need help in determining the best course of action. Unfortunately these complex imbalances are very difficult to detect on your own feet, so the first you hear of the problem might be when you are told by a doctor.

Size and Shape of Your Foot

Look at the top surface of both your feet and identify any unusual bumps or projections. Check particularly the area over the joints, where the big and little toe meet the forefoot. Remember that nylon uppers are not going to mold to any abnormality, but will continue to apply pressure to it for the life of the shoe. This is likely to make the condition considerably worse. Leather uppers are a must for abnormally shaped feet, and they may need some prestretching in the right places to insure a trouble-free performance during the first few weeks.

As we saw in Chapter 7 there is no reason to suppose that the width and length of your left and right feet are the same. Before you go to the store it is a good idea to know some facts about your foot size, so that you know what to expect from any measurements taken.

Take a large piece of paper and have someone draw a pencil outline around both your feet while you're standing. Make sure that they compress some of the soft tissue and hold the pencil vertical all the way around the feet. Have them mark the bulges at the ball, which represent the joints between the forefoot and the first and fifth toes.

When the outlines have been taken, join these two points on the side of the foot together, and also join the tip of the longest toe to the middle of the heel. You should end up with something which looks like Figure 14.2. Take a ruler and measure the length of the two lines on both feet as shown.

You can check the actual correspondence between the lengths and widths that you measure against the dimensions given in Chapter 9. Pay particular attention to width, because more than ninety percent of all running shoes are made in D width. If you diverge far from this width you may be forced to select from manufacturers who make width sized shoes.

The real purpose here though is to determine any differences there might be between left and right. Width sizing is, strictly speaking, done on the basis of circumference, the distance all the way around the foot, not just across it. So if you have found a substantial width difference (greater than four millimeters) on the tracing, you may want to take a tape measure around your foot to confirm the differences.

You will recall that the length difference between a half size in shoes is one-sixth of an inch (0.16 inches) or 4.2 millimeters. Width sizing, as we are measuring it, varies by approximately the same amount for a full width size.

If you have found width or length differences between your feet the general advice is to fit the shoe to the larger and wider foot.

Width is easier to take care of than length. If you have a width difference, choose a shoe which has the possibility of drawing the upper in on the narrower side. This will mean a long throat, with seven lace holes and sufficient width for the laces to draw in the sides of the throat without overlapping, to allow adjustment on the smaller foot. Several lacing designs which permit this are described in Chapter 8.

Many people advise that the toe of the shoe on the smaller foot should be padded to fill out the extra space. Length differences will also have to be accommodated to some extent by tighter lacing on the smaller foot. So if you have a length difference, make sure the

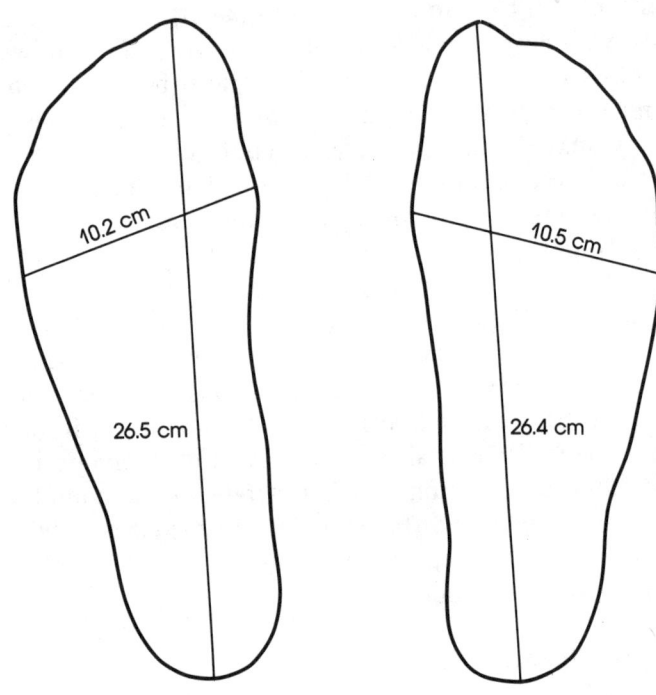

Fig. 14.2 Foot outlines with two measurements you can make to see if your right and left feet are different in size.

upper can be closed on the smaller foot without the sides of the throat coming too close.

If the difference is greater than half a size, you may be forced to buy two pairs of shoes so that one from each will accommodate your feet. As expensive as this sounds it may be the best solution to a seemingly intractable problem. Ideally, you would find someone with exactly opposite length discrepancies to your own, but this is rather unlikely. Perhaps someone will start a "National Register for Runners with Different Size Feet" to arrange the exchange.

Looking at Your Legs

There are certain skeletal problems above the feet that might influence your choice of a running shoe. In particular you should be aware of the two known as tibial varum and valgum.

In these conditions the normal, near-vertical alignment of the shank is not present in an easy standing position with the feet apart. The knees are either together (tibial valgum) or bowed (tibial varum). Both of these should be easily visible if they are at all pronounced.

Tibial varum is by far the more common. We described the functional varum which is a natural part of the running gait in Chapter 4. If the alignment of the leg heightens this even further the foot and knee will have to cope with additional stresses. Most likely the runner who has tibial varum will pronate excessively, as the foot tries to get flat on the ground despite the severe angulation of the leg. If the varum is severe professional help should be sought. An initial attempt to ward off problems would involve a shoe with a varus wedge. Although rearfoot control is important to this foot, by the time most of the conventional rearfoot control features begin to act, tremendous abnormal pronation has already occurred.

No shoes on the market cater to the problem of tibial valgum or knock knees. A runner with pronounced tibial valgum who already has pain or is contemplating increased mileage should seek professional help.

Self-examination of your feet and legs will provide you with key information about your needs in footwear. Also, you now know more about your feet than the salesperson in the shoe store, and this has to be to your advantage.

Your Body Weight

The runners who should be most concerned about including body weight in the shoe selection equation are the heavyweights. We describe several factors which they should consider in Chapter 15. In particular, most racing shoes are a bad idea for men weighing more than 170 pounds and women over 140.

There is no doubt that the future will bring shoes which are specially built for different body weights. It may be, for example, that women's shoes are over-designed in terms of cushioning for the average build of women runners. Heavyweight individuals may need more protection than they can currently obtain. All this is in the future.

POINT NUMBER THREE—CONSIDER YOUR INJURY HISTORY

For the vast majority of serious runners, injury prevention should be a strong guiding principle in selecting a running shoe. The shoe is first and foremost a protective device. If you have had injuries in the past these should help your choice of certain features in the shoe. If you have been injury-free, then good performance on features important to injury prevention will be important.

It would be nice to be able to report that it is easy to find shoes which will prevent specific injuries, but the whole question of injury prevention and causation by running shoes is not well understood, as we discussed in Chapter 13.

Since there are almost no well-controlled studies indicating which features of footwear cause or prevent certain injuries, the best we can do is make some intelligent guesses. We can also lean on the advice of practitioners who have seen injured runners and have made some connections between the type of shoe and type of injury.

Sometimes a change in shoes will cause an injury to disappear completely, but most often the injured runner will not be so fortunate. Perhaps a change in shoes, treatment, rest, and exercises will be needed. In this section we will give some pointers on what to look for if you have had one of the more common running injuries. We are going to look at the top five categories of injuries mentioned in Chapter 13 from the Saint Elizabeth's Hospital survey.

Knee Injuries

Where else to start but knee injuries? Out of every one hundred running injuries knee problems are claiming about thirty victims. The spectre was raised in Chapter 13 that running shoes may be as much a part of the problem as they are the solution.

Most knee injuries are the result of alignment and overuse problems. There is no traumatic "ouch" when the moment of catastrophe can be identified. The onset is insidious and relentless.

Pain around the kneecap (peripatella pain) seems most likely to be shoe related. Shoes that allow the foot which overpronates to continue its motion without resistance will in all likelihood be adding to this problem. Rearfoot control is a vitally important feature for runners with a history of knee injury. Good performance on the test of "rearfoot stability" (see Chapter 7) is particularly important. Most knee problems are not impact injuries; if a shoe is getting good impact results from a soft and compressive midsole, it will be bad news for the knee. Excessive flare at the heel should also be avoided by runners with knee pain. Many clinicians feel that this will, if anything, exacerbate any pain, particularly on the outside of the knee, that might exist.

The causes of many other types of knee pain are not well understood. Once a clear idea is obtained then defining the type of shoe needed will be possible. But so far, the difficult task of identifying the cause has not been completed.

Heel Spur Syndrome

The origins of heel spur syndrome are still shrouded in mystery. You will recall that this includes pain at the heel, plantar fasciitis, and other complaints not necessarily accompanied by a bony spur at the heel (see Figure 3.7). In many instances there is pain whenever pressure is exerted underneath the front edge of the heel bone. If this is present a shoe with good rearfoot impact properties should be sought. This will offer a first line of defense.

It is likely that an excessive twisting motion between the rearfoot and forefoot will also irritate the plantar surface. This will dictate shoe type in two ways. First, rearfoot control will be important to a runner with any or all of the symptoms of heel spur syndrome. If this applies to you, you should buy a shoe which scores well on the standard tests of rearfoot control.

Second, resistance to twisting about the long axis of the shoe will probably be helpful. No standard tests yet measure this property which we will call torsional stiffness. The stiffer the shoe, the better it will be for this particular injury. But there is a problem here. Shoes which are stiff under the ball of the foot may also lead to plantar fascia problems. The choice must be a compromise between good flexibility under the ball and stiffness around the long axis.

Some other extras will probably be needed by sufferers from heel spur syndrome. Heel pads will be useful for symptomatic relief. Some direct relief of painful pressure, such as that described under self help in Chapter 12, may also be beneficial. This might include a heel pad, with a cut out area under the painful site.

A good arch support can help. The controversy surrounding the use of prescription or over-the-counter devices is also discussed in Chapter 12. It is very likely that if treatment was received from a doctor for heel spur syndrome that a custom-made arch support was prescribed. If this was the case, all of the features above should be considered, together with the fact that there must be adequate room for the orthotic to fit inside the shoe.

In summary, rearfoot impact, rearfoot control, flexibility at the ball, and tortional stiffness are features to be looked for if heel spur syndrome has been part of your injury history.

Shin Splints

Shin splints are, as we discussed in Chapter 13, many things to many people. Originally the term described any pain in the shank, frequently because the accurate site and cause of the injury could not be determined. But more recently two important categories have been identified. These are tendonitis of the posterior tibial muscle and stress fractures of the shank bones.

In our simplified runner's anatomy in Chapter 3 the location of the posterior tibial muscle was given. You will recall that this muscle is in a good position to resist pronation of the foot. It is generally runners with excessive pronation who develop posterior tibial tendonitis, since the muscle is being worked considerably harder than normal. Therefore a shoe which controls rearfoot motion will be extremely important to sufferers of this condition.

Because other maladies besides posterior tibial tendonitis are included in this "grab bag" term, you should try to pin down the site of your particular shin splint problem. Certain of these other injuries are impact related, and good forefoot and rearfoot impact properties are recommended for most shin splint type injuries. Don't forget that shin splints can also be the result of training habits which perhaps try too much, too fast, and too soon. Consider this as you search for desirable qualities in a running shoe.

Stress Fractures

The most common sites of stress fractures in runners are the front of the bones of the shank, the tibia and fibula. It is generally agreed that stress fractures are "impact" type injuries. They result from the continual application of stresses which, although not large enough to do damage in a few cycles, accumulate with repetition until a small fracture occurs.

The overwhelming need in a shoe for a runner who has had stress fractures is protection from impacts during ground contact. As we saw when discussing the biomechanics of distance running, the forces are greatest in the forefoot region; forefoot impact response is clearly important in this case. For rearfoot strikers the rearfoot impact properties are also crucial, since the initial shock from landing is cushioned by this region of the shoe.

Although it is now a less frequent injury, a stress fracture of the metatarsal bones in the forefoot, particularly the second and third, can still happen. This was originally known as a "march fracture" since it was first noticed in German soldiers during march training.

This problem can be attributed to inadequate forefoot cushioning and inflexible shoes. The reason it has declined is that shoes have improved in their forefoot cushioning properties and have become more flexible. Nevertheless there is still a considerable difference between the best and worst shoes in forefoot impact values. For example, women's training shoes in the 1980 *Runner's World* survey were scattered over a 230 percent range. So if you have had a march fracture look over the table of forefoot impact values carefully and make this your number one priority in choosing a shoe. Be particularly wary of racing flats; although they are more flexible than training flats they generally lose out in forefoot cushioning (see Chapter 11).

Achilles Tendonitis

This is another category of injury which has improved in recent years. The range of motion at the ankle joint, and consequently of the Achilles tendon, has been reduced by greater elevation of the heel platform with respect to the forefoot. But Achilles tendonitis still is a debilitating injury for many runners.

One source of the problem may be differences in heel and forefoot height among the various shoes that a runner uses during the week. Suppose for example that you have a solid pair of training shoes with a good heel raise, but on weekends you use a skinny pair of racing shoes for a ten kilometer race. Your Achilles tendon and its associated structures will have adjusted to the range of motion needed during training. Even though the race is only for a short duration, the added stretching of the Achilles tendon enforced by the racing shoe may be enough to start the inflammation. Once you establish a given heel-forefoot height difference, try not to make sudden changes. In general Achilles tendon problems dictate a good heel raise in a running shoe if this is not incompatible with other requirements.

There is another important property to search for if you have suffered from Achilles tendonitis. In 1980 one or two shoes appeared with spectacular impact response, which was achieved by placing extremely soft and compressible material under the heel. But these shoes produced a rash of Achilles tendonitis injuries. This particular feature is measured in *Runner's World* by the penetration test. The more penetration the worse the shoe will be for your Achilles tendon.

Some runners find that the so-called Achilles tendon protector irritates the tendon. This problem is easily solved by cutting the protector completely off. When you try on the shoe make sure that this part of the upper does not exert undue pressure on the tendon.

Ankle Sprains

Habitual ankle sprainers should, if their knees allow, go with a shoe with flared heels, to make the foot placement more stable. As we discussed earlier, people who sprain their ankles on the outside should avoid shoes with varus correction since this will encourage the tendency to turn the ankle inwards. This type of sprain is known as an inversion sprain, and is the most common type of ankle sprain.

If the Achilles tendon is not prone to inflammation,

it makes sense for runners who sprain their ankles to choose as low a heel height as possible. This reduces the risk of turning an ankle by literally falling off the platform of the shoe.

POINT NUMBER FOUR—DEFINE YOUR RUNNING STYLE

Analysis of running style is something coaches have been doing for many years. Only recently has science attempted to document the variations in such factors as foot placement, limb movement, and the forces and pressures generated under the foot. The subtleties of running style are difficult to judge simply by looking. In the future it is likely that we will be providing a scientific style analysis to our elite athletes.

Despite the complexity of determining running style, there are things you may be able to detect with the help of a shrewd observer. In particular, aspects of the interaction of your foot with the ground may yield to a visual analysis.

The idiosyncracies of your running style will affect your choice of shoes. First try to determine which part of your foot makes initial contact with the ground. (Remember that this is speed dependent; make your test runs at your most common training speed.) This can be difficult to see because the foot becomes flat so quickly. But have someone else watch your foot carefully from the back and side, and take another look at the wear pattern on your shoe, which should give some information.

If the foot makes first contact with the back outside corner, you are a rearfoot striker. In this case both forefoot and rearfoot impact properties will be important, because your foot needs to be protected throughout its length.

If your initial contact occurs further forward, toward the midfoot and forefoot, then forefoot impact protection will be of special concern to you. We have seen that forefoot cushioning of shoes was ignored for many years because of the mistaken idea that all distance runners land on their heels.

This does not mean that rearfoot impact is not important to a midfoot or forefoot runner. Many midfoot runners strike first with the midfoot and then move backwards onto the heel. Also, running on a gradient changes the way you strike the ground. Running downhill, almost everyone becomes a rearfoot striker, while in uphill running the initial contact is generally with the forefoot.

Next, try to determine what happens to your rearfoot during the early part of the support phase. This should confirm the information given by the lean of the heel counters in your old shoes. Have someone watch carefully to see if you pronate excessively, or if the rearfoot is neutral or even in a varus position, during support.

If you do pronate excessively, get the best rearfoot

control you can find. If you are running pain-free at present it's in your best interest to get rearfoot control which is at least as good as that offered by your present shoe. A shoe with a varus wedge may also be helpful if its other rearfoot properties are good.

Runners who maintain a neutral position during stance can compromise on rearfoot control to some extent. This may help if some other feature is called for that cannot easily be found combined with good rearfoot control. Runners who run on the outside of their foot (either in the rearfoot or forefoot) should avoid shoes with varus correction. They should look for a substantial heel counter to resist this tendency.

A final thing worth looking at in your running style is how much movement occurs while the foot is "planted" during mid-support. After initial placement, many runners snap the rearfoot towards the midline of the body in an action known as an abductory twist. If you do this your shoes will probably reflect it in excessive wear under the ball. If you do have a tendency to twist the foot in mid-support, be especially careful about the wear characteristics of the outsole.

The choice is not a simple one, though. This twisting movement will wear down waffles faster than a flat outsole, but the waffles may ease the effect of the twisting at the knee and ankle joints. Start with a flat sole, but if this is a change for you, watch during the first few runs for knee pain.

Getting Professional Help

You may feel that some questions concerning foot type, injury history, and running style that I have posed in points 2, 3, and 4 are beyond your current knowledge. If this is the case, don't feel despondent. Many people have spent years studying the foot and leg and still do not have a clear idea about how to meet footwear requirements. If you believe that you have special needs in a running shoe, dictated perhaps by injury or an unusual anatomical feature, you should seek professional help before deciding what shoe to buy. The best person to ask is not the clerk in the store but a doctor who sees runners, their shoes, and their injuries on a regular basis. Such a consultation will cost money, but it will be money well spent.

At present, runners' clinics are filled with injured runners. I would be happier if more people at those clinics were seeking advice and prevention rather than help for injuries already sustained. We see our dentist regularly on a preventative basis. Running many miles a week is as demanding on the musculoskeletal system as eating three meals a day is on the teeth. The sooner we get into a preventative frame of mind the better.

Sports medicine practitioners should be able to advise you about shoes for your needs—if you choose the right person.

If you are a runner who is habitually injured, then

seeking professional help before choosing a shoe is a must. We will discuss this further in Chapter 15. If you've been running with a nagging pain that you think is not worth seeing the doctor about, it may be that a change of shoe would solve the problem.

POINT NUMBER FIVE—CONSIDER YOUR RUNNING HABITS

Consumer organizations often talk about the "end use" of a product. The end use for a running shoe is not simply running. Since there are many types of running, the terrain, speed, and environmental conditions will influence your choice of shoe.

If you run for enjoyment and not for top-class racing, shoe weight should not be of particular concern. If the shoe is a little heavier, the additional energy cost will be of no great consequence. Elite athletes are a special case and I shall save discussion of their needs for Chapter 15.

If you are going to run on the roads protection from the pounding your feet will take is essential. Concrete is about as hostile a surface as one could find to run on. Road runners should look carefully for a shoe which, among other virtues, has good protection where they need it. If the surfaces you run on are less harsh the impact properties of the shoe can take second place to other features. Over rough terrain flare at the heel might help with stability, and good tread could help with traction.

Most running shoes provide good traction on dry pavement, but when the going is slick, shoes separate rapidly into good and bad. Friction tests for *Runner's World* showed that coefficients of friction between 0.3 and 0.75 could exist under wet and greasy conditions. Since 0.5 or above is generally regarded as acceptable, you can see that there are shoes which you'd rather not be wearing on a wet day. This could be particularly important in racing. We know that car races are won and lost by the properties of the tires used, and it is my belief that many foot races are the same. It may be worthwhile having a pair of your favorite shoes resoled with a material that will perform well in wet weather. This way, regardless of conditions you can be sure of good traction.

Paradoxically enough a deep tread may be more of a hindrance than a help in muddy conditions. The gaps between individual treads tend to clog up with mud adding enormous weight to the shoe. A smaller pattern may give equally good traction without the adverse effects. If you run in snow a lot you may want to try one of the add-on traction devices mentioned in Chapter 8.

The temperature and humidity during your runs will dictate what kind of upper you need. If you frequently run in high temperature and humidity, nylon mesh which has as broad a knit as you can find is recommended. Be sure to check the material on both the outside and inside of the shoe; an impermeable lining on a wide mesh will prevent any cooling effect. You may also need an insole which will allow cooler air to circulate underneath your foot. These are described in Chapter 8. If you cannot find the shoes you need with a mesh upper, cutting ventilation holes may help. Unfortunately this may prove disastrous in a nylon upper since the material will probably fray very quickly, but it will be successful in a leather shoe.

In cold conditions either leather or nylon weave uppers should prove satisfactory. Rarely do runners complain of cold feet unless they've been thoroughly soaked by icy water. Several new fabrics for uppers are now on the market which purport to be both breathable and water resistant. If they live up to their billing they could provide a good all-weather shoe. In snow and ice the thermal conductivity of the soles may lower the temperature of the platform of the shoe considerably making the soles of your feet noticeably cold. You can use an additional sockliner as insulation.

Finally, running shoes are not multipurpose, the way an "all-court" shoe is. In fact, it can be dangerous to play sports like tennis, racquetball, or basketball, which involve lateral motion, in a running shoe. The latter is just not designed for quick changes of direction. It can also accelerate the wear of the shoe and break down the heel counter, making it worse for running. Walking is perhaps a special case, and we shall cover that later.

POINT NUMBER SIX—MULLING OVER WHAT YOU HAVE LEARNED

By now you have been battered by questions about everything from your black toenails to the temperature outside. It is time to organize the knowledge you have gained into a usable prescription for a shoe.

Points one through five are repeated in the Shoe Search Charts. Go through these and check off the categories which fit your description. For each entry in the chart, some property of a shoe will be recommended or rejected. For example, a wider toe box or good forefoot impact properties might be suggested by two of your answers.

When the questions have all been answered use the summary chart. Go through the various features one by one as represented in this chart. Look down the shoe search charts you have filled in and see what was recommended or rejected in the preceding five steps.

For example, taking the first entry in the summary chart—did the analysis of your old shoes suggest a larger or wider shoe? Did your foot measurement reveal differences between left and right? Note the implications in the summary chart. "Left foot bigger — also try wider shoe" might be a typical entry.

If a feature is recommended by more than one of the five steps, mark it each time it occurs so that its importance will be highlighted. For example, if you have had knee pain, find that you tend to overpronate, and noticed the heel counters of your old shoes turning in, you would have three entries on the summary table where rearfoot control was recommended. This suggests that rearfoot control is what you should look for above all other factors in your running shoe. If you have a particularly troublesome pain or injury and a feature has been suggested to help with this, it may be worthwhile to buy a shoe for that feature alone.

As you sift through the recommendations your answers suggested, a consensus should emerge. You should see which features were recommended most often and which you were warned against. Occasionally there are apparent contradictions. Some runners may find, for example, that they are advised to look for both a high and low heel on the basis of two different problems. In cases like this you will have to make compromises and choose the most critical features for your needs.

If you find that few recommendations have emerged it is likely that you will be served equally well by many different shoes. Such a finding means you will have a wider selection to choose from.

Consult a Friend—and *Runner's World*

Before you leave for the store, there are a few other ingredients you might want to throw into the pot. If you have been running for some time you have a better idea of what the recommendations mean. If you are a beginner you might want to consult a knowledgeable friend. The problems of shoe buying for the beginner receive special attention in Chapter 15.

The *Runner's World* shoe issue is now an essential companion as you match your requirements with a particular make and model. Scan the tables of characteristics which are important to you, trying to obtain the best overall performance you can on your own criteria. Read the description of each shoe and see if it fits your needs.

There is no doubt that shoes priced substantially below the usual bracket are running shoes in appearance only. Their performance is in no way comparable to a serious running shoe. Stay away from the "look-alikes."

But remember that paying a high price is no guarantee that you are getting the best running shoe for you. More money does not simplify the process. Sometimes a manufacturer's most expensive shoe actually costs less to produce than a lower-priced model.

I compiled some statistics on the *Runner's World* survey results by taking the overall point totals for each shoe and correlating them with shoe price. A perfect correlation of 1.0 would indicate that the more you pay the better shoe you get. The actual result was a correlation of less than 0.2 between price and score. Statisticians will tell you that this low score means that there is almost no relationship between the two factors. Remember that this correlation is specific to the sample used and did not include any of the "look-alike" shoes which would have been the exception to this rule.

So the moral is: let price be your guide only at the bottom end. Be prepared to pay enough money to get you into the range of serious running shoes. But from that point use the criteria that we have talked about so far and not the price tag.

What About Imports?

In a quiet moment most shoe manufacturers will tell you that it is possible to make good shoes almost anywhere in the world if management is sufficiently diligent. This does not mean that all shoes are the same quality. Neither does it mean that it's as easy to produce shoes in the Far East as it is in America. In fact it is considerably more difficult since the management has to keep constant tabs on the manufacturing process from a great distance. But it might surprise you to know that names as well known as Nike and Adidas make some of their shoes in the Orient.

So while staying away from imports is not a good general rule it does pay to look extra carefully at shoes that are imported. Is the shoe well made? Was the quality control good? Were the materials as good as you might find in an American-made shoe? Occasionally the prices of some imports are considerably higher than others. Europe is an expensive place these days for an American, and European shoes generally come at a higher price.

Orderly marketing agreements which the United States has established with some of the Oriental countries have imposed quotas and a twenty percent import duty on some categories of imported shoes. This has cut into the price advantage resulting from the cheaper labor cost enjoyed in foreign countries.

Are You Safe With A Big Name Manufacturer?

As of January 1980 the best estimates of market share for running shoes sold in general sporting goods stores in the United States were as follows: Nike—27.4 percent; Adidas—19.0 percent; Brooks—18.0 percent; Converse—5.9 percent; Puma—5.6 percent; New Balance—5.0 percent; and Tiger—2.3 percent. Just how reliable this data is no one knows. Surveys taken in specialty shoe stores would probably move the percentages up or down by ten percent. Exact figures aside, these companies have risen to prominence because they do make good shoes. But they all make several models, some of which may be quite wrong for you. Buying by manufacturer alone is not enough.

In general, reputable manufacturers will use good materials, and it is in their interests to insist on good workmanship. Companies like Etonic, Brookfield, Rebok, Pony, Osaga, and Saucony have all been making running shoes for many years and their products have been widely accepted by runners.

But staying with the big names cuts you off from some new and potentially good shoes. In the last few years companies such as Fastrack, Wilson, Autrey, Spalding, Kaepa, Ambi, and Uniroyal have begun making running shoes. When you look through the test results in *Runner's World* you should be guided more by the performance of the shoe than the shape of the logo or the name that the shoe bears.

The Short List

At the end of the process described under this point, you should have identified four or five shoes which represent your "short list"—those shoes included in the final consideration. It will help if these are made by different manufacturers, since you will have a better chance of finding both the right properties and a good fit. The next step is finding somewhere you can look at, try, and buy the shoes.

POINT NUMBER SEVEN—FIND A GOOD RUNNING SHOE STORE

One of my outstanding moments in shoe buying happened one rainy Saturday when I took my daughter to a big department store for new rubber boots. The girl who waited on us proceeded to slip the left shoe on the right foot. As my daughter squirmed a little I pointed out the problem to the clerk, who had a ready answer, "Well, I'm new at this. I only started this week." This level of expertise would obviously be of little help in guiding a shoe purchase.

Although the same shoe might be sold in several stores in your area, it will pay to ask around to determine the best place to buy running shoes.

Recently running shoe shops have appeared all over the country, and they are generally staffed by people who have had a lot of running experience. Several of the franchises will only accept runners as store managers. I'm not saying that someone who doesn't run could not do a satisfactory job of selling you a pair of shoes, but I do think that a runner will give advice that comes from understanding and experience rather than from reading the trade literature.

Go to a store with as wide a selection of shoes as possible. A small store that carries mainly one brand is unlikely to be able to satisfy your needs. If the last used by that company is not right for your foot, you'll never find a good fit. The clerk will also be anxious to convince you that one of their line of shoes is exactly right for you.

POINT NUMBER EIGHT—WHAT TO DO IN THE STORE

Manufacturers and retailers could make life a little easier than they do. It would be nice if stores had demonstrator models, at least in the most popular sizes. This might be a sizeable investment for small retailers, but manufacturers could take the lead. If they are sure of their product, they could offer one pair of each size at a reduced cost to the dealer on condition that the shoes were used as demonstrators. Logging a mile or so in a pair of shoes would tell a lot more than simply walking up and down on the nice soft carpet inside the store.

Another of my hopes for the future is that shoes will carry a tag indicating how the shoe performs on a number of accepted tests. This would allow the more informed users to meet their own needs.

When you head for the store, take the information gained from this chapter along, either in your head or written on the charts from the book. Don't forget to take the socks that you usually wear when running. This will be a better test of fit than if you wear your regular socks or none at all. While talking of size, we should recall that foot volume is likely to increase throughout the day, so it is probably best not to try on new shoes first thing in the morning.

When you first get to the store have the clerk measure your feet for both length and width. Watch carefully and ask them what they have found. You will already know any differences between the left and right feet from measurements you made earlier, and it will be interesting to see whether the clerk confirms your results. Some of the measuring devices are calibrated for use in non-weightbearing while others require that the person stand for measurement. Ask the clerk what you should be doing. Remember, use the size read off the measuring device as a preliminary guide. Start with the size indicated but be ready to move up or down depending upon the feel of the shoe.

While your feet are being measured, get to know a little about the store. Ask what their policy is on returns for poor workmanship; this could be quite important. Some stores will give you an instant replacement for an obviously defective product. This is the best situation for you because it means the dealer will absorb the loss until the shoe company reimburses the store. Other stores insist that credit or replacement is not possible until the shoes have been inspected at the factory and a credit slip issued. This could take weeks; meanwhile you are without running shoes.

Also ask the clerk if they have any demonstration shoes that you could wear for a short run. Find out what shoes they have in width sizing if you're going to need it, and whether they can special order certain items for you.

Make it clear to the clerk that you already have a good idea of what you are looking for. Try to establish a dialogue because, as we mentioned earlier, many who work in running shoe stores are running afficionados who have seen a lot of shoes sold and returned. Tell him or her the names of the shoes on your "short list," find out if they are in stock, and ask the clerk about the shoes you are interested in.

When the time comes to try the shoe on, try both the left and right, and lace them as tightly as you normally would. In Chapter 9 we discussed how the right shoe is invariably on top of the box, but the chances are that your left foot will be slightly bigger. If you do have a difference in foot length pay particular attention to your larger foot for sizing. Don't neglect the fact that you have to be able to take up some of the excess upper material by the lacing on your shorter foot. We also mentioned that most people recommend at least half an inch between the end of the longest toe and the end of the toe box. This should be considered a rough guide because the shape and size of your foot will affect fit in other parts of the shoe.

While you are in the store take advantage of the variety in stock and try on a number of different designs. For example, try on a straight-lasted shoe and an in-flared shoe to see which feels more comfortable. Keep the shoes on for a while so that any fit problems in the toe box will become apparent. Also try on a slip-lasted shoe and a cement-lasted shoe and see if you find either one more to your liking. Look at the toe box to see if the upper is tightly stretched and if your toes are pressing not only the end of the toe box but the roof and sides as well. Try on a few shoes with special features even though they may not be on your list. The feel of something different will give you perspective on the shoes you have already tried.

One of the big problems with comfort is that the shoe will change its "feel" during the first part of its active life. What you feel when the shoe is new will not be maintained. There is no good way to anticipate this other than through experience.

If you wear an orthotic, make sure there is going to be room to accommodate your inshoe device, and take a good look at the back of the shoe to make sure that the heel counter is not going to break down easily.

Don't let the shoe clerk convince you that a particular model performs beyond what you know to be its capacity. If the clerk strongly recommends one particular shoe, ask why, and be sure the answer makes sense both in terms of the shoe's performance on the tests and your own needs. Get them to spell out the shoe's strong and weak points. Remember that a shoe that is good for one person's foot may be completely wrong for someone else's foot.

Most stores have copies of the October issue of *Runner's World* for buyers to look at, and if statements are being made about a shoe that you are unsure of, ask to see the data on that shoe for a particular test. Stick firmly to your overall requirements. You spent a lot of time thinking about what you need; don't make an impulsive change based on a pleasing appearance.

Two places where your search strategy may break down are unfortunately completely beyond your control. Despite a written pledge from manufacturers that shoes entered in the *Runner's World* survey would be available in the stores, some companies have not kept their side of the bargain. Some highly rated shoes have had availability problems in the past.

More serious is the case of manufacturers who enter a shoe in the survey only to change its construction immediately afterwards. And the change is not usually for the better; it involves cheaper materials or simpler manufacturing techniques. The buyer must be on guard against obvious changes in a shoe but is almost powerless to detect subtle, ones which may affect performance. The only solution is more honesty on the part of the manufacturer. Companies who try these manuevers should be encouraged to change their ways.

POINT NUMBER NINE—BE TOUGH ON QUALITY CONTROL

However hard the manufacturer tried to control the production process, the final arbiter of quality is always the buyer. Careful examination of the shoe in the store can save a lot of potential trouble.

Running shoe manufacturers have been assailed most often by irate customers for lack of quality control, and rightly so. As running has become more popular shoe companies have exploded. Some have responded by increasing their capital investment. They have bought more machines and taken on more staff. Others have simply turned the screws and increased production, so that more shoes are produced with the same number of employees. Quality control inevitably suffers.

First look at the shoes and check that there is indeed a left and right shoe in the same box. Next see if the sizes are the same, for both width and length. Look both at the size printed on the shoes and hold the shoes up sole to sole to make sure the length and width are identical.

Next stand the shoes on an even surface like a counter or table. Make sure that the seam on the back of the heel counter is vertical, and that the shoes are not leaning to one side or another. If the shoes are designed to have a varus wedge, make sure that the wedges are equal on both sides and that both shoes turn away from the midline when they are standing on the table.

Look at the upper and make sure that the material is not snagged or ripped. There should be no creases in the upper material around the featherline; they would be signs of poor lasting work.

Convince yourself that the soling process has been well done. Look for early signs of delamination, particularly at the heel and toe. If there is a wrapover of the sole material onto the foxing, make sure the bond is good. Look to see if there is any cement on the upper. This probably won't affect the performance but it is sloppy shoemaking and deserves to be rejected. Take a look inside the shoe. Make sure the arch cookie, if present, is on the inside border and not the outside, and that it is the same distance forward in each shoe. Try the tongue to see if it is firmly attached, and if you can lift the sockliner take a look at the insole board to make sure it isn't creased. Check the stitching both inside and out. Double stitching around the foxing will provide a longer lasting shoe than single. Look also for loose or frayed stitching.

If any of these quality control factors do not meet your expectations, ask for another pair of shoes. I have known runners who tried three or four pairs of the same model to find one that met their quality control requirements. Although this might leave the clerk exasperated, the more trouble you take now the less you will have later.

The Moment Arrives—You Find Your Shoe

By a process of elimination, one of the shoes on your short list should emerge as the top candidate. Time in the store is spent plugging factors which are unique to you into the overall equation. You want a shoe that has the right properties on all the criteria we have mentioned, but it also has to fit well and feel right. That is why buying by mail order is such a risky business unless you are buying a shoe which you already know well.

If you are equally happy with two or more shoes then price could be used to tilt the decision. You might think it strange that I have left consideration of price until this late stage. The reason is that, within the price bracket we are discussing, the maximum price difference between shoes might be fifteen dollars. If the shoes are really the same in all respects then saving that much makes sense. But if the more expensive shoe will provide better protection and fit, then trying to save money is dangerous and irrelevant.

So after all the hard work, the moment arrives. The clerk breathes a sigh of relief as you point to the pair you want. But before you leave the store there are a couple of things to consider.

If you do a lot of running buying two pairs of shoes at this point may be a wise move. This is particularly true if your search has led to two different shoes which seem to suit your needs equally well. Although this seems an extravagant suggestion it really isn't, because you will be able to rotate shoes by the day or week. This will give the shoes time to dry out, from both perspiration and rain, and it will slow down the wear on each pair.

Many runners also find that switching to a different model during a week of hard running gives them some relief from minor aches and pains. This relates to the subtlety of the running process. Shoes which apparently have only minor differences in design can result in major differences in feeling.

Be advised, however, that a good argument can be made against buying two pairs of the same make and model at the same time. It doesn't give you the opportunity to see if the shoe feels as good during running as it felt in the store. Also you don't yet know how it will wear over the long term.

While in the store you may want to pick up various accessories, such as a spare pair of inserts or sockliners, a pair of heel cups, additional or special laces, or a tube of repair solution. While shoes are foremost in your mind, this is a good time to lay in the supplies you will need in the future.

POINT NUMBER TEN—WHAT TO DO AFTER THE SALE

It's a good idea to wear your new shoes around the house for a couple of days. This way the store might take them back if the shoes aren't completely right. But they certainly won't take back shoes in which you've run even ten miles.

The first few runs in a new pair of shoes should be exploratory and easy. Both the shoe and your body will undergo some adjustments, particularly if the purchase has involved a change of shoe type for you. Give this process time to happen in a controlled and relaxed manner.

The worst thing you could do is run a race in a new pair of shoes. Although there have been some notable exceptions to this rule, such a debut invariably leads to trouble. Derek Clayton ran his first world record in a new pair of shoes, but Abebe Bikila's widely publicized barefoot marathon in Rome actually started with Abebe wearing a new pair of shoes he had been given the day before. They were so uncomfortable that he threw them away a short time after the start.

You should be prepared to rip out the "arch cookie" if it feels uncomfortable. Either move it or replace the complete sockliner with something more to your liking, perhaps a device which will take a form fit to your foot.

During the first fifty miles or so listen carefully to your body. If the new shoes have caused an ache or a pain that won't go away, you may be forced to stop using the shoes and switch to another pair at least temporarily. This is a hard thing to do after you have spent a lot of money, but there are times when it can be the wisest policy. It may well be a temporary problem which will resolve itself if you use another pair of shoes for a while or change your training habits.

Keep an eye on the shoes during these early miles. Although you can't expect to exchange the shoes simply because the alignment of your body is such that the shoe makes you ache, there are some basics that you can expect from the shoe.

It should certainly not start breaking down during the first few weeks of running. Occasionally the layers of the sole will begin to separate, particularly in the toe region. The uppers may rip or tear (especially if they are nylon mesh), and the stitching may begin to come apart. Other early signs of poor manufacturing include lacing holes which break, a tongue which pulls out, or leather foxing which roughens up badly.

If any of these things occur during the first few weeks of normal wear, you should return to the shoe shop and state your case. Be fair about the process, though. Don't try to return a shoe if you know it's gone through some traumatic event of your own doing. The more unlikely claims a store gets, the harder it will be for genuine problems to find a solution.

Retailers and manufacturers expect a small percentage of shoes to be returned. In any manufacturing process there will always be defects that do not show up until the product is used. The unfortunate thing for the runner is that getting a new pair of shoes will often involve waiting while the dealer sends the problem shoes back to the manufacturer. Some weeks later a rebate will arrive. There are retailers who will absorb the cost of the return until a rebate is given. This is obviously the best solution since it does not leave you without shoes for an undetermined period.

Computerizing the Search Process

It is one of the odd effects of a free market that runners in the United States have more than 100 training flats to choose from. My feeling is that this number will shrink considerably in future years as some of the fringe manufacturers move into other fields.

The process of sorting out your needs and matching them to a shoe is involved enough so that a computerized search procedure could be helpful. One or two services have appeared where for a fee runners can receive a list of shoes that the computer "thinks" are right for them.

Unfortunately the computer programs presently used can be criticized on two counts. They do not require enough detailed information of the kind the questions in this chapter were designed to elicit. In addition, they do not incorporate information like that given in the October issue of *Runner's World*.

Such a system, though, is a possibility for the future. It would be most effective in the hands of someone trained to evaluate questions concerning body structure, injury history, and running style. The *Runner's World* test data lends itself well to the concept of matching these needs through a computerized process.

For most of us the search will have to be conducted with the computer between our own ears. If enough thought is put into the process beforehand the methods described in this chapter will help you reach that holy grail—the perfect running shoe for you.

15

Groups with Special Needs

Like any consumer industry, shoemakers make their products for the "average person" who exists only in the computers of the census bureau. But the garment and footwear industry is unluckier than most. You can get by making tables, chairs, books, tools, and a host of other products in one size even though they are used by different size people. But "one size fits all" shoes are not a possibility.

As a consequence a shoe manufacturer makes and a retailer stocks more than ten different sizes of the same product. It is therefore with more than a little reluctance that any manufacturer will make shoes for runners with special needs. Width sizing is ignored by most companies, women hardly receive the design attention they need, and heavy individuals are left groping for an adequate shoe. So runners who belong to these "minority groups" will have to sort through available shoes with their special needs in mind, in addition to the criteria discussed in Chapter 14.

In this chapter we will consider the special needs that

beginners, women, heavyweights, habitually injured runners, elite athletes, children, and walkers bring to the search for a running shoe.

Beginners

You often hear the phrase, "that shoe is okay for beginners, but wouldn't do for an experienced runner." I feel this advice is misguided. The only justification for this view is that a beginning runner is not running as far as someone who had been running for several years, and would therefore not be prone to overuse injuries. But in general, beginners need as much, if not more, attention to their shoes and feet as do experienced runners.

Why is this so? First, the transition from no running at all to twenty miles a week is probably a more drastic change for the body than a slow increase from twenty to sixty miles per week. It is very important that during this rapid transition the body receives as much protection as possible. Also, someone who begins running is never going to progress unless their experience is a good one. This in itself is a good reason to provide the best footwear available. Finally, beginners have no experience with the problems they may encounter during running on which to base their purchasing decision. So it is far better to make a mistake on the safe side and buy a good shoe to begin with.

The initial expenditure required to start running is relatively modest. There is no elaborate equipment to buy, there are no court fees or waiting lists to endure. If the beginner decides not to continue the running program, the shoes are still useful, so there really are very few good arguments for buying a cheap pair of shoes at the start.

Women Runners

Women are a majority of the world's population but a minority of the running community in the United States. Despite the fact that their numbers are growing, women runners still remain a mystery to sport scientists and shoe designers.

Last year I was asked to write a chapter on biomechanics for a handbook of women's running. I decided not to write the chapter, not because I wasn't interested, but because the number of serious experiments on the special needs of women runners can be counted on the fingers of one hand. We have very little evidence about a woman's needs in a running shoe.

To be sure, there is plenty of folklore. "Women have a wider pelvis and so they tend to cross over more." Plausible, but unproven. "Women have a lower center of gravity than men." True. But show me some evidence indicating what that has to do with their running shoes and I'll give you a degree in Biomechanics. "Women have a narrower foot than men." Now, women runners all over the world have had problems finding shoes that fit well, but is there any data? Not really.

What most manufacturers actually do to make women's shoes is to use a small men's last. For example, a 5E men's shoe might be used to make a 7D women's. So the only concession to difference is one width increment. The temptation to do this is strong because the lasts and patterns already exist for the men's shoes.

Although there is very little direct evidence, most experts will say that there are even more subtle differences between the foot of a man and a woman. In particular it is generally agreed that the heel of a woman's foot is narrower in relation to the ball. This is a difference in proportion and not just size. Therefore a scaled down men's shoe, even if it is reduced one width, will just not fit well.

Women runners should support companies who genuinely use women's lasts for their shoes. This is not easy because there have been cases of plainly deceptive advertising. But the fit should tell all. If you know you can be fitted well for dress or casual shoes but cannot find a good fit in a particular brand of running shoe, you are probably trying on a small man's shoe.

If a good-fitting shoe just cannot be found, there are several things that can be tried. First, you might buy shoes that offer the possibility of pulling in the uppers with the lacing. A shoe which has a wide throat and a "lace to the toe" pattern will allow the most adjustment. Next try a heel cup to fill any extra space in the back of the shoe. A thick sockliner which conforms to the foot will also take up space and may improve the fit.

So at present the best that women runners can expect to find is a shoe which is sized for them, and not simply a scaled down men's shoe. But there are other important differences besides fit, and the future should bring important developments in women's footwear. First, the question of weight differences between the average male and female runner has implications for the amount of shock absorption required from the midsole and wedge. It may be that women's shoes are presently overdesigned in terms of shock absorption, and that studies will show that a lighter shoe can be made that is equally safe. If it can also be shown that women cross the midline more with their feet than men, there may be reasons for building a slight varus wedge as a standard feature of women's shoes.

All that is in the future. At the moment, we may have to settle for shoe manufacturers who believe that a woman's shoe is rather like a man's shoe, but made in powder blue and blessed with some romantic name.

Heavyweights

Although bigger people have bigger bones, ligaments, and muscles, it is still likely that their joint surfaces experience greater pressures than those of lighter people. This is certainly true if the person is overweight.

It is probable that many people in the top ten percent

of the weight distribution may not have engaged in endurance activities in the past. A typical history would be that of a contact sports player who needs to do something to stop the middle-age spread. The athlete may also have sustained an injury along the way, and footwear is, therefore, a very important consideration.

No manufacturer has yet made a shoe designed for the heavier runner. The stereotypical male distance runner is light, perhaps around 140 pounds, and this is certainly lighter than athletes in most any other sport which does not involve a horse.

The heavier person will want support and protection to a greater degree than can probably be obtained in present footwear. This has led to some unusual recommendations. Podiatrist Dick Schuster, for example, suggests that heavier runners should run in Army boots (see Chapter 16) although many of his colleagues disagree. The idea is that the heavier person may bottom out the shock absorbent material in the shoe; no one yet knows whether this really happens.

Beyond trying to buy a shoe which is suited to their foot structure and injury history, heavier runners should seek out the best possible combination of impact, stability, and rearfoot control. Racing shoes are not a good idea for heavier runners. Their lightweight construction will not provide adequate control for the larger forces that heavy runners generate.

Habitually Injured Runners

The runner who is habitually injured should take extreme care in selecting running shoes. These runners cannot afford to take chances with footwear; yet they have to compromise between experimentation with shoes which may help, and conservatism in shunning features which may make their injury worse. Professional help from a podiatrist or orthopedist is strongly recommended for these individuals. The injury patterns should dictate the features of the shoe, and it is far safer to get a professional opinion on what characteristics will most help or hurt a particular injury.

As we discussed in Chapter 14, runners with knee injuries should focus on rearfoot control properties of the shoe, as well as the overall alignment of their lower extremity. A history of stress fractures would make energy absorption crucial. Runners who pronate excessively might try a varus wedge as a prelude to personalized correction of their alignment difficulty. Problems on the plantar surface of the foot call for good impact properties combined with good stability.

Unfortunately there cannot be an unequivocal guide to which shoe will help which injury, because a more accurate prescription of shoes would require epidemiological studies that have not yet been conducted. But individual clinicians do develop a feeling and good practical knowledge of which shoes help runners with particular problems.

One idea that I tried to interest a shoemaker in several years ago, was a shoe specifically made so that injured runners could recover while continuing to run. The premise is that we should accept the reality that despite being told to rest, most injured runners will ignore the advice. So why not give them something in a shoe that has more cushioning and protection than a runner would normally want or need?

I think the idea has merit, but I could not persuade any manufacturer that it did. In a sense it came to pass in 1979 with some early versions of Nike's airshoe, the Tailwind. I have heard a number of people, in the middle of a chronic injury cycle, say that they were able to run in the Tailwind without slowing down the healing process.

Of course, it would be easy to see how this concept could be misused, and would lead to more injuries if the idea became current that a certain shoe was guaranteed to provide injury-free running. Injured runners all over the country would suffer further injuries, because they would ignore the warning signs and continue to run. But with the right approach, this concept might alleviate some of the genuine anxieties that runners have about stopping their running, and help maintain basic fitness during certain types of injury.

Shoes for Elite Athletes

This is one issue that I am prepared to release some adrenalin on. World class runners deserve better service from shoe manufacturers than they are getting at the moment. In the process of collecting information for this book, I have spoken to many manufacturers and athletes. What has become clear is that neither of these groups believes that anything other than fit is really important.

But for an elite athlete trying to go beyond present world records, fit is perhaps only twenty-five percent of the problem. And fit, in most people's minds, is a static phenomenon. But running is a dynamic activity.

I am not saying that shoe companies are not doing anything for athletes. I think it's great that athletes receive large sums of money for their endorsement of a particular shoe. The AAU and the IAAF are lightyears behind in their understanding of what it takes to be a top athlete, particularly a marathoner. But money is not enough. If you are going to pay an athlete thousands of dollars to wear a shoe, then putting a few thousand more dollars into research to build a pair of shoes for that individual is to my mind essential.

First, it's just plain ethical. Athletes who have struggled for perhaps ten years to reach a level required to win an Olympic medal have invested much of their life in this effort. And not on a part-time basis, either. Their bodies are extremely valuable tools which deserve the best help in order to function at an optimal level.

Second, it makes good business sense for the shoe

company. The athlete they are sponsoring is as important an investment as the machines which make the shoes. If the athlete's career can be extended or improved it will mean better recognition and presumably higher sales. It seems to me that we take better care of our thoroughbred horses than we do of our top athlete's feet.

So what am I talking about if I don't simply mean making shoes that fit? Well, suppose that the runner is a forefoot striker at their marathon pace. Then, if the course is a flat one with not much downhill running, it makes good sense to build a shoe specifically designed for forefoot running. In a more complex case, subtle alignment problems such as leg length discrepancies, or forefoot and rearfoot alignment, should be corrected in the manufacture of the shoe. There should be no need for an Olympic runner to wear an orthotic. The shoe itself should be the correction, and should be built with a full knowledge of a particular athlete's running style, injury history, and body structure.

The question of efficiency in racing shoes is also something that should be given further thought on an individual basis. Weight is critically important to an elite distance runner, and on some courses it may be possible to eliminate parts of the shoe in the interests of saving weight.

There are other ways to improve running efficiency which should be explored. Energy absorbed by the shoe should not be energy lost. Theoretically it should be possible to build a shoe which returns some of its stored energy to the runner, making the process more efficient and ultimately faster. Making shoes for a specific race—"tuning" them to the characteristics of a runner or a particular course—may be a reality in the near future. Fast running shoes for super athletes are within reach if shoe companies are willing to spend the time and money in research.

Children

Although there are many look-alike running shoes for children, the number of serious shoes for them is small. Children bring unique problems to running; so much so that many authorities believe that children under fifteen should be banned from distances longer than ten kilometers, and definitely from the marathon. That children are capable of running marathons has been proven beyond question by the many sub-three hour performances of ten and twelve year olds. The questions revolve not on their ability to complete the distance, but on the long-term effects of running and training at such long distances.

The steady skeletal growth during the first ten years of life imposes certain requirements on footwear. Children's feet are definitely deformable in the worst sense. Figure 15.1 shows the result of the ancient Chinese practice of binding the feet at a very early age.

Groups with Special Needs

average child will grow a half size in six months. Expensive as it might be, children should get new shoes when their growth patterns dictate it. They should not wait until shoes are worn out before getting new ones.

Of course, children typically wear shoes not only for their intended purpose. If they like them, they will wear them twenty-four hours a day unless forced to take them off. This leads to incredibly quick wear. To say children are tough on shoes is nearly trite, but there is a temptation to buy cheap shoes because "well, they will wear out anyway."

The solution, I think, is for some manufacturer to develop a "super kids shoe" which has all the protective characteristics of a running shoe, but is built to be almost indestructible. In particular, the uppers would have to have the ultimate wear characteristics, since the uppers break down quickly when the shoes are used for general play as well as running.

Walkers

Industry estimates of how many running shoes sold are actually used for running vary from forty to seventy percent. No one disputes the fact that at least thirty percent never get to run a single step. Running shoes have become required wear on campuses throughout the country, and for casual wear in general. But is the running shoe good for walking?

First let's take a brief look at the mechanics of walk-

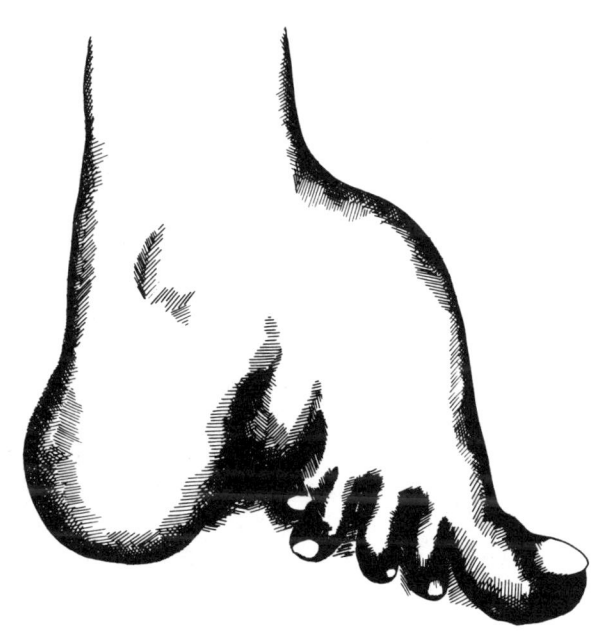

Fig. 15.1 A drawing of a lotus foot, the result of the once popular Chinese custom of binding children's feet.

I am not suggesting that wearing running shoes one hour per day will produce the changes we see in Figure 15.1, but the worst example should help us to avoid the intermediate pitfalls that ill-fitting shoes could create.

Fit is absolutely critical in children's footwear. The

ing, considering two important determinants. In Figure 15.2, we show a center of pressure pattern during walking similar to those shown for running in Chapter 4.

Notice first that there is a clear difference between the pressure distribution pattern in the two activities. In walking, most people make first contact at the furthest rear part of the heel, and then the pressure moves up the midline of the shoe. So walking is very much a back-to-front activity; it starts at the back of the shoe, and moves progressively down the middle until toe-off occurs somewhere under the heads of the metatarsals. But in running, this same individual starts on the outside, moves to the middle, and then moves toward the front in what we call the LMF pattern.

All this refers back to the statement I made in Chapter 4, that running shoes are presently designed as if running were a back-to-front activity, when in fact it is not. It is my feeling that running shoes have simply developed from walking shoes, and do not necessarily create the optimum distribution pattern for the pressures created in running. So it does follow that most running shoes are quite suitable for walking.

Some of our own experiments have shown that the forces generated in walking can be equally or sometimes more intense than those during running. The forces are smaller in walking, but they build up very rapidly. The resulting shock is transmitted up the whole leg. So the shock absorption characteristics of the running shoe are certainly not misplaced.

The heel lift present in almost all running shoes is greater than the heel lift in walking shoes. This should come as a pleasant surprise to the Achilles tendon of most walkers. The increased heel height, however, could result in more ankle sprains when used for activities that require more than the simple walking pattern shown in Figure 15.2.

We should note here that using running shoes for sports which involve lateral movements, such as racquetball or tennis, is extremely ill-advised. Running shoes are simply not designed to provide any stability for lateral movement, and may be downright dangerous for such activities. The shoe will also wear very badly and rapidly erode the properties, such as rearfoot control, which depend on the lateral stability of the shoe.

One reason why running shoes may be more comfortable than street shoes is that they are not subject to the

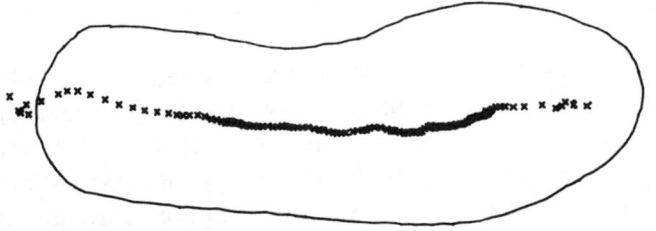

Fig. 15.2 A typical center of pressure pattern during slow walking. Notice how it moves from heel to forefoot down the middle of the shoe, and compare it with the running patterns in Figure 4.9.

constraints of fashion. There is no need for a slim toebox, or a square toebox, or whatever the current styles happen to be. There is also much more room inside a running shoe for devices that are likely to increase comfort (see Chapter 8). Apart from the forces noted earlier, walking creates conditions which are less severe than those during running. For example, the temperature differences will be less extreme and the range of motion in the shoe is probably smaller. Certainly a shoe used for walking will wear out in different places than one used for running.

From all these factors, it can be seen that the balance is in favor of using running shoes for walking, a conclusion which has already been reached by a large proportion of the non-running population.

16

Views on Shoes

Giving life to all of the ideas on running shoes that we have discussed are, of course, people. In this chapter you will have a chance to meet some of the interesting people that I have encountered during my search for information about the running shoe.

They are a diverse group, twenty-five altogether. They include shoe makers, athletes, doctors, scientists, journalists, and coaches. The group is unified by a common interest in running and running shoes and by the fact that they were willing to spend some time sharing their views on shoes. I hope you enjoy meeting them as much as I did, and I think you will agree that their presence here goes a long way toward humanizing the running shoe, which we have, after all, subjected to fairly rigorous dehumanization in the analyses of previous chapters.

DICK SCHUSTER
DOYEN OF SPORTS PODIATRISTS

There were not many runners on the streets when Dick Schuster graduated from the New York School of Podiatric Medicine back in 1937. It was only after twenty-five years of treating feet that a significant number of runners started to come through his office door. Schuster is the Tip O'Neill of the podiatry profession; a man who, through his teaching at the New York school, has exerted a powerful influence on a generation of podiatrists.

To open our discussion on a controversial note, I asked Schuster to comment on the bad press that podiatry had been getting from the *New York Times*, among others, on the question of fees for services. "I think there are podiatrists who are taking advantage of runners, yes, but I certainly don't think there are any more than there would be in any other profession. I'm not proud of it, but it does happen."

Schuster was an early pioneer in the use of orthotic therapy for athletic injuries, a treatment which was also hit by the *New York Times* as overused and overpriced. Most observers felt that the newspaper was off base in many of its sweeping statements, but Schuster is concerned about the trends. "Orthotics are not for everybody. I think there is an attempt to call orthotics an essential part of a runner's equipment, and I think

this is absolutely wrong. Only about forty percent of our patients get orthotics."

The secret is in the delay of symptoms, as far as Schuster is concerned. He has found that the patients who respond best to orthotic therapy are those who feel just fine when they start out on a long run, but perhaps in the fourth or fifth mile start to feel a nagging pain which stays with them until they are forced to stop. Another good respondent is the runner who has a mileage limit, say fifty miles a week, but gets injured if he or she exceeds this limit. "This is the delay aspect.

You can be reasonably sure that using orthotics properly on that individual will help. I won't say it will cure the problem, but it will certainly help because this is an overuse injury related to structure."

Another idea that Schuster expounds is that many of his runners are patients only when they run; thus he tells most of his orthotic wearers to use their devices just for running and not walking. The point is that alignment problems become much more severe under the more intense strain of running.

Many of his former students recall the large repertoire of simple "fixes" that Schuster had up his sleeve that proved useful to them in practice. Several of these techniques came up during our talk. "I tell my students often, 'if you don't know what to do, raise the heels.' This is the answer in many cases for compartment-type shin splints, for anterior ankle pain, and for many Achilles tendon problems."

He frequently modifies a running shoe, shaving some off the outsole, putting incisions in the upper, generally performing minor surgery on the shoe. With women who had problems with the shoe slipping off their narrow heels, Schuster has drilled a hole through the midsole and used a supplementary lace which goes through the hole and ties up on the instep.

Schuster is unabashed when it comes to one of his more hotly debated ideas—that heavy people should run in army boots. Was it true or had he been misquoted? "Absolutely true. The big guys, the one hundred and ninety pounder running, he has one hell of a time in the ordinary running shoe . . . in a relative sense . . . it's really like running in bedroom slippers. Until their bones toughen up, and bones do toughen up, do this for a few weeks and then . . . gradually get into the running shoe."

Doesn't this conflict, I inquired, with studies like those quoted in Chapter 13 that show Marine recruits get injured during their first few weeks of running in such boots? "Not at all. These kids have never run before, and all of a sudden they get put into walking and running long distances . . . it's too much too soon."

Before all my heavier readers go out and buy army boots I should add that this idea, like many expressed in this book, has supporters on both sides of the fence.

The concept of shoes for special foot and body types is one that Schuster feels is particularly important, but is likely to fail because of economics. He thinks that some shoe companies will have to be adventurous enough to make shoes for people with, for example, high arch (cavus) feet, although the retailer won't be at all happy about carrying an extra line. An idealistic but attractive idea is that each shoe company would make one type of shoe for a particularly difficult foot. Brooks, perhaps, might agree to make a shoe for the cavus foot, Nike might make a shoe for the heavyweight, Etonic for a rigid flat foot, and so on.

Like many observers of the running shoe scene, Schuster feels that the major problem today is quality control. One in particular he has noticed is the tendency of new shoes to lean inward when they are placed on a level surface. This forms a "valgus wedge" which can encourage the runner to pronate.

What is it that keeps a person young after forty-two years of practice? One thing that helps Schuster is that he is seeing a completely new group of patients. The running patients now rub shoulders with the geriatric patients, the diabetics, and the others who were the standard fare of podiatric medicine in the past. "But," Schuster adds, "you have to be in the right frame of mind for a runner. He comes in with his check-off list, his shoes, his log book—he wants to unburden his soul to you."

And, as many runners can testify, they often leave Schuster's office with not only an unburdened soul, but, to use an inexcusable pun, an unburdened sole.

DEREK CLAYTON
MARATHON WORLD RECORD HOLDER

Derek Clayton's first marathon was a race he would rather forget. His training was six weeks confinement on a boat plying from England to Australia, and his intention was to run ten miles with a friend and then drop out. But the iron will that was to lead Clayton to greater

things intervened. He found himself incapable of stopping, despite the leg and foot pains which were made no easier by the Dunlop tennis shoes he was wearing. He remembers someone shouting with a half mile to go that he might break three hours, so he stopped walking and jogged to the finish. His time was three hours and three seconds. So take heart, all first-time marathoners. Within five years Clayton demolished the world record mark with a time of 2:08:33, a performance which has been inviolate for over a decade.

The initial meeting of man and marathon could hardly be described as love at first sight. In fact, as the memory of the pain lingered, Clayton did not attempt another marathon for four years. He concentrated on track running. Although he never had a coach, it was hard to live and run in Australia in the mid-sixties without falling under the spell of Percy Cerutty or Arthur Lydiard. Both were advocating "overdistance" training, and Clayton put himself on a marathoner's regimen, although his competitive aspirations were at three and six miles.

In 1966, Clayton returned to the marathon when some of his training partners decided to enter a local race. At twenty miles he found himself in the lead and went on to win a surprise victory in an Australian record time of two hours twenty-two minutes. This was the point of no return. Within a year, Clayton had slashed the Aussie record by another four minutes, and went on to his first world record of 2:09:36.

Shoes have always been a problem for Clayton. He has very tender feet which are easily blistered. Even though comfort was something that he neither expected nor received from running shoes, the stiff leather uppers of conventional models ripped his feet to shreds. He tried hammering the shoe, then employed the more subtle approach of rubbing cooking oil into the leather, but nothing helped. So the main criterion for "good" running shoes became the absence of blisters after a race, and tennis shoes with their canvas uppers met this requirement.

It took five years of running in inadequate shoes before the wear and tear began to show. Clayton's running weight was almost 170 pounds, and the combination of high mileage, high weight, and poor protection led to chronic Achilles tendon problems. Nine operations followed, and today a nagging back problem is a reminder of what Clayton firmly believes is the legacy of poor running shoes. "I feel quite sure that if I'd have had the range of shoes when I started that are available today, I could have avoided a lot of the nasty injuries I've had. Even this back injury . . . it's been caused by hard running with no protection—nothing at all."

Understandably, on his first trip to Japan, Clayton was on the lookout for new ideas in footwear. Australia was a backwater of athletic endeavor and few foreign shoes had made it there. However, a pair of Tiger Cubs had come Clayton's way. These were the early canvas shoes with thin white rubber soles that sold for about $4.00. In Fukuoka, Tiger gave him a "deluxe" version of the Cub, with kangaroo leather uppers, but the same delicate sole. Breaking sacred vows to not run a race in new shoes, Clayton laced up and proceeded to the 2:09 world record with only a minor blister along the way (see Fig. 2.28).

So did a new world record bring shoe manufacturers to his door waving lucrative promotion contracts?

"Look. I never received a cent from any shoe company during my career. It was only toward the end they were offering money to athletes. But not marathoners, mind you. Marathons were for guys who weren't good at anything else. I'm sometimes envious but not bitter about the money athletes get today. Good luck to them. Why shouldn't they be getting paid in dollars and cents? They don't have an easy road to success."

Although the contracts weren't forthcoming, a letter from Adi Dassler did arrive on the desk of Ron Clarke, the legendary miler and the representative in Australia for Adidas. Why, it asked, was this new world record holder not wearing Adidas shoes? The answer, relayed through Clarke, was a characteristic piece of Clayton candor. "Because they are terrible shoes—beautifully made but terrible." Despite this inauspicious start, a relationship grew between Clayton and Adidas which lasted for the remainder of Clayton's career. He told Adidas what he wanted in a shoe and they built it for him. Adidas provided him with all the shoes he needed, and this engendered a loyalty which transcended some minor financial enticements at the Mexico Olympics. Describing the horsetrading at the Olympic Village, Clayton says, "It was really sickening. Some of these guys would switch from one company to another for less than $100. Adidas had taken good care of me, seen to all my requests, so why should I suddenly turn on them? I'm money oriented, but not at the expense of logic."

The long years of battling injury have left Clayton with a clear view of the worth of good running shoes. "The most important advice I can give is not to skimp on shoes. Injury is just around the corner for all of us. One way of reducing the odds is to make sure you wear the best shoes. I also had a tendency to ignore wear on my shoes, to let the heels wear down, which I now fully regret."

Clayton was an athlete who was at least a decade ahead of his time. It is an irresistible fantasy to imagine the diminutive figure of Bill Rodgers shoulder to shoulder with the towering Derek Clayton with one mile to go at Boston. Who would dare to predict the outcome? It is a simpler task to document the present. Rodgers' name is a household word and his endorsement is worth many thousands of dollars to any company. Clayton must just sit and wait to see if Rodgers, or any other marathoner, can make up for a lost decade and erase the name of Derek Clayton from the record book.

JERRY TURNER
PRESIDENT OF BROOKS

Visiting the factory of the Brooks Shoe Company was proving more of an adventure than I had bargained for. I had left the comparative safety of United Airlines in San Juan and was now sitting in a claustrophobic twin-engine twelve-seater belonging to Prinair of Puerto

Rico. I recognized the plane well. I had seen one just like it twenty years before in my native England. It may even have been the same one!

As a thunderstorm raged overhead, we waited patiently with the first engine running as the pilot tried in vain to start the second. Fifteen minutes later the engine coughed violently, breathed a cloud of purple smoke, and lazily started in a semblance of activity. By this time no one on the plane was particularly anxious to continue the trip to Mayaguez but there seemed to be no choice; the pilot had taken to the air instantly, as if to get there before the engine stalled.

So it was with more than a little relief that I greeted Jerry Turner when I finally arrived at the company's main factory in Aguadilla, Puerto Rico. Turner had moved the factory to Puerto Rico ten years earlier when, at a time of full employment in the hometown of Hanover, Pennsylvania, qualified labor was difficult to find. It is a move he has not regretted. The work force is diligent, in part because there are at least twenty other people who would willingly take every available job.

As a sportsman, the best that can be said is that Turner's qualifications in business are superb. He graduated from the University of Pennsylvania's Wharton School and has an MBA from the University of California at Berkeley. He dimly remembers playing a little tennis and golf along the way but has managed to avoid

addiction to running. As he showed me around the plant it became clear that Turner gets more than his share of exercise from routine sixteen-hour days on the shop floor. He didn't seem to have an office, but on the brief occasions when he sat down, he held court next to the Coke machine, planning strategy to deal with the current crisis on the floor. Here was an executive who was not happy pontificating from the boardroom. He could only be satisfied by intimate involvement in each stage of the production process.

Brooks has been making sports shoes for more than fifty-five years, but it is only in the last ten that they achieved their substantial share of the running shoe market. Their first entry was a shoe called the Drake in 1973. Turner realized that foreign manufacturers, notably Tiger, Adidas, and Puma, were dominating the American market partly because there was no viable domestically made running shoe. Curiously enough, the biggest problem he encountered was getting domestic raw materials, and to this day Brooks still imports twenty-five percent of what it needs from Germany. Eventually, through contact with David Schwaber at the Monarch Rubber Company in Baltimore, Brooks moved into the era of what Turner calls "space age materials."

Turner knew his limitations in understanding the needs of the runner, so he recruited Olympian Marty Liquori to help develop the product line. The two first met at a sporting goods show. "Marty stopped by at our booth and asked if we realized what a good shoe we really had. And, of course, we didn't. He was in the process of committing himself to another shoe company so we 'uncommitted' him. He played an extremely important role, because in the early years we just didn't know what we were doing."

The interaction with Liquori led to the development of the Villanova shoe, which carried Brooks through the mid-1970s with considerable success. Turner then moved to recruit podiatrist Steve Subotnick, who helped develop the next link in the chain, the Brooks Vantage. At this point one or two clouds appeared on the horizon.

After a massive initial production run, the mesh upper of the shoes proved defective; runners found that their shoes would fray and tear within the first few miles. This problem, together with the dramatic growth that Brooks experienced, has left Turner fighting to escape the stigma of poor quality control. "It really hurt our credibility at the outset and many people were disappointed, but no one was more disappointed than Jerry Turner. Unfortunately it was a poor beginning and one which we lived with for a while."

His way of fighting back has been innovation in both design and marketing. Air shoes have been a major development project in the last few years, and Turner hopes to have an air shoe on the market in the near future. His latest coup has allowed Brooks to become the first manufacturer with a shoe bearing the name of an international athlete who is still actively competing. The John Walker series was the result of a landmark deal between Turner and the New Zealand Amateur Athletic Association on terms the former is not willing to disclose. It is the first time an amateur athlete had been allowed to endorse a product. Is Turner willing to try the same thing with the AAU or the Athletics Congress? "The answer is yes. We would be just as happy to do the same thing with American athletes if the AAU is willing to let it happen. The problem so far is that the organizations want to take all the money, so why should an athlete give his name to a shoe?"

Turner sees running "maturing" at a high level of participation, rather than declining as some have predicted. Like most progressive running shoe companies Brooks has grown exponentially as the sport has exploded. If his forecast is correct his company's future looks bright. The only uncertainty seems to be with air travel—and I mean Prinair—not air shoes. Turner's air shoes might take off in the market, but will the local planes be able to get them there?

JEFF JOHNSON
THE NIKE STORY

At the age of nine, Jeff Johnson was convinced that he was the world's fastest kid over 100 yards. While his pals were playing baseball, Jeff huddled over the intricacies of Charlie Paddock's training program, convinced that if he duplicated or perhaps exceeded the great runner's workouts he too would become a world class sprinter. Unfortunately, in sixth grade, some smart aleck named Bruce Miller had the audacity to thrash Jeff over the 100. So at the tender age of twelve, a serious reevaluation of his life's ambition was required.

As this story shows, Jeff had running coded into his DNA. He made sure he was close to runners throughout his life, whether it was mowing the lawn of *Track and Field News* editor Bert Nelson, or corresponding with Fred Wilt and exchanging photographs. It was not surprising, then, that a planned career in anthropology did not have the magnetism that Johnson needed as an outlet for his considerable energy. While doing graduate work at UCLA he became disillusioned with his chosen field. "Here I was, studying the social implications of three hair nets found in an ancient garbage dump in Wisconsin. One day I just said, 'Hey, this really is not important.'" And naturally he turned toward running and running shoes.

The critical moment was a chance meeting with ex-Oregon runner Phil Knight at a Los Angeles track meet in the summer of 1964. After leaving Oregon, Knight had travelled the world looking for business opportunities, and found what he thought was a good one in Japan. A company called Tiger was making shoes which Bill Bowerman, Knight's coach at Oregon, thought could become the best of the bunch with a little work. So Knight and Bowerman entered into a partnership to import the shoes, but neither had the time to run the marketing side of the business. Jeff Johnson took it on.

It is not Jeff's style to do things by half measures. Spending most of his waking hours writing advertisements, photographing shoes, running a mail order business, Johnson was so successful that by 1966 Tiger shoes were the required footwear for serious road runners.

There were also some opportunities for innovation. Johnson made a prototype with a shower slipper sandwiched between the outsole and midsole of a conventional shoe, for a runner whose legs became "dead" during a marathon. The shoe eventually became the Tiger Boston, featuring the first full-length midsole unit.

Although many track and field enthusiasts had probably seen Jeff Johnson's name in the credits of photographs, they first read his work in the April 1967 issue of *Distance Running News.* Jeff had corresponded with publisher Bob Anderson on a number of occasions, and it soon became clear to Anderson that he was the person who knew more than anyone about the state of the art in running shoes. So Jeff was recruited to write what was actually the first shoe survey.

There were fifteen models of shoes available at that time and after writing a small narrative about each model, Jeff included the preferences expressed in a poll he made of the entire Road Runner's Club of America. Embarrassing as it was for him, because of possible conflict of interest charges, the runners gave Tiger shoes an overwhelming first place vote, by 2 to 1 over the nearest competition. However no one questioned the results, because the evidence could be seen at the starting line of every race in the country.

The partnership between Tiger and Blue Ribbon Sports disintegrated in 1972. Tiger wanted to expand their marketing base using regional distributors, to which Blue Ribbon Sports said no thank you. The parting was not a happy one. The American contingent felt that so many of their own ideas had been incorporated into the existing line of Tiger shoes that they should receive compensation. As the case dragged through the courts business had to go on. The split was final.

Phil Knight was temporarily the president of a company that had no product. The first order of business was a name and a logo. The now familiar "swoosh" came not from a multimillion dollar ad agency, but from the pen of a young student named Carolyn Davidson, who was enrolled in an accounting class at Portland State College that Phil Knight was teaching. But what about a name? No one at Blue Ribbon Sports could come up with a suitable one. Jeff Johnson, by now in charge of east coast operations for Blue Ribbon Sports, got an urgent call from Oregon. They had to have a name by the next morning. Did he have any ideas?

What happened next, Johnson recalls clearly. "It was one of those experiences that you remember all your life. I went to bed that night—I'd thought about it but didn't really come up with anything. But I woke up the next morning, sat up in bed, and said 'Nike.' I went right to the phone and told them the name and why I thought it worked. First, it fit the mark which we had already adopted which looked like a wing. Nike was the winged goddess of victory in Greek mythology. I had also read somewhere that the perfect brand name should have two syllables and contain at least one exotic letter, a K, W or Q." The proposed name was not well received, but it was adopted as the best of a bad bunch.

Next on the agenda was building some shoes. Knight and Johnson spent a fortnight in Japan working with a new supplier. They finalized the running and tennis lines and got home to start selling. The results are well known. From having no product in 1972 Nike grossed 140 million dollars in 1979.

Having seen running shoes evolve in the last twenty years, Jeff Johnson is convinced that the next twenty will see even greater changes. He thinks that new materials technology will open doors, and has great hopes for the air shoe concept. "If you sat back in 1971 and looked at the Tiger Cortez and the Tiger Marathon you could have said 'there isn't much more you guys can do to a running shoe' . . . but a lot has been done and I see a lot ahead in the next decade. I personally live on the edge of total dissatisfaction with everything we've ever done. I want to make things better and better and there's so much available."

Jeff Johnson appears to be a one-man answer to the energy crisis. His endless drive, which feeds a sharp intellect, has carried him from the rigors of preadolescent sprint competition to the upper echelons of one of the world's largest sports shoe companies. It is likely that if he is forced to retire on schedule in the year 2008, he will turn his hand to designing running shoes for his fellow retirees. Who knows? He may even start dreaming of being the world's fastest sixty-five year old over 100 yards.

JOHN LUCAS
SPORT HISTORIAN

The sport of running has a glorious history, yet few historians. If one was to set out the qualifications of such an historian, the definition would probably read like a summary of the achievements, interests, and experiences of John Apostle Lucas.

What better beginning than to be born in the right town—Boston, Massachusetts—and in the right era—1928—when Clarence DeMar and both Johnny Kellys were household names. John remembers his early involvement with "the long and honorable tradition of cross-country and long distance running among schoolboys in the city of Boston." There was a strong interest in track at Harvard, Tufts, and Northeastern. Community events such as the Scottish Highland Picnic Games and the Irish Italian Games had open footraces, which also spurred local interest in running.

As a youngster just out of high school John found himself in Korea serving under Captain Lou Gregory, who had been runner-up in the Boston Marathon in 1941 and several time AAU 10,000 meter champion. Their hill runs together through a battle-torn landscape

were a real education for a young greenhorn "trying to run with a ruthless runner who—even in his late thirties—asked no quarter and gave none."

The next important milestone was a first flirtation with the spirit of the Olympics, which was to lead to a lifelong obsession. The place was Los Angeles and the event was the 1952 Olympic 10,000 meter trial. Lucas finished back in the pack, but the magic of competing against the likes of Horace Ashenfelder, who went on to take the gold medal in Helsinki, was addictive. John Lucas has been running ever since, receiving a citation from the President's Council on Physical Fitness for 50,000 lifetime miles in 1975, and is now well over the 60,000 mile mark.

Besides his own running, Lucas had been a highly successful coach. His high school record was 77-0-0 in cross-country and both indoor and outdoor track, and he was head coach of cross-country and track at Penn State for seven years. So the running credentials are flawless.

But on the other side of the coin is the academician. Lucas has a Ph.D. in Sports History, has co-authored a respected textbook on the topic, and is regarded as one of the country's leading experts on the Olympic movement and the history of pedestrianism.

Thus when the parts of his personality are integrated John Lucas offers a perspective on the history of running and running shoes which is unparalleled. A casual mention during our conversation of the Indian runner Tewanina, whose picture is shown back in Chapter 2, triggered a flow of information which is a mere token of the total store of knowledge.

"Yes. Ninety-eight pounds, 5 foot 1 Louis Tewanina was a Sac and Fox Indian and a brother Indian to Jim Thorpe. Both of them were brought from the Oklahoma Reservation to high school in Carlisle, Pennsylvania, which was a kind of finishing school for the 'illiterate and wild' as they were called. And you couldn't find two more contrasting athletes—the thin, sparrowlike Tewanina, who had loved to run long distances ever since he was a boy on the reservation, and a bully of a lad—185 pounds, 6 foot 1 Thorpe."

John Lucas recalls a high point from his own past when he placed in the top five finishers in the Hyde ten-mile race in 1954, and won a pair of Hyde road shoes for his efforts. These must have been quite like the shoes in Figure 2.23, and were a far cry from the $1.98 Blucher plimsoles from the Hood Rubber Company in which he started his running career. The advice of his coach at the time was never to wear your good shoes in training. So even the boys who could afford the expensive Spalding or Hyde shoes (which Lucas could not) kept them in the closet until race day. As might be expected, the boys were resourceful in their own defense. Since the soles were paper thin, felt and rubber inserts were the order of the day and they probably made running tolerable.

Years later the picture changed dramatically, and Lucas recalls coaching just as running shoes began to proliferate. Suddenly there was a wider choice. "It was a period of great transition in the knowledge of shoes among coaches. That's a kind way of saying that there had been mass confusion among athletes and coaches about what was needed in a running shoe."

Many of the trends that most of us see as new, the historian recognizes as simply another swing of the pendulum. Such is the case with the commercialization of running in the last five years. Lucas sees some parallels and some dangers in the substantial purses that many of today's runners can command.

"(Today's runners are) . . . following historical precedent. We can go back to the nineteenth century foot racers, who were caught up in this syndrome of fame, glory, and commensurate under-the-table payments. There is some inherent danger in this because the temptation is enormous to come back much too quickly to do it again. And in the pedestrian races there was regrettably the matter of compromises in finishing the races, throwing the races, and in winning by small or large margins depending on what the promoters or gamblers insisted upon."

Not that it is happening now, but at the start of the pedestrian era running was as idealistic as it is today. And yet it almost disappeared from sight as public awareness of and disgust with corrupt practices grew. We would do well to rest a while on our dash to the "million dollar marathon" and listen to the John Lucases of the sport, who frequently have seen it all before.

GEORGE SHEEHAN
PHILOSOPHICAL PHYSICIAN

He had probably given at least 300 lectures in the previous five years. Enough, you might think, to make

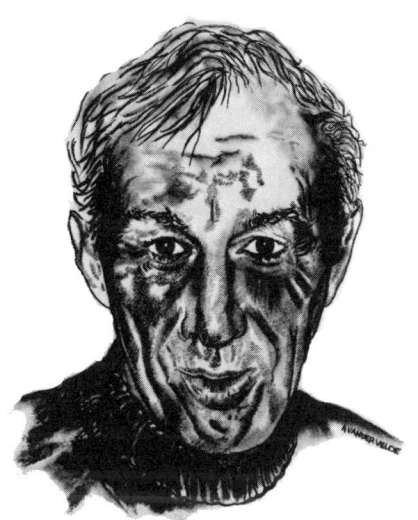

this one at Slippery Rock State College in Western Pennsylvania just another arduous hour of saying the same things and answering the same questions.

But as we sat in the cafeteria a full hour before the lecture was scheduled to begin, George Sheehan excused himself by saying, "I am going upstairs to get nervous." And he was bitterly serious about it. He took the stage in an empty auditorium, sweated, fidgeted, adjusted the microphone, and constantly paced back and forth engaging delighted early birds in conversation. As the hall slowly filled he warmed himself and the audience up simultaneously, answering questions, savouring each one as if tasting a fine wine before giving his answer. It became clear that his secret is to approach each talk, each question, as a virgin approaches her first date.

When the appointed moment arrived he launched into a ninety minute monologue which kept his audience of 500 college students, most of whom were less than one-third his age, entirely spellbound. Their first movement in one and one-half hours was to stand and give Sheehan a warm and long ovation.

What kind of man—and what kind of message—can have this effect? There are two distinct aspects to the person who is George Sheehan. First, there is Sheehan the Doctor, who, as Medical Editor of *Runner's World* magazine, retails medical advice to an enormous constituency of injured runners. Should they run during pregnancy? Do orthotics work? What about blood in the urine? More than 100 runners a week receive handwritten notes on the bottom of their own inquiry, often written from Sheehan's armchair as he watches television.

But the other Sheehan would rather debate the workings of the mind than the body. And it is the psychologist-philosopher that is an experience to treasure. He leans heavily on a variety of nineteenth century poets and philosophers. The New England Transcendentalists such as Emerson and Thoreau, are particular favorites, with the Spanish philosopher Ortega y Gasset a close third. Sheehan's own distillation of Western thought from Aristotle to Auden strikes his audience as an appealing blend of existentialism and disciplined hedonism. The message, simply stated, is that we have lost the ability to engage in pure play. By experiencing the sensuousness of exercise and play we are led to a deeper understanding of our purposes and goals in life.

When the doctor and philosopher are viewed together it is apparent that Sheehan's personality is not so clearly dichotomized as I have drawn it. After all, there are elements of play in many of his statements about the medical problems of runners. I was present at the General Meeting of the American Podiatry Association in 1977 when Sheehan told the assembled prescribers of orthotic devices that he buys his eyeglasses at Woolworth's, so why shouldn't he and his patients buy their orthotics there too? He has proposed that runners drink beer during a race, that repairing shoes is not a good idea, and that the correct style of running involves running off the big toe.

Not unexpectedly, Sheehan's views on shoes are fairly unconventional. His own requirements in a running shoe were frozen ten years ago, when he tried on the Tiger Cortez. I asked him what running shoes will look like in ten years. "Mine will look just the same as these, if I can get them," he responded, pointing down to a battered pair of Cortez which appear to be inseparable from his feet during all waking hours. "What about shoe surveys," I asked, "are they useful?" Without a moment's hesitation came the reply, "Frankly, Peter, I ignore them."

Sheehan believes the right approach to shoe selection is to consider the individual factors such as body weight, sex, foot type, and so on, in the manner we have attempted in Chapter 14. He will continue to go by his own judgments until he sees these factors being considered. Sometimes, though, the best evidence is in direct contradiction of Sheehan's views. At one point our conversation went this way:

Sheehan: "Sometimes I tell people with high-arched feet that they should take the shoe that wears the worst, because that's probably going to give you the best shock absorption."
Cavanagh: (Wanting to say "But the evidence shows that is not true.") "No comment."
Sheehan: "No comment, huh! Well, you're not being interviewed, I suppose."

What is important about George Sheehan's ideas is not their absolute truth for all individuals. Each time he writes or speaks he is proclaiming his independence from conventional wisdom and constantly chiding the reality of his audience. He is encouraging us to take ourselves a little less seriously in the short term in the interest of greater truth in the long term. Seen in this wider context, his irreverence on such things as running shoes, orthotics, and drinking beer during marathons seems entirely inconsequential.

STEVE SUBOTNICK
THE RUNNING FOOT DOCTOR

One of the things that gets Steve Subotnick hot under the collar is when a 200-pound runner hobbles into his office with a flimsy pair of racing shoes, wondering why he is injured. Choosing different shoes for different runners is something Subotnick has championed during his ten years of podiatric practice, much of which has been spent looking at runners' feet. More than one hundred a week stop by the offices of Subotnick and his partner Barry Scurran, a volume that has been sustained for almost five years. This adds up to an astonishing total of 25,000 runners who have come to Subotnick in search of help.

The kind of help they have found is well documented in Subotnick's two popular books, *The Running Foot Doctor* and *Cures for Common Running Injuries*. A conventional doctor he certainly is not. In the early days Subotnick would run with many of his patients, trying to spot clues to their injuries in style and alignment problems which would not show up during a clinical examination. Today he has a treadmill in the office which gives the same opportunity in a more controlled

and cost effective manner. He also has a chiropractor on his staff, a bold and open-minded move at a time when many of his orthopedic and podiatric colleagues are adamant about the exclusion of chiropractors from the Olympic medical team.

Subotnick's style is characterized by empiricism, energy, and more than a little panache. His frequent lectures are upbeat and eagerly digested by audiences, who feel that Subotnick gives advice that comes from a runner who has been there as well as a clinician who has been at the battle front long enough to see a wide variety of ailments.

Subotnick is never at a loss for ideas. In 1976 he approached the Brooks Shoe Company with a couple of suggestions that could be incorporated into a running shoe. The result was the Brooks Vantage, which became the top rated shoe in 1977. The major design innovation was the varus wedge, described in Chapter 8, which raised the inside border of the shoe by incorporating a four degree angle into the midsole. This was an idea that had been suggested many years before for basketball shoes, but had never been tried in production running shoes. It was a controversial idea which some of Subotnick's colleagues criticized, on the grounds that the four degree varus wedge was in fact a form of "non-prescriptive treatment" that would not be suitable for all runners.

But the idea has stood the test of time and Subotnick feels that the shoe is good for two-thirds of all runners. He acknowledges that the problem is educating the other runners so that they know to avoid a shoe with a varus wedge.

Many of Steve's more extreme ideas are, as he readily admits, based on intuition and acumen rather than hard evidence. He described a current experiment in his effusive style, which involves enunciating about 400 words a minute. "If you are hurt because you have been running forwards, why not run backwards, that way you you can avoid the forward progression injuries like some knee problems."

He also believes that a runner's style can be modified both to improve performance and reduce the likelihood of injury. "We blame a lot of things on shoes but probably there is more error from running style . . . because just about all the shoes are pretty good now . . . you have to teach people how to use the ankle—your knees hurt, you don't have to use your knees when you are running. You can run with just your ankles." Vintage Subotnick. Part fact, part overstatement designed to drive the point home.

When I asked him to speculate on the worst problem runners have with their shoes, it took Steve about half a second to respond. "By and large runners are a cheap group of people, not because they don't have the money, but because they just don't like to spend it properly. They wear the same shoe until it is well beyond the ability of the rubber to rebound and recover for the next step, until the shoe is grossly deformed, until the shoe itself will cause the injury. Then they come into the office . . . expect an immediate cure . . . spend money . . . go through the whole rehabilitation program . . . and eight months later they are back in the office again with an old pair of shoes completely worn out."

A sad tale seen only too often by doctors who treat runners. But times are changing, partly because of Subotnick's missionary efforts to raise the level of consciousness among runners. And it is not only runners who owe Subotnick a debt. His own profession of podiatry has certainly benefited from the visibility he has garnered. His colleagues may not always agree with him, but there is no denying that in a word association test, most runners would utter "Subotnick" when the white card with the word "podiatrist" was placed in front of them.

GIDEON ARIEL
COMPUTERIZED BIOMECHANICAL ANALYSIS, INC.

There is little doubt that what Steve Subotnick has done for sports podiatry Gideon Ariel has done for sports biomechanics. Ariel has a sixth sense for finding the limelight, and through appearances on television and articles about his work in such magazines as *Sports Illustrated*, the word biomechanics has passed into the everyday vocabulary of sport.

Ariel grew up in Israel and graduated from the Wingate Institute with a degree in physical education. His own prowess as an athlete landed him a place as a discus thrower on the Israeli national team at the Olympics. His next stop was North America, specifically the University of Wyoming where he learned, among other things, about the omnipotent status of a collegiate football coach. One fall afternoon Ariel arrived at the deserted fieldhouse and started work in earnest on his discus technique. After some time one or two football players appeared, and the coach gruffly gestured Ariel to leave, expecting the usual obedient response to divine authority. But the new kid on the block, who didn't speak much English anyway, figured that he was there first and was not going to leave. The resulting altercation confirmed Ariel's squatters rights—at least temporarily—but it was his last afternoon practice session after the football barons asserted their power.

On the day we met in the Amherst, Massachusetts offices of Ariel's company (Computerized Biomechanical Analysis), he had just returned from an unusual recruiting trip in Europe. The plan was to have various European countries send their entire national track and field squads to Ariel's new facility in California to undergo a technique analysis in an attempt to diagnose any faults in style. But while Ariel was in Europe members of the United States Olympic Committee learned of the plan and registered their violent objections. They felt that his involvement with the USOC disqualified Ariel from such activity. What they forgot is that Ariel's commitment to USOC was on a cost-only basis, and that his livelihood depended on income from biomechanical analysis of athletes and equipment. The USOC logic could presumably be extended to keep foreign athletes from wearing American shoes and using American made drugs.

This controversy highlights the current dilemma of Olympic sport in the United States. We realize that it is no longer possible for a solitary athlete to battle his way to the top, untrammeled by interference from govern-

ment and science. Yet we are not willing to pay the price needed to win under today's conditions.

Controversy is nothing new to Ariel; indeed he seems to thrive on it. He estimates that he has spent more than one million dollars on legal fees over the last five years. He has taken on a variety of adversaries, from close associates to large corporations, and cheerfully shrugs it off as part of the game.

He is now Director of Research for Pony USA, continuing an involvement with running shoes that began in 1972 with a project for Uniroyal. In the interim he has conducted experiments on a number of innovative ideas for running shoes, including variable composition midsoles and outsoles, and a variety of inflatable shoes. A prototype air shoe designed in 1975 convinced Ariel that stability would be the barrier to further progress in air shoes. The air would have to be packaged in such a way that the shoe would be safe, efficient, and stable. Not finding any immediate solution to these problems, the air shoe was put on the back burner.

Ariel feels that many of today's shoes are overdesigned for a recreational runner. He expressed this view in 1979 when *Running Times* labelled the J.C. Penney USA Olympics line, which Ariel had helped design, unsuitable for running and potentially dangerous. Ariel's response was that the shoe, which carried a price tag of under twenty dollars, was not designed for serious running and that for a person who jogs two or three miles a day, the shoe would be entirely adequate.

As a former academic now firmly entrenched in industry, Ariel is acutely aware of the potential "no man's land" which he inhabits. He is between both communities as a citizen of neither. He laments the difficulty in communicating the results of research to marketing people in a large corporation. If an idea has a good theoretical basis but no obvious marketing advantage then, as often as not, it will be left out of a shoe. There have even been occasions when one of Ariel's innovations was advertised when in fact the suggestion had been ignored in favor of an entirely cosmetic change which simulated the substantive improvement.

If his relationships with industry have been far from smooth, Ariel's links with the scientific community can also generate differences. On the PBS television special Nova called "The Race for Gold," he and I were set back to back giving opposite views of what was currently possible from a biomechanical analysis of athletes. Ariel feels that we should be willing to take a top athlete and modify his technique as a result of biomechanical analysis. My view is that we should be wary of promising too much too soon, and that there is still a long way to go before a valid basis for suggesting such changes will exist.

But differences of opinion are the hard currency of science, and it is difficult not to be impressed by Ariel's energetic pursuit of a more quantitative approach to sport. It seems that running shoes have taken a back seat in Ariel's day-to-day work to the more lucrative areas of strength training machines, tennis racquets, and other sports equipment. However, if he has moved on from running shoes professionally he still meets one pair at least daily. Throwing the discus in downtown Amherst would carry with it even more risks than throwing in the Wyoming fieldhouse, so Ariel puts his 200-pound-plus frame through five miles of running a day. It's safe and healthy and there is little chance of meeting an irate football coach.

JOAN BENOIT
AMERICAN MARATHON RECORD HOLDER

After Joan Benoit won the Boston Marathon in 1979 strange things began to happen. Among the strangest was an offer to go into movies. But who was she going to portray? A woman marathoner, an Olympic heroine, or some other wholesome role where her "joie de vivre" would come shining through? Actually, none of the above. The Hollywood mogul on the telephone wanted Joan to be a cheerleader in his movie. She was to send a portfolio of pictures immediately so the casting director could be convinced.

Surely the irony of the offer was lost on this man. Women had fought for many years to enter what was thought to be "man's territory," and here he was, asking the best female marathoner in the United States to take a part which could not be more stereotypical in its presentation of a woman's role.

To report that Joan turned down the offer does not do justice to her considerable integrity. There were more acceptable offers which would have been financially rewarding without requiring that she trade in her ideals. But she knew that college could be a cocoon to protect her from the real world for a while, and she chose to let it be just that way, doing occasional clinics, lectures, and appearances but letting training and racing be the focus of her life. She knew that to survive as a runner after college such deals would put food on the table, but that could wait until after graduation.

Joan won her first marathon by accident during early 1979 in Bermuda. She had run hard in a ten kilometer race the day before and decided to do a half-marathon as a training run. "I got to thirteen and said that will be bad luck if I drop out here, so I got to fifteen and I said that's an odd number, I might as well make it eighteen. Eighteen's so close to twenty—I'll go twenty. Then, gee, only six miles left and I've done the whole thing."

At the end the clock showed two hours and fifty minutes for a run that had been far from an all-out effort. But the race took its toll, or at least the running immediately afterwards did. Joan headed straight back

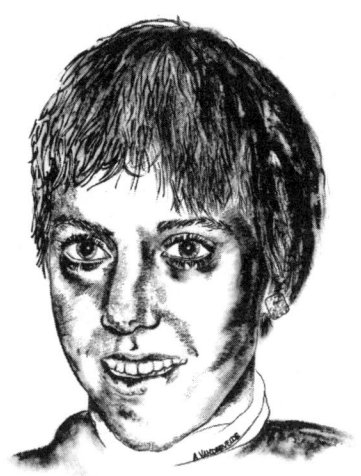

to Bowdoin College in Brunswick, Maine, where winter was firmly entrenched. She put on a pair of spikes for the first time since fall and proceeded to run the one- and two-mile races in a dual meet. "I know it was stupid, but I learn from my mistakes."

And a mistake it was. Joan had broken her leg in a skiing accident while a sophomore in high school, and as so often happens to growing bones that are broken, she ended up with one leg shorter than the other. Despite special shoes to balance the shorter side, she frequently was aware of some pain or another in this leg. After the indoor races, her Achilles tendon became inflamed and excruciatingly painful. Cutting back on running didn't help, and a Boston orthopedist finally convinced her by more than the power of suggestion that complete rest was needed. The doctor took her upstairs to the hospital to meet a European runner who was in bed with a tidy cut over each Achilles tendon. Knowing that he had in Joan a patient who needed a stern warning, he said, "If you don't get off your feet right now, this is what's going to happen to you." The warning was heeded and two weeks of rest cured a problem that has, so far, not returned.

In addition to a maturity well in excess of her twenty-three years, the fear of disabling injury has allowed Joan to keep her running in perspective at a time when many of her peers have gone overboard. She knows that the halo around a champion runner can evaporate when injury occurs. Suddenly a name that was on everyone's lips is difficult to remember. But Joan sees running shoes as parachutes that let you move through otherwise hostile air space with reduced risk of injury. "I really like heavy training shoes. With a little more weight you work a bit harder, and I just feel more secure and protected in a heavy shoe. And it's so much more of a psychological boost when I get my racing shoes on."

Joan has always worn men's shoes because her foot is wide. But working in a running shoe store made her aware of how lucky she was to find a shoe that fits. "The biggest complaint we had from women runners was that the heel region would slip up and down. We had far more women with fit problems than men. . .". Like many top runners, she doesn't really have to worry about buying shoes that fit. All the shoes she needs come free in the mail. In college Joan was part of the Nike Assistance Program. This is a broadbased program, not just for a few top athletes, which provides shoes, encouragement, and help with travel expenses, but not the vast amounts of under-the-counter money that we often read about. Joan displayed a fierce loyalty to Nike that many of their athletes show. "What Nike does is to keep me supplied with shoes, and if a race promoter won't pay my way, then they will take care of it. I've had numerous and very inviting offers from other shoe companies, but I like what Nike stands for and what they have done for me."

If the Olympic Games in 1984 do not have distance events for women, Joan is ready to be in the vanguard of a protest movement. "I mean Grete (Waitz) runs a 2:27 marathon. She would beat half the guys in the Olympics. So I just don't see how they can put on any more excuses that women are not capable of competing at such distances."

As we talked during the last year of her college career, Joan showed a sense of calm about her status as a student and a feeling of uncertainty about life after college, which was to come all too soon. "It's going to be really hard for me in a couple of months. When the Olympics are all over, shoe companies will make their money by having their shoes displayed on the road. There will be offers—I just wish I could put all that off."

Now twenty-three years old, and with a 2:35 marathon which was "an easy run" behind her, Joan Benoit could well be approaching her prime by the 1984 Olympics. It is more than an even bet that this accomplished and intelligent New Englander will have pushed the American women's marathon record several minutes lower by then, and that she will be the leading United States contender for medal honors. As long as she can continue to resist the lure of the Hollywood chauvinists.

JOCK SEMPLE
BOSTON VETERAN

I was lost, and possibly dreaming. Feeling like Gulliver in Lilliput I leaned backwards to try to look eye to eye with these giants who seemed to be surrounding me. A pinch confirmed that I was in the Boston Celtics front offices. The object of my search was Jock Semple, veteran Boston Marathon organizer, who I knew had his office somewhere in the inner caverns of the Boston Garden.

One of the 7-footers obligingly showed me the way to

"Old Jock's place," as he called it, and as I entered, surrounded by a cloud of liniment and not much else except for a small towel, there was Jock Semple about to take a "sweat bath" after a hard day's work.

Jock is a physical therapist who in years past looked after the Celtics and Bruins and now continues in private practice. His office is one small room in the Garden with a couple of couches, a few heat lamps, and walls completely covered with running memorabilia. He is a warm and likeable man with an incredible storehouse of knowledge on runners and races of the past. Unfortunately for his public image, Jock is probably best known to non-runners as the man who tried to eject Kathy Switzer forcibly from what was an all-male Boston Marathon in 1967. Thanks to Kathy's sturdy male escort, he was unsuccessful and she carried on to finish the race.

Of far greater significance, but far less newsworthy, is the fact that Jock has licked the envelopes, sorted the entries, taken the phone calls, and cared for the other details needed to keep the Boston Marathon alive in the days when 400 runners seemed like a multitude and something close to the limit of what the race could hold.

As the number of entries has skyrocketed, the Boston Athletic Association has depended less on this seventy-six year old stalwart and more on a committee of organizers. It is not as if Jock is losing any of his enthusiasm or alertness. His mental and physical prowess

would easily fit someone twenty years younger. He admits his wife has been encouraging him to slow down. His solution, he told me with a grin, is that "now I only work six days a week instead of seven."

Over the last several years he has been at odds with the Boston Athletic Association, particularly on the subject of qualifying times for entry in the Boston Marathon. "I still get mad with the BAA," Jock told me in a Scottish brogue that has been minimally tainted by more than fifty years in the United States. "I'm against all these qualifying times; 2:50 might be alright but 3:20 for the Masters and 3:30 for the women—you're cutting an awful lotta people off."

His empathy for the average rather than the elite runner is interesting, because he was a top-flight competitor in his day. His career started and ended with marathons in Philadelphia in 1926 and 1953, and included almost 100 marathons in the intervening decades. Highlights included a sixth place finish in the 1928 Olympic trial and a seventh in the 1930 Boston Marathon.

Jock's memories of the shoes he used at various stages of his career are still vivid. This is not surprising since the early leather shoes were murderous on the feet. Despite taping every toe, foot problems were often the limiting factor for Jock and his fellow racers in the 1920s. He recalls that "the old BAA clubhouse was like a butcher's shop after the race—everyone was patching up their blisters." One of his early advisers was a man named Abraham Lincoln Monteverde who had been a six-day pedestrian racer in his youth. At his prompting Jock would pickle his feet twice a week for half an hour in a mixture of corned beef brine, sea water, and rock salt.

It was not the pickling, but a shoemaker named Old Man Richings who made the difference to Jock Semple's feet. During the Depression, Jock was holding down an eleven dollar a week job at the YMCA and running in a pair of soft leather bowling shoes. Richings had long ago retired from shoemaking, but was tempted to start up again because he felt the youngsters in the trade were making inferior shoes. He tried to get Clarence DeMar as a guinea pig. DeMar, who would eventually win the BAA race seven times, was not known for his personal charm and he abruptly refused.

So Richings approached Jock Semple. As any true Scotsman would, Jock jumped at the chance of free shoes, and as every runner having foot problems would be, he was willing to spend time and energy to find a solution. Richings set up shop in his garage in Peabody, Massachusetts, and Jock would run to his house for modifications or repairs on the shoes. They were lighter, softer, and wider than any he had worn, and the final design became a hot item among New England runners. Unfortunately Jock did not keep any of these shoes, but a direct descendant of the Richings shoe is shown in Figure 2.18.

Shoe repair was a necessary art for runners in the 1930s and Jock was a master at the craft. He often used old car inner tubes which he would cement to worn heels and uppers. Crepe was a particular favorite for which he never lost a liking. During a trip to the 1948 Olympics as physical therapist for the American hockey team, Jock bought up all the crepe he could find. Worrying about Customs, he stuffed it inside hockey helmets before the trip home. Then, feeling like Santa

Claus, he distributed the haul to the grateful runners of the BAA who cemented it to the heels and soles of their leather-soled shoes.

As I was about to leave, Jock told me about his autobiography, which as yet does not have a publisher. He pulled out letters from Jim Fixx and Hal Higdon commenting on sections of it. Of particular pride was a nice note from Kathy Switzer testifying to the absence of hard feelings between the former adversaries.

Jock Semple is one of the truly great characters of our sport. Talking with him is to live through an era which, despite its hardships, seems in retrospect incredibly romantic in the best sense of the word. As I emerged from Boston Garden into the dusty street outside, I had the urge to organize a Jock Semple Society with the goal of erecting a life-size bronze of Jock somewhere along the Boston Marathon course. And that still doesn't seem like a bad idea. Do I hear a second?

ROB ROY McGREGOR
A PIONEER OF RUNNERS' CLINICS

When his picture first appeared in the pages of *Runner's World* magazine, Rob Roy McGregor was looking out at the reader not from an article on foot care but from an advertisement for Etonic shoes. "The Dr. Rob Roy McGregor one-piece heel and arch support" was

hailed as a revolutionary advance, but Rob Roy was seen by some of his colleagues as the first podiatrist who had "gone commercial." It was not a decision that he came to lightly. "I'll tell you, I had sleepless nights over that. I was willing to be used as a promotional vehicle for a very simple reason. What bothers me about advertising is when they say 'designed by a podiatrist' or an orthopedic surgeon. Well, you know, is that like being designed by a computer? I would rather they come right out and say this was designed by Dr. Jones, and here are Dr. Jones' qualifications, and then let me as a consumer decide if I give a damn about Dr. Jones, and who is he to be saying this?"

These animated words ruffled the linen on the breakfast table as Rob Roy and I met in the stately splendor of Boston's Copley Plaza Hotel. The waitress appeared and blushed slightly as she recognized Rob Roy from his weekly fitness program on local television. It gave us both time to gulp some coffee before his all-out commitment to talking and mine to listening began again.

Listening to Rob Roy talk requires the concentration of a chess player and the alertness of a detective. This is principally because his mind is working in several different directions at once, and there appears to be equal probability that any one of the ideas will take precedence during a particular unit of speech. The following passage from our conversation, in which three separate ideas are being discussed simultaneously, illustrates the point.

"The feet I'm seeing in our running population are free of lesions. One of the reasons for this is that they are wearing running shoes. But I guess I'm trying to say the need for a profusion of widths—I argue against it because the shoe will seat the foot. The shoe will accept some of those changes. And so in the same breath I can say the need for a different shoe for women, there may be a need, but the number of women who can wear men's shoes comfortably is greater than the women might be willing to admit."

At this point I felt like shouting for help or at least calling time out. But Rob Roy definitely fits under the umbrella of a "philosophical podiatrist" and his ideas and opinions have had an important influence on the development of sports podiatry. He knew little about runners and their problems when he was asked in 1974 to assist with foot care at the end of the Boston Marathon. He had devoted the majority of his professional life to care of the diabetic foot, and the running patients who began knocking on his door were "the first healthy people that I had ever seen in my practce. They came in healthy and challenging—and you had to be challenged because they were challenging themselves."

Rob Roy took up the gauntlet and immersed himself in running and runners with an enthusiasm bordering on religious fervor. He had always run a modest weekly mileage, but when Patriots Day 1975 rolled around one of those 2090 souls packed into the tiny main street of Hopkinton was Rob Roy McGregor. He finished the race in three hours and thirty-seven minutes and began to feel a closer communion with his running patients. At about that time he developed the idea of a runner's clinic and implemented it at The Deaconess Hospital in Boston. "It seemed to me that the runner required an attitude, time, and an environment different from the sick patient."

And so the experiment began, and was to prove so successful that several other runners' clinics were spawned in the Boston area. Today that city can rightfully claim to be offering its runners the most accessible and affordable health care in the nation. Included in Rob Roy's conception was a team of health care professionals who could provide a comprehensive approach to a runner's special needs; an orthopedist, a podiatrist, a physical therapist, and an athletic trainer. The total Sports Medicine Center was designed for a patient who was suffering from a running-related problem but was otherwise in the best of health.

To complement his sports medicine center, Rob Roy has developed what he calls a "global theory of sports medicine." He explains: "You get three kinds of problems—those with inadequate joint motion, those with excessive joint motion, and those with an abnormal relationship of the bones that make up the joint. Almost all of our problems are a function of joint inadequacy. You treat by either stopping motion, increasing motion, or you treat mechanically, and that's what orthotics are."

He insists that orthotics should be seen as a means of facilitating function and not correcting it. He uses the example of eyeglasses as an analogy. The hallmark of Rob Roy's approach to the runner is that he does not treat what he sees until it is causing pain. "I refuse to see people who are not in pain . . . (some doctors) want to make a disease out of forefoot varus. It isn't a disease any more than brown eyes are a disease. I don't treat forefoot varus. I will address a forefoot varus because it's causing pain, but that is a different matter."

But doesn't this exclude the possibility of preventive medicine, I asked? What about someone who comes in with a hyperpronated gait pattern and says, "I'm sure that I will have a problem if I keep on running?" I say, 'do ankle exercises,' I say, 'be healthy, be fit, and come on in when you have the problem.'"

Rob Roy highlights the importance of a person we often forget to include in the running shoe equation—the clerk in the store. "I call him the first point practitioner in the sports medicine delivery system, just like the pharmacist in general medicine. He has an incredible responsibility and is called on to make all sorts of decisions . . . 'my knee hurts, what shoe do I get?', 'what do I get for heel pain?' I'm going to suggest that the runner should buy his shoes from a trained equipment technician. That may raise the cost of shoes but it's well worth it if it helps you through the jungle of 108 models."

When the dust from our conversation had cleared, I was left with the impression that Rob Roy McGregor would be the ideal occupant of a think tank. It would be organized something like this. He would sit inside a sealed chamber facing a television monitor for eight hour periods. Every five minutes a new word from a sports medicine vocabulary would appear on the screen to trigger associations in Rob Roy's mind. A committee of informed listeners, working fifteen minute shifts, would listen in as Rob Roy talks, noting down the good ideas, discarding the rest. They would pass on their recommendations to an action committee, who, after further screening, would set about implementing the top one percent of his ideas. And one last thing: there would have to be a treadmill in the chamber to allow Rob Roy to exercise. It sounds like an attractive idea—are you game, Rob Roy?

THE GERMAN GIANTS

At either end of the main street of Herzogenaurach are two large towers. They are striking pieces of architecture, perhaps 150 feet tall. After a rectangular ascent, they curve gently outward to support a watchtower, and then, just as neatly, they terminate in a smooth gothic pinnacle. To the traveler who knows the history of this little town, these two towers could as well be electrodes thrust into a bath of acid. The town is polarized as sharply as any battery.

Looking down from the clock tower to the right, one sees the sign in bold orange letters—Puma Shop. Across the street, offset just enough so that two men don't look into each other's eyes, the sign reads, Hans Hoffman—Adidas. These are two small retail shops, but Herzogenaurach is the site of the international headquarters of both Adidas and Puma.

The feud within the Dassler family which led to the formation of the two companies was played before the world as a grandstand. But nowhere is the rivalry felt so intensely as in this small Bavarian town where 30,000 inhabitants express their allegiance daily on their feet rather than at the ballot box. Herzogenaurach has two amateur soccer clubs. Predictably, one is outfitted by Adidas, the other by Puma. The cars of the workers display either a leaping Puma or an Adidas trefoil. The management doesn't request it, but it's a way of life to state your position.

Until the explosion of the sporting goods business in the last five years, Adidas and Puma were suppliers of sports shoes to the world. Their shoes were like gold in the Soviet Union, worn by Presidents of the United States, on the feet of royalty in England, and generally regarded as the shoes to be seen in all over the globe.

At the outbreak of war in 1945, the brothers Adolf and Rudolf Dassler had been making shoes together for almost twenty years. Their work was widely considered the best in athletic footwear. Already athletes were starting to make specific requests that the Dassler brothers make their shoes. But suddenly, the rift came. The specifics of the argument have been blurred by the passage of time, but Franconians by nature are stubborn, determined creatures, and once the decision to go their separate ways had been made, the town may as well have had a wall down the main street. Rudolf retreated to the north side of the river, Adolf set up shop on the south. Until Rudy Dassler died in 1974, the brothers never spoke a kind word about each other again.

Adolf Dassler

Rudolf Dassler

Adidas—The Magic of Adi Dassler

On September 9th, 1978, long after the workers had left the factory, Adi Dassler was doing what he did best. He and his chief technician, Horst Widman were crouched over a table in Adi's office, brainstorming some new ideas for the outside of a soccer shoe. Like most West Germans, Adi was a soccer fanatic. He traveled constantly with the German team, and loved the company of soccer players and coaches.

Before they finished work that night, Dassler and Widman had formulated a design that would allow a shoe to bend in one direction but provide resistance in the other, and perhaps help protect the foot from injury. But on September 10, Adi Dassler died, at age seventy-eight, of a massive heart attack. And the athletic world was robbed of an acknowledged genius.

Adi Dassler made his fortune from making shoes, but the world of sport made a fortune from Adi Dassler; a wealth of ideas and innovations in sports as diverse as basketball and bobsled, high jump and hammer throw, parachuting and pentathalon. The museum at the Adidas headquarters is a testament to his ingenuity. In the search for better materials to make shoes that would meet his special needs, Adi at various times tried dogskin, badgerskin, kangaroo skin, and even sharkskin. From the beginning the company philosophy reflected his belief that good materials are the key to good shoe-making.

While today's polymer chemist has largely taken over the realm of material selection, the shoes in the museum indicate the profound influence that Adi Dassler has had on running since the first model which the Dassler brothers made in 1925. Jesse Owens' shoes from the 1936 Olympics stand proudly on display. Kip Keino's steeplechase shoes (with a sharkskin patch on the outsole) are there, inscribed as a Christmas present to Adi Dassler.

There are shoes that have won gold medals, shoes that have set world records; each shoe tells its own story, usually a story of extreme interest in the athlete shown by Dassler. Certainly he was getting good advertising, but he had a very real concern for the athlete, and worked hard to make a shoe that would suit any special requirements an athlete might have.

After Adi Dassler's death, the responsibility for the company was taken over by his wife Kathe. But it is likely that Adi's eldest son Horst, who currently heads Adidas France, will soon be at the helm of the entire corporate structure.

But while Horst Dassler is heir apparent to the financial empire, the legacy of working on a daily basis with some of the world's best athletes has fallen on Horst Widman, a short, intense, slightly bowed man who probably worries about shoes twenty-five hours out of every day.

When I arrived in Herzogenaurach, a regular sort of

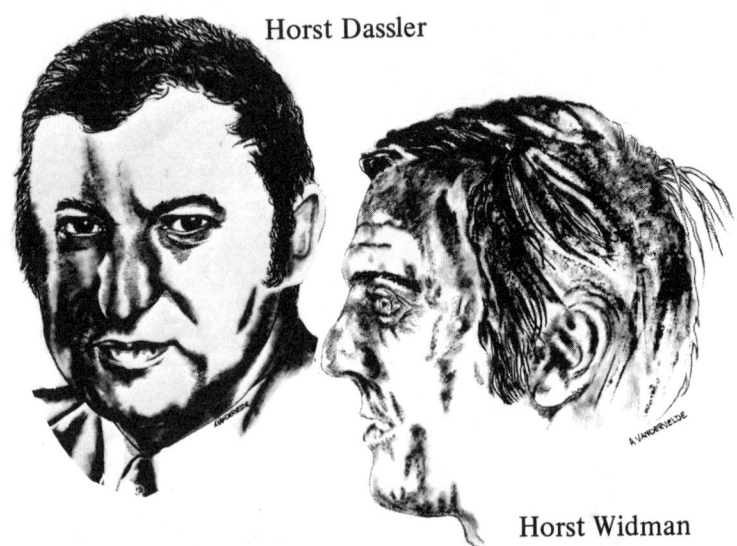

Horst Dassler

Horst Widman

Adidas day was in progress. Widman had just finished showing a new custom made shoe to the young European 5,000 meter champion, Marcus Ryfels, and word had spread that world champion Edwin Moses was in town to collect some new shoes. On that same day my luggage had arrived in Tehran, and I sat, having coffee and homemade pie, with Mrs. Kathe Dassler, feeling scruffy in four-day-old clothes, and probably smelling worse.

Out of kindness to me, and in deference to my hosts, I was ushered into a large room that has appeared in many athlete's wildest dreams. Amid larger than life photographs of Ilie Nastase, Franz Beckenbauer, and Grete Waitz were shelf upon shelf of shoes, clothes, racquets, skis, and every conceivable item of sports equipment. This was the holy of holies, where the world's best athletes are clothed from head to foot in the Adidas stripes and trefoil. For a few brief moments I was allowed to imagine that my marathon time had miraculously improved by thirty minutes or more, and I was suddenly among the ranks of elite runners. The room was a giant sporting goods store, except there was no cashier. Warm-ups, shirts, tee shirts, socks, and of course shoes were there for the taking, complete with luggage to carry away the haul.

Suitably re-clothed and smelling sweeter, I settled down to talk with Horst Widman in the office where Adi Dassler used to work. It became clear that the spirit of Adi still dominates the thoughts and actions of Widman and the other shoe technicians.

"He tried all his life, with all his energy, to produce better shoes," mused Widman. "There is a saying, 'One year of working with Adi Dassler was like ten years at University.'"

And it probably was. Dassler was a compulsive worker, a "shoe-aholic" who would never rest on his laurels. Improvement was the only game allowed. His basic techniques were trial and error, constant discussion with his technicians, and continual interaction with top athletes. During my stay I had the feeling that if only Dassler had been born twenty years later, so that the scientific discipline of sports biomechanics had been available to him, his advances and innovations would have been even more spectacular.

In many respects things at Adidas have not really changed. They still search for the best materials available, setting up a development program if nothing is available. They still build their shoes with pride and good workmanship. But they are still reluctant to admit that experimentation and measurement on athletes wearing the finished product are anywhere near as valuable as simply asking the athlete, "How do they feel?" Of course, almost no other manufacturer believes in science either, but one might reasonably expect the giant to seize the opportunity that science provides.

Fun runners frequently wonder if the Adidas they see more serious runners wearing have anything in common (except the three stripes) with the shoes that they wear themselves. Some do and some don't. Most runners who come to Adidas for shoes start off with off-the-shelf models. As they become more aware of their special needs, requests for special features will be met by Widman and his team. But the burden of proof is on the athlete. If he or she is content with production line shoes, then the matter goes no further.

Ed Moses, for example, has special needs. He is flat footed and has a very broad foot. The hurdles place special demands on his feet, but it would clearly be uneconomical for any manufacturer to make a shoe just for hurdling. Marcus Ryfels needed more protection in the mid- and rearpart of the foot than conventional spikes provide. So like 1700 other athletes, the feet of Moses and Ryfels became shapes on a shelf. Special lasts were made so that their shoes would be more than production models in the right size.

There have been signs in the last few years that Adidas has finally begun to listen to the needs of not just the superior athlete but to the everyday runner. For many years in the seventies it appeared that training flats were something beneath the dignity of Adidas. While other manufacturers were quick to provide protection from impact, Adidas continued stolidly with models like the Country, which was well made but hard as a rock.

One reason for the slow response was probably a lack of transatlantic communication. As American runners hit the streets by the millions, runners on European streets were few and far between, still something which provoked a smirk or a whistle. So the Europeans had a hard time realizing both the magnitude of the American avocation and the needs of the thirty mile a week runner.

Adi Dassler is the patron saint of sports shoes. If Adidas or any other company can ever combine the genius of Adi Dassler with the technical capability that modern sport science offers, the game will be all over.

Puma—The Sign of the Cat

It would have made eminent sense to bid farewell to the Adidas group and stroll across town to the Puma factory, but somehow it just didn't seem the diplomatic thing to do. The intrigue surrounding the thirty year rivalry between the two companies was exerting a powerful influence on me, and I dutifully drove back to Frankfurt, hardly daring to glance at the Puma plant as I left town.

Armin Dassler

Six months later, as Pennsylvania struggled to free itself from the last traces of winter, I boarded a plane for Europe to make my second visit to the small town in Bavaria which has become the capital of the sports shoe world. This time I would visit Puma and wouldn't breathe the name beginning with A.

When Rudolph Dassler died in 1974, the grooming process for his successor was already complete. His son Armin had literally grown up in the factory and moved easily into the president's chair. Armin Dassler is a large, impressive man who has the aura and bearing of an aristocrat. His control over the company is clearly total, and it seemed unimaginable that any of his directives would not be carried out.

Our first meeting came at a brief talk I gave to a group of Puma technicians. He listened closely, and it was clear from the incisive questions that he had a good understanding of the practical problems of running shoe design in addition to his firm grasp of the business aspects.

Later that same day we sat together in his office, and he reminisced about the origins of shoemaking in the Dassler family. His grandfather had been a shoemaker and produced a slipper or "schlaper" of camel hair uppers and car tire soles. It became a family enterprise in 1924 when Armin's father Rudolph and Uncle Adolph joined the business which was run from the family home. "My grandfather had a used typewriter, and I think this was half the value of the company. They made shoes in the laundry kitchen of our home."

The first venture into sports shoes was the "turnschuhe," a shoe for gymnastics, a natural extension from slippers. But the critical event was a meeting that the brothers had with Waitzer, the coach of the national German track and field team. He told the brothers that there was a real need for German-made shoes, and helped them design their first spiked track shoe. The resulting shoe bore the names of both Dassler and Waitzer (Figure 2.21a) and it became an instant success with German athletes who wore the shoe at the 1928 Olympics in Amsterdam. This began the relationship between the name Dassler and the Olympics which has continued, with increasing intensity, to this day.

By 1939 there were more than 100 employees, but when the war was finished, so was the partnership of Adolph and Rudolph Dassler. The reasons for the split are private family history, as shown by the following excerpt from our conversation.

Dassler: So they decided to separate, I think it was on June 20, 1948. I don't want to go into the details of what did happen and what did not happen."
Cavanagh: There have been a lot of different stories about . . .
Dassler: Let's forget it.

Cavanagh: So you do not want to put the record straight?
Dassler: That's right.

So Puma was born. Armin's father took the sales force and a building which had been earmarked for a new factory, while his Uncle took the old factory and most of the work force. Both sides agreed not to use the name Dassler on their products. For a time the brothers used some combination of letters from their name; Adolph used Addas and Rudolph, Ruda. The substitution of the letters P and M to give Puma was suggested by an advertising agency on the grounds that it conveyed speed and power, and was easily pronounced in many languages.

Armin's family actually lived in part of the new factory. In keeping with the permanence which pervades so many European institutions, Armin now has his desk about six feet from where his childhood bed was.

Rudolph Dassler categorically refused to let his son go to University. Instead Armin attended the Technical School for Shoe Making and learned everything else about the business from practical experience. That the learning process was successful is evident from Puma sales figures. Each day the company produces 70,000 pairs of shoes in its factories all over the world. One-tenth of this total is running shoes. Since many of these end up in the United States I asked Dassler what his opinion of American import quotas was. There was a visible increase in his blood pressure. "Well, I am a fighter for free and fair trade worldwide so don't ask me that question. I am against quotas of any kind."

Although Puma began to make some shoes in the Far East in 1972, Dassler feels that one element of truly fair trade is to try to increase the wages of workers in the "sweatshops" of the Orient. "Of course, it is not fair trade when workers in our Taiwan factories or in China earn ten dollars a week while in Germany we pay ten dollars an hour. But my philosophy is that to get fair trade it has to be free first."

One of the men responsible for keeping the quality of shoes produced by Puma at a high level is the former San Jose State coach Don Riggs, now Director of Research and Development for the company. Don's involvement originally was as a link to the top athletes who worked with Puma, but as his enormous appetite for work and fundamental understanding of the shoe-making process became apparent, Armin Dassler knew when to keep a winning horse. Riggs' idol is General Patton, and he walks into a shoe factory with a no less commanding presence. His travel schedule would make an air hostess weary but somehow Riggs comes up asking for more.

While I was at Puma headquarters, the American decathalete Bob Coffman was also passing through. His presence prompted me to ask Dassler for his views on the financial support of amateur athletes. Since Bavarians are living in the shadow of the East German border it did not surprise me that the East-West rivalry loomed large in his answer. "This is such a complex question. First, I think we should give them some reimbursement for the advice they are giving us on shoe design. Then, of course, there is the advertising benefit for us. But a method should be worked out so that it does not affect their amateur status. You know our athletes, the German, British, the Americans, they have to live from their own resources and fight against athletes from Eastern countries who have been brought up for nothing. If it were not for the Eastern bloc countries I would still be a great supporter of amateur athletics. But if we really want to see our athletes winning, we have to do something."

The 'something' in West Germany, Dassler explained, includes large lump sum contributions from Puma and other running shoe manufacturers to the National Track and Field Federation. The individual athletes still make an agreement with the particular company they want to work with, but the Federation handles the financial aspects of the relationship.

As a parting question I asked Dassler what he wanted the image of Puma to be among runners. He nodded slowly and then in his excellent English said, "Well, first I would like Puma to be known as the best shoemaker in the world—to have the best quality shoe. Also, the average runner, he is not looking to be the fastest in the world, he wants to enjoy his own ability to run for an hour or two hours each day. And our job is to make it comfortable for him. Give him a light shoe, and make it suitable for any terrain. That's our basic philosophy."

And certainly there will always be a mystique about wearing a Puma shoe. Runners have the feeling that the shoes are like grapes from a mature vine. They were around yesterday, and they will be around tomorrow. Armin has certainly laid the groundwork for the future. His two oldest sons are soon to graduate from University, one in law and one in mathematics. So we may again see "Dassler Brothers" written on a running shoe. With one brother who can legislate and another who can calculate they would make a powerful management combination.

SHELDON LANGER
FATHER OF "SPORTHOTICS"

For Sheldon Langer there is no doubt that the egg came before the chicken. Langer is president of Langer Laboratories, the company that produces "Sporthotics." The egg in this case was the steel Schaffer plate that Langer wore inside his shoe to help with a foot problem while he was a collegiate lacrosse player. Through a series of personal difficulties with his foot, the egg gave birth to the chicken—a corporation which now produces more than 50,000 orthotic devices a year.

When Langer graduated from podiatry school in 1950 he started a running program to keep fit. But he soon found that the device he wore inside his shoe, a Rohadur orthotic still used to some extent today, was fine for walking but could not be tolerated during running. So rather than use it, he used nothing, which turned out to be a very bad move.

As we discussed in Chapter 13, ankle and foot problems frequently affect the knee joint and Langer found himself, after two years of running, with a serious knee injury and subsequent phlebitis. During recovery from surgery there was plenty of time to think, and the association between an orthotic that was inadequate for running and the damage he had inflicted on himself was only too clear. So Langer resolved to make the best of a bad situation. "I wanted to continue to run, so I decided that I would look into materials which could offer the necessary control without the side effects of rigid materials such as steel and Rohadur. And that's when 'Sporthotics' came into being." The extent to which he was successful is shown by the volume of devices which are produced by his company today to the order of doctors from around the world.

In addition to the product, the name was also a stroke of genius; it seems to be going the way of "Xerox" in becoming a generic noun for a particular article, in this case an orthotic device used in sports. This does not make Langer particularly happy since he has to spend a good deal of time on "cease and desist" letters to competitors who are riding the name in the interest of sales.

Not unnaturally orthotics were the main topic of our conversation, and I asked Langer to take all the success stories for granted for a moment and tell me what he could about the reasons orthotic therapy was, on occasion, unsuccessful. Langer is known to his colleagues for his forthright views and he immediately enumerated four reasons for failure. "First of all is the problem of the runner's expectations, and here it is the doctor who has failed to communicate properly to the patient. If the doctor would be candid with a patient who he feels has only a fifty percent chance of successful treatment, then if that patient got fifty percent relief he would be getting all of what the doctor promised.

"Next, some patients are given orthotics which are poorly made. Anyone can take a piece of plastic and mold it over a piece of plaster. But there's got to be more care taken in the creation of an orthotic.

"If the device is well made, another possible problem is the runner who puts on the orthotic and goes out and does too much too soon. In this case he's actually fighting the device.

"Finally, a common thing is that a five mile a day runner who is doing nicely with his orthotic might decide that he's going to go out and run a marathon. He is no longer a short distance runner but a long distance runner who is running with the wrong device."

The question of fees for podiatric services has been raised in a number of forums, and Langer's view is that if a patient thinks he is being overcharged he should say so and give the doctor an opportunity to explain what he is doing for the money. "If the doctor cannot explain then indeed he may be overcharging. But we should bear in mind that it is not the device that determines the fee. It is the doctor's time, his knowledge, his overhead, and so on."

Although podiatry is now emerging as a respectable discipline in its own right, Langer has lived and practiced through the times when prejudice from other members of the health care professions was strong. Today there is still animosity between some podiatrists and orthopedic surgeons, and I asked Langer to give his views on the present climate. "The relationship between podiatry and orthopedics should be a firm and steadfast one, but unfortunately it is not. I believe that orthopedists are wrong to relegate the feet to a minor role in total body health, and I also believe that podiatrists handle the feet better than anyone else. It has much to do with economics. Orthopedists are involved with acute trauma and emergency situations in which they are superb. Podiatrists live with the feet all the time."

One sure thing is that the patient would be the loser in such a tussle, because he or she may feel free to consult only one of the specialists in the interest of being able to obtain treatment without fear of prejudice.

As his comments indicate, Sheldon Langer is an earnest and outspoken podiatrist who cares deeply about the profession he has chosen and the patients he is helping, either directly or indirectly. Although they don't know it, the army of runners who are wearing "Sporthotics" should be grateful that Langer himself suffered foot problems in his younger days. If he had been a symptom-free runner, they might not be running today.

BRUCE TULLOH
BAREFOOT TRACK RUNNER

In 1958 a diminutive runner named Bruce Tulloh wrote his name into British track archives by winning the national three-mile championship in record time. Tulloh went on to lower the British and European records at 5,000 and 10,000 meters, and only a bout of measles prevented what seemed a certain medal at the Mexico Olympics. He became a favorite with the British people. They admired the way he ran, hanging in doggedly at whatever pace his rivals cared to set during the first part of the race, only to dig down into seemingly endless reserves to leave the field behind in the final laps.

But there was something beyond his superb abilities that fixed an image of Tulloh in the minds of all who saw him run. He was the first runner in living memory who chose to run barefoot in track races. With a band-aid on the big toe as his only footwear, Tulloh lined up against the best the world could offer and usually won.

In seeking out people with important views on shoes, it was therefore natural that I should visit Marlborough, England, where on a warm June day I talked with Bruce about his running career over a pint of beer and a "ploughman's lunch." I found a man forced to acclimatize himself to considerable success in a new role as the Jim Fixx of England. The popularity of running in England has lagged about two years behind similar events in America. Random House was now demanding such enormous sums for the British rights to Fixx's book that an Anglo-Saxon book on running was requested with Tulloh as the author. This was duly written and in the first three weeks 25,000 copies of the book were sold. The face of its author became familiar once more to the British television and newspaper audiences, as public appearances to promote the book were arranged.

Tulloh is unquestionably one of the most cerebral runners who has ever competed on the international circuit. His approach to running reminds one of a hard fought but well won battle. Following meticulous and often solitary training to prepare for competition, Tulloh would carefully analyze both the responses of his own body and the possible threats from the competition. During training sessions on grass in college, he began to perceive that running barefoot felt surprisingly easy compared to running in shoes. As a biologist, Tulloh knew that some of the energy expended during running was dissipated simply to accelerate and decelerate the limbs. Anything that could reduce the mass of these parts would cause a reduction in energy expenditure and perhaps leave that small but significant margin available for faster times. Since the university actually had a grass track on which some of their dual meets were held the obvious experiment was to race barefoot. This he did successfully and never used shoes in a race again unless the surface was too hostile to the foot.

Because the majority of his walking hours were spent in shoes, Tulloh's feet never really calloused the way some of the African runners' feet do. Remarkably enough he was never injured during his ten-year running career. He was "spiked" only once and often blistered (particularly at ten kilometers), but a blister seemed a small price to pay for increased running efficiency.

Two other highlights of Bruce Tulloh's career deserve mention; one for its irony, the other for its enormity. During a stint as National Coach in Kenya, Tulloh sometimes found himself the only person in the race not wearing running shoes. To the Kenyan runners who had been barefoot throughout their childhood owning a pair of running shoes was a status symbol which meant they had arrived. Tulloh continued to feel better and faster without shoes and found it impossible to convince his athletes that they might run better without theirs.

To crown his career following the disappointment of missing the Munich Olympics, Tulloh searched for a challenge which would prove to himself and anyone else who would take notice that he was an athlete of unrivalled ability. It was to be his own personal rebuke of fate, his own private Olympic event, an event so extreme that there would be only one competitor. The event he chose began one morning in Los Angeles and ended sixty-four days, twenty-one hours, and thirty minutes later in New York City. Bruce Tulloh had achieved the fastest ever crossing on foot of the American continent, gaining the distinction with an incredible average of forty-eight miles per day—without a single day of rest.

This time he ran in shoes, and back in England following the run Bruce was tested by the eminent British physiologist Griffith Pugh. Physiological measurements confirmed Tulloh's belief that he was actually one or two percent more efficient without shoes. The acute perception of a superior athlete had been confirmed. Should everyone follow his example? Definitely not. Tulloh obviously has a unique and robust anatomy. Anyone who can run 3500 miles without injury is clearly made differently from almost every other human being. For most of us the decision to discard our running shoes would be a disaster and would probably mark the end of our running careers. But for Bruce Tulloh it worked, and history will surely keep its place for him.

STAN JAMES
THE COURT OF LAST RESORT

Stan James knows he could cure ninety percent of all running injuries if only the athletes would give him a chance. Perhaps better stated, if only they would give themselves a chance. It is not that runners don't come to James' office. They do in droves—so much so that he has had to cut down on running patients in order to concentrate on his specialty of knee surgery. But when they come many runners bring with them one problem which seems insurmountable. James puts it this way: "Runners have a communication gap between their minds and bodies. Their minds tell them they must go out and run 150 miles every week, and they can't hear their bodies screaming NO, NO, NO!"

James was among the first to identify overuse as a principal cause of running injury. He believes that there is an accumulation of stress which will result in injury if intense racing and training is not accompanied by adequate rest. "Training errors" is the phrase he uses to include both high mileage fanaticism and rapid changes in training patterns.

That Stan James has become an acknowledged expert on running injuries seems, in retrospect, the product of a certain determinism. When a man of James' interest and ability was planted in the fertile running atmosphere of Eugene, Oregon, osmosis took over to generate the finished product.

Stan James arrived in Eugene in 1967 to take his first job with a well established sports medicine practice. He had both interest in and insight into sports medicine, having majored as an undergraduate in General Science and Physical Education before going on to medical school and an orthopedic residency.

When he lined up at the start of road races in Eugene in the early days, runners began to take notice. It wasn't long before they were knocking on his door with their aches and pains. James began rather self-consciously learning the runner's language and exploring various treatment avenues—without charging because he felt it was so much trial and error with unpredictable results. Over a period of time a coherent philosophy evolved, and his success in treating running injuries brought Olympians and overweights alike into his office seeking relief.

The mystical cure that James has found for running injuries is rest—relief from the stresses of running. Not so very complicated, unless you are a runner. Runners seem totally incapable of believing that, at least for a few weeks, it would make good sense if they found some other way to keep their pulse rate at 150 for two hours.

James is not telling injured athletes to go to bed or to keep off their feet. He is more of a realist than that. He is asking them to spare their lower extremity the pounding which can be temporarily eliminated by other forms of cardiovascular exercise. Cycling, for example, is one of his frequent prescriptions. Not biking for fun, but planned, hard exercise which can be as demanding as running. Many local runners have ended up in the basement of James' home, pedalling his exercise bicycle.

But a person can be ignored only so much. James is to the point now where his tolerance of runners who won't heed his advice is on the low side of empty. He has been known to put a cast on the ankle of a persistent offender who might otherwise have gone out and run himself into oblivion. He has bluntly told runners to look elsewhere for treatment if they won't follow his suggestions. "Runners are extremely difficult patients," recounts James. "You cannot see runners in five or fifteen minutes. You must spend half an hour or more learning about their history, examining their body in great detail, and looking at their shoes. And if at the end of all this they disregard your advice, well, was it worth it?"

As time has gone by and James' reputation has grown, he acknowledges that he has become somewhat of a "court of last resort." When an outstanding runner comes to his office after seeing five or six other doctors, the athlete is more likely to listen. Even if the advice is no different and stopping running is recommended, the runner has the message that this is journey's end.

One of the major formative influences in James' approach to treating runners has been University of Oregon coach emeritus Bill Bowerman. James has seen the results of Bowerman's "hard-easy" approach to coaching. Or rather, he hasn't seen the results as far as injuries are concerned. James was there to pick up the remains when, on the advice of a Swedish physiologist, Bowerman tried intense workouts every day for one part of the squad. The results were injury rates far higher than before.

Bowerman and James have also worked together on shoe design. With prosthetist Dennis Vixie they hold a number of patents including the original "waffle sole" (see Chapter 8). But communication has not always been smooth between design and manufacture. The old Nike LD 1000 is a case in point. James had a part in the conception of the shoe, but was shocked to see how far the production model diverged from his original idea. He was even more surprised when the shoe was advertised as being made for the knee. The excessive flare turned out to actually cause knee pain in some athletes.

Stan James now has an added responsibility which may prove as hard as all those that have gone before. He is orthopedist in charge of Athletics West, the group of twenty-five athletes sponsored by Nike. Since the group works together in such an atmosphere of intensity it is easy for them to overtrain. James has the difficult job of trying to temper the reality for athletes who have finally been given the chance they always dreamed of. They can train without worrying about where the next meal is coming from or how they can pay their doctor bills.

Whether or not James' moderate view of training will be assimilated by coaches and athletes as time goes by is an open question. With overuse injuries sidelining or slowing down some of the world's top distance runners, it is hard to imagine that his words will go unheeded. One thing is certain, though. In ten years time, Stan James will still be running half marathons, doing a little weight training, and skiing twenty kilometer cross-country races while many of his more famous patients have their feet up in front of the television. If only they would listen now!

BOB ANDERSON
PUBLISHER, RUNNER'S WORLD MAGAZINE

Everyone in the running shoe business knows the name of Bob Anderson. Some people like him, some dislike him, and many wish that he would just go away and raise cattle instead of publishing *Runner's World* magazine. But Bob Anderson won't go away. He is tenacious in his role of maverick to the running shoe industry, a function served by the October issue of *Runner's World* which incorporates the annual shoe survey. This survey considers all available running shoes and groups them into ratings from five stars to one star.

Views on Shoes

Because of the influence on the survey on the vast consumer market, Anderson has been the target of shoe makers who are unhappy because their product has not received a top rating. Some of the major shoe companies regard Anderson rather like General Motors treats Ralph Nader. He recalls a meeting with executives of a large shoe company. "My advertising man came over and said, 'Bob, this is going to be a strange discussion. I just wanted you to know.' We went over to the table where these men were sitting. I reached out my hand—'Hi, I'm Bob Anderson.' No comment. They just looked at my hand and refused to talk to me. And they refused many times after that."

These kinds of pressures, some more subtle than others, became something Anderson either had to learn to live with or quit. So why didn't he just publish an inoffensive description of available shoes which would be enthusiastically endorsed by shoe manufacturers? "Frankly, if we let up on shoes, I think the manufacturers will let up on shoes. I know that the things they have been forced to do have cost a lot of dollars. And the survey has cost us a lot too. It doesn't make good business sense for a publisher to rank the products of his advertisers."

But Anderson keeps going with the survey because he feels that it is an important service to runners. He still remembers standing in a shoe store in the mid-1960s and hearing a clerk explain why a pair of tennis shoes would be ideal for running. And the fact that the consumer had no place to go for reliable information left its mark on Anderson.

He became a "track nut" while going to high school in Kansas at a time when Jim Ryun was better known than the governor of Kansas. He still remembers his first pair of running shoes which were Converse "Chuck Taylors" (see Figure 2.29). Performances of 2:08 in the half mile and 9:38 for two miles were encouraging enough to suggest participating in track at Kansas State University. But college competition was a disappointment. Being a star in high school and then a "C" team runner in college was not an easy transition. So Anderson left the team to concentrate on another project he was sure he could excel at. It was a newsletter called *Distance Running News*. At first there were four issues a year, and the format was a typewritten sheet which Anderson himself wrote, typed, duplicated, and mailed. By 1967 there were about 1500 subscribers and a team of interested runners who contributed occasional features.

One such contribution was a lengthy feature in the April 1967 issue written by Jeff Johnson, now an executive with Nike (see profile earlier in this chapter). This was the first shoe issue, describing and rating the offerings of the five companies who made running shoes. The results from this survey were not earth-shaking. Tiger shoes, which did well in the survey, certainly experienced a greater sales volume, but they were already popular with runners. But responses to the shoe survey from runners were encouraging enough for Anderson to plan more.

As the running boom gathered momentum, *Distance Running News* attracted subscribers and eventually outgrew its roots and name, moving to Palo Alto, California to become *Runner's World*.

In 1980, *Runner's World* has a circulation of about four hundred thousand and is the flagship of a magazine and book publishing company. The annual shoe issue is treated by many runners as a buyer's guide to the year's shoes, and by many retailers as an index of what shoes they will carry. Anderson is cognizant of the influence he has had on the development of running shoes, but also admits that there have been some wrong turns along the way. "We have called some wrong shots, such as advocating that the wider the shoe was in the rearfoot the better, not realizing that too wide could cause problems. We must be ready to change our ideas as better evidence comes along."

He doesn't intend to let the magazine rest on its laurels. A major current interest is using running as a vehicle for corporate fitness. Anderson has pioneered the Corporate Cup, in which teams of runners from some of the country's major businesses battle each other over a variety of distances on the road and track. The result has been not just an increased awareness of the importance of fitness, but improved morale and sense of corporate identity in those companies who have taken part. Anderson hopes that corporate involvement in running will produce new avenues for the support of our finest athletes. "A lot of people complain about Japanese companies sponsoring volleyball teams, or East German athletes working for the government. Just because we're not doing it in the States they think it's unfair. Well, the long-term thinking in the Corporate Cup is that companies might sponsor running teams of super athletes who would run and work for the company."

The story may only be half told. Still only thirty-three years old, Bob Anderson could publish *Runner's World* for another thirty-three years. Running and *Runner's World* have catapulted him into a position of power in the running shoe hierarchy. While some shoe-making companies would like to see this power eliminated, it is reassuring to runners to know that someone is representing their interests in the halls of industry.

BILL BOWERMAN
EMERITUS COACH, UNIVERSITY OF OREGON

Bill Bowerman saw his first track meet as a college freshman at the University of Oregon in 1929. He had come to college to study, not to run, but this first track meet changed his mind. He saw "a long skinny fellow" named Ralph Hill break the American collegiate 5,000 meter record by six seconds. Right there and then, with the determination that flows instead of blood in his veins, Bowerman said to himself, "If that fellow can make a letter at Oregon then I can make a letter at Oregon." And true to his word, he did make a letter as a quarter-miler. Thus began an illustrious career in track and field which nurtured athletes like Steve Prefontaine and Kenny Moore, and nudged forward the

growing pastime of jogging until it became a national obsession.

Almost exactly fifty years after this catalytic track and field meet, I met with Bowerman in a crowded basement workshop in the center of Eugene, surrounded by all the paraphernalia of running shoe manufacture. In this small den there were brightly colored uppers of various sizes, sheets of midsole and soling material, and the machines and an assistant needed to convert ideas into real shoes. The pungent smell of shoe cements gave the room its final stamp of authenticity, reminding me of similar smells in the huge shoe factories I had visited. Bowerman descends on this workshop from his farm in the hills, dividing his days of retirement among cattle, shoes, and athletes.

Now circling seventy, a time when most coaches sit back and reflect on their accomplishments, I found him excited and enthusiastic. He had just agreed to coach a young woman athlete, and that sixth sense told him it would be no ordinary assignment. "When Prefontaine came to Oregon I said to myself, 'Bill, this is a very serious responsibility,' and I feel that way about this young lady."

A challenge has always had an effect more powerful than gravity on Bowerman. That's why he got involved in shoemaking. In 1956 he was putting European shoes on the feet of his track team. He saw prices going up and quality going down. Inquiries to local shoemakers were rebuffed. They told him it would be impossible to make shoes as good as those already on the market. "Well, I never take a challenge lightly, so I got a set of lasts, started fiddling around, and by 1958 I was making a better shoe than I could buy out of Europe."

Bowerman's fiddling resulted in a unique generation of shoes. He would take a standard last and shave it down or pad it out to suit various foot types. Then using the best and lightest materials, he hand-built track spikes for many of his athletes on a custom basis. His garage today is like a "Track Hall of Fame" with lasts and shoes which he made for some of the nation's best athletes.

Phil Knight was one of Bowerman's runners who graduated in 1959. After an interlude of traveling around the world, Knight suggested partnership in a running shoe business to Bowerman. They called the company Blue Ribbon Sports, with Knight at the helm and Bowerman responsible for the designs. The shoes were made by Onitsuka Tiger in Japan. Soon Jeff Johnson entered the picture to promote Tiger shoes to the nation's runners. The growth was spectacular, as we saw in Chapter 2, but in 1972 disagreements forced an end to the Blue Ribbon-Tiger link. As Bowerman puts it, "They wanted fifty-one percent of the company for nothing, so we split." The rest is well worn history (see the Jeff Johnson profile). Nike was born from nothing to become a $100 million company by 1978.

Bowerman's perfect shoe has a straight lasted design, with a broad, high toe box, a good heel counter, and a midsole which provides both support and cushioning. When we talked he lamented the lack of quality control in the mass produced shoes of today. As his eyes moved from direct contact, it was easy to imagine him focusing on an old pair that he had painstakingly put together for a former athlete.

But the contribution that Bowerman will probably be remembered for most is the waffle. "The waffle story is quite true," he recalled. "I was trying to make a shoe that could be worn on roads, grass, or on the tracks. I used my wife's waffle iron and put urethane in it. The only problem was that I couldn't get it out!" The process was soon perfected and has become a very common feature of outsoles in today's running shoes.

What Bowerman brought to shoe design was a strong background in coaching, applied common sense, and an ear for the needs of his athletes. He must be one of the few coaches in history who took care of his athletes, literally, from the ground up.

MARY DECKER
AMERICA'S PREMIER FEMALE TRACK RUNNER

I tracked down Mary Decker in Northern California during the first week of 1980. Her record breaking performances were still six weeks away, but it was already clear that her personal renaissance was in full swing.

Our breakfast conversation turned first to the disqualification of East European women for using steroids. Since Mary was contemplating a mountain of pills as an appetizer, I posed the obvious question of whether or not she would consider using steroids. Her reply was immediate and prophetic. "Well, right now, I am so far from reaching my potential, why should I take something when I've got so much more I haven't even used—naturally, I mean." Within a month of speaking those words, some of that potential was realized as Mary broke the women's records for the mile and 1500 meters indoors, as well as the outdoor mile mark. What made these performances even more remarkable were the injuries that Mary overcame after her early exploits as track and field's child prodigy seemed to have taken their toll and forced her into premature retirement.

She started running competitively at the age of eleven. For the first few days Mary ran in a pair of deck shoes—a dry but irresistible pun. She recalls that they were so uncomfortable that she took them off and ran barefoot in a successful effort to con her parents into buying a pair of running shoes. At twelve she ran a marathon in three hours and nine minutes and went on to capture a string of age group records as well as a place on the United States senior track and field squad.

Injuries first appeared when Mary was fourteen years old. First was a stress fracture in her right leg, and when she emerged from six weeks in a cast, her first shin splint pain was noticed. There followed a coincidence of unfortunate circumstances: hard training after six weeks of inactivity, pressure to repeat the glories of her past season, and a period of accelerated growth—over six inches in height in one year. Every step became a torment, and even sleep was difficult. "I would lie in bed and just couldn't go to sleep because my legs were throbbing so much."

And so Mary's dark ages began. She slipped from the limelight and read articles telling the story of "Little

Mary Decker's" early flowering and quick demise from competition. The round of doctors was endless. Over a dozen cortisone shots in a year, physical therapy, acupuncture, and ". . . rest, good old rest. I could rest forever, and a week later the intense pain would come back after the first mile."

She came to hate her image as running's Shirley Temple, but found the comments spurred her on to continue the search for a solution. "People said that my body had changed, my interests would change, and how much I would hate running again. I was determined to prove everyone wrong. Especially people who were calling me a has-been."

The daylight came after Mary first met Dick Quax, the 5,000 meter silver medalist in the 1976 Olympics. Mary had casts on both her legs, and as soon as they were removed she felt the same shin pain all over again. Quax had experienced identical problems and pointed to the scars which were evidence of his cure. Surgery, to release the envelope of connective tissue around the muscles on the front of the shin, had allowed him to escape from the spiral of injury, and perhaps it would work for Mary. "After so much time and so many no-hope cures, I went into surgery with the frame of mind that I had absolutely nothing to lose, and everything to gain." And gain she did. The success of the surgery can be read in the record books.

Those frustrating years of injury have given Mary a

new perspective on her training and on running shoes. Her old regime gave very little room for long easy runs, and she would always train in racing shoes. "I hated heavy shoes, so for me weight used to be everything in a shoe. Now I'm more cautious and I look for good cushioning as well as a good fit and reasonable weight. I also put in some easy days instead of long progressions of hard intervals on the track."

Most of her shoes are custom made because her feet are hard to fit. She has long, narrow, high-arched feet, which means a lot of extra space if length is used as the criterion for fit. A last has been made in the shape of Mary's foot for all her racing shoes.

As far as the future is concerned, Mary would turn professional at the drop of an eyelash if conditions were right. "If it were possible for me to make a living at what I do best, I would love to—but I can't see it happening." Those days of wondering where the money is coming from to pay the next bill have left Mary envious of her Eastern European counterparts. "They told us that they live in government subsidized camps for eight months of the year. Every bit of medical care is paid for, every bite of food is paid for."

Recently Mary has become the lone woman on the Athletics West Team, and this has eased her problems considerably. She is aggressive in her assault on the record books, and thinks a women's four minute mile a possibility in the next ten years. But first she wants four minutes and ten seconds for herself. "All these high school boys run 4:10 and they don't put in the training that I do, they don't train as intelligently." Seeing the determination that has brought her back from the depths of injury, it is hard not to view a healthy Mary Decker as an endless natural resource. One is left with the distinct impression that she could trounce her rivals even if she were wearing army boots.

JOE HENDERSON
THE RUNNER'S WRITER

In 1957 Coyne, Iowa had about 300 residents and one runner. "There goes the Henderson boy," the farmers would say, rolling their eyes as Joe ran along the dusty roads packing in his miles. In those days no one could quite understand why any sane person would waste energy running, particularly when there was work to be done in the fields.

All of which is to say that Joe Henderson started running several years B.B. (Before the Boom). For many people he personifies the boom. Joe has probably written more words on running than any other living person. His first published article on running was in 1960. Since then he has become widely known as the editor of *Runner's World* in the early seventies, and as the author of a series of popular books, including *Long Slow Distance— The Humane Way to Train; Jog, Run, Race;* and *The Long Run Solution.* He is compulsive when it comes to writing about running, keeping a daily log of his personal program from which many ideas for books and articles are born.

Joe's books and columns are aimed at runners like himself; people who will never be in serious contention for a medal, but to whom running is as essential as breathing. He sees himself as a missionary for the sport. In the introduction to *Jog, Run, Race* there is no pre-

tense about the book's intent. It could have been extracted verbatim from a revival meeting leaflet. "I want others to see the same light and to share this activity from which so many blessings seem to flow."

It took ten years of writing before Joe wrote his first words about running shoes. But when they came they were important and wide-ranging. In 1971 he wrote a pamphlet called *All About Distance Running Shoes*, which in many ways was the precursor of this book. All available shoes were examined and a survey of runners' preferences (and injuries) was done. The results were skillfully woven into a readable and informed text which gave runners the first publication devoted completely to running shoes.

After a rerun in 1973 called *Shoes for Runners*, Joe's next important contributions were the *Runner's World* shoe surveys in 1975 and 1976, which he wrote the bulk of. He recalls the response of manufacturers after those surveys. "In 1975 not too many people took us seriously, but when we put numbers to shoes in 1976, all hell broke loose." Manufacturers who had done well were ecstatic, but others who wanted the top ranking and didn't get it applied whatever pressures they could to change the system. Some were subtle, others were simply brutal. And much of the pressure was exerted directly on Joe. He is reluctant to talk of the specifics, but it is clear that those years are not a time in his life he will remember with much pleasure.

Outside the fray today, Joe is still a firm believer in shoe surveys. "Not only do I think they will and should continue, but I think shoe surveys are more essential all the time. It just isn't possible for one person to go out and compare all the shoes for themselves. There are so many shoes, if a survey can winnow down the choices to five or six, then the runner is way ahead."

His own running career has been plagued by Achilles tendon problems. They started during basketball in junior high and were probably solidified by four early years of road running in basketball shoes. He has tried the gamut of orthotics, rest, reduced mileage, reduced speed, and increased stretching, but still the problem lingers.

As one would expect from a writer on running and shoes, Joe has kept a log of every shoe he has ever worn (for more than a month) in his running career. The list, reproduced here, includes five years of "bare feet." This was mostly running on a grass track and in cross-country races in high school. Ironically enough, 1960-64 were his healthiest years.

SHOE DIARY

1. Various canvas sneakers—1958-1961
2. Various spiked shoes—1958-1968
3. Bare feet—1960-1964
4. New Balance Trackster I—1962-1966
5. Tiger Road Runner—1966-1967
6. Tiger Cortez—1967
7. Tiger Bangkok—1967-1968
8. Tiger Marathon—1968-1969, 1971-1972, 1972-1973*
9. Tiger Boston—1969-1970, 1973-1974*
10. Lydiard Road Runner—1970
11. Adidas Dragon—1972, 1974*
12. Tiger Jayhawk—1974*
13. Tiger Montreal—1975*
14. New Balance 320—1976*
15. New Balance 305—1976-1977*
16. Brooks Victor—1977-1978
17. Etonic Streetfighter—1978
18. Brooks Vantage—1978-1979
19. Brooks RT-1, 1979-

*indicates worn with orthotics

Joe has a better awareness of his needs in a running shoe than most. He has had personal and professional contacts with many doctors and sport scientists and slips easily into the vernacular of sports medicine. "I have a rigid cavus foot so I can take a shoe with a lot of motion," he expounds. "I know pretty much what my needs in a shoe are."

As one of the sport's elder statesmen (in years running, not lived), Joe has firm ideas on what shoe companies should be doing for runners. I asked him to imagine that he was president of the Henderson Shoe Company, which had just experienced a boom year and sold more running shoes than all of its rivals. What would he do?

"Well, I would plough money back into the sport. Support research, put more money into the education of runners—create some publications that could be sold at low cost or given away with shoes. I'd try to support athletes at both ends of the spectrum. Not just for the top athletes who are reaping it in from every direction, but to encourage the up and coming runners."

"Could such idealism actually work, without the message being complicated by commercial half-truths?"

I asked.

"I think it could. For example, George Sheehan and I worked on a pamphlet for Anheuser-Busch on basic running. They printed half a million copies, didn't mention beer at all, and their own name appeared only once."

Joe's success in writing has allowed him the opportunity to fashion his own existence exactly the way he would like it. He has assembled the elements of a lifestyle which is almost primeval in its simplicity. There is a family, a pair of running shoes by the door, and a blank page on the table. Each is an essential component in a symbiosis, each feeding the other in a relationship which is solid and enduring. His writings are not so much things written as they are things lived. It is small wonder that the "Gospel according to Joe" has been so widely read and so well accepted.

MARTY LIQUORI
PRESIDENT, ATHLETIC ATTIC

In 1964 Marty Liquori found running shoes hard to come by. He was on the Adidas Top 100 list, a group of athletes who got five free pairs of shoes a year. By 1980 the picture was brighter. He was the president of Athletic Attic, a chain of 170 stores specializing in athletic footwear with a growth rate of thirty percent per year.

Marty's progress is a uniquely American success story. Using athletic ability, good business sense, and the ability to weld the two, he rode the tidal wave of popular interest in running to an enormously successful conclusion.

An unexpected piece of the puzzle is that he was not a retired jock lending his name to a promotional venture. As he planned the growth of Athletic Attic, he continued to run, staying in the upper echelon of American middle distance running for more than a decade. The former prospect of a summer Olympics in 1980 drove him to a winter and spring of 140-mile weeks, greater mileage than ever before.

Marty's involvement with running shoes started with a pair of Converse Chuck Taylors (Figure 2.29) in high school. Running began as a way of getting in shape for basketball, but early successes in cross-country caused a change of direction. By sophomore year in high school, Marty had run a 4:17 mile, and he went under four minutes as a senior. The neon signs were already beginning to spell out his name. In 1971 he was rated the top miler in the world.

But then disaster struck. A favorite for the Munich gold medal, Liquori joined the ranks of the walking wounded with chronic plantar fasciitis. Was it shoe-related? Liquori reminisces: "Well, it started during the cross-country season, but I am sure shoes had a lot to do with it. Shoes were not very sophisticated back then, and had I known about orthotics I possibly could have forestalled the problem." But when the injury struck Liquori ignored the warning signs. "Villanova was defending NCAA champion when it happened, so I ran even though I should have taken a month or two off."

And so began the rounds of doctors, advice, and endless cortisone shots, each providing little more help than the last. Some of the treatments were, in retrospect, stunningly incompetent. In his book *On the Run* Marty tells of one doctor who told him to go out and run the hardest interval session he had ever run, despite the fact that each step was agony. Dutifully, he ran twenty very fast quarters, supposedly to break up scar tissue as a preliminary to a cortisone injection. Then he hobbled to the doctor's office to receive the promised shot. The doctor, it turned out, had suffered an ulcer attack and would see him in a week's time.

Such early skirmishes bred a realism which has taught Liquori not to expect miracle cures for his current back injury. "All I expect from a doctor is to lead me through the woods, to discuss various possibilities and to give me some guidance. If I go to a doctor and within minutes he's all opinions, certainly I am skeptical. Running injuries are complex. They need time for thought and reflection and many doctors are not willing to give that."

Fifteen years of lacing up running shoes have also bred a conservatism that is Liquori's guiding principle in shoe selection. This is true both in his personal use and shoes which the Athletic Attic will retail. "I was hesitant about the waffle at first. I didn't use it and we didn't carry it in our stores until it stood the test of time. I have been turned off by extreme flares, things jutting out the back of shoes, air pockets, and all the rest. We have never yet sold air shoes."

For his own use he sometimes has special training flats made with a reduced heel height. The rationale is that, as a track man, the change from a high heel to no heel in a spiked shoe can be devastating to the Achilles tendon.

Through his currently massive mileage, Marty has developed the firm belief that a runner should rotate shoes on different days even if the workout remains unchanged. "Right now, I have four different shoes and I change for every single workout. I believe that each shoe has a slightly different foot strike. I rotate depending upon how I feel and how my legs feel after the last workout. I have been wearing a shoe that totally destroyed every toenail on my foot, but seems just right to ease my back problem."

Liquori came close to becoming a distributor for Adidas, Karhu, and Brutting. He was responsible for giving free Adidas shoes to chosen athletes in the early seventies, and made a few design suggestions to the Adidas technicians.

But many shoe companies consider an injured athlete dead weight, and so in 1972 he was in the cold when he started Athletic Attic in partnership with Jimmy Carnes. "Soon after we started I went to the Brooks booth at a sporting goods show and saw that they had a pretty good shoe for an outrageously low price. I don't think they knew how good it was until I showed interest." Many of Liquori's early ideas were embodied in the Brooks Villanova. Jerry Turner (see profile) had not yet approached the AAU, so calling a shoe the Villanova was next best to naming it the Marty Liquori. The relationship with Brooks has endured ever since.

"Athletic Attic" vests have been popping up in magazines and on television in recent years. These athletes are sponsored, in Liquori's words, ". . . both as an advertising medium and to help win a gold medal for the United States. We are not out to encourage jogging, promote physical fitness, or anything like that. There are many vehicles to do that. We support a select group of elite athletes who have a chance of being the best in the world."

For the future, there are signs of a graceful retirement from competition to enjoy the fruits of an empire built on running and running shoes. "This year warrants putting up with my back problem but next year, if it continues this way, I won't run."

Liquori's road to success has taken him from the cinders at Villanova, to his first running shoe store (literally in the attic of a small shop in Gainesville, Florida), to the presidency of a large and flourishing company. It is an intriguing commentary on the sport that whatever else they may do, running shoes can also make people millionaires.

KENNY MOORE
MARATHONER AND JOURNALIST

After a distinguished career as a marathoner, Kenny Moore told me that he had decided to become a miler. At least a fantasy miler. The cause of this change was several days spent in England with Sebastian Coe collecting information for a magazine article. Coe and Moore had lived, talked, and run together, and that communion had aroused Moore's competitive juices anew.

Kenny Moore is a product of the Oregon mold. He went to the University of Oregon because it was home; he is a Eugene native. He wasn't recruited or on a scholarship, although track had always been a keen interest. He recalls doing a six mile run in high school—his longest ever—the day that Dellinger, Grelle, and Burleson came to visit right after the 1960 Olympics. The taste of the fast pace and sight of the Olympians in the distance still lingers in his mind.

Those early runs were in tennis shoes, but soon the high school team switched to an Adidas with "... stiff leather uppers and Bakelite soles. There was no informed selection process," Moore recalls, "we just ordered them out of a catalog. I'm not sure what they were designed for. We didn't ever try anything on." Those early "bone breakers" soon gave way to training shoes, Adidas Olympias, and when Moore walked into Coach Bill Bowerman's office as a freshman, those were the shoes he was wearing.

Whether Bowerman recognized latent ability in this stringy young athlete, or if the attention made Moore determined to perform, is uncertain. But improve he did, cutting his best quarter mile time from fifty-nine to fifty-two seconds by the end of his sophomore year.

Freshmen at Oregon in the mid-sixties were guinea pigs for Bowerman's continuing shoe experiments. Participation, though, was born out of respect and loyalty rather than coercion. "I was there ready, able, and certainly willing to lose a toenail if Bowerman wanted me to do prototype work," says Moore. And there was plenty to do. In 1964 Bowerman was excited about ripple soles, having seen early versions of the New Balance Trackster. Moore ran in shoes with all types of ripple designs, from tiny waves to gigantic tire treads, giving his feedback on each design.

Bowerman's role as shoemaker and coach was to have personal benefit for Moore in his junior year, after a stress fracture which could have threatened his career. After two hard races in a Pac 8 Conference meet, Moore went out for a long road run in a Tiger shoe with heel and forefoot cushioning but with a complete cutout in the middle (see Figure 2.28). "There was a strange pressure, nothing painful. It felt like I'd popped a shoelace. I sat down at a gas station to tie the alleged shoelace and it wasn't untied."

After a preliminary "chewing out" for disobedience, Bowerman reasoned that there might be something besides Moore's stubbornness which aggravated the injury. He worked with a full-cushioned shoe, producing something that enabled Moore to run again six weeks after the injury. This shoe was the model for the Tiger and later Nike Cortez.

Curiously, it was this shoe which led Moore to the witness stand in the Tiger vs. Nike feud. The judge wanted to know if Bowerman's modification of the Tiger shoe had been a quantum jump, something definitively different from what had gone before. Moore's responses and other evidence convinced the judge that it was, and Nike was able to use the name.

Moore's turn to marathoning was as much a geographical accident as a planned move. His roommate the first year at Oregon was NCAA steeplechase champion Bruce Mortenson. Since Moore had the local knowledge, the two went out on long runs, twenty-seven or more miles of punishing six minute miles. His first marathon was at nineteen, a painful 2:43 which included several frustrating miles of walking. By the Munich Olympics in 1972 this had fallen to 2:14, good for fourth place.

Munich was Moore's second Olympic marathon. Foot problems had held him back in the thin air of Mexico City. He never wore socks for racing, but always taped his feet in tender areas to save weight, putting lanolin on the tips of his toes. In Mexico the tape unravelled and caused irritation rather than prevented it.

Although he is still capable of Olympic caliber marathon times, it is likely that Moore will be known to the next generation of runners as a sportswriter rather than an athlete. Moore is a staff writer for *Sports Illustrated*. His contributions on track and field are often solitary islands of literacy in seas of baseball jargon and gridiron hyperbole. His dual abilities in journalism and athletics were well used in 1978 when Moore was secretary of the committee which made recommendations for the federal support of amateur sport.

From a personal standpoint, Moore seems torn between the "moral force" of amateurism and the stark reality of the need for financial support. He sparks into life recalling how Frank Shorter rebuked an Olympic yachtsman who could not see beyond his stock portfolio when preaching the need for amateurism. "After Frank's speech the man sat down, chastised properly for his narrow view. You know there are not too many ghetto yachtsmen." But support of the idea of sponsorship never went as far as support in practice. "I could never conceive of a shoe company paying me to engender loyalty to a particular shoe. My only loyalty is to my feet. When I was racing hard, I always preferred to go out and get the shoes I thought were the best."

Moore thinks that better shoes will provide a major contribution to the mythical two-hour marathon. "In my experience, what keeps you from sustaining that 4:34 per mile speed is not a physiological inability to hold the pace, but the feeling that your legs are going to come apart from the pounding. We all feel that way. After a hard marathon your legs are just bruised and hemorrhaged."

Certainly future shoes will help marathoners in their pursuit of the two-hour hurdle. But whether they will help this 2:11 marathoner run a 3:48 mile, even in his dreams, is something I don't think even Bowerman would presume to judge.

GRETE WAITZ
WORLD MARATHON RECORD HOLDER

At twelve she was putting the shot. At sixteen she was a 400 meter runner on the Norwegian national team. At twenty-six she conquered New York with a stunning world record for the marathon. She of course is Grete Waitz, who has established her position unassailably as the greatest athlete in the short history of women's distance running.

In these days of "bionic" women athletes who are nurtured on steroids and in danger of failing chromosome tests, Grete Waitz is like a wild flower in winter. She leaves you with the distinct impression that no one could be more surprised than she at the success which has propelled her far above her competition at distances from 3,000 meters to the marathon. Such humility is almost unique among the egocentric and extroverted ranks of world champion athletes.

During our conversations, it became clear that she finds the American preoccupation with every last detail of distance running curious and occasionally irksome. "Why are you asking me all these questions? Look, sometimes I sleep six hours, sometimes ten hours, no I don't have any special diet. No, I don't know my muscle fiber type. Yes, of course I'm nervous before a race."

Her irritation with my attention to minutiae was in

retrospect understandable, because Grete is the archetypal born champion. She is successful not because she trains right, eats right, or has been guided by the right scientists, but because she has that unique alignment of DNA. Her gift is a fortunate accident of heredity that no training schedule, drug, or diet can imitate.

She has virtually never been injured, losing only three weeks training due to knee pain in ten years. She has suffered Achilles tendonitis, shin splints, and knee problems, but when injury strikes she generally grits her teeth a little harder, and in three or four days it disappears.

She has worn Adidas shoes since she was twelve years old, and despite approaches from many manufacturers she has no plans to switch. Like many Europeans, she thinks that American shoes made for running on the roads are too soft. "You understand I run on trails in spring and summer and on snow in winter, so great cushioning is not something I need in a training shoe."

"But surely training for the marathon you run on the roads?" I asked what turned out to be a crucial question.

"But I don't train for the marathon."

And so it turns out that this world record Norsewoman never ran longer than twelve miles before her first marathon at New York City in 1978. And winning that race didn't change her training habits either. She completely forgot about the marathon until October

1979, when the five-borough race beckoned her back.

In a sense, Grete, like our own Joan Benoit, is a hostage of the male chauvinism embodied in the International Olympic Committee. To date, the pronouncements of this group have implied that women are not capable of running distances greater than 1500 meters. And since the ultimate glory for all track and field athletes is an Olympic medal, Grete and other women distance runners are trying to excel at shorter events which are not necessarily their best distances.

Of course her 1500 meter time is far from ordinary. She was fifth in the world in 1979 with a 4:07. But the fact that her marathon time is five minutes faster than any other woman in the world must indicate a special talent, especially since there was no specific training for this run.

In a habit that carries over from track running, Grete goes through a track runner's ritual before a marathon. She warms up in training flats and then ten or fifteen minutes before the race slips on a pair of racing flats. She likes shoes that fit like a glove. You can feel her big toe at the end of the toe box, but she does not suffer from black toenails. Her shoes are mostly "off the shelf" models, the same as you and I can buy. When too much training in the snow one winter caused Achilles tendonitis to flare up, a special shoe was made with added heel height. But the majority of the time she uses production models. Lightness is not something of prime importance to Grete in a marathon shoe. When she starts looking for ten second improvements it might be, but so far the increment each race has been far greater than this.

For another of her loves, cross-country running, she feels that there is a dearth of good shoes, pointing out that the design effort has been mostly dichotomized into track spikes and road running shoes. Grete was of course the winner of the world cross-country championships in 1978, 1979, and 1980.

Just which of her many roles will emerge as dominant in the next few years is dependent upon many factors, personal, political, and sociological. To the Norwegians, the New York marathon is as incongruous as a fifty kilometer cross-country ski race would be to the average New Yorker. Thus the recognition Grete receives in America for her marathon performances far outstrips the ripples it causes in her home country. But if there are Olympics in 1984, and if those Olympics have a marathon for women, it is my guess that an Olympic victory will be the final building block of the legend of Grete Waitz—the eternal first lady of women's distance running.

KIHACHIRO ONITSUKA
PRESIDENT, TIGER SHOE COMPANY

Distance can be an insurmountable barrier. I was able to meet in person with the twenty-four other people whose views on shoes are presented in this chapter at one time or another during 1979 or 1980. The one elusive person on my list was the president of the Tiger Shoe Company, Mr. Kihachiro Onitsuka, and after narrowly missing a meeting with him during one of his visits to the United States I resigned myself, as deadlines approached, to the fact that there would be no chance to include him.

But the message came from Japan that Mr. Onitsuka would very much like to answer any questions I had by mail. So I dashed off more than twenty questions on a broad range of topics and sat back to await the response. Soon a large manila envelope arrived from Japan, and, judging by the weight of it, I thought it would be possible to write a book on Tiger shoes alone. Eagerly, I opened the envelope, and a sample of what I found is shown below.

衝撃を緩和する作用を発揮して、防止し、長距離用マラソンに最適

Altogether, there were eleven closely packed pages of information, presumably about Mr. Onitsuka and Tiger shoes—each page a work of art—which I could only admire but not read. And because of the compact nature of Japanese characters where each small symbol represents a group of syllables, I estimated that this letter was probably equivalent to forty pages of English. More than 12,000 words and I could not read one!

Actually, there is one piece of the puzzle that I have omitted. A visitor from Japan happened to be working in our laboratory when the letter arrived, so with his help I can share with you some facts about Tiger.

When Tiger made their first running shoes back in 1951 they made what must be one of the most unique shoes of all time. The shoe (shown in Figure 2.24) had a divided toe box, with a small pocket for the big toe and a larger pocket for the other four. The shoes were just like a pair of mittens for the feet; they could only be worn by Japanese athletes who had developed a wide space between the first and second toes from many years of wearing the geta, the traditional Japanese shoe with a thong in this location.

From this esoteric beginning Tiger went on to become one of the world's largest manufacturers of running shoes, making a total of 2.5 million pairs in 1979 alone. But the statistic that Mr. Onitsuka is most proud of is his rate of returns, the magic number for any consumer product, telling how many units are brought back by the customer because of a quality control problem. The official line on rate of returns is 0.1 percent, or one shoe in every thousand that are made. This is a staggeringly low figure and must be the result of employees who take pride in their work and a quality control system on the production line which is extremely rigorous.

In recent years the name of the corporation has been changed from Tiger to ASICS. One of my questions was "What on earth does ASICS mean?" The answer is neither Japanese nor English. It stands for "anima sana in corpore sano," which, approximately translated from the Latin, means "healthy mind in a healthy body," a phrase often used by the champions of physical education and sport as a means of promoting morality. This motto, as high-sounding as it might seem, really captures the evangelism that Onitsuka feels about sport. He declares as a principal goal in life "to give hope to youth who have lost their purpose" and he sees sport as a major means of achieving this. I wonder how many businessmen in America would state similar goals.

Whether we like to admit it or not, the United States has become somewhat protectionist in its international trade policies. There are import quotas on Japanese cars, television sets, and running shoes, so I asked Mr. Onitsuka to be frank about his feelings on the difficulty of being an exporter of shoes to the United States. ". . . (the taxes) have caused the price of our products to increase and our total sales have fallen as a result. It shows a tendency toward protecting American trade interests which goes against the concept of free world trade. Also we think it is irrational to impose a tax retroactively."

The American manufacturers are probably nodding contentedly at these comments; it is evident that international trade is not without its frustrations. And the difficulties are not only confined strictly to business. A shoe made to sell in Japan cannot be sold in any other market because the average Japanese foot is much wider than the average American or European foot.

Not surprisingly, Onitsuka counts good fit in a running shoe as his number one priority, because any Japanese company selling shoes overseas has had to go through a long learning process to achieve a good fit in a foreign population. On the question of shoe surveys, he was polite but insistent about other factors which should be considered. "We recognize that these tests are valuable because they offer some standards for the industry. An integrated test should also include such factors as how the shoes feel, their thermal properties, and evidence about any injuries that may be caused by the shoes."

It is an interesting footnote that Tiger shoes were preferred over the next most popular brand by 2 to 1 in a survey published by *Distance Running News* in 1968. As the running boom gathered momentum it was hard for foreign manufacturers to appreciate the magnitude of the growth and to understand the requirements of the American runner. Onitsuka feels that the rapid growth of new manufacturers, the decline of the American dollar, and the appearance of "budget shoes" contributed to the decline in Tiger's market share. He is clearly out to regain that share and states: "We think it is most important to manufacture some shoes in the United States to fit the needs of the American market." At present there is no Tiger plant in the United States, but this statement suggests that one may be on the way.

Japanese runners have triumphed in the Boston Marathon on five occasions since their first appearance in the early 1950s, and I could not resist asking Onitsuka about his predictions for possible Japanese victory in the Olympic marathon in 1980, which, at the time of our correspondence, still seemed like a relevant question. The Japanese equivalent of *Track and Field News* couldn't have given me a better answer. "We think it is possible that four of our Japanese runners may win medals in the marathon race. We have four excellent distance runners whose best records are as follows: Seko 2:10:12, the So twins 2:09:05 and 2:10:40, and Kita 2:13:30."

The national pride in top marathoners is obviously as strong in Japan as it is in America. And if there is ever a competition involving marathon letter writing, my money will be firmly placed on Kihachiro Onitsuka regardless of what shoes he happens to be wearing. He is, after all, the author of the longest handwritten letter that I have ever received!

BILL RODGERS
AMERICAN MARATHON RECORD HOLDER

You might be forgiven for thinking that Bill Rodgers, the most outstanding marathon runner of our time, is surrounded by an array of health care professionals, has his own shoe designer on call, and has more running shoes than he knows what to do with. Unfortunately, you would be wrong on all three counts. The fact that Bill has none of these things is, to my mind, an indictment of our way of treating top athletes. Take, for example, the events surrounding the 1976 Olympic marathon and what Bill describes as his worst-ever experience with his feet.

He limped into the Olympic Village with severe metatarsalgia after a build-up period devoid of speed work, in case speed would irritate his injury. "Here I was, the fastest man in the field and the kind of medical care I got . . . well, while they were watching another event on television some guy used ultrasound on my foot and told me to go and ice it. They never looked at my shoes or anything—there was no holistic approach." So Bill gritted his teeth and ran the race. "It was very strange. Something was wrong with my style and my stride was off a little bit. I was feeling fatigue and burning in my feet as early as eight, ten miles, you know, which shouldn't happen in a good marathon race. I'd gotten a terrible blister. I thought it would be hot and slow but it turned out to be hot and still fast."

Long after the Olympic race was forgotten, the solution to Bill's metatarsal problem came, not from sophisticated scientific inquiry or high-powered medical care, but from the casual observation of his wife Ellen that he was bulging out of the forefoot of his shoe, which was simply too narrow. He went to a wider shoe and so far the problem has not returned.

A major part of the problem for the elite athlete is the AAU, now The Athletics Congress, and Bill has always had a stormy relationship with this organization, which was designed to administer the sport but frequently ends up stifling it. The advertisements for his "BR" sportswear line tell how the AAU "prohibits Bill Rodgers' picture, or any reference to his accomplishments from appearing in his company's advertising." The headline neatly catches the feeling. "If we showed you the man behind this running clothing we'd have another kind of suit on our hands."

I asked Bill if he had plans to do a "John Walker" and have his name appear on a running shoe. "Oh yes, it could be done, but the American AAU is more greedy than the New Zealand AAA; they want a higher share of the money, something that is pretty prohibitive to an athlete's chances of making such arrangements. I would like athletes to become involved in the development of their own shoes. There has to be some legal arrangement whereby athletes can endorse a shoe or have a shoe named after them. I hope that the officials of the sport are listening—you know."

The struggle is to make a good living, as top men and women in other sports do, without having someone from a governing body label you as dishonest, as has happened to Coe and Moses. Rodgers has been walking the knife edge for some time now with little more than posturing from both sides. The alternative is to say "no payment," but total and complete support of the athlete and all of his or her needs. But right now we have neither. We have accusations that Rodgers and others like him are bending the rules together with half-hearted care—like ultrasound from television viewers.

It was tempting to talk about the AAU all night, but I asked Bill to tell me what he looked for in a running shoe. What was important to him? "In a racing shoe, I must have a good fit—a comfortable shoe—psychologically that's so important, particularly in a marathon. Next, forefoot cushioning is important because I tend to land more on the forefoot. If I ever have problems it's never my Achilles or my heel, it's the ball of my foot or toes that get sore. I don't know how important an arch support is, but I've had one or two arch problems, you know, that might be something nice."

Bill is not a subscriber to the theory that you should rotate shoes during training, using one type one day and a different one the next. He wears one training flat until it's gone, until he feels the forefoot cushioning begin to go and he can feel the rocks. At this point the shoes go to the garbage, and he starts on a new pair.

In the various promotional agreements that he has made with shoe companies, he finds their chief concern is that he wears their shoe during races, because that's where they get maximum exposure. This has left him free to experiment with a number of shoes during training. Bill's experiments with running shoes actually began early, when his high school coach Frank O'Rourke nailed a piece of wood onto the heel of Bill's spikes. The reason for doing this is now obscure, but Bill recalls winning the Connecticut Class A Cross-Country Championship in those shoes.

His racing shoes are specially made to an outline of his foot (Figure 9.8) so that a good fit is obtained, but as far as I could gather, no special design features of the kind I discussed in Chapter 15 have ever been incorporated into any of his shoes.

For an athlete who has raced more than anyone else in recent history, Bill Rodgers has been amazingly injury-free. Apart from the dark days of 1976, Bill describes his injury history this way. "I got shin splints once, from running in the corridors in high school, and once as a freshman in college. Then I had a muscle pull. It lasted about a week. I have occasional arch problems when I do hard training—150 miles a week and track work—then it can give me trouble. But that's about it."

He has tried orthotics for the arch problem on a couple of occasions, but never really got over the break-in period of the first hundred miles or so before losing patience and tossing them out. He thinks a runner training at a high level has to expect occasional trouble and will frequently stop and walk on a training run if he feels a twinge of pain.

So there it is. Bill Rodgers gets the kind of care and the sort of shoes that are not much different from what you or I get. But we must remember that Bill is the ultimate survivor. He has run fast races and a grueling schedule in spite of the lack of special attention to his needs. How many promising runners have been lost because they were not as robust as Bill? If they had received the care they deserved, who knows what the record book would look like today? Our top athletes deserve more than they are getting—isn't it time we demanded it on their behalf?

Index

AAPSM (American Academy of Podiatric Sports Medicine), 251
AAU (Athletics Congress), 315, 328, 374, 383-384
Abductor muscle group (of hip), 76
Abrasion test — see outsole wear test
Absorption of water, 206, 207, 208, 211
Acceleration, 87-89
Accelerometer, 143
Accommodation (of shoe to foot), 124
Accommodative devices, 252
Achilles tendon, 43, 68, 77, 237, 244, 264-268, 270-272, 282, 297, 318, 322, 324, 341, 370, 378, 379, 384.
Achilles Tendon Protector, 43, 49, 97, 98, 297
Adams, Tom, 158, 176
Adductor muscle group (of hip), 76
Adidas (see also Dassler Brothers, Adi Dassler, Rudi Dassler, Armin Dassler, Horst Dassler, Horst Widman), 33, 34, 36, 41, 42, 49, 134, 195, 303, 325, 327, 348-352, 371, 372, 374, 375, 378
Adidas Falcon, 165
Adidas Formula I, 166-167
Adidas L.A. Trainer, 183-184
Adidas Olympia, 42, 267, 375
Adidas Runner, 48
Adidas SL 72, 45, 47
Adidas SL 76, 47
Adjustable shoes, 184
Advertising, 159
Aerobics, 38
Ageing, 4, 146, 152
Air Shoes, 49, 50, 176-180, 184, 327, 339, 373
Ajax, 10
Albert, Bob, 187
Alexandra, Queen, 22, 24
Alignment, 5, 68, 73, 74, 85, 146, 148, 169, 170, 228, 229, 243, 247, 249, 250, 251, 259, 267, 268, 273-275, 281, 290-291, 293, 294, 309, 314, 316
All court shoes, 301
Ambi, 304
Anatomy, 3, 52-77, 289, 290
Anderson, Bob, 41, 47, 329, 362-365
Ankle joint, 70, 237, 337
Ankle sprain, 67, 70, 167, 170, 231, 264, 266, 270, 272, 273, 282, 286, 297-298, 318
ANSI, 199
Anterior Tibial Muscles — see Tibialis Anterior
AOSSM — (American Orthopedic Society for Sports Medicine), 251
Arch bandage, 97, 98, 290
Arch cookie, 99, 120, 121, 133-134, 245, 275, 308, 309
Arch Ease, 248
Arches of the foot, 60-62, 193, 237, 241-260, 289-290
Arch injuries, 264, 266, 270, 272, 274, 275
Arch length, 198
Arch Support, 33, 48, 99, 133, 182, 241-260, 275, 290, 295, 383
Ariel, Gideon, 337-340
Army Boots, 262, 314, 322
ASICS — see Tiger Shoes
Astley, Sir John, 17, 20
ASTM, 199
Asymmetry, 194-195, 217, 281, 292, 293, 301, 341

Athlete's foot, 212, 262
Athletic Attic, 372-374
Athletic Trainer, 269
Autrey, 304
Australia, 124, 323, 324
Axis of the foot, 64
Back pain, 270
Bacteria, 131, 211
Badger skin, 124
Ball girth, 189, 196
Bannister, Sir Roger, 100, 236
Barefoot Running, 9-13, 16, 358-360, 367, 371
Basketball, 230, 301, 336
Basketball Shoe, 155, 370
Batcheler, Jack, 43, 336
Bates, Barry, 142, 268
Beginning runners, 312
Benoit, Joan, 340-342, 378
Bensel, Carolyn, 262-263
Best running shoe, 277, 310
Big toe, 72, 73
Bikila, Abebe, 309
Biomechanics of Running, 3, 78-95, 140, 142, 177, 185, 238, 240, 259-260, 296, 298, 337
Biomechanics of Walking, 317-319
Blisters, 43, 210, 211, 230, 262, 288, 324, 382
Blisterstop, 210, 211
Blue Ribbon Sports (see also Nike), 39-41, 329, 330, 366
Body Segments, 94, 95
Body Weight, 282, 293-294, 313
Bone, 53-63
Bone Scan, 55, 273
Bone Spur — see Heel Spur
Boot camp, 262
Boston Marathon (BAA), 1, 23, 29, 30-32, 35, 44, 49, 55, 234, 331, 340, 342-346, 382
Bostonian Ltd, 181, 209
Bottom of the shoe, 96, 97
Boulanger, J.P., 204
Bowerman, Bill (see also Nike), 39, 41, 45, 46, 158, 162, 329, 362, 365-367, 375-377
Bow legs (genu varum), 85, 282, 293
Braking phase of contact, 88, 89, 91
Brannock device, 198-199
Breaking In, 209, 230, 240
Breathability — see Permeability
Brookfield Shoe Company, 303
Brooks Drake, 47, 327
Brooks Hugger GT, 172
Brooks Shoe Company, 46, 47, 49, 132, 170, 179, 180, 303, 325-328, 336, 371, 374
Brooks Vantage, 48, 180, 327, 336, 371
Brooks Vantage Supreme, 169
Brooks Villanova, 47, 48, 208, 327, 374
Bunions, 202
Bursa, 66, 68, 270
Buying a Running Shoe, 6, 277-310
Callus, 262
Cameltrotter Heel Pad, 244
Camp, Walter, 16
Cantilever Outsoles, 163
Carbon black, 131
Carnes, Jimmy, 374
Carter, President Jimmy, 49
Cartilage, 66
Casting for an orthotic, 253-254
Catlin, Mike, 233
Cavus foot — see high arch foot
Cement, 102, 111, 116-118, 307
Cement lasting, 99, 102-103, 108, 111, 119, 120, 188

Center of Pressure, 89-93, 318
Cerutty, Percy, 324
Changes in foot size, 200-201
Changes with age — see ageing
Children, 6, 53, 192, 200, 316-317, 367
Choosing a Running Shoe, 155
Clancy, Bill, 268
Clarke, Ron, 325
Clayton, Derek, 40, 309, 323-325
Clicking, 105
Closed cell foam, 46, 49, 129, 132, 142
Coach, 79
Coe, Sebastian, 375, 383
Coefficient of Friction, 150
Cold feet, 205
Cold Weather Running, 177, 182, 184
Collar, ankle, 97-98
Combining (uppers), 127-128
Comfort, 4, 204-212, 281, 288, 306
Compensation, 274, 289, 291
Competition, 232-240, 283, 300
Compliance, 209
Component shoes, 183-184
Compression Set, 130, 134, 180-181, 201, 224-227, 229, 280, 288
Compromise in buying a shoe, 302
Computer, 80-81, 90, 94, 144-145, 147, 153, 157, 190-191, 269, 310
Conduction, 205
Conforming footbed, 180-181, 184, 210, 285, 313
Conneff, Thomas, 19
Consumer Testing, 138-139, 141
Convection, 205
Converse, 303
Converse Chuck Taylor Shoes, 40, 363, 373
Cooper, Kenneth, 38-39
Copy lathe, 190
Corfam, 125
Cork orthotics, 252
Corks (or Running Grips), 28-29
Cornstarch, 212
Corporate Cup, 364-365
Cosmetic aspects of shoe, 161-162, 173, 175, 188, 306, 319, 339
Cost of shoes, 7, 19, 25-26, 30, 32, 47, 49-51, 135, 146, 178, 188, 239, 285, 302, 303, 308, 312, 339
Cost of Treatment, 252, 356-357
Cotton socks, 206, 207
deCoubertin, Baron Pierre, 21
Cressman, Luther, 9
Cricket, 17-18
Cross over, 312-313
Cruciate ligaments, 66
Curved last — see inflared last
Cushioning — see shock absorption
Custom Fitting, 203
Cutting, 105-106, 190
"D" ring lacing, 173-174
Dark Ages, 15
Dassler, Adi (see also Dassler Brothers and Adidas), 25, 33, 124, 158, 325, 348-353
Dassler, Armin, 158, 352-355
Dassler Brothers (see also Rudi Dassler, Adi Dassler, Puma, Adidas), 33-34, 173, 348-355
Dassler, Horst, 355
Dassler, Rudi (see also Dassler Brothers, Armin Dassler and Puma), 33, 34, 348, 353-354
Davis, Steven Andrew, 212
Debriefing your old shoes, 286-288
Decker, Mary, 367-369
Defects in running shoes — see Quality Control

Density, 129
Demonstrator Models, 6, 304-305
Demoya, Richard, 262
Density, 49
Diebschlag, W., 200
Digitizing, Film (see Film Analysis)
Diocletian, Emperor, 14
Distance Running News, 2, 39, 41, 278, 329, 364, 381
Dogskin, 124
Do-it-yourself devices, 246-247
Downhill Running, 298
Dressendorfer, Rudy, 233
Dunlop shoes, 323
Durability (see Wear)
E.B. (Lydiard) shoes, 42, 199, 371, 374
Economics of wear, 231
Edema, 200
Edward II of England, 195
Edward III of England, 15
Efficiency of Running, 95, 179, 316
Elite Athletes, 6, 30, 35, 51, 203, 238-239, 283, 300, 315-316, 384-385
Endorsement by Athletes, 30, 44-45, 315, 325, 327-328, 333, 342, 355, 369, 371, 377, 383-384
Energy Absorption — see Shock Absorption
Energy cost, 234, 300, 359-360
Energy storage in a shoe, 316
England, 15-20, 23, 26, 36, 323
English, Dianne, 269
Environmental factors, 283, 300
Epidemiology, 263, 314
Eternal Sole, 218
Ethics of over the counter orthotics, 242-243, 247
Etonic Shoes, 48, 182, 199, 303, 345, 371
Etonic KM, 48
Etonic Stabilizer, 172
E.V.A. (ethylene vinyl acetate), 46, 49, 117, 129, 130-132, 136, 177, 223
Evaporation, 205, 206, 208
Evolution, 9
Eyestay, 97-98, 104, 107, 108
Fastrack, 104
Featherline, 97, 98, 115, 118-119, 190, 222, 307
Feet — see Foot
Felt orthotics, 246-247, 259-260
Fiberboard Heel Counter, 111, 134-135, 226
Fibula (see also shank), 55, 58, 274
Filler (in lasting process), 116-117
Filler in rubber manufacture), 130-131
Film Analysis, 80, 83, 85
Film, High Speed, 80-81, 83, 85, 90, 144, 252
Fit, 4, 124, 145, 180, 182, 186-212, 281, 285, 288, 291-293, 304-306, 308, 315, 317, 368, 379, 381, 38
Fitting Room, 106-109
Fixx, Jim, 345, 358
Flack, Edwin, 22
Flaming (upper materials), 128
Flare — see flared heel and inflare
Flared Heel, 47-49, 167-168, 281, 285, 295, 297, 30 362, 373
Flat feet, 64, 241, 281, 284, 290
Flexible feet, 281, 289-290
Flexibility, 48, 131-132, 144-145, 167-169, 204, 23 235-236, 239, 262, 275, 281-282, 284, 295-297
FoamGard Footbed, 180-181, 210
Foam rubber (see also polymeric foams), 134, 245
Follow up with orthotics, 258-259
Foot, 54, 59-65, 70-77, 82, 95, 169, 178, 180-1 192-212, 242-243, 245-251, 253-254, 262-276, 2 289, 290-292, 295-296, 298, 314, 316-317, 322, 3
Footbed, 209, 210

Foot Book, The (see also Harry Hlavac), 247
Foot infection, 212
Foot measurements, 193-195
Foot outline, 192-193, 291-292
Foot placement, 57, 68, 297
Foot Powder, 211, 212
Footprint, 63-65, 192-193, 289-290
Foot strike, 79-80, 82, 83, 85, 89-93, 131, 145, 150, 374
Footraces, 16
Foot types, 63-65, 281, 289-291
Foot volume, 200-201, 305
Force, 6, 58-59, 87-93, 124, 146, 147, 150, 163, 175, 201, 209, 221, 274, 290, 296, 318
Force Platform, 87, 89, 142
Forefoot, 47-49, 62, 90, 234, 250-251, 254, 257-258, 266, 272, 281, 290, 296, 316, 384
Forefoot control, 85, 173
Forefoot strike, 215-216, 282, 288, 298
Forepart of shoe, 91, 93
Fort Knox Study, 193-194, 200
Foxing, 97-98, 104, 107, 135, 173, 307, 308, 310
Frederick, E.C. (Ned), 178-179
French sizes, 196
Freon gas, 178
Friction (see also Traction), 131-133, 163, 173, 175, 210
Friction Forces (see also Front to Back Forces and Traction), 89, 92
Front to Back Forces (see also Friction Forces) 88-89, 175
Fukuoka Marathon, 40, 324
Functional Varus, 82, 169
Fungal infection, 131, 211
Gallica, 14
Geta, 36, 380
Gimmicks, 157-185
Girth — see shoe width
Glutaraldehyde, 212
Goodyear, Charles, 17, 49
Goodyear Welt Stitcher, 102
Gore, 31, 35
Grades — see shoe size
Greeks, 6, 9, 12, 16, 21-22
Greenberg, Joseph, 212
Growth, 200, 316
Habitually Injured Runners, 314-315
Half-sliplasting, 103, 108, 115
Hallux valgus, 6, 73, 77
Hamstring muscles, 76, 266
Hardness, 223
Hard Orthotics, 252-260
Hayes, John J., 24
Heavy runners, 184, 239, 293-294, 311, 313-314, 322, 335
Heel, 43
Heel bruise, 273
Heel counter, 43, 45, 60, 97-99, 111, 134-135, 145-146, 226-229, 258, 280, 282, 285, 286-287, 290, 301, 307, 366
Heel counter stiffness, 145-147, 229, 235, 287
Heel counter wear, 226-229, 280, 286-287, 298
Heel cup, 199, 229, 243-245, 285, 309, 313
Heel fitting, 199, 244
Heel flare — see flared heel
Heel-forefoot height differential, 32, 38, 40, 98, 178, 237, 239, 266, 272, 290, 374
Heel lift, 32, 40, 98, 237, 244, 281-282, 290, 297, 318, 322
Heel pads, 244-245, 282, 290, 295
Heel pain, 244, 262, 264-265, 270, 273, 274-275

Heel spur syndrome, 60, 241, 265, 270, 272-275, 282, 295
Heel strike — see foot strike
Heel wedge, 38, 43, 47, 93, 98-99, 117-118, 128-130, 142, 144-146, 166-171, 267, 272, 276, 280, 285, 287-288
Heel wedge wear, 222-226, 229, 274
Henderson, Joe, 41, 157, 159, 369-372
Hertzogenaurach, 348, 350
Higdon, Hal, 41, 345
High arch feet, 64-65, 281, 289, 290, 322, 371
High top shoes, 32
Hip bones (Pelves), 56-57
Hip joint, 68, 264, 266, 272-273
History, 8-51, 99-102, 123, 331-333, 344-345
Hlavac, Harry, 85, 247, 267
Holister, Jeff, 46
Homer, 10
Homo Erectus, 8
Hot air drying, 222, 224
Hot glue gun, 218, 220
Hot weather running, 177, 182, 184, 300-301
Human Tolerance Data, 141
Humidity, 207, 208, 300
Hyde Athletic Co. (see also Saucony), 35, 332
Hygiene, 211, 212
Hytrel, 181
Impact tests — see Shock Absorption
Imported Shoes, 303, 354, 381-382
Incidence of injury, 263
Industrial Revolution, 102
Infection, 211, 212
Inflammation, 145, 262, 270, 271, 272, 297
Inflare, 20, 188, 191-193, 196, 237, 290
Inflared last, 191-193, 237, 306
Injection molding, 99, 103-104, 168, 178
Injuries, 5, 6, 42, 49, 53-56, 79, 88, 93-94, 139, 141, 159, 239, 241-243, 250-252, 261-276, 279, 282, 294-300, 302, 310, 314-316, 324-325, 335, 341, 356-357, 367-369, 370-371, 373-374, 376, 378, 384
Inserts — see: sockliners; heel cups; heel pads; orthotics; morthotics; do-it-yourself devices; arch supports
In-shoe devices — see inserts
Insole — see sock liner
Insole board, 98, 102-103, 108, 110-117 131-132, 146, 209, 220, 229, 258, 308
Instep girth, 189
Insulation, 182, 283, 301
Internal training, 238
Interweb space, 212
Inversion sprain, 297
Isoprene, 130
James machine, 150
James, Stan, 158, 162, 167, 192, 268, 360-362
Japan, 35, 39, 40, 324, 330, 379-382
Johnson, Jeff, 39-41, 43, 45, 328-331, 364, 366
Joints, 64-74
Joint forces, 88
Jones and Vining, 187
Kaepa shoes, 134, 171-172, 176, 304
Kangaroo leather, 35, 124
Kangoran, 125
Karhu shoes, 177, 374
Keds shoes, 184
Keino, Kip, 350
Kelley, Johnny the Elder, 30-31, 37, 269
Kennedy, John F., 38
Kidd, Paul, 37
Kinetic Energy, 94-95
Kneecap (Patella), 58

Knee joint, 69, 83, 145, 337
Knee pain or injury, 58, 69-72, 162, 167, 264-276, 282, 294-295, 302, 314, 362, 378
Knight, Phil (see also Nike and Blue Ribbon Sports), 39, 45, 329-330, 366
Knock knees, 282, 292
Korea, 128
Koroibos of Eli's, 11, 14
Lab tests of running shoes (see also Shoe Survey), 139-156, 204, 223
Labor costs in shoemaking, 96-97, 107, 121
Lace irritation, 212
Lace to the toe throat, 175
Laces — see Shoe laces
Lacerda, John, 187
Lacing patterns, 171-176, 197, 281, 285, 292-293
Langer, Sheldon or Laboratories, 242, 253, 355-358
Last, 32, 100-103, 112-115, 118-119, 187-193, 200, 203, 313, 352, 366
Last bottom paper, 190-193
Lasting allowance, 102, 108, 113, 116-117
Lasting operation, 109-116
Lasting room, 109-116
Lateral border of shoe (outside border), 82-83, 90-91, 145, 148, 214-217
Lateral flare — see flared heel
Lateral knee pain, 270, 274
Lateral motion, 301, 318
Law family, 100, 236
Leather, 9, 18, 20, 32, 35, 43, 47, 100-101, 105, 122-125, 201-202, 209, 220-222, 230, 280-281, 287, 291, 301, 324
Leather orthotics, 258
Leather uppers, 20, 32, 43, 47, 122-125, 201-203, 207, 221-222, 280-281, 287, 291, 301, 324
Left-right asymmetry — see Asymmetry
Leg fractures, 54-56, 272-274
Leg weight, 94
Ligaments, 54, 59, 66
Liquori, Marty, 155, 327, 372-374
Littlewood, George, 20
LMF pattern of running, 83, 90-91, 318
Long heel girth, 189
"Look alike" running shoes, 302-303
Lorz, Fred, 23, 43
Lotus foot, 317
Louis, Spiridon, 22
Lucas, John A., 13, 20, 35, 331-333
Lydiard, Arthur, 137-138, 199, 249, 324
McArthur, Kenneth, 29
McGillicuddy, John, 269
McGregor, Rob Roy, 182, 199, 242, 267, 289, 345-348
McKay stitcher, 102
Mail order shoe buying, 308
Maloney, Matt, 24, 47
Manufacturers (see also under individual names) 153-154, 304-305, 307
Manufacture of running shoes, 96-121
Marathon, plains of, 12, 22
Marathon race, 18, 21-23, 26-27, 29-30, 34, 43, 234, 238-239, 255, 316, 323-325, 367, 375-377, 378-379, 382-384
March fracture, 282, 296-297
Marines, 261-263, 266, 267, 322
Market share, 303
Marron, Don, 176
Materials for shoemaking, 104, 122-136
Mayflower, 187
Memory foams — see conforming footbed
Metatarsal arch support, 245-246, 248

Metatarsal fractures (see also march fracture), 264, 272, 296
Metatarsalgia, 382
Meyer, Herman, 192
M-F heel cup, 244
Microcellular rubber, 46, 129
Microclimate of foot, 204-212
Middle Ages, 16, 192
Midfoot, 59-61
Midfoot strike, 92-93, 149, 215, 282, 288, 298
Midsole, 38, 41, 98, 117-118, 128-130, 142, 144, 146, 166-171, 183-184, 220, 222-226, 267, 274, 276, 280, 282, 285, 287-288, 329, 336, 339, 366
Midsole plugs, 183-184
Midsole wear, 222-226, 229
Midtarsal joint, 72
Mileage limit on shoes, 231
Misalignment of joints — see alignment
Mizuno, 174
Moccasin, 99-100, 103
Moccasin construction — see sliplasting
Moccasin toe, 97
Model maker (see also last), 187-191
Monarch Rubber Company, 46, 49, 129, 327
Moore, Kenny, 43, 365, 375-377
Morthotics (Mail Order orthotics), 243, 247-249, 250
Morton's Extension, 246-247
Morton's Toe, 201-202
Moses, Edwin, 350-352, 383
Muddy conditions, 300
Mudguard tip, 97
Muscle, 74-77
Muscle pulls, 264, 266, 270, 272, 273, 384
Muller-Limroth, 200
Nails, 103, 113, 114
Nail seating (of heel counter), 113-114, 135
Neatsfoot oil, 222
Nelson, Burt, 41
Neolithic period, 9
Neutral position, 73-74, 83-85, 169-170, 247, 253, 268, 299
New Balance, 32, 36-39, 41, 47, 175, 303
New Balance 3:05, 47-48, 371
New Balance 320, 48, 371
New Balance Speed Star, 39
New Balance Trackster, 37-39, 371, 376
New shoes, 275, 309
Newton, Sir Isaac, 87
New York Marathon, 24, 32, 49, 378-379
Nike, 45, 48-49, 158, 210, 303, 330, 342, 366, 376
Nike Bermuda, 173-174
Nike Boston, 41
Nike LD-1000, 48, 167, 362
Nike LDV, 179
Nike Liberator, 180
Nike Tailwind, 49, 178-180, 315
Nonaligned eyelet holes, 173-174
Nonuniform outsoles, 163-164
Normal feet, 281, 289
Novel lacing techniques, 174-176
Nylon mesh (knit), 48, 126-128, 203, 209, 219-220, 283, 287, 300-301, 310
Nylon socks, 206, 207
Nylon taffeta (weave), 48, 125-128, 203, 209, 287
Nylon uppers, 40-41, 45, 48, 97, 105, 123, 125-128, 207, 219-222, 267, 280, 287, 291
Odysseus, 10
Office visit to doctor, 251-252
Old shoes, looking at your, 279-281, 286-288
Olympia, 11, 13
Olympic Games, 10, 13, 16, 21-25, 29, 33, 34, 43-44,

315, 325, 331–332, 336, 342, 353, 359, 373, 375–377, 378–379, 382–383
Onitsuka, Kihachiro, 379–382
Open cell foams, 129
Oregon, 3, 9, 39, 329–330, 360–361, 365–366, 375–376
Orient, shoemaking in the, 97, 303, 354
Orthopedic shoes, 36–37
Orthopedic surgeon, 54, 243–260, 267–269, 299–300, 314, 336, 357, 360–362
Orthotics, 5, 7, 85, 94, 241–260, 267–268, 275, 281, 285, 290, 295, 306, 316, 321–322, 334–335, 347, 355–357, 370, 371, 373, 384
Orton, George, 26–27
Osaga Moscow 80 Shoe, 48
Osaga Shoes, 48, 163, 303
Osternig, Louis, 268
Outflare, 194
Outpatient Injury Survey, 263, 271
Outsole, 17, 25, 26, 32, 36, 38, 40, 43, 45–48, 117–118, 128, 142, 144, 162–166, 280, 285, 288, 359
Outsole wear, 25, 26, 48–49, 130–131, 136, 138, 148–149, 162–164, 214–219, 236–237, 280–282, 288, 298–299, 325
Outsole wear test, 148–149, 236–237, 284, 288
Overpronation — see pronation, excessive
Over the counter devices, 243–246
Overuse syndrome, 67, 69, 73, 229, 267–268, 273, 312, 362
Owens, Jesse, 33, 350
Oxford shoe, 98
Oxygen uptake, 233
Pacer, 181–182
Package, upper, 126–127
Pagliano, John, 242, 267
Pain, 55, 86, 148
Patents, 17, 34, 38, 157–185, 362
Pattern maker, 190
Pausanius, 11
Pedestrians, 3, 17–18, 20–21, 332–333
Pelvis (see also hip bones), 82
Penetration, 144, 147, 230, 235, 282, 297
Pennsylvania State University, 137, 210, 259, 272
Periosteum, 54
Periostitis, 270
Peripatella pain, 69, 270, 274, 294
Permeability (to water vapor), 123, 126, 128, 151, 212, 283, 300–301
Peroneus longus muscle, 77, 270
Perspiration, 131–132, 204–208, 209, 211, 212
Peters, Jim, 34
Pheidippides, 12–13, 21
Photography, high speed, 80
Pietri, Dorando, 23–24
Plantar fascia, 60, 270
Plantar fasciitis (see also heel spur syndrome), 60, 264, 268, 270, 272, 274, 295, 373
Plastozote, 252
Plimsolls (see also pumps), 16
Plugs — see wear plugs, midsole plugs
Podiatrist, 85, 160, 170, 242–244, 246–247, 250–260, 267–269, 299–300, 314, 321–323, 336, 345–348, 355–358
Points (or pikes), 15
Polydactylism, 202
Polymer, 104, 117, 129
Polymeric foams, 46, 49, 129, 132, 142, 144, 146, 245
Polyolefin foams (see also EVA), 128
Polyurethane, 99, 103–104, 131, 164, 178
Polyethylene, 173, 227
Pony Shoes, 49, 179, 303

Posterior tibial muscles — see tibialis posterior
Potential energy, 94
Powder, 212
Prefontaine, Steve, 365–366
Premolded heel counters, 134
Pressure measurement, 93–94, 168, 208, 209, 290, 318
Preventative medicine, 299–300, 347
Price — see cost
Pronation, 49, 70–72, 77, 82–85, 145, 226, 242, 259, 296, 323
Pronation, excessive, 83–85, 145, 169, 170, 247, 250–251, 259, 268, 274, 275, 280, 281, 290, 293–294, 296, 298, 302, 314
Propulsive phase of contact, 88–89, 91–92
Puma (see also Dassler Brothers, Rudi Dassler, Armin Dassler, Don Riggs), 34, 41, 134, 163, 174, 195, 199, 303, 327, 348, 352–355
Pumps (see also plimsoles), 16–17
Pushers, 28
Quadriceps, 75–76
Quality control, 6, 106–107, 119–120, 151–152, 279, 307–310, 323, 327, 355, 366, 380
Quarters of the shoe, 97
Quota system (for shoe import), 128, 354, 381–382
Racing flats, 5, 19, 39, 40, 49, 183, 232–240, 282, 293, 297, 314, 368, 379, 384
Racing last — see inflared last
Racquetball, 301, 318
Radiation, 205
Rearfoot, 59–60, 83–86, 90–91, 169, 250–251, 254, 257–260, 268, 272, 281, 290–291
Rearfoot control, 49, 85, 135, 144–148, 167, 173, 178, 227, 230, 235, 239, 248, 259–260, 274, 280–284, 286, 289–290, 293–296, 299, 302, 314, 318
Rearfoot stability, 146–147, 178, 230, 235, 294, 314
Rearfoot strike, 90–92, 149, 166, 168, 214, 273, 282, 288, 296, 298
Reebok, 303
Rejects, 138
Repair of shoes, 148
Replaceable wear plugs, 164–165
Research and development, 4, 48, 138–139, 153, 160–162, 339
Resoling, 219, 226, 236, 300
Rest, 264–265, 267–268, 315, 361, 370
Retailer — see shoe store
Return of defective shoes, 305, 309–310, 380
Richings, "Old Man", 31–32, 35, 37, 51, 344
Riggs, Don, 354
Rigid feet, 280, 281, 286, 289–290, 322, 371
Riley Company, 36
Ripple Sole, 38, 45, 47, 376
Rodgers, Bill, 7, 80, 193, 202, 234, 269, 325, 382–385
Roman Empire, 13–15, 187, 191–192
Ross, Browning, 41
Rotation of shoes, 308, 374
Roughing, 116, 119
Rubber, 17, 24–26, 30, 32, 34, 36, 38, 40, 43, 45–47, 49, 128–131, 134, 164
Rudi, Frank, 158
Runners clinics, 263, 268–269, 346–347
Runners knee (see also peripatellar pain), 58, 264–265
Runners Wedge, 248–249
Runner's World Magazine, 2, 4, 41, 45, 47–48, 139–140, 143–155, 178, 223, 262, 265–266, 269–271, 278–280, 284–285, 287–288, 297, 302, 304, 306–307, 310, 334, 362–365, 369–370
Running cycle, 80
Running habits, 279–280, 283, 300–301

Running style, 78–95, 185, 213, 279, 280, 282–283, 298–299, 316, 337
Running style centers, 185
Runski, 248
Ruptured tendons, 67
Ryfels, Marcus, 350, 352
Saddle, 97–98, 290
SATRA (Shoe and Allied Trades Research Association), 138
Saturation, 206, 207, 208
Saucony, 173, 303
Saucony TC 84, 172
Scholl's, Dr., 244–246, 248–249
Schuster, Richard, 199, 267, 314, 321–323
Schwaber, David M. (see also Monarch Rubber Company), 46–47, 327
Scuffing (at foot strike), 148
Sears Roebuck, 19, 30
Self-help in injury, 243–249
Self-report injury studies, 263–265, 271
S.E.M. (Scanning Electron Microscope), 53, 123, 125–127, 129–134
Semple, Jock, 26, 30, 31, 37, 222, 342–345
Sewing, 107
Sewing machine, 102, 106, 110
Shampoo, 222
Shank, lower leg (see also tibia, fibula), 58–59, 296
Shape of shoe outline, 191–193
Shark skin, 124
Sheehan, George, 242, 265, 266, 333–335, 372
Shin splint syndrome, 77, 241, 264–268, 270–274, 282, 294, 322, 368, 378, 384
Shock absorption, 2, 40, 43, 45–49, 66, 98, 104, 128–132, 139, 141–144, 146–147, 159, 163, 167, 169, 178–179, 181, 183, 184, 204, 209, 219, 223–224, 226, 230, 234–235, 238–239, 244, 255, 262, 266, 272–273, 281–283, 288–289, 294–298, 300, 313–314, 318, 352, 384
Shoe gerontology, 213–231
Shoe Goo, 218
Shoe laces (or strings), 28, 35, 173–176, 309
Shoe length — see shoe size
Shoemaking, 3, 14, 15, 96–136
Shoe Search Chart, 279, 280–283, 301
Shoe size, 4, 6, 105–106, 189, 191, 194–201, 284, 287, 291–293, 305–306, 311, 317
Shoe store, 154, 279, 284–286, 310
Shoe Survey (Runner's World), 139–156, 178, 186, 229, 234–236, 239, 278–279, 288, 302, 306–307, 335, 362–365, 370, 381
Shoes for orthotic wearers, 257–258
Shoe tag, 305
Shoe testing (see also shoe survey and various individual tests), 4, 7, 48, 136, 137–156
Shoe volume, 201
Shoe wear, 85, 337
Shoe weight, 5, 18, 32, 43, 45–47, 94–95, 131, 229, 232–234, 237, 239, 267, 280, 284, 288, 300, 316, 341, 368, 379
Shoe width, 38, 195–198, 235, 280, 284, 287, 291–292, 301, 305, 311, 381, 383
Short heel girth, 189
Short leg, 245, 250–251
Short list, 304, 306
Shorter, Frank, 43, 377
Shrinkage, 217
Shrubb, Alfred, 26–27, 172
Six Day Races (see also Pedestrianism), 20
Size — see shoe size
Ski boots, 180
Sliplasting, 6, 99, 103, 108–110, 114, 118–120, 188, 217

Slipsock, 103, 114
Smith, Lloyd, 242, 269–271, 274–275
Sneakers, 1, 16, 30, 37
Snow, 166, 300
Sockliner, 48, 98, 120–121, 129, 131–133, 142, 180–182, 184, 188, 210, 230, 243, 258, 308, 309, 313
Socks, 21, 205–208, 211, 305
Soft orthotics, 252
Soft support, 48, 132, 180–181
Sole — see outsole, midsole, insole
Sole assembly, 117–119
Sole laying, 118–119
Sole wear — see outsole wear, midsole wear
Spalding, 19, 24–28, 30, 32, 35, 50, 130, 172, 203, 304, 332
Sparta, 13
Special needs, 311–319
Speed lacing, 33–34, 47, 173, 174
Spencer, Alan, 195
Spencer, Lord, 18
Spenco, 132, 244–246
Spike last — see inflared last
Spikes, 17–20, 22, 30, 32, 40, 353
Split leather, 123
Split vamp, 171–172
Spoiler, 166
Sponge rubber, 128
Sporthotics (see also Langer), 242, 355–358
Sports Illustrated, 337, 376
Sports medicine, 261, 264–265, 269–276, 299, 347, 371
Sport science, 78–79, 351–352
Springing the last, 119–120
St. Elizabeth's Hospital, Boston, 269–270, 273, 294
Stability (see also rearfoot stability), 18, 47, 339
Standards for running shoes, 155–156
Steaming the upper, 111
Stick length, 189, 196, 198
Stiffness — see heel counter stiffness
Stitches, 102, 107, 287, 308, 310
Stone bruises, 264, 270, 274
Store — see shoe store
Straight last, 191, 193, 290, 306
Strain gauges, 144
Stress fractures, 54–56, 59, 239, 262, 264–265, 268, 270–273, 282, 296–297, 314, 367, 376
Stride Rite, 164, 219
Strike index, 89–90
String lasting, 103–104
Stripes (as shoe logo), 33, 173
Subotnick, Steven I., 49, 148, 170, 267, 278, 290, 327, 335–337
Subtalar joint, 70–72, 82–83, 145, 169, 247, 253
Sullivan, James E., 25–28
Summary Chart (for shoe buying), 279, 284–285, 301–302
Suophas, 182
Supination, 70, 82–85
Supplementary lacing systems, 172–173
Surefoot, 170
Surface for running, 273–274
Sweat glands, 229
Sweating, 204–208
Swing phase, 94, 166
Switzer, Kathy, 343, 345
Symptomatic treatment, 265
Syndrome, 270
Synovial joints, 65–66
Synthetic uppers, 206
Taffeta — see nylon taffeta
Talus (see also subtalar joint), 59, 169

Tanaka, Shigeki, 35
Tanning leather, 123
Tendons, 54, 58, 67
Tendonitis, 68, 262, 264, 265-268, 270-272, 296
Tendon sheath, 67
Tennis, 230, 301, 318
Ten Point Plan (for buying a shoe), 6, 278-310
Tensile tester, 138
Tensor fascia lata, 76
Terrycloth, 132-133
Texon, 132
Thermaflex K, 182
Thermal properties, 4, 151, 182, 204-208, 283, 300-301
Thigh bone (femur), 57-58
Thompson, D'arcy, 137-138
Thornton, John, 174, 192
Thread, 107
Throat of shoe, 97-98, 173, 175-176, 292
Tibia (see also shank), 55, 58, 274
Tibialis anterior muscle, 75-76, 271
Tibialis posterior muscle, 77, 270-271, 274, 296
Tibial valgum (see knock knees)
Tibial varum (see bowlegs)
Tiger Boston, 42-43, 329, 371
Tiger Cortez, 42-43, 330, 334, 371, 376
Tiger Cub, 324
Tiger Marathon, 39-40, 45, 330, 371
Tiger Olympiad, 40
Tiger Road Runner, 39-40, 50, 371
Tiger Shoes (Asics Tiger), 35-36, 39-45, 123, 174, 193, 267, 303, 327, 329, 330, 334, 366, 371, 376, 379-382
Toe box, 32, 35, 97-98, 108, 119, 196, 199, 202, 209, 217, 280, 281, 284-285, 287, 306, 366, 378
Toe box stiffener, 97-98, 111
Toenails, 175, 220, 262, 281, 288, 374, 376, 379
Toe off, 216
Toes, 62, 194, 199, 281, 288, 306
Toe spring, 170-171
Tongue, 173, 175, 308, 310
Torsional stiffness, 282, 295
Torque, 58
Trabeculae, 54
Traction, 45, 49, 98, 131, 149-150, 165-166, 236, 284, 300
Traction test, 149-150, 166, 236, 300
Training habits, 261-263, 266, 268, 273-275, 282, 296, 360-361, 368, 378, 384
Training shoes (as distinct from training flats) 36
Trans America Run, 359
Tread design, 92, 131, 149-150, 162-166, 276, 283, 300
Treadmill, 252, 336
Tred 2, 168-169
Tricot lining, 127
Tudor Period, 15
Tulis heel cup, 244
Tulloh, Bruce, 183, 358-360
Tuned shoes, 183-184, 316
Turner, Jerry (see also Brooks Shoe Company), 46, 325-328, 374
Turnshoe, 15, 100
U.K. sizes, 195-196
Uniroyal, 304, 339
Uphill running, 298
Uppers, 4, 36, 40, 41, 45, 47, 97, 102-103, 105, 108, 111-118, 123, 125-128, 182-183, 190, 202-203, 208, 209, 211, 219-222, 267, 280-281, 283-284, 287, 291, 293, 300-301, 307, 310, 317
Upper care, 222

Upper wear, 219-222, 280, 287, 310
U.S. Army, 5, 151, 193-196, 261-263
U.S. Customs, 128
"U" throat, 175, 197
Valgus, 73, 184, 217, 281, 291
Valgus wedge, 227, 323
Vamp, 97, 171, 172-173, 175
Varus, 73, 82, 169, 184, 221, 250-252, 254, 281, 291, 298
Varus wedge, 48, 169-170, 241, 247-251, 258, 280-282, 285-286, 288, 291, 293, 297, 299, 307, 313-314, 336
Vector last — see straight last
Velcro closure, 174
Velour, 132-133
Vertebral column, 57
Videotape, 252
Viren, Lasse, 44
Vixie, Dennis, 362
Vulcanization, 17, 50
Waffle outsoles, 46, 49, 117, 158, 162-163, 216, 226, 283, 288, 299, 362, 366-367, 373
Waist girth, 189
Waitz, Grete, 342, 351, 377-379
Walker, John, 327, 383
Walking, 6, 16, 230, 301, 317-319
Wear, 4, 126, 130, 213-231, 317
Wear bars, 149, 288
Wear plugs, 164, 184, 219, 288
Wear test — see outsole wear test, consumer testing
Weave — see nylon weave
Wedge — see heel wedge, varus wedge
Wedgee Patch, 218
Weight — see shoe weight
Weighting, of shoe test results, 147, 152-153
Wells, Jeff, 234
Welt, 15, 18, 101-102, 290
Weston, Edward Payson, 20
Wet weather running, 149-151, 166, 207, 222, 226, 236, 283, 300
Where to buy a shoe, 304
Widman, Horst, 349-351
Width sizing (see shoe width)
Wilson, 304
Wilt, Fred, 41
Wing tip, 97-98, 104
Wooden shoes, 14
Women runners, 6, 12, 16, 49, 57, 82-83, 87, 244, 311, 312-313, 340-342, 367-369, 377-379
Women's sizes, 196, 313, 341-342, 369
Wool socks, 206, 207, 208, 209
Wraparound at heel, 228-229, 307
Wrapover of toe, 119-120, 307
X-ray, 53-56, 130, 252, 267, 273
Z-scores, 153
Zatopek, Emile, 34-35

About the Author

Peter R. Cavanagh was born and raised in England. He attended Loughborough College and earned his doctorate in Human Biomechanics from the Royal Free Hospital School of Medicine in London.

He is currently Associate Professor of Biomechanics at The Pennsylvania State University, where he teaches in the graduate program and conducts research in locomotion and footwear studies. He is also science editor of *Runner's World* magazine and has directed the research team that conducts the laboratory tests for the *Runner's World* shoe survey since 1977.

Cavanagh is co-author of the book *Physiology and Biomechanics of Cycling* and author of many articles in professional and popular journals. He lists among his dislikes mediocrity, meetings, and television, while on the positive side he claims work, classical guitar music, his family, and his running provide the "essence of life." His best marathon time is 2:44:11, run at the Avenue of the Giants in 1980.

About the Illustrator

Ann E. Vandervelde is a graphic illustrator in the College of Agriculture at Penn State. She graduated from the University of Wisconsin with a B.A. in Art and has painted on a freelance basis for several years. She runs when the bathroom scale dictates and vows never to run a marathon. She enjoys pottery, historical novels, and Welsh history. Her ambition is to have time to paint for pleasure.

The author and illustrator live with their three children in Pine Grove Mills, Pennsylvania.